ANNUAL 1991-92
D0794739

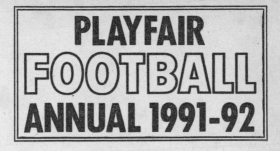

PLAYFAIR FOOTBALL ANNUAL 1991-92

EDITED BY JACK ROLLIN

Macdonald
Queen Anne Press

A *Queen Anne Press* BOOK

First published in Great Britain in 1991 by
Queen Anne Press, a division of
Macdonald & Co (Publishers) Ltd
165 Great Dover Street
London SE1 4YA

A member of Maxwell Macmillan Publishing Corporation

Cover photograph: Lee Sharpe, Manchester United (Bob Thomas Sports Photography)

A CIP catalogue record for this book
is available from the British Library

ISBN 0-356-20163-5

Typeset by BPCC Whitefriars, Tunbridge Wells, Kent
Printed and bound in Great Britain by
BPCC Hazell Books
Aylesbury, Bucks, England
Member of BPCC Ltd.

CONTENTS

Other Football

Information and Records

EDITORIAL

The concept of a Super League is not a new idea. In the last five years there have been several attempts to put one into operation, originally through a breakaway of leading clubs and more recently by the Football Association-inspired Blueprint for Soccer.

Envious glances have been cast abroad at the set-up in Italy and West Germany, both of whom have strong domestic competitions. On the face of it, they represent ideal models. The Serie A in Italy has 18 teams but at the end of each season four teams are relegated and naturally another four come up from Serie B. This would not suit an English Super League which intends to restrict the amount of promotion and relegation to ensure the elite are not too unduly disturbed.

In the West German Bundesliga, there are two teams automatically relegated but another has to fight through the play-offs. But the criterion in both leagues is that the translation into effectiveness at international level is not what it seems.

The Italians probably have more of the best players from around the world than any other country. But the best the national team could manage was to finish third in the 1990 World Cup when they were the host nation. They had previously done better than this of course, but also in the days when the numbers of foreigners were either more restricted or banned completely.

In Germany, the cream of the footballing talent does not even play in the Bundesliga, but in Italy. They won the 1990 World Cup largely because their leading players benefited from the exposure in the Serie A.

Of course the Super League idea was mooted as a guide to help the England national team. No competition at club level can be organised with such an end in view. It would be a naive proposition. Football would still continue much as it does at present if the England team never played another match, sad though this would undoubtedly be if it happened, which is unlikely. However, there is always the threat that with places in the World Cup finals at a premium, FIFA might still one day be forced by its members to demand that Great Britain enters as one country with England, Northern Ireland, Scotland and Wales losing their identity completely.

Since the Football Association abandoned the Home International Championship in 1984, there was always the possibility that the lobby, which is jealous of the position enjoyed by the four home countries, would be encouraged to act against them. If England could not be bothered to play the other three, what was the point in pretending they existed as serious opposition at all.

But of course the real motive behind the Super League was to allow the big clubs to flourish at the expense of the rest. The spectators were not consulted and more importantly neither were the players themselves.

FOOTBALL LEAGUE CLUBS AND THEIR PLAYERS

ALDERSHOT DIV. 4

Brown, Kevan B.
Burvill, Glen
Coombs, Paul A.
Cooper, Leigh V.
Flower, Johannes G.
Henry, Charles
Hopkins, Anthony
Hucker, Peter, I.
Ogley, Mark A.
Puckett, David C.
Randall, Adrian J.
Stewart, Ian E.
Whitlock, Mark

League Appearances: Banton, D.C. 13(8); Beeks, S.J. –(2); Brown, K.B. 40; Burvill, G. 34(7); Coles, D.A. 2; Coombs, P.A. 1(2); Cooper, L.V. 33; Cornish, R.G. 7(2); Dunwell, R.K. –(1); Fisher, A.J. 2; Flower, J.G. 30(2); Gray, M.D. 3(2); Halbert, P.J. –(3); Henry, C. 41; Hopkins, A. 9(1); Hucker, P.I. 27; Joyce, A.J. 3; Lange, A. 2; Murphy, J. 1(2); Ogley, M.A. 31(3); Puckett, D.C. 46; Randall, A.J. 34(2); Reinelt, R.S. 3(2); Sheffield, J. 15; Stewart, I. 33(3); Talbot, B. 10; Terry, P.E. 1; Tucker, J.J. –(1); Whitlock, M. 28(1); Wignall, S.L. 14; Williams, J.S.J. 37(2); Yanushevski, V. 6.
League Goals (61): Puckett 21 (3 pens), Henry 13, Randall 8, Williams 6, Banton 2, Burvill 2, Cooper 2, Flower 2, Whitlock 2, Yanushevski 1, own goals 2.
Rumbelows Cup (3): Puckett 3 (1 pen).
FA Cup (9): Henry 2, Puckett 2, Randall 2, Stewart 2, Williams 1.
Ground: Recreation Ground, High St., Aldershot GU11 1TW (0252–20211)
Nearest Station: Aldershot
Manager: Brian Talbot **Secretary:**
Colours: Plain red shirts with blue trim; blue shorts
Record home gate: 19,138 v Carlisle U, January 1970 (FA Cup)
Honours: Nil

ARSENAL DIV. 1

Adams, Tony A.
Ampadu, Kwame
Bacon, John, P.G.
Bould, Stephen A.
Campbell, Kevin J.
Clements, Steven
Cole, Andrew A.
Davis, Paul V.
Dickov, Paul
Dixon, Lee M.
Flatts, Mark M.
Gaunt, Craig, J.
Groves, Perry
Heaney, Neil A.
Hillier, David
Jonsson, Sigurdur
Joseph, Matthew N.A.
Limpar, Anders
Linighan, Andrew
McKeown, Gary J.
McKernon, Craig A.
Marshall, Scott
Merson, Paul C.
Miller, Alan, J.
Morrow, Stephen J.
O'Leary, David A.
Parlour, Raymond
Pates, Colin G.
Rocastle, David
Seaman, David A.
Smith, Alan M.
Thomas, Michael L.
Webster, Kenneth D.
Will, James A.
Winterburn, Nigel

League Appearances: Adams, T.A. 30; Bould, S.A. 38; Campbell, K.J. 15(7); Cole, A.A. –(1); Davis, P.V. 36(1); Dixon, L.M. 38; Groves, P. 13(19); Hillier, D. 9(7);

Jonsson, S. 2; Limpar, A. 32(2); Linighan, A. 7(3); Merson, P.C. 36(1); O'Leary, D.A. 11(10); Pates, C.G. –(1); Rocastle, D. 13(3); Seaman, D.A. 38; Smith, A.M. 35(2); Thomas, M.L. 27(4); Winterburn, N. 38.
League Goals (74): Smith 23 (1 pen), Merson 13, Limpar 11, Campbell 9, Dixon 5 (5 pens), Davis 3, Groves 3, Rocastle 2, Thomas 2, Adams 1, O'Leary 1, own goal 1.
Rumbelows Cup (10): Groves 3, Smith 3, Adams 2, Merson 2.
FA Cup (9): Limpar 2, Smith 2, Adams 1, Campbell 1, Dixon 1, Merson 1, Thomas 1.
Ground: Arsenal Stadium, Avenell Road, N5 1BU (071–226 0304)
Nearest Stations: Arsenal (Piccadilly Line), Drayton Park (British Rail) or Finsbury Park (BR, Piccadilly Line or Victoria Line)
Manager: George Graham **Secretary**: Ken Friar
Colours: Red shirts, with white sleeves; white shorts
Record home gate: 73,295 v Sunderland, March 1935 (League)
Honours – Champions: Division 1: 1930–1, 1932–3, 1933–4, 1934–5, 1937–8, 1947–8, 1952–3, 1970–1, 1988–9, 1990–1.
FA Cup winners: 1929–30, 1935–6, 1949–50, 1970–1, 1978–9
League Cup winners: 1986–7
Fairs Cup winners: 1963–4, 1969–70

ASTON VILLA DIV. 1

Blake, Mark A.
Bullivant, Russell P.
Butler, Lee S
Callaghan, Nigel
Carruthers, Martin G.
Cascarino, Anthony G.
Comyn, Andrew J.
Cowans, Gordon S.
Cox, Neil J.
Crisp, Richard I.
Daley, Anthony M.
Duffy, Darrell G.
Froggatt, Stephen J.
Gage, Kevin W.
Gray, Stuart
Jones, David
Livingstone, Glen
McGarth, Paul
Mountfield, Derek N.
Nielsen, Kent
Olney, Ian D.
Ormondroyd, Ian
Parrott, Mark A.
Penrice, Gary
Platt, David
Price, Cristopher J.
Small, Bryan
Spink, Nigel P.
Stas, Ivo
Williams, Gareth J.
Williams, Lee
Yorke, Dwight

League Appearances: Birch, P. 6(2); Blake, M.A. 6(1); Butler, L.S. 4; Callaghan, N. 2; Cascarino, T.G. 33(3); Comyn, A.J. 9(2); Cowans, G.S. 38; Daley, A.M. 22(1); Gage, K.W. 20(1); Gallacher, B. 2; Gray, S. 22; McGrath, P. 35; Mountfield, D.N. 32; Nielsen, K. 37; Olney, I.D. 13(5); Ormondroyd, I. 13(5); Penrice, G. 9(3); Platt, D. 35; Price, C.J. 38; Spink, N.P. 34; Yorke, D. 8(10).
League Goals (46): Platt 19 (6 pens), Cascarino 9, Mountfield 4, Olney 3, Daley 2, Nielsen 2, Yorke 2, Cowans 1 (pen), Ormondroyd 1, Price 1, own goals 2.
Rumbelows Cup (8): Platt 3 (2 pens), Daley 2, Ormondroyd 2, Cascarino 1.
FA Cup (1): Gray 1.
Ground: Villa Park, Birmingham B6 6HE (021–327 6604)
Nearest Station: Witton and Aston
Manager: Ron Atkinson **Secretary:** Steven Stride
Colours: Claret and blue shirts; white shorts
Record home gate: 76,588 v Derby Co, March 1946 (FA Cup)
Honours – Champions: Division 1: 1893–4, 1895–6, 1896–7, 1898–9, 1899–1900, 1909–10, 1980–1; Division 2; 1937–8, 1959–60; Division 3: 1971–2

FA Cup winners: 1886–7, 1894–5, 1896–7, 1904–5, 1912–3, 1919–20, 1956–7.
League Cup winners: 1960–1, 1974–5, 1976–7
European Cup winners: 1981–2
Super Cup Winners: 1982–3

BARNET — DIV. 4

Bodley, Michael
Bull, Gary
Carter, Mark
Cooper, Geoff
Evans, Nicholas
Hayrettin, Hakan
Horton, Duncan
Howell, David
Lowe, Kenneth
Lynch, Anthony
Murphy, Frank
Nugent, Richard
Payne, Derek
Phillips, Gary
Poole, Gary
Stein, Edwin
Tomlinson, David
Willis, Roger
Wilson, Paul

Ground: Underhill Stadium, Barnet Lane, Barnet, Herts EN5 2BE (081–441 6932)
Nearest Station: High Barnet and New Barnet
Manager: Barry Fry **Secretary:** Bryan Ayres
Colours: Amber shirts, black shorts
Record home gate: 11,026 v Wycombe W. 1952 (Amateur Cup)
Honours – GM Vauxhall Conference Winners 1990–1
Amateur Cup winners: 1945–6

BARNSLEY — DIV. 2

Agnew, Stephen M.
Archdeacon, Owen D.
Baker, Clive E.
Banks, Ian F.
Bullimore, Wayne A.
Connelly, Dean
Cross, Paul
Deehan, John M.
Dobbin, James
Fleming, Gary J.
Gridelet, Philip R.
Hoyle, Colin R.
McCord, Brian J.
Marshall, Colin
O'Connell, Brendan J.
Rammell, Andrew V.
Rimmer, Stuart A.
Robinson, Mark J.
Saville, Andrew V.
Smith, Mark C.
Taggart, Gerald P.
Tiler, Carl
Whitehead, Philip M.

League Appearances: Agnew, S.M. 38; Archdeacon, O.D. 45; Baker, C.E. 46; Banks, I.F. 31(2); Connelly, D. 5(4); Cooper, S.B. 8(4); Cross, P. 1(1); Deehan, J.M. 3(8); Dobbin, J. 8(6); Fleming, G.J. 44; Gridelet, P.R. 1(3); Joyce, J.P. 3; McCord, B.J. 23(1); Marshall, C. –(1); O'Connell, B.J. 39(6); Rammell, A.V. 32(8); Rimmer, S. 10(5); Robinson, M.J. 15(7); Saville, A.V. 45; Smith, M.C. 36(1); Taggart, G.P. 28(2); Tiler, C. 45.
League Goals (63): Rammell 12, Saville 12, O'Connell 9, Agnew 8 (2 pens), Smith 6, Archdeacon 2 (1 pen), Banks 2, Cooper 2, Deehan 2, Taggart 2, Tiler 2, McCord 1, Rimmer 1, Robinson 1, own goal 1.
Rumbelows Cup (1): Cooper 1.
FA Cup (1): Deehan 1.
Ground: Oakwell, Grove Street, Barnsley S71 1ET (0226–295353)
Nearest Station: Barnsley
Manager: Mel Machin **Secretary:** Michael Spinks

Colours: Red shirts white trim; white shorts
Record home gate: 40,255 v Stoke 1936 (FA Cup)
Honours – Champions: Division 3 North: 1933–4, 1938–9, 1945–5
FA Cup winners: 1911–12

BIRMINGHAM CITY — DIV. 3

Aylott, Trevor K.C.
Bailey, Dennis
Clarkson, Ian S.
Dolan, Eamonn J.
Downs, Gregory
Fox, Mathew C.
Frain, John W.
Francis, Sean R.
Gayle, John
Gleghorn, Nigel W.
Gordon, Colin K.
Harris, Andrew
Larkins, Nigel K.
Masefield, Paul D.
Matthewson, Trevor
Overson, Vincent D.
Peer, Dean
Rodgerson, Ian
Rutherford, Mark R.
Sturridge, Simon A.
Tait, Paul R.
Thomas, Martin R.
Williams, Dean
Yates, Mark J.

League Appearances: Ashley, K.M. 3; Aylott, T.K.C. 23(2); Bailey, D. 25(7); Bell, D.G. 1; Clarkson, I.S. 34(3); Dolan, E.J. 5(5); Downs, G. 16(1); Fox, M.C. 9(2); Frain, J.W. 42; Francis, S.R. (3); Gayle, J. 20(2); Gleghorn, N.W. 42; Gordon C.K. 3(2); Hopkins, R.A. 18(5); Matthewson, T. 46; Moran, R. 2(6); O'Reilly, G.M. 1; Overson, V.D. 40; Peer, D. 37(3); Robinson, P. 9; Rodgerson, I. 25; Rutherford, M.R. 1(2); Sturridge, S.A. 33(5); Tait, P.R. 17; Thomas, M.R. 45; Williams, D. 1; Yates, M.J. 8(1).
League Goals (45): Gayle 6, Gleghorn 6, Sturridge 6, Bailey 5, Frain 3 (2 pens), Hopkins 3, Matthewson 3, Tait 3, Overson 2, Peer 2, Rodgerson 2, Dolan 1, Moran 1, Yates 1, own goal 1.
Rumbelows Cup (1): Downs 1 (pen).
FA Cup (2): Aylott 1, Sturridge 1.
Ground: St Andrews, Birmingham B9 4NH (021–772 0101 and 2689)
Nearest Station: Birmingham, New Street
Manager: Terry Cooper **Secretary:** H.J. Westmancoat FFA, MBIM.
Colours: Blue shirts with white trim; white shorts
Record home gate: 66,844 v Everton, February 1939 (FA Cup)
Honours – Champions: Division 2: 1892–3, 1920–1, 1947–8, 1954–5
League Cup winners: 1962–3
Associate Members Cup winners: 1990–1

BLACKBURN ROVERS — DIV. 2

Atkins, Mark N.
Brown, Richard A.
Collier, Darren
Dewhurst, Robert M.
Dobson, Anthony J.
Donnelly, Darren C.
Duxbury, Michael
Garner, Simon
Gayle, Howard A.
Gennoe, Terence W.
Hill, Keith J.
Irvine, James A.
Johnrose, Leonard
Livingstone, Stephen
May, David
Mimms, Robert A.
Moran, Kevin B.
Reid, Nicholas S.
Richardson, Lee J.
Sellars, Scott
Shepstone, Paul T.A.
Skinner, Craig R.
Sulley, Christopher S.
Wilcox, Jason M.

League Appearances: Atkins, M.N. 35(7); Beckford, J. 3(1); Beglin, J.M. 6; Collier, D. 10; Dewhurst, R.M. 13; Dobson, A.J. 17; Donnelly, D.C. 1(1); Duxbury, M. 20(2); Gallacher, B. 4; Garner, S. 11(1); Gayle, H.A. 22(2); Gennoe, T.W. 1; Grew, M.S. 13; Hill, K.J. 19(3); Irvine, J.A. 23(4); Johnrose, L. 9(17); Livingstone, S. 18; May, D. 19; Millar, J. 34; Mimms, R.A. 22; Moran, K.B. 32; Oliver, N. 2(1); Reid, N.S. 29(1); Richardson, L.J. 32(6); Sellars, S. 9; Shepstone, P.T.A. 15(10); Skinner, C.R. 4(3); Stapleton, F.A. 38; Starbuck, P.M. 5(1); Sulley, C.S. 25; Wilcox, J.M. 15(3).
League Goals (51): Stapleton 10, Livingstone 9, Johnrose 7, Atkins 4, Gayle 4, Sulley 3 (2 pens), Hill 2, Irvine 2, Reid 2, Richardson 2, Garner 1, May 1, Moran 1 (pen), Sellars 1, Shepstone 1, Starbuck 1.
Rumbelows Cup (3): Hill 1, Johnrose 1, Stapleton 1.
FA Cup (1): Garner 1.
Ground: Ewood Park, Nuttall Street, Blackburn BB2 4JF (0254–5432)
Nearest Station: Blackburn
Manager: Donald Mackay **Secretary:** John W. Howarth FAAI.
Colours: Blue and white halved shirts; white shorts
Record home gate: 61,783 v Bolton Wanderers, March 1929 (FA Cup)
Honours–Champions: Division 1: 1911–2, 1913–4; Division 2: 1938–9; Division 3: 1974–5
FA Cup winners: 1883–4, 1884–5, 1885–6, 1889–90, 1890–1, 1927–8
Full Members Cup winners: 1986–7

BLACKPOOL DIV. 4

Bamber, John D.
Bradshaw, Mark
Briggs, Gary
Brook, Gary
Burgess, David J.
Davies, Michael J.
Eyres, David
Garner, Andrew
Gore, Ian G.
Gouck, Andrew S.
Groves, Paul
Hawkins, Nigel S.
Hedworth, Christopher
Horner, Philip M.
Lancaster, David
McIlhargey, Stephen
Murray, Mark
Richards, Carroll L.
Rodwell, Anthony
Sinclair, Trevor L.
Taylor, Peter M.R.
Wright, Alan G.

League Appearances: Bamber, J.D. 23; Barber, F. 2; Bradshaw, M. 1; Briggs, G. 30; Brook, G. 3(1); Davies, M.J. 30(7); Eyres, D. 30(6); Garner, A. 34(2); Gore, I.G. 40(1); Gouck, A.S. –(5); Groves, P. 46; Hedworth, C. 20; Horner, P.M. 39; Lancaster, D. 7(1); McIlhargey, S. 44; Owen, G. –(1); Richards, C.L. 16(6); Rodwell, A. 43(2); Sinclair, T.L. 19(12); Smalley, P.T. 6; Stant, P. 12; Taylor, P.M.R. 13(6); Wright, A.G. 45; Wright, M.A. 3.
League Goals (78): Bamber 17, Garner 13 (4 pens), Groves 11 (2 pens), Horner 7, Rodwell 7, Eyres 6, Stant 5, Richards 4, Taylor 3, Davies 1, Lancaster 1, Sinclair 1, own goals 2.
Rumbelows Cup (1): Brook 1.
FA Cup (4): Groves 2, Garner 1, own goal 1.
Ground: Bloomfield Road, Blackpool FY1 6JJ (0253–404331)
Nearest Station: Blackpool North
Manager: Bill Ayre **Secretary:** D. Johnson
Colours: Tangerine shirts with white collar and cuffs; tangerine shorts
Record home gate: 38,098 v Wolves, September 1955 (League)

Honours – Champions: Division 2: 1929–30
FA Cup winners: 1952–3
Anglo-Italian Cup winners: 1970–1

BOLTON WANDERERS — DIV. 3

Brown, Philip
Burke, David I.
Came, Mark R.
Comstive, Paul T.
Cowdrill, Barry J.
Cunningham, Anthony E.
Darby, Julian T.
Felgate, David W.
Fisher, Neil J.
Green, Scott P.
Henshaw, Garry
Jeffrey, Michael R.
Lee, Samuel
Neal, Philip G.
Oliver, Darren
Patterson, Mark A.
Philliskirk, Anthony
Reeves, David
Rose, Kevin P.
Seagraves, Mark
Spooner, Nicholas
Storer, Stuart J.
Stubbs, Alan
Thompson, Stephen J.
Winstanley, Mark A.

League Appearances: Brown, P. 45; Burke, D.I. 13(1); Came, M.R. 8; Comstive, P.T. 12(6); Cowdrill, B.J. 35(1); Crombie, D. 2; Cunningham, A. 9; Darby, J.T. 45; Felgate, D.W. 46; Green, S.P. 33(8); Henshaw, G. 1(3); Lee, S. 4; Patterson, M.A. 18(1); Philliskirk, A. 43; Reeves, D. 36(8); Seagraves, M. 32; Stevens, I.D. 1(4); Storer, S.J. 30(5); Stubbs, A. 16(7); Thompson, S.J. 45; Winstanley, M.A. 32.
League Goals (64): Philliskirk 19 (7 pens), Reeves 10, Darby 9, Green 6, Storer 5, Thompson 5 (1 pen), Cunningham 4, Comstive 2, Patterson 2, Cowdrill 1, own goal 1.
Rumbelows Cup (9): Philliskirk 5 (2 pens), Darby 3, Stubbs 1.
FA Cup (7): Philliskirk 2, Comstive 1, Darby 1, Reeves 1, Storer 1, Thompson 1.
Ground: Burnden Park, Manchester Rd., Bolton BL3 2QR (0204–389200)
Nearest Station: Bolton
Player/Manager: Phil Neal **Secretary:** Des McBain, FAAI.
Colours: White shirts; navy blue shorts
Record home gate: 69,912 v Manchester City, February 1933 (FA Cup)
Honours – Champions: Division 2: 1908–9, 1977–8; Division 3: 1972–3
FA Cup winners: 1922–3, 1925–6, 1928–9, 1957–8
Associate Members Cup winners: 1988–9

AFC BOURNEMOUTH — DIV. 3

Blissett, Luther L.
Bond, Kevin J.
Brooks, Shaun
Coleman, David H.
Cooke, Richard E.
Ekoku, Efan
Fereday, Wayne
Guthrie, Peter J.
Hedges, Ian A.
Holmes, Matthew J.
Jones, Andrew M.
Lawrence, George R.
Mitchell, Paul R.
Morrell, Paul D.P.
Mundee, Denny W.J.
O'Driscoll, Sean M.
Peyton, Gerald J.
Pulis, Anthony R.
Rowland, Keith
Shearer, Peter A.
Teale, Shaun
Watson, Alexander F.
Williams, William J.

League Appearances: Aylott, T.K.C. 8(1); Blissett, L.L. 45; Bond, K.J. 29(1); Brooks, S. 12(1); Coleman, D.H. 4(3); Cooke, R.E. 10; Ekoku, E. 5(15); Fereday, W. 17(1); Guthrie, P.J. 10; Holmes, M.J. 38(4); Jones, A.M. 30(3); Lawrence, G.E. 17(17); Miller, P.R. 14(2); Mitchell, P.R. 2; Morrell, P.D.P. 42; Morris, D.K. –(1); Mundee, D.W.J. 16(5); O'Driscoll, S.M. 45; Peacock, G.K. 15; Peyton, G.J. 36; Pulis, A.R. 12(3); Redknapp, J.F. 5(4); Shearer, P.A. 5; Teale, S. 46; Watson, A.F. 23; Wood, P.A. 20(1).
League Goals (58): Blissett 19 (8 pens), Jones 8, Peacock 4, Teale 4, Ekoku 3, Watson 3, Bond 2, Cooke 2, Holmes 2, Lawrence 2, Mundee 2, O'Driscoll 2, Miller 1, Morrell 1, Pulis 1, own goals 2.
Rumbelows Cup (3): Blissett 2, Aylott 1.
FA Cup (7): Jones 3, Brooks 1, Ekoku 1, Fereday 1, Teale 1.
Ground: Dean Court, Bournemouth, Dorset BH7 7AF (0202–395381)
Nearest Station: Bournemouth
Manager: Harry Redknapp **Secretary:**
Colours: All red
Record home gate: 28,799 v Manchester United, March 1957 (FA Cup)
Honours – Champions: Division 3: 1986–7
Associate Members Cup winners: 1983–4

BRADFORD CITY DIV. 3

Abbott, Gregory S.
Babb, Philip A.
Bairstow, Scott
Campbell, David A.
Duxbury, Lee E.
Evans, Mark
James, Robert M.
Jewell, Paul
Leonard, Mark A.
McCarthy, Sean C.
McHugh, Michael B.
Mitchell, Charles B.
Oliver, Gavin R.
Reid, Wesley A.
Sinnott, Lee
Stuart, Mark R.N.
Tinnion, Brian
Tomlinson, Paul
Torpey, Stephen
Treacy, Darren

League Appearances: Abbott, G.S. 21(5); Adcock, A.C. 8(2); Babb, P.A. 27(7); Duxbury, L.E. 45; Evans, M. 3; James, R.M. 46; Jewell, P. 35(3); Leonard, M.A. 15(3); McCarthy, S.C. 42; McHugh, M.B. –(1); Megson, K.C. 3(1); Mitchell, C.B. 16(4); Oliver, G.R. 46; Reid, W.A. 14(2); Sinnott, L. 44; Stuart, M.R.N. 13; Tinnion, B. 41; Tomlinson, P. 43; Torpey, S. 28(1); Tracey, D. 16.
League Goals (62): McCarthy 13, Babb 10, Torpey 7, Duxbury 5, Oliver 5, Tinnion 5 (4 pens), Jewell 4, Leonard 4, James 3 (1 pen), Stuart 2, Tracey 2, Adcock 1, Sinnott 1.
Rumbelows Cup (7): McCarthy 2 (1 pen), Abbott 1, James 1, Leonard 1, Oliver 1, own goal 1.
FA Cup (1): Jewell 1.
Ground: Valley Parade, Bradford BD8 7DY (0274–306062)
Nearest Station: Bradford Exchange
Manager: John Docherty **Secretary:** T.F. Newman
Colours: Claret and amber striped shirts; black shorts
Record home gate: 39,146 v Burnley, March 1911 (FA Cup)
Honours – Champions: Division 2: 1907–8; Division 3: 1984–5; Division 3 North: 1928–9
FA Cup winners: 1910–11 (first holders of present trophy)

BRENTFORD DIV. 3

Bates, Jamie
Bayes, Ashley J.
Benstead, Graham M.
Birch, Paul A.
Blissett, Gary D.
Buckle, Paul J.
Cadette, Richard R.
Cousins, Jason
Driscoll, Andrew
Evans, Terence W.
Fleming, Mark J.
Gayle, Marcus A.
Godfrey, Kevin
Holdsworth, Dean C.
Jones, Keith A.
Line, Simon J.
Millen, Keith
Peters, Robert A.G.
Ratcliffe, Simon
Rostron, John W.
Smillie, Neil

League Appearances: Bates, J. 30(2); Benstead, G.M. 45; Blissett, G.D. 22(4); Brooke, G.J. 8(3); Buckle, P.J. 24(2); Cadette, R.R. 19(9); Cash, S.P. 11; Carstairs, J.W. 8; Cockram, A.C. 7(13); Cousins, J. 8; Evans, T.W. 36; Fleming, M.J. 18; Gayle, M.A. 23(10); Godfrey, K. 26(6); Goodyear, C. 10; Holdsworth, D.C. 27(3); Jones, K.A. 45; May, E. 16(1); Millen, K. 31(1); Parks, A. 1; Peters, R.A.G. 6; Ratcliffe, S. 34(4); Rostron, J.W. 18(4); Smillie, N. 33(3).

League Goals (59): Blissett 10 (2 pens), Cadette 6, Gayle 6, Jones 6 (1 pen), Holdsworth 5 (1 pen), Godfrey 4, Cockram 3, Smillie 3, Bates 2, Evans 2, May 2, Millen 2, Ratcliffe 2, Rostron 2, Brooke 1, Fleming 1, Peters 1, own goal 1.
Rumbelows Cup (4): Bates 1, Evans 1, Godfrey 1, Jones 1 (pen)
FA Cup (9): Holdsworth 3, Blissett 2, Jones 2, Godfrey 1, May 1.
Ground: Griffin Park, Breamar Road, Brentford TW8 0NT (081–847 2511)
Nearest Station: Brentford (BR) or South Ealing (Piccadilly Line)
Manager: Phil Holder **Secretary:** Polly Kates
Colours: Red and white striped shirts; black shorts
Record home gate: 39,626 v Preston North End, March 1938 (FA Cup)
Honours – Champions: Division 2; 1934–5; Division 3 South: 1932–3; Division 4: 1962–3

BRIGHTON & HOVE ALBION DIV. 2

Barham, Mark F.
Beeney, Mark R.
Blissett, Nicholas
Bromage, Russel
Byrne, John F.
Chapman, Ian R.
Chivers, Gary P.S.
Codner, Robert A.G.
Crumplin, John L.
Digweed, Perry M.
Iovan, Stefan
McCarthy, Paul J.
McGrath, Derek B.J.
Munday, Stuart C.
Nelson, Garry P.
O'Dowd, Gregory H.
Robinson, John R.C.
Savage, David P.T.
Small, Michael A.
Stemp, Wayne D.
Wade, Bryan A.
Walker, Clive
Wilkins, Dean M.

League Appearances: Barham, M.F. 32; Bissett, N. 3; Beeney, M. 2; Bromage, R. 1; Byrne, J.F. 34(4); Chapman, I.R. 15(8); Chivers, G.P.S. 39; Codner, R.A.G. 42; Crumplin, J.L. 45(1); Digweed, P.M. 42; Gatting, S.P. 43; Gurinovich, I. 3(1); Iovan, S. –(2); McCarthy, P.J. 21; McGrath, D.B.J. 1(4); McKenna, B.F.J. 1; Meola, A.M. 1; Nelson, G.P. 12(11); Owers, A.R. 2(1); Pates, C. 17; Robinson, J.R.C. 13(2); Small, M.A. 39; Stemp, W.D. 2; Wade, B.A. 5(6); Walker, C. 45; Wilkins, D.M. 46.
League Goals (63): Small 15 (5 pens), Byrne 9, Codner 8 (2 pens), Wilkins 7, Wade 6, Nelson 5, Barham 4, Chivers 3, Walker 3, Gatting 1, Gurinovich 1, own goal 1.
Rumbelows Cup (1): Small 1.

FA Cup (7): Barham 2, Byrne 2, Small 2 (1 pen), Gurinovich 1.
Ground: Goldstone Ground, Old Shoreham Road, Hove, Sussex BN3 7DE (0273–739535)
Nearest Station: Hove
Manager: Barry Lloyd **Secretary:** Steve Rooke
Colours: Blue and white striped shirts; white shorts
Record home gate: 36,747 v Fulham, December 1958 (League)
Honours – Champions: Division 3 South: 1957–8; Division 4: 1964–5

BRISTOL CITY DIV. 2

Aizlewood, Mark
Allison, Wayne
Bailey, John A.
Bent, Junior A.
Bryant, Mathew
Campbell, Gary
Donowa, Brian L.
Edwards, Robert W.
Honor, Christian R.
Leaning, Andrew J.
Llewellyn, Andrew
Mardon, Paul J.
May, Andrew M.P.
Mellon, Michael
Morgan, Nicholas
Newman, Robert N.
Paterson, Andrew
Rennie, David
Scott, Martin
Shelton, Gary
Sinclair, Ronald M.
Smith, David A.
Taylor, Robert
Weaver, Steven A.

League Appearances: Aizlewood, M. 41(1); Allison, W. 18(19); Bailey, J.A. 6(1); Bent, J.A. 15(5); Bryant, M. 22; Donowa, B.L. 11(13); Humphries, G. 1(1); Leaning, A.J. 29; Llewellyn, A. 42; Mardon, P.J. 6(1); May, A.M.P. 44(1); Morgan, N. 43(1); Newman, R.N. 46; Rennie, D. 29(3); Scott, M. 27; Shelton, G. 43; Sinclair, R.M. 17; Smith, D.A. 32(2); Taylor, R. 34(5).
League Goals (68): Morgan 13, Taylor 11, Newman 8, Shelton 8, Allison 6, Smith 5 (1 pen), Donowa 3, May 3, Aizlewood 2, Bent 2, Rennie 2, Bryant 1, Scott 1 (pen), own goals 3.
Rumbelows Cup (5): Morgan 4, Smith 1.
FA Cup (1): Allison 1.
Ground: Ashton Gate, Bristol BS3 2EJ (0272–632812)
Nearest Station: Bristol Temple Meads
Manager: Jimmy Lumsden **Secretary:** Jean Harrison
Colours: Red shirts; white shorts
Record home gate: 43,355 v Preston North End, February 1935 (FA Cup)
Honours – Champions: Division 2: 1905–6; Division 3 South: 1922–3, 1926–7, 1954–5
Associate Members Cup winners: 1985–6

BRISTOL ROVERS DIV. 2

Alexander, Ian
Bloomer, Robert
Boothroyd, Adrian
Browning, Marcus T.
Clark, William R.
Hazel, Ian
Holloway, Ian S.
Jones, Vaughan
Kelly, Gavin
Mehew, David S.
Nixon, Paul
Parkin, Brian
Pounder, Anthony M.
Purnell, Philip
Reece, Andrew J.
Saunders, Carl S.
Twentyman, Geoffrey
White, Devon W.
Willmott, Ian M.
Yates, Steven

League Appearances: Alexander, I. 37(2); Bailey, D. 6; Bloomer, R. 7(6); Boothroyd, A. 2(1); Clark, W.R. 13(1); Gordon, C.K. 1(3); Hazel, I. 2(4); Holloway, I.S. 46; Jones, V. 44; Kelly, G. 7; McClean, C.A. –(2); Mehew, D.S. 30(11); Nixon, P. 10(6); Parkin, B. 39; Pounder, T.M. 39(6); Purnell, P. 6(3); Reece, A.J. 46; Saunders, C.S. 36(2); Sealy, A.L. 9(9); Twentyman, G. 46; White, D.W. 45; Wilmott, I.M. 2(1); Yates, S. 33(1).
League Goals (56): Saunders 16 (1 pen), White 11, Mehew 8, Holloway 7 (4 pens), Sealy 4, Pounder 3, Alexander 1, Bailey 1, Clark 1, Jones 1, Nixon 1, Reece 1, own goal 1.
Rumbelows Cup (2): Alexander 1, Twentyman 1.
FA Cup (0).
Ground: Twerton Park, Bath, Avon BA2 1DB (0272–352508)
Nearest Station: Bath Spa
Manager: Martin Dobson **Secretary:** R.C. Twyford
Colours: Blue and white quartered shirts; white shorts
Record home gate: 38,472 v Preston North End, January 1960 (FA Cup)
Honours – Champions: Division 3 South: 1952–3

BURNLEY — DIV. 4

Bray, Ian M.
Davis, Steven P.
Deary, John S.
Eli, Roger
Farrell, Andrew J.
France, Michael P.
Francis, John A.
Futcher, Donald
Hamilton, David
Hardy, Jason P.
Howarth, Neil
Jakub, Yanek
Lawrie, Graham
McKay, Paul W.
Measham, Ian
Monington, Mark D.
Mumby, Peter
Pearce, Christopher L.
Pender, John P.
Sonner, Daniel J.
Williams, David P.

League Appearances: Bray, I.M. 10(1); Davis, S.P. 46; Deakin, R.J. 37; Deary, J.S. 43; Eli, R. 15(11); Farrell, A.J. 30(7); France, M.P. 1(1); Francis, J.A. 45; Futcher, R. 30(4); Grewcock, N. 21(9); Hamilton, D. 8(3); Jakub, Y. 46; Lancashire, G. –(1); Measham, I. 44(1); Mumby, P. 15(5); Pearce, C.L. 43; Pender, J.P. 40; Smith, N.P. 2; Sonner, D.J. 1(1); White, E.W. 26(3); Williams, D.P. 3.
League Goals (70): Futcher 18 (6 pens), Francis 14 (2 pens), Eli 10, Deary 7, Davis 5, Mumby 5, Jakub 3, Farrell 2, Grewcock 2, White 2, own goals 2.
Rumbelows Cup (3): Futcher 1, Hamilton 1, Mumby 1.
FA Cup (5): White 2, Francis 1, Mumby 1, own goal.
Ground: Turf Moor, Brunshaw Road, Burnley BB10 4BX (0282–27777)
Nearest Station: Burnley Central
Manager: Frank Casper **Secretary:** Albert Maddox
Colours: Claret shirts; white shorts
Record home gate: 54,775 v Huddersfield, February 1924 (FA Cup)
Honours – Champions: Division 1: 1920–21, 1959–60; Division 2: 1897–8, 1972–3; Division 3: 1981–2
FA Cup winners: 1913–14

BURY — DIV. 3

Bishop, Charles
Bradley, Patrick
Greenall, Colin A.
Hulme, Kevin
Kearney, Mark J.
Kelly, Gary A.

Knill, Alan R.
Lee, David
Mauge, Ronald C.
Parkinson, Philip J.
Robinson, Spencer L.
Stanlislaus, Roger
Valentine, Peter
Walsh, Michael

League Appearances: Atkin, P.A. 8(3); Bishop, C. 25(4); Bradley, P. –(1); Cunningham, A. 30(3); Feeley, A.J. 20(7); Greenall, C.A. 29(2); Hill, A. 12; Hulme, K. 17(7); Kearney, M.J. 22; Kelly, G.A. 46; Knill, A.R. 19(1); Lee, D. 45; McGinlay, J. 16(9); Mauge, R.C. 26(3); Parkinson, P.J. 44; Patterson, M.A. 22; Price, G. 1(2); Robinson, S.L. 41(2); Sheron, M. 1(4); Stanislaus, R. 40(4); Valentine, P. 42.
League Goals (67): Lee 15 (2 pens), Cunningham 9, McGinlay 9 (2 pens), Hulme 7, Mauge 6, Patterson 6, Robinson 4, Bishop 2, Parkinson 2, Stanislaus 2, Valentine 2, Kearney 1, Knill 1, Sheron 1.
Rumbelows Cup (3): Cunningham 1, Mauge 1, Valentine 1.
FA Cup (1): Mauge 1.
Ground: Gigg Lane, Bury BL9 9HR (061–764 4881/2)
Nearest Station: Bury Metro Interchange
Manager: Mike Walsh **Secretary:** John Heap
Colours: White shirts; navy blue shorts
Record home gate: 35,000 v Bolton, January 1960 (FA Cup)
Honours – Champions: Division 2: 1894–5; Division 3: 1960–61
FA Cup winners: 1899–1990, 1902–3

CAMBRIDGE UNITED DIV. 2

Bailie, Colin J.
Chapple, Philip R.
Cheetham, Michael M.
Claridge, Stephen E.
Clayton, Gary
Daish, Liam S.
Dobie, Mark W.G.
Dublin, Dion
Fensome, Andrew B.
Kimble, Alan F.
Leadbitter, Christopher
O'Donohue, Fergus
O'Shea, Daniel E.
Philpott, Lee
Proctor, Matthew T.
Taylor, John P.
Vaughan, John
Wilkins, Richard

League Appearances: Bailie, C.J. 27(5); Berryman, S.C. 1; Chapple, P.R. 43; Cheetham, M.M. 42(2); Claridge, S.E. 16(14); Clayton, G. 5(1); Cook, M.J. 1(1); Daish, L.S. 13; Dennis, J.A. 6(14); Dublin, D. 44(2); Fensome, A.B. 36; Kearns, J.A. 1; Kimble, A.F. 43; Leadbitter, C. 30(9); O'Shea, D.E. 39(1); Philpott, L. 36(9); Sheffield, J. 2; Taylor, J.P. 37(3); Vaughan, J. 43; Welsh, S. –(1); Wilkins, R. 41.
League Goals (75): Dublin 16 (2 pens), Taylor 14, Claridge 12, Cheetham 7, Chapple 5, Philpott 5, Kimble 4 (3 pens), Wilkins 3, Bailie 2, Dennis 2, Daish 1, Leadbitter 1, own goals 3.
Rumbelows Cup (4): Leadbitter 2, Cheetham 1, Dublin 1.
FA Cup (12): Taylor 5, Dublin 4, Kimble 1 (pen), Leadbitter 1, Philpott 1.
Ground: Abbey Stadium, Newmarket Road, Cambridge CB5 8LL (0223–241237)
Nearest Station: Cambridge
Manager: John Beck **Secretary:** Terry Coad
Colours: Yellow and black shirts: Yellow and black shorts
Record home gate: 14,000 v Chelsea (friendly), May 1970
Honours – Champions: Division 3: 1990–1; Division 4: 1976–7

CARDIFF CITY DIV. 4

Abraham, Gareth J.
Blake, Nathan A.
Gibbins, Roger G.
Griffith, Cohen
Hansbury, Roger
Heard, Timothy P.
Jones, Mark
Lewis, Allan
Matthews, Neil P.
Perry, Jason
Pike, Christopher
Searle, Damon P.
Ward, Gavin J.

League Appearances: Abraham, G.J. 2; Baddeley, L.M. 2; Barnard, L.K. 26(2); Blake, N.A. 33(7); Chandler, J.G. –(1); Daniel, R.C. 13; De Mange, K.J.P.P. 15; Fry, C.D. 14(9); Gibbins, R.G. 43; Griffith, C. 43(2); Hansbury, R. 46; Heard, T.P. 38; Heath, P.A. 11; Jones, M. 20(2); Lewis, A. 16(11); MacDonald, K.D. 8; Matthews, N.P. 36(1); Morgan, J.P. 1(3); Perry, J. 43; Pike, C. 37(2); Rodgerson, I. 14; Russell, K.J. 3; Searle, D.P. 34(1); Stephens, L.M. 1(2); Summers, C. –(3); Taylor, P.M.R. 6; Toshack, C.J. 1(3); Unsworth, J.J. –(1); Ward, G.J. –(1).
League Goals (43): Pike 14 (5 pens), Griffith 9, Gibbins 5, Blake 4, Heard 3, Taylor 3, Barnard 1, Heath 1, Jones 1, Matthews 1, own goal 1.
Rumbelows Cup (6): Griffith 5, Pike 1.
FA Cup (0).
Ground: Ninian Park, Sloper Road, Cardiff CF1 8SX (0222 398636)
Nearest Station: Cardiff Central and Queens Street
Manager: **Secretary:** Eddie Harrison
Colours: Blue shirts; white shorts
Record home gate: 61,566 Wales v England, October 1961 (Club record); 57,893 v Arsenal Division 1: 22 April, 1953
Honours – Champions: Division 3 South: 1946–7
FA Cup winners: 1926–7

CARLISLE UNITED DIV. 4

Bennett, Michael
Dalziel, Ian
Edmondson, Darren S.
Fitzpatrick, Paul J.
Fyfe, Tony
Gates, Eric L.
Graham, Michael A.
Halliday, John R.
Jeffels, Simon
Jones, Alexander
Miller, David B.
Priestley, Jason A.
Proudlock, Paul
Sendall, Richard A.
Shepherd, Anthony
Siddall, Barry
Taylor, Ian
Walsh, Derek

League Appearances: Armstrong, L.W. 4(2); Bennett, M. 16(1); Dalziel, I. 13; Edmondson, D.S. 30(1); Edwards, R.W. 36; Elliott, E.G. 3(1); Fitzpatrick, P.J. 29(3); Fyfe, T. 8(8); Gates, E.L. 33(5); Goldsmith, C.S.W. –(4); Graham, M.A. 13; Halpin, J. 18(3); Halliday, J.R. 1; Jeffels, S. 21; Jones, A. 26; Lillis, J. 4; Methven, C. 12; Miller, D.B. 41; Norris, S.M. 2(3); Owen, G. 4(1); Priestley, J.A. 22; Proudlock, P. 43(2); Sendall, R.A. 15(10); Shepherd, A. 43(1); Siddall, B. 24; Thorpe, J.R. 6(7); Walsh, D. 19; Walwyn, K. 20(2); Wilkes, D.A. –(1).
League Goals (47): Gates 8, Proundlock 7, Shepherd 6 (2 pens), Edwards 5 (4 pens), Miller 4, Walwyn 4, Fyfe 3, Jeffels 3, Norris 2, Sendall 2, Halpin 1, Lillis 1, own goal 1.
Rumbelows Cup (3): Fitzpatrick 1, Proudlock 1, Walwyn 1.
FA Cup (0).
Ground: Brunton Park, Warwick Road, Carlisle CA1 1LL (0228-26237)

Nearest Station: Carlisle Citadel
Manager: Aidan McCaffery **Secretary:** Miss Alison Moore
Colours: Blue shirts; white shorts
Record home gate: 27,500 v Birmingham, January 1957 (FA Cup) and v Middlesbrough, February 1970 (FA Cup)
Honours – Champions: Division 3: 1964–5

CHARLTON ATHLETIC DIV. 2

Bacon, Paul D.
Balmer, Stuart M.
Barnes, Anthony
Bolder, Robert J.
Brown, Steven B.
Caton, Thomas S.
Curbishley, Llewellyn C.
Dyer, Alexander C.
Gorman, Paul M.
Grant, Kim, T.
Gritt, Stephen J.
Leaburn, Carl W.
Lee, Robert
Minto, Scott C.
Mortimer, Paul
Peake, Andrew M.
Pitcher, Darren E.J.
Reid, Mark
Salako, Andrew O.
Salmon, Michael B.
Tivey, Mark R.
Walsh, Colin D.
Wareham, Daniel
Webster, Simon P.

League Appearances: Bacon, P.D. –(1); Balmer, S.M. 19(5); Bolder, R.J. 39; Caton, T.S. 20; Crooks, G.A. 2(5); Curbishley, L.C. 20(5); Dyer, A.C. 34(1); Gorman, P.M. 2(6); Grant, K.T. 11(1); Gritt, S.J. 5(5); Jones, A.M. 5(2); Kernaghan, A.N. 13; Leaburn, C.W. 11(9); Lee, R. 43; MacKenzie, S. 15; Minto, S.C. 42(1); Mortimer, P. 32; Peake, A.M. 45; Pitcher, D.E.J. 42(2); Reid, M. 23(1); Salako, A.O. 1; Salmon, M.B. 7; Walsh, C.D. 10(3); Watson, G.W.G. 18(4); Webster, S.P. 40; Wilder, C.J. 1; Wilson, D.G. 6(1).
League Goals (57): Lee 13, Dyer 7, Mortimer 7, Watson 7, Peake 4, Caton 3 (3 pens), Pitcher 3 (2 pens), Gorman 2, Grant 2, Reid 2 (1 pen), Wilson 2, Crooks 1, Leaburn 1, MacKenzie 1, Minto 1, own goal 1.
Rumbelows Cup (2): Minto 1, Watson 1.
FA Cup (1): Dyer 1.
Ground: The Valley, Floyd Road, Charlton, London SE7 8BL (081-293 4567)
Nearest Station: Charlton
Player Coaches: Alan Curbishley and Steve Gritt **Secretary:** Miss Anne Payne
Colours: Red shirts; white shorts
Record home gate: 75,031 v Aston Villa, February 1938 (FA Cup)
Honours – Champions: Division 3 South: 1928–9, 1934–5
FA Cup winners: 1946–7

CHELSEA DIV. 1

Barnard, Darren S.
Beasant, David J.
Burley, Craig W.
Clarke, Stephen
Cundy, Jason V.
Dickens, Alan W.
Dixon, Kerry M.
Dorigo, Anthony R.
Durie, Gordon S.
Freestone, Roger
Hall, Gareth D.
Hitchcock, Kevin J.
Johnsen, Erland
Lee, David J.
Le Saux, Graeme P.
McAllister, Kevin
Matthew, Damian
Mitchell, David S.
Monkou, Kenneth J.
Newton, Edward J.I.
Sinclair, Frank M.
Stuart, Graham C.
Townsend, Andrew D.
Wilson, Kevin
Winters, Jason
Wise, Dennis F.

League Appearances: Beasant, D.J. 35; Bumstead, J. 8(5); Burley, C.W. –(1); Clarke, S. 17(1); Cundy, J.V. 28(1); Dickens, A.W. 13(3); Dixon, K.M. 33; Dorigo, A.R. 31; Durie, G.S. 24; Hall, G.D. 24; Hitchcock, K.J. 3; Johnsen, E. 6; Lee, D.J. 17(4); Le Saux, G.P. 24(4); McAllister, K. 5(8); Matthew, D. 6(2); Mitchell, D.S. 1; Monkou, K.J. 27; Myers, A. –(3); Nicholas, P. 11(1); Pearce, I.A. –(1); Sinclair, F.M. 4; Stuart, G.C. 17(2); Townsend, A.D. 34; Wilson, K. 17(5); Wise, D.F. 33.
League Goals (58): Durie 12, Dixon 10, Wise 10 (6 pens), Wilson 7, Le Saux 4, Stuart 4, Dorigo 2, Townsend 2, Bumstead 1, Clarke 1, Cundy 1, Lee 1, Monkou 1, Nicholas 1, own goal 1.
Rumbelows Cup (18): Dixon 4, Durie 3, Townsend 3, Wilson 2, Wise 2 (2 pens), Lee 1, Le Saux 1, McAllister 1, Stuart 1
FA Cup (1): Dixon 1.
Ground: Stamford Bridge, Fulham Road, London SW6 1HS (071–385 5545)
Nearest Station: Fulham Broadway (District Line)
Manager: Ian Porterfield **Secretary:** Janet Wayth
Colours: All royal blue
Record home gate: 82,905 v Arsenal, October 1935 (League)
Honours – Champions: Division 1: 1954–5; Division 2: 1983–4, 1988–9
FA Cup winners: 1969–70
League Cup winners: 1964–5
European Cup Winners Cup winners: 1970–71
Full Members Cup winners: 1985–6, 1989–90

CHESTER CITY — DIV. 3

Abel, Graham	Dale, Carl	Preece, Roger
Barrow, Graham	Ellis, Neil J.	Pugh, David
Bennett, Gary M.	Hinnigan, Joseph P.	Stewart, William I
Bishop, Edward M.	Lightfoot, Christoipher	Whelan, Spencer
Butler, Barry	Morton, Neil	
Croft, Brian G.A.	Painter, Peter R.	

League Appearances: Abel, G. 29; Barber, F. 8; Barrow, G. 20; Bennett, G.M. 23(7); Bertschin, K.E. 14(5); Bishop, E.M. 19; Brightwell, D. 6; Butler, B. 42(1); Croft, B.G.A. 31(7); Dale, C. 41(3); Ellis, N.J. 13(8); Lane, M.J. 38(2); Lightfoot, C. 33(4); Lundon, S. 4(1); Morton, N. 31(3); Painter, P.R. 34(8); Preece, R. 35; Pugh, D. 33(4); Reeves, A. 3(7); Stewart, W.I. 38; Whelan, S. 9(2); Withe, C. 2.
League Goals (46): Dale 10, Bishop 7, Morton 7, Butler 5, Abel 4 (4 pens), Bennett 3, Painter 3, Pugh 3 (1 pen), Lightfoot 2, Ellis 1, own goal 1.
Rumbelows Cup (5): Croft 2, Abel 1 (pen), Ellis 1, own goal 1.
FA Cup (11): Dale 4, Croft 2, Painter 2, Abel 1 (1 pen), Bennett 1, Bertschin 1.
Ground: Moss Rose Ground, Macclesfield
Nearest Station: Macclesfield
Manager: Harry McNally **Secretary:** R.A. Allan
Colours: Royal blue shirts; white shorts
Record home gate: 20,500 v Chelsea, January 1952 (FA Cup)
Honours: Nil

CHESTERFIELD DIV. 4

Brien, Anthony J.
Caldwell, David W.
Cooke, John
Dyche, Sean M.
Francis, Lee
Gunn, Brynley C.
Hewitt, James R.
Lemon, Paul A.
Leonard, Michael C.
McGugan, Paul J.
Morris, Andrew D.
Rogers, Lee J.
Ryan, John B.
Turnbull, Lee M.
Waller, David H.
Williams, Steven B.

League Appearances: Albiston, A.R. 3; Allison, M. 16; Barnes, P.L. 1; Benjamin, C. 5(6); Boyd, C.M. –(1); Brien, A.J. 41(2); Caldwell, D.W. 22(1); Cooke, J. 19(1); Cordner, S. 1(3); Dyche, S.M. 22(6); Francis, L. 26(3); Godfrey, P. 2; Gunn, B.C. 34(2); Hart, N. 18(1); Hewitt, J.R. 42(1); Lancaster, D. 12; Lemon, P.A. 39; Leonard, M.C. 30; McGugan, P.J. 22; Morris, A.D. 11(4); Plummer, C.A. 23(4); Rogers, L.J. 31(3); Rolph, A.J.P. 7(8); Ryan, J.B. 38(1); Shaw, A. –(1); Turnbull, L.M. 19; Williams, D. 4(1); Williams, S.B. 18(7).
League Goals (47): Turnbull 9 (3 pens), Caldwell 4, Lancaster 4, Morris 4, Plummer 4, Williams S 4, Brien 3, Dyche 2, Gunn 2 (1 pen), Lemon 2, Ryan 2, Albiston 1, Benjamin 1, Cooke 1, Cordner 1, Francis 1, McGugan 1, Williams D. 1.
Rumbelows Cup (3): Morris 3.
FA Cup (6): Caldwell 2, Barnes 1, Cooke 1, Morris 1, own goal 1.
Ground: Recreation Ground, Chesterfield S40 4SX (0246–209765)
Nearest Station: Chesterfield
Manager: Chris McMenemy **Secretary:** R.F. Pepper
Colours: Royal blue shirts; white shorts
Record home gate: 30,968 v Newcastle United, April 1939 (League)
Honours – Champions: Division 3 North: 1930–31, 1935–6; Division 4: 1969–70, 1984–5
Anglo-Scottish Cup: 1980–81

COVENTRY CITY DIV. 1

Billing, Peter G.
Booty, Martyn J.
Borrows, Brian
Clark, Howard W.
Clarke, Timothy J.
Drinkell, Kevin S.
Edwards, Paul
Emerson, Dean
Gallacher, Kevin W.
Greenman, Christopher
Gynn, Michael
Hurst, Lee J.
Kilcline, Brian
MacDonald, Kevin
McGrath, Lloyd A.
Middleton, Craig D.
Ogrizovic, Steven
Peake, Trevor
Pearce, Andrew J.
Rosario, Robert M.
Sansom, Kenneth G.
Smith, David
Titterton, David S.J.
Wilson, Carl N.
Woods, Raymond G.

League Appearances: Billing, P.G. 15; Borrows, B. 38; Butcher, T. 6; Clark, H.W. –(2); Dobson, A.J. 5(1); Drinkell, K.S. 11(4); Edwards, P. 22(1); Emerson, D. 20(4); Fleming, T.M. –(2); Gallacher, K.W. 32; Gynn, M. 35; Hurst, L.J. 3(1); Kilcline, B. 14; Livingstone, S. 6(4); McDonald, K. 7(2); McGrath, L.A. 12(2); Ogrizovic, S. 37; Peake, T. 36; Pearce, A.J. 11; Perdomo, J. 4; Regis, C. 31(3); Robson, S.I. 3(1); Rosario, R.M. –(2); Sansom, K.G. 9; Smith, D. 30(6); Speedie, D.R. 18; Sutton, S.J. 1; Thompson, K.A. –(1); Titterton, D.S.J. –(1); Woods, R.G. 12.

League Goals (42): Gallacher 11, Glynn 8, Borrows 6 (4 pens), Regis 4, Kilcline 3 (1 pen), Speedie 3, Livingstone 2, Dobson 1, Peake 1, Pearce 1, Smith 1, Woods 1.
Rumbelows Cup (15): Gallacher 5, Livingstone 5, Regis 3, Glynn 1, Speedie 1.
FA Cup (3): Glynn 2, Kilcline 1.
Ground: Highfield Road Stadium, King Richard Street, Coventry CV2 4FW (0203–257171)
Nearest Station: Coventry
Manager: John Sillett **Secretary:** G.P. Hover
Colours: Sky blue and white stripes; navy blue shorts
Record home gate: 51,455 v Wolverhampton, April 1967 (League)
Honours—Champions: Division 2: 1966–7; Division 3: 1963–4; Division 3 South: 1935–6
FA Cup winners: 1986–7

CREWE ALEXANDRA DIV. 4

Callaghan, Aaron J.
Carr, Darren J.
Curran, Christopher P.
Disley, Martin
Edwards, Paul
Gardiner, Mark C.
Greygoose, Dean
Gunn, Andrew C.
Hignett, Craig J.
Jasper, Dale W.
Jones, Robert
Lennon, Neil F.
McKearney, David
Murphy, Aiden J.
Naylor, Anthony J.
Rose, Collin J.
Smart, Jason
Sussex, Andrew R.
Swain, Kenneth
Walters, Stephen

League Appearances: Beresford, M. 3; Callaghan, A.J. 35(4); Carr, D.J. 32(4); Clayton, P.S. 16(6); Curran, C.P. 1(3); Doyle, M. 6(1); Edwards, P. 9; Edwards, R. 21(8); Foreman, D. 7(2); Gabbiadini, R. 1(1); Gardiner, M.C. 30(3); Garvey, S.H. –(1); Gorton, A. 3; Greygoose, D. 31; Gunn, A.C. 1(2); Hignett, C.J. 31(7); Jasper, D.W. 23(2); Jones, R. 29(3); Lennon, N.F. 32(2); McKearney, D. 23(8); Moore, J. –(1); Murphy, A.J. 13(3); Naylor, A.J. 5(9); Rose, C.J. 15(2); Scott, I. 12; Smart, J. 37; Sussex, A.R. 44; Swain, K. 39(2); Walters, S. 3(1); Ward, M.D. 4.
League Goals (62): Hignett 13 (1 pen), Edwards R 11, Sussex 11, Gardiner 10 (1 pen), Lennon 3, Clayton 2, Doyle 2, Murphy 2, Foreman 1, Jasper 1, Jones 1, McKearney 1, Naylor 1, Rose 1, Scott 1, Ward 1.
Rumbelows Cup (4): Sussex 4.
FA Cup (8): Hignett 2, Callaghan 1, Carr 1, Gardiner 1, McKearney 1, Sussex 1, Ward 1.
Ground: Gresty Road, Crewe CW2 6EB (0270–213014)
Nearest Station: Crewe
Manager: Dario Gradi **Secretary:** Mrs G.C. Palin
Colours: Red shirts, white trim; white shorts
Record home gate: 20,000 v Tottenham, January 1960 (FA Cup)
Honours: Nil

CRYSTAL PALACE DIV. 1

Barber, Phillip A.
Bodin, Paul
Bright, Mark A.
Collymore, Stanley V.
Gray, Andrew A.
Hopkins, Jeffrey
Humphrey, John
McGoldrick, Edward J.P.
Martyn, Anthony N.

Moralee, James D.
Newman, Richard A.
Osborn, Simon E.
Pardew, Alan S.
Rodger, Simon L.
Salako, John A.
Shaw, Richard E.
Southgate, Gareth
Suckling, Perry J.
Thomas, Geoffrey R.
Thompson, Garry L.
Thorn, Andrew C.
Whyte, David A.
Witter, Anthony J.
Woodman, Andrew J.
Wright, Ian E.
Young, Eric

League Appearances: Barber, P.A. 13(6); Bodin, P. 5; Bright, M.A. 29(3); Collymore, S.V. –(6); Dennis, M.E. –(1); Gray, A.A. 27(3); Hedman, R.G. 1; Hodges, G.P. 5(2); Humphrey, J. 38; McGoldrick, E.J.P. 21(5); Martyn, A.N. 38; Osborn, S.E. 2(2); Pardew, A.S. 15(4); Salako, J.A. 35; Shaw, R.E. 36; Southgate, G. 1; Thomas, G.R. 38; Thompson, G. 8(3); Thorn, A.C. 34; Wright, I.E. 38; Young, E. 34.
League Goals (50): Wright 15, Bright 9, Salako 6, Thomas 6, Gray 4 (2 pens), Young 3, Barber 1, Humphrey 1, Pardew 1, Shaw 1, Thompson 1, Thorn 1, own goal 1.
Rumbelows Cup (11): Bright 4, Wright 3, Hodges 1, Salako 1, Thompson 1, Young 1.
FA Cup (2): Salako 1, Wright 1.
Ground: Selhurst Park, SE25 6PU (081-653 4462)
Nearest Station: Selhurst, Norwood Junction of Thornton Heath
Manager: Steve Coppell **Secretary:** Alan J. Leather
Colours: Red and blue shirts; red shorts
Record home gate: 51,482 v Burnley, May 1979 (League)
Honours – Champions: Division 2: 1978–9; Division 3 South: 1920–21
Full Members Cup winners: 1990–1

DARLINGTON DIV. 3

Borthwick, John
Coatsworth, Gary
Coddington, Matthew J.
Cork, David
Corner, David E.
Coverdale, Drew
Elison, Anthony L.
Evans, Allan J.
Geddis, David
Gill, Gary
McJannet, William L.
Mardenborough, Stephen A
Prudhoe, Mark
Smith, Kevan
Tait, Michael P.
Toman, James A.
Trotter, Michael
Willis, James A.

League Appearances: Borthwick, J. 46; Burke, M.S. 5; Coatsworth, G. 6(6); Cook, M. 9; Cork, D. 31(3); Corner, D.E. 13(2); Coverdale, D. 14(2); Ellison, A.L. 9(4); Emson, P. 12(2); Evans, A.J. –(1); Geddis, D. 2(11); Gill, G. 36; Gray, F. 43; Linacre, P. 6(2); McJannet, W.L. 38(1); Mardenborough, S.A. 17(18); Prudhoe, M. 46; Smith, K. 46; Tait, M.P. 45; Toman, J.A. 43; Trotter, M. 11(13); Willis, J.A. 28.
League Goals (68): Borthwick 10, Cork 8, Gill 8 (1 pen), Gray 7 (6 pens), Toman 5, McJannet 4, Smith 4, Coverdale 3, Ellison 3, Linacre 3, Tait 2, Trotter 2, Willis 2, Burke 1, Coatsworth 1, Cook 1, Mardenborough 1, own goals 3.
Rumbelows Cup (4): Cork 2, Borthwick 1, Gray (1 pen).
FA Cup (1): Gill 1.
Ground: Feethams Ground, Darlington DL1 5JB (0325–465097 and 467712)
Nearest Station: Darlington
Manager: Frank Gray **Secretary:** Brian Anderson
Colours: All white
Record home gate: 21,023 v Bolton, November 1960 (League Cup)
Honours – Champions: Division 3 North: 1924–5; Division 4: 1990–1

DERBY COUNTY DIV. 2

Briscoe, Robert D.
Chalk, Martyn P.G.
Cross, Stephen C.
Davidson, Jonathan S.
Forsyth, Michael E.
Gee, Phillip J.
Hartford, Michael G.
Hayward, Steve L.
Hebberd, Trevor N.
Kavanagh, Jason C.
McMinn, Kevin C.
Micklewhite, Gary
Patterson, Mark
Phillips, Justin L.
Pickering, Nicholas
Ramage, Craig D.
Round, Stephen J.
Stage, Melvyn
Saunders, Dean N.
Shilton, Peter L.
Sleeuwenhoek, Kris
Straw, Robert G.
Taylor, Martin J.
Taylor, Stephen M.
Weston, Kingsley P.
Williams, David G.
Williams, Paul D.
Wright, Mark

League Appearances: Briscoe, R.D. 2(1); Callaghan, N. 12; Cross, S.C. 19(2); Davidson, J.S. 2(3); Forsyth, M.E. 35; Francis, K.M.D. –(2); Gee, P.J. 1(1); Harford, M.G. 36; Hayward, S.L. –(1); Hebbard, T.N. 12(9); Kavanagh, J.C. 5(6); McMinn, K.C. 13; Micklewhite, G. 35; Patterson, M. 6(3); Phillips, J.L. 3; Pickering, N. 12(1); Ramage, C.D. 15(2); Sage, M. 33(1); Saunders, D.N. 38; Shilton, P.L. 31; Taylor, M.J. 7; Watson, A.F. 5; Williams, D.G. 31; Williams, P.D. 17(2); Wilson, I. 11; Wright, M. 37
League Goals (37): Saunders 17 (4 pens), Harford 8 (1 pen), Williams P 4 (1 pen), Micklewhite 2, Callaghan 1, Hebberd 1, Patterson 1, Phillips 1, Ramage 1, Sage 1.
Rumbelows Cup (10): Harford 3, Saunders 3, Ramage 2, Micklewhite 1, own goal 1.
FA Cup (0).
Ground: The Baseball Ground, Shaftesbury Crescent, Derby DE3 8NB (0332–40105)
Nearest Station: Derby
Manager: Arthur Cox **Secretary:** M.J. Dunford
Colours: White shirts; black shorts
Record home gate: 41,826 v Tottenham, September 1969 (League)
Honours – Champions: Division 1: 1971–2, 1974–5; Division 2: 1911–12, 1914–15, 1968–9, 1986–7; Division 3 North: 1956–7
FA Cup winners: 1945–6

DONCASTER ROVERS DIV. 4

Boyle, Lee D.
Crichton, Paul A.
Douglas, Colin F.
Gormley, Edward J.
Harle, David
Jones-Quartey, David
Morrow, Grant R.
Muir, John G.
Nicholson, Maximilian
Noteman, Kevin S.
Ormsby, Brendan T.
Rankine, Simon M.
Reddish, Shane
Redhead, Christopher A.
Rowe, Brian
Samways, Mark
Stiles, John C.
Whitehurst, William

League Appearances: Adams, S. 2(3); Ashurst, J. 29; Bennett, C. 1(1); Brevett, R.E. 27; Brockie, V. 1(6); Crichton, P.A. 20; Cullen, D. 1; Douglas, C.F. 46; Gormley, E.J. 32(8); Grayson, N. 17(6); Harle, D. 16(6); Holland, S.L.D. 1; Holmes, A.J. 10(1); Jones, M. 5; Jones-Quartey, D. 7(6); Limber, N. 1; Mardon, P.J. 3; Morrow, G.R. 9(5); Muir, J.G. 35(4); Nicholson, M. 1; Noteman, K.S. 41(1); Ormsby, B.T. 43; Parsley, N.R. 2(1); Place, M.G. 1; Rankine, S.M. 40; Reddish, S. 9(2); Rowe, B.

3(1); Samways, M. 26; Smalley, P. 14; Stiles, J.C. 37; Turnbull, L.M. 13(6); Whitehurst, W. 13.
League Goals (56): Muir 13, Noteman 7, Turnbull 6 (1 pen), Gormley 5 (1 pen), Grayson 5, Ormsby 5 (1 pen), Brevett 3 (1 pen), Brockie 2 (2 pens), Harle 2 (1 pen), Jones 2, Rankine 2, Adams 1, Ashurst 1, Morrow 1, Whitehurst 1.
Rumbelows Cup (3): Brockie 1 (pen), Jones 1, Muir 1.
FA Cup (3): Gormley 1, Noteman 1, Rankine 1.
Ground: Belle Vue Ground, Doncaster DN4 5HT (0302–539441)
Nearest Station: Doncaster
Manager: Billy Bremner **Secretary:** Mrs K.J. Oldale
Colours: White shirts with red trim; red shorts
Record home gate: 37,149 v Hull City, October 1948 (League)
Honours – Champions: Division 3 North: 1934–5, 1946–7, 1949–50; Division 4: 1965–6, 1968–9

EVERTON DIV. 1

Atteveld, Raymond
Barlow, Stuart
Beagrie, Peter S.
Cottee, Anthony R.
Ebbrell, John K.
Hinchcliffe, Andrew G.
Kearton, Jason B.
Keown, Martin R.
McCall, Stuart M.
McDonald, Neil R.
Milligan, Michael
Nevin, Patrick K.F.
Newell, Michael C.
Quinlan, Philip E.
Ratcliffe, Kevin
Sharp, Graeme M.
Sheedy, Kevin M.
Snodin, Ian
Southall, Neville
Warzycha, Robert
Watson, David
Whiteside, Norman
Youds, Edward P.

League Appearances: Atteveld, R. 17(3); Barlow, S. –(2); Beagrie, P.S. 14(3); Cottee, A.R. 20(9); Ebbrell, J.K. 34(2); Hinchcliffe, A.G. 21; Jenkins, I. 1; Keown, M.R. 21(3); McCall, S.M. 33; McDonald, N.R. 27(2); Milligan, M. 16(1); Nevin, P.K.F. 31(6); Newell, M.C. 20(9); Ratcliffe, K. 35(1); Sharp, G.M. 24(3); Sheedy, K.M. 20(2); Snodin, I. 1; Southall, N. 38; Watson, D. 32; Whiteside, N. 1(1); Warzycha, R. 7(1); Youds, E.P. 5(3).
League Goals (50): Cottee 10, Nevin 8, Newell 7, Sheedy 4 (1 pen), Ebbrell 3, McCall 3, Sharp 3, Beagrie 2, McDonald 2, Warzycha 2, Watson 2, Hinchcliffe 1, Milligan 1, own goals 2.
Rumbelows Cup (12): Cottee 4, Sharp 3, McDonald 2, Ebbrell 1, Nevin 1, own goal 1.
FA Cup (9): Cottee 2, Ebbrell 2, Sharp 2, Watson 2, Sheedy 1.
Ground: Goodison Park, Liverpool L4 4EL (051–521 2020)
Nearest Station: Liverpool Lime Street
Manager: Howard Kendall **Secretary:** Jim Greenwood
Colours: Royal blue shirts; white shorts
Record home gate: 78,299 v Liverpool, September 1948 (League)
Honours – Champions: Division 1: 1890–91, 1914–15, 1927–8, 1931–2, 1938–9, 1962–3, 1969–70; 1984–5, 1986–7; Division 2: 1930–31
FA Cup winners: 1905–6, 1932–3, 1965–6, 1983–4
European Cup Winners Cup winners: 1984–5

EXETER CITY DIV. 3

Brown, Jonathan
Cawley, Peter
Cooper, Mark N.
Dryden, Richard A.
Frankland, Tony
Hiley, Scott P.
Hobson, Gordon
Jones, Murray L.
Kelly, Thomas J.
Marshall, Gary
Miller, Kevin
Morgan, Trevor J.
Neville, Steven F.
Rowbotham, Darran
Taylor, Shaun

League Appearances: Bailey, D.S. 17(1); Batty, P.W. 9(2); Boughey, D.J. 8; Brown, J. 26(3); Cawley, P. 7; Cooper, M.N. 42; Dryden, R.A. 41; Eshelby, P. 9(9); Frankland, T. –(3); Hiley, S.P. 46; Hobson, G. 37; Jones, M.L. 16(4); Kelly, T.J. 13(9); McDermott, B.J. 8; McNichol, J.A. 9; Marshall, G. 31(1); Miller, K. 46; Morgan, T.J. 14(3); Neville, S.F. 35(5); O'Toole, C.P. 6; Owen, G. 4; Rogers, L. 16(1); Rowbotham, D. 9(4); Rowe, B.P. 1(1); Taylor, S. 45; Whitehead, C.R. 8; Young, R.A. 3(4).
League Goals (58): Cooper 11 (2 pens), Neville 11, Hobson 7 (3 pens) Dryden 6, Taylor 4, Jones 3, Marshall 3, Morgan 3, Rowbotham 3, Hiley 2, Bailey 1, Boughey 1, Eshelby 1, Kelly 1 (pen), own goal 1.
Rumbelows Cup (1): Dryden 1.
FA Cup (1): Neville 1.
Ground: St James' Park, Exeter, Devon EX4 6PX (0392–54073)
Nearest Station: Exeter Central or St David's
Manager: Alan Ball **Secretary:** M. Holladay
Colours: Red and white vertical striped shirts; black shorts
Record home gate: 20,984 v Sunderland, March 1931 (FA Cup)
Honours – Champions: Division 4· 1989–90

FULHAM DIV. 3

Baker, Graham E.
Brazil, Gary N.
Cobb, Gary E.
Eckhardt, Jeffrey E.
Ferney, Martin J.
Finch, John
Haag, Kelly
Hails, Julian
Kelly, Mark D.
Lewington, Raymond
Marshall, John P.
Milton, Stephen
Morgan, Simon C.
Nebbeling, Gavin M.
Newson, Mark
North, Stacey S.
Onwere, Udo A.
Pike, Martin R.
Rocastle, Steven O.
Scott, Peter R.
Skinner, Justin
Stannard, James
Stant, Philip R.
Thomas, Glen A.
Tucker, Mark J.

League Appearances: Baker, G.E. 5(1); Batty, L. 2; Brazil, G.N. 41(1); Cobb, G.E. 4(7); Cole, M.W. –(2); Davies, G.J. 19(11); Eckhardt, J.E. 28(1); Ferney, M.J. 12(2); Finch, J. 1; Gray, P. 3; Haag, K. 12(11); Joseph, F. 2(2); Kelly, M.D. 17(1); Langley, R.J. –(4); Marshall, J.P. 34(1); Milton, S. 12(11); Morgan, S.C. 32; Nebbeling, G.M. 5(1); Newson, M. 31; North, S.S. 38; Onwere, U.A. 5(2); Parks, A. 2; Pike, M.R. 45(1); Rosenior, L.D.G. 11; Scott, P.R. 23; Skinner, J. 24(8); Stannard, J. 42; Stant, P. 19; Talbot, B. 5; Thomas, G.A. 32(2).
League Goals (41): Davies 6, Skinner 5 (2 pens), Stant 5, Brazil 4 (1 pen), Haag 3, Pike 3, Rosenior 3, Eckhardt 2, Marshall 2, Scott 2, Baker 1, Newson 1, Onwere 1 (pen), Talbot 1, Thomas 1, own goal 1.

Rumbelows Cup (1): Joseph 1.
FA Cup (3): Brazil 1 (pen), Davies 1, Pike 1.
Ground: Craven Cottage, Stevenage Road, Fulham SW6 6HH (071–736 6561)
Nearest Station: Putney Bridge (District) or Hammersmith (Metropolitan, District and Piccadilly)
Manager: Alan Dicks **Secretary:** Mrs Yvonne Haines
Colours: White shirts, black trim; black shorts
Record home gate: 49,335 v Millwall, October 1938 (League)
Honours – Champions: Division 2: 1948–9; Division 3 South: 1931–2

GILLINGHAM — DIV. 4

Arnott, Andrew J.
Beadle, Peter C.
Berkley, Austin J.
Burke, Paul G.
Butler, Philip A.
Carpenter, Richard
Clarke, Brian R.
Crown, David I.
Dempsey, Mark A.P.
Dunne, Joseph
Eeles, Anthony G.
Hague, Paul
Lim, Harvey C.
Lovell, Stephen J.
Manuel, William A.J.
Martin, Eliot J.
O'Connor, Mark A.
O'Shea, Timothy J.
Palmer, Lee J.
Trusson, Michael S.
Walker, Alan

League Appearances: Beadle, P.C. 12(10); Butler, P.A. 6; Carpenter, R. 6(3); Clarke, B.R. 20; Crown, D.I. 29(1); Dempsey, M.A.P. –(2); Docker, I. 26(5); Dunne, J. 25(1); Eeles, A.G. 1(5); Gleasure, P.F. 3; Hague, P. 6(1); Haines, I. 12; Harle, M.J.L. 1(1); Heritage, P.M. 8(7); Hillyard, R.W. 4; Johnson, P.E. 22(2); Jordan, D.C. –(2); Kimble, G.L. 23(11); Lim, H.C. 39; Lovell, S.J. 46; McDonald, D.H. 10; Manuel, W.A.J. 31(7); O'Connor, M.A. 39(2); O'Shea, T.J. 26(3); Owers, A.R. 9(1); Palmer, L.J. 18(3); Trusson, M.S. 39; Walker, A. 44; West, G. 1.
League Goals (57): Lovell 19 (3 pens), Crown 11, Beadle 7, Trusson 4 (2 pens), Walker 4 Docker 3, O'Connor 3, Heritage 2, Carpenter 1, Kimble 1, Palmer 1, own goal 1.
Rumbelows Cup (1): Lovell 1.
FA Cup (1): Crown 1.
Ground: Priestfield Stadium, Gillingham, Kent ME7 4DD (0634–51854 and 576828)
Nearest Station: Gillingham
Manager: Damien Richardson **Secretary:** Barry Bright
Colours: Blue shirts, white trim; white shorts and blue trim
Record home gate: 23,002 v Queen's Park Rangers, January 1948 (FA Cup)
Honours – Champions: Division 4: 1963–4

GRIMSBY TOWN — DIV. 2

Agnew, Paul
Childs, Gary P.C.
Cockerill, John
Cunnington, Shaun G.
Futcher, Paul
Gilbert, David J.
Hargreaves, Christian
Jobling, Kevin A.
Knight, Ian J.
Lever, Mark
McDermott, John
Reece, Paul J.
Rees, Anthony A.
Sherwood, Stephen
Smith, Mark
Watson, Thomas R.
Woods, Neil

League Appearances: Agnew, P. 6(1); Alexander, K. –(1); Baraclough, I.R. 1(3); Birtles, G. 15(8); Childs, G.P.C. 20(5); Cockerill, J. 34(1); Croft, G. –(1); Cunnington, S.G. 46; Futcher, P. 22; Gilbert, D.J. 44; Hargreaves, C. 8(10); Jobling, K.A. 44(1); Knight, I.J. 4(4); Lever, M. 40; McDermott, J. 43; Rees, A.A. 36; Sherwood, S. 46; Smith, M. 1(10); Tillson, A. 18; Watson, T.R. 36(5); Woods, N. 42(2).
League Goals (66): Gilbert 12 (6 pens), Woods 12, Rees 10, Watson 9, Cockerill 7, Childs 4, Hargreaves 3, Cunnington 2, Lever 2, Birtles 1, Knight 1, own goals 3.
Rumbelows Cup (2): Gilbert 1, Hargreaves 1.
FA Cup (0).
Ground: Blundell Park, Cleethorpes, DN35 7PY (0472–697111)
Nearest Station: Cleethorpes or Grimsby Town
Manager: Alan Buckley **Secretary:** I. Fleming
Colours: Black and white striped shirts; black shorts
Record home gate: 31,651 v Wolverhampton, February 1937 (FA Cup)
Honours – Champions: Division 2: 1900–1, 1933–4; Division 3 North: 1925–6, 1955–6; Division 3: 1979–80; Division 4: 1971–2

HALIFAX TOWN DIV. 4

Barr, William J.
Butler, Brian F.
Donnelly, Paul A.
Ellis, Mark
Evans, David
Fleming, Craig
Fleming, Paul
Gould, Jonathan A.
Graham, Thomas
Gregory, Anthony G.
Juryeff, Ian M.
Megson, Kevin C.
Norris, Stephen M.
Richardson, Nicholas

League Appearances: Barr, W.J. 34(3); Broadbent, G.R. 3(4); Brown, D.J. 11; Butler, B.F. 19(7); Cook, M. 16(1); Cooper, G. 13(4); Dobson, P. 1, Donnelly, P.A. 8(3); Ellis, M. 27(3); Evans, D. 42; Fleming, C. 46; Fleming, P. 39; Futcher, P. 15; Fyfe, T. 3(1); German, D. –(1); Gore, S.M. 15; Gould, J.A. 23; Graham, T. 23; Gregory, A.G. 11(1); Griffiths, N. 1; Hall, D.R. 8; Hutchinson, I.N. 3; Juryeff, I.M. 34; Leonard, M.C. 3; McPhillips, T. 3(2); Martin, D. 26(2); Megson, K. 5; Norris, S.M. 39; Patterson, J.R. 3(3); Richardson, N. 23(3); Whitehead, P.M. 9.
League Goals (59): Norris 30 (8 pens), Juryeff 9, Ellis 4, Graham 3, Richardson 3, Barr 1, Broadbent 1, Butler 1, Cooper 1, Dobson 1, Evans 1, Gregory 1, Martin 1, Patterson 1, own goal 1.
Rumbelows Cup (4): Evans 1, Fyfe 1, Gregory 1, Richardson 1.
FA Cup (5): Juryeff 2, Norris 2, Graham 1.
Ground: The Shay, Halifax HX1 2YS (0422–53423)
Nearest Station: Halifax
Manager: Jim McCalliog **Secretary:** Mrs A. Pettifor
Colours: Blue and white shirts, blue shorts
Record home gate: 36,885 v Tottenham, February 1953 (FA Cup)
Honours: Nil

HARTLEPOOL UNITED DIV. 3

Allon, Joseph B.
Baker, David P.
Bennyworth, Ian R.
Dalton, Paul
Davies, Andrew J.
Fletcher, Steven M.

Gabbiadini, Ricardo
Honour, Brian
McKinnon, Robert
MacPhail, John
Nesbitt, Mark T.
Nobbs, Alan K.
Olsson, Paul
Smith, Michael
Southall, Nicholas
Tinkler, John
Tupling, Stephen

League Appearances: Allon, J.B. 46; Baker, D.P. 43(3); Bennyworth, I.R. 42(1); Cox, B.R. 34; Dalton, P. 40(6); Davies, A.J. 2(2); Davies, K.F. 1(2); Duggan, A.J. 2; Dunbar, I. –(2); Fletcher, S.M. 5(9); Gabbiadini, R. 1(4); Heaney, N.A. 2(1); Honour, B. 39(3); Hutchison, D. 7(4); Lamb, A. –(4); MacDonald, G. 1(1); McKinnon, R. 45; MacPhail, J. 42; Nesbitt, M.T. 1; Nobbs, A.K. 38(2); Olsson, P. 29(2); Poole, K. 12; Shotton, J. –(1); Smith, M. 11(1); Tinkler, J. 23(3); Tupling, S. 40(2).
League Goals (67): Allon 28 (3 pens), Baker 12, Dalton 11, Honour 4, Fletcher 2, Tinkler 2, Tupling 2, McKinnon 1, MacPhail 1, Olsson 1, Smith 1, own goals 2.
Rumbelows Cup (5): Allon 2, Baker 1, Dalton 1, Honour 1.
FA Cup (3): Allon 3.
Ground: Victoria Ground, Clarence Road, Hartlepool TS24 8BZ (ground 0429–272584; office 0429–222077)
Nearest Station: Hartlepool
Manager: Alan Murray **Secretary:** M. Kirby
Colours: All blue
Record home gate: 17,426 v Manchester United, January 1957 (FA Cup)
Honours: Nil

HEREFORD UNITED — DIV. 4

Bradley, Russell
Brain, Simon A.J.
Devine, Steven B.
Elliott, Anthony R.
Goddard, Karl E.
Heritage, Peter M.
Jones, Richard
Lowndes, Stephen R.
Narbett, Jonathan V.
Pejic, Melvyn
Vaughan, Nigel M.
Wood, George

League Appearances: Benbow, I.R. –(1); Bradley, R. 39(2); Brain, S.A.J. 20(2); Burton, P.S. 1(1); Devine, S.B. 38; Dobson, P. 6; Elliott, A.R. 5; Goddard, K.E. 8; Gordon, C.K. 6; Hemming, C.A.J. 5(1); Heritage, P.M. 17(1); Jones, M.A.W. 46; Jones, R. 40; Jones, S.G. 3(15); Juryeff, I.M. 3; Lowndes, S.R. 16(1); Miller, P.W. 5; Mitchell, I.D. –(3); Narbett, J.V. 44; Peacock, D. 15; Pejic, M. 46; Phillips, S.G. 31(6); Robinson, C.R. 16(19); Tester, P.L. 41(3); Vaughan, N.M. 1; Wheeler, P. 13(20); Wood, G. 41.
League Goals (53): Narbett 11 (6 pens), Phillips 10, Brain 8, Wheeler 4, Tester 3, Bradley 2, Millar 2, Robinson 2, Dobson 1, Goddard 1, Hemming 1, Heritage 1, Jones M A 1, Jones R 1, Jones S 1, Juryeff 1, Lowndes 1, Peacock 1, Pejic 1.
Rumbelows Cup (1): Phillips 1.
FA Cup (2): Narbett 1, Pejic 1.
Ground: Edgar Street, Hereford HR4 9JU (0432–276666)
Nearest Station: Hereford
Manager: John Sillett **Secretary:** D.H. Vaughan
Colours: White shirts; black shorts
Record home gate: 18,114 v Sheffield Wednesday, 1958 (FA Cup)
Honours – Champions: Division 3: 1975–6

HUDDERSFIELD TOWN DIV. 3

Barnett, Gary L.
Byrne, Brian J.
Campbell, David M.
Charlton, Simon T.
Donovan, Kevin
Dyson, Jonathan P.
Edwards, Keith
Haylock, Gary A.
Ireland, Simon P.
Jackson, Peter A.
Kelly, John
Lewis, Dudley K.
Marsden, Christopher
Martin, Lee B.
Mitchell, Graham L.
O'Doherty, Kenneth B.
Onuora, Iffem
O'Regan, Kieron
Parsley, Neil R.
Roberts, Iwan W.
Trevitt, Simon
Wilson, Robert J.

League Appearances: Barnett, G.L. 19(3); Campbell, D.M. 1; Charlton, S.T. 29(1); Donovan, K. 4(2); Edwards, K. 10(8); Hardwick, S. 42; Haylock, G.A. 9(3); Ireland, S.P. 3(3); Jackson, P.A. 38; Kelly, J. 3(1); Lewis, D.K. 4(2); Maguire, P.J. 1(3); Marsden, C. 43; Martin, L.B. 4; Mitchell, G.L. 46; O'Doherty, K.B. 8; Onuora, I. 32(11); O'Regan, K. 46; Parsley, N.R. 6(2); Quinlan, P.E. 7(1); Roberts, I.W. 44; Smith, M.C. 29(3); Stant, P.R. 5; Trevitt, S. 38; Wright, M.A. 10; Wilson, R.J. 25(4).

League Goals (57): Roberts 13, O'Regan 11 (8 pens), Onuora 7, Marsden 5, Edwards 4, Haylock 4, Quinlan 2, Smith 2, Wilson 2, Barnett 1, Donovan 1, Jackson 1, Maguire 1, Stant 1, Wright 1, own goal 1

Rumbelows Cup (1): O'Regan 1.

FA Cup (2): Onuora 1, Roberts 1.

Ground: Kirklees Stadium, Leeds Road, Huddersfield HD1 6PE (0484–420335/6)

Nearest Station: Huddersfield

Manager: Eoin Hand **Secretary:** G.S. Binns

Colours: Blue and white striped shirts; white shorts

Record home gate: 67,037 v Arsenal, February 1932 (FA Cup)

Honours – Champions: Division 1: 1923–4, 1924–5, 1925–6; Division 2: 1969–70; Division 4: 1979–80

FA Cup winners: 1921–2

HULL CITY DIV. 3

Atkinson, Graeme
Brown, Nicholas L.
Buckley, Neil A.
Calvert, Mark R.
Cleminshaw, David C.
De Mange, Kenneth J.P.P
Hesford, Iain
Hockaday, David
Hunter, Paul
Jacobs, Wayne G.
Jenkinson, Leigh
McParland, Ian J.
Mail, David
Palin, Leigh
Payton, Andrew P.
Shotton, Malcolm
Swan, Peter H.
Waites, Paul
Warren, Lee A.
Wilcox, Russell

League Appearances: Allison, N.J. 1; Atkinson, G. 14(2); Bamber, J.D. 6(3); Brown, N.L. 2(1); Buckley, N.A. 30(1); Butler, L.S. 4; Calvert, M.R. 7; Dearden, K.C. 3; De Mange, K.J.P.P. 5(1); Doyle, S.C. 11; Finnigan, A. 15(3); Hesford, I. 31; Hobson, G. 4; Hockaday, D. 35; Hunter, P. 6(12); Jacobs, W.G. 19; Jenkinson, L. 12(14); Jobson, R.I. 2; McParland, I.J. 7(9); Mail, D. 35(1); Ngata, H. 1(9); Norton, D.W. 15; Palin, L. 35; Payton, A.P. 43; Roberts, G.W. 8; Shotton, M. 26; Smith, M.K. 4(2); Swan, P.H. 38; Thomas, D.G. 10(1); Thompson, L. 19(1); Waites, P. 10; Walmsley, D.G. 1; Warren, L.A. 15; Wilcox, R. 24(7); Wilson, S.L. 2; Wright, T. 6.

League Goals (57): Payton 25 (1 pen), Swan 12, Palin 5 (3 pens), Bamber 2, Buckley 2, Hunter 2, Thompson 2, Finnigan 1, Hockaday 1, Jacobs 1, McParland 1, Mail 1, Walmsley 1, Wilcox 1.
Rumbelows Cup (1): Swan 1.
FA Cup (2): Buckley 1, McParland 1.
Ground: Boothferry Park, Hull HU4 6EU (0482–51119)
Nearest Station: Hull or Boothferry Park Halt
Manager: Terry Dolan **Secretary:** Frank Boughton
Colours: Black and amber striped shirts; black shorts
Record home gate: 55,019 v Manchester United, February 1949 (FA Cup)
Honours – Champions: Division 3 North: 1932–3, 1948–9; Division 3: 1965–6

IPSWICH TOWN — DIV. 2

Bernal, Andrew
Dozzell, Jason A.W.
Fearon, Ronald T.
Forrest, Craig L.
Gayle, Brian W.
Goddard, Paul
Gregory, David S.
Hill, David M.
Honeywood, Lee B.
Humes, Anthony
Johnson, Gavin
Kiwomya, Christopher M.
Linigan, David
Lowe, David A.
Milton, Simon C.
Palmer, Stephen L.
Parkes, Philip B.N.F.
Pennyfather, Glenn J.
Redford, Ian P.
Stockwell, Michael T.
Thompson, Gary M.
Thompson, Neil
Whelan, Philip J.
Whitton, Stephen P.
Yallop, Frank W.
Zondervan, Romeo

League Appearances: Dozzell, J.A.W. 27(3); Forrest, C.L. 43; Gayle, B.W. 33; Goddard, P. 18(1); Gregory, D.S. 14(7); Hill, D.M. 18(5); Houghton, S.A. 7(1); Humes, A. 15(1); Johnson, G. 5(2); Kiwomya, C.M. 34(3); Linighan, D. 45; Lowe, D.A. 12(1); Milton, S.C. 27(4); Palmer, S.L. 18(5); Parkes, P.B.N.F. 3; Redford, I.P. 23(3); Stockwell, M.T. 44; Thompson, N. 33(5); Whitton, S.P. 10; Yallop, F.W. 44(1); Zondervan, R. 33(1).
League Goals (60): Kiwomya 10, Dozzell 6, Goddard 6, Milton 6, Stockwell 6, Thompson 6 (2 pens), Gayle 4, Redford 4 (1 pen), Linighan 3, Humes 2, Whitton 2, Gregory 1, Houghton 1, Palmer 1, own goals 2.
Rumbelows Cup (4): Redford 2, Kiwomya 1, Milton 1.
FA Cup (2): Dozzell 2.
Ground: Portman Road, Ipwsich IP1 2DA (0473–219211)
Nearest Station: Ipswich
Manager: John Lyall **Secretary:** D.C. Rose
Colours: Royal blue shirts; white shorts
Record home gate: 38,010 v Leeds United, March 1975 (FA Cup)
Honours – Champions: Division 1: 1961–2; Division 2: 1960–61, 1967–8; Division 3 South: 1953–4, 1956–7
FA Cup winners: 1977–8
UEFA Cup winners: 1980–81

LEEDS UNITED — DIV. 1

Batty, David
Beglin, James M.
Chapman, Lee R.
Curtis, Leonard P.
Davison, Robert
Day, Mervyn R.

Fairclough, Courtney H.
Grayson, Simon N.
Haddock, Peter M.
Kamara, Christoipher
Kerr, Dylan
Lukic, Jovan
McAllister, Gary
McClelland, John
O'Dowd, Anthony T.
Pearson, John S.
Shutt, Carl S.
Snodin, Glynn
Speed, Gary A.
Sterland, Melvyn
Strachen, Gordon D.
Varadi, Imrie
Whitlow, Michael
Whyte, Christopher
Wigley, Russel D.C.G.
Williams, Andrew

League Appearances: Batty, D. 37; Chapman, L.R. 38; Davison, R. 2(3); Fairclough, C.H. 34; Haddock, P.M. 10(5); Jones, V. 1; Kamara, C. 5(2); Lukic, J. 38; McAllister, G. 38; McClelland, J. 3; Pearson, J.S. 4(9); Shutt, C.S. 25(3); Snodin, G. 14(6); Speed, G.A. 35(3); Sterland, M. 38; Strachan, G.D. 34; Varadi, I. 5(1); Whitlow, M. 14(4); Whyte, C. 38; Williams, A. 5(7).
League Goals (65): Chapman 21, Shutt 10, Speed 7, Strachan 7 (4 pens), Sterland 5, Fairclough 4, Whyte 3, McAllister 2, Varadi 2, Davison 1, Pearson 1, Whitlow 1, own goal 1.
Rumbelows Cup (13): Chapman 4, Speed 3, McAllister 2, Fairclough 1, Strachan 1, Whyte 1, own goal 1.
FA Cup (7): Chapman 3, McAllister 1, Sterland 1, Strachan 1 (pen), own goal 1.
Ground: Elland Road, Leeds LS11 0ES (0532–716037)
Nearest Station: Leeds
Manager: Howard Wilkinson **Secretary:** D.J. Dowse
Colours: All white
Record home gate: 57,892 v Sunderland, March 1967 (FA Cup)
Honours – Champions: Division 1: 1968–9, 1973–4; Division 2: 1923–4, 1963–4
FA Cup winners: 1971–2
League Cup winners: 1967–8
European Fairs Cup winners: 1967–8, 1970–71

LEICESTER CITY DIV. 2

Baraclough, Ian R.
Gibson, Colin J.
Hill, Ricky A.
Hodge, Martin J.
Holden, Stephen A.
Hoult, Russell
James, Anthony C.
Johnson, Robert S.
Kelly, David T.A.
Kitson, Paul
Linton, Desmond M.
Mauchlen, Allster H.
Mills, Gary R.
Muggleton, Carl D.
Oakes, Scott, J.
Oldfield, David C.
Peake, Jason W.
Ramsey, Paul C.
Reid, Paul R.
Russell, Kevin J.
Smith, Richard G.
Walsh, Steven
Williams, Darren
Wright, Thomas E.

League Appearances: Davies, W.M. 5(1); Fenwick, T.W. 8; Gavin, P.J. 1(2); Gibson, C.J. 17(1); Hill, R.A. 19(7); Hodge, M.J. 10; Hooper, M.D. 14; James, A.C. 35(3); Johnson, R.S. 8(4); Kelly, D. 41(3); Kitson, P. 2(5); Linton, D.M. 5(3); Madden, L.D. 3; Mauchlen, A.H. 40; Mills, G.R. 45; Muggleton, C.D. 22; North, M.V. 35(4); Oldfield, D.C. 32(10); Paris, A.D. 10(3); Peake, J.W. 4(4); Ramsey, P. 20(4); Reid, P.R. 24(9); Russell, K.J. 13; Smith, R.G. 2(2); Spearing, A. 16(1); Walsh, S. 35; Wright, T.E. 40(4).
League Goals (60): Kelly 14 (2 pens), James 8, Oldfield 7, Wright 7, Mills 5 (1 pen), Russell 5 (1 pen), Walsh 3, North 2, Reid 2, Fenwick 1, Gibson 1, Mauchlen 1, Peake 1, own goals 3.
Rumbelows Cup (1): Kelly 1 (pen).

FA Cup (1): James 1.
Ground: Filbert Street, Leicester LE2 7FL (0533–555000)
Nearest Station: London Road, Leicester
Manager: Brian Little **Secretary:** A.K. Bennett
Colours: Blue shirts; white shorts
Record home gate: 47,298 v Tottenham Hotspur, February 1928 (FA Cup)
Honours – Champions: Division: 2: 1924–5, 1936–7, 1953–4, 1956–7, 1970–71, 1979–80
League Cup winners: 1963–4

LEYTON ORIENT DIV.3

Achampong, Kenneth
Baker, Adam
Baker, Stephen
Berry, Greg J.
Burnett, Wayne
Carter, Darren S.
Castle, Stephen C.
Cobb, Paul
Cooper, Mark D.
Day, Keith
Dickerson, Kevin J.
Hackett, Warren J.
Hales, Kevin P.
Harvey, Lee D.
Heald, Paul A.
Howard, Terry
Newell, Paul C.
Nugent, Kevin P.
O'Neill, Mark A.
Otto, Ricky
Sayer, Andrew
Sharman, Keith E.
Whitbread, Adrian R.

League Appearances: Achampong, K. 25(9); Baker, S. 23(2); Bart-Williams, C. 19(2); Berry, G.J. 32(3); Burnett, W. –(1); Carter, D.S. 38(4); Castle, S.C. 45; Cobb, P. 2(2); Cooper, M.D. 18(4); Day, K. 21(3); Dickenson, K.J. 6(1); Fee, G. 4(1); Hackett, W.J. 4; Hales, K.P. 3(2); Harvey, L.D. 21(5); Heald, P.A. 38; Hoddle, C. –(2); Howard, T. 46; Hull, A.E. –(2); Newell, P.C. 8; Nugent, K.P. 33; Otto, R. –(1); Pike, G.A. 30; Sayer, A. 6(5); Sitton, J.E. 22(2); Taylor, R. –(3); Tomlinson, M.L. –(1); Whitbread, A.R. 38; Zoricich, C.V. 24(4).
League Goals (55): Castle 12 (2 pens), Cooper 9, Berry 5, Carter 5, Nugent 5, Achampong 4, Harvey 3, Howard 3, Bart-Williams 2, Sayer 2, Day 1, Pike 1, Taylor 1, Tomlinson 1, own goal 1.
Rumbelows Cup (9): Castle 3 (1 pen), Nugent 3, Berry 2, Harvey 1.
FA Cup (8): Castle 3, Pike 2, Carter 1, Howard 1, Nugent 1.
Ground: Leyton Stadium, Brisbane Road, Leyton E10 5NE (081–539 2223/4)
Nearest Station: Leyton (Central Line)
Manager: Frank Clark **Secretary:** Miss C. Stokes
Colours: Red shirts; white shorts
Record home gate: 34,345 v West Ham United, January 1964 (FA Cup)
Honours – Champions: Division 3: 1969–70; Division 3 South: 1955–6

LINCOLN CITY DIV. 4

Alexander, Keith
Bowling, Ian
Bressington, Graham
Brown, Grant A.
Carmichael, Matthew
Casey, Paul
Clarke, David A.
Dobson, Paul
Dunphy, Sean
Lee, Jason B.
Lomor, Anthony
Nicholson, Shane M.
Puttnam, David P.
Schofield, John D.
Scott, Keith
Smith, Neil
Smith, Paul M.
Stoutt, Stephen P.
Thompson, Steven P.
Ward, Paul

League Appearances: Alexander, K. 21(2); Bowling, I. 16; Bressington, G. 36(1); Brown, G.A. 32; Carmichael, M. 20(6); Casey, P. 26(3); Clarke, D.A. 14(1); Crombie, D.M. –(1); Davis, D.J. 29(1); Dickins, M. 7; Dobson, P. 9(1); Lee, J.B. 17; Lormor, A. 31(3); Nicholson, S.M. 38(2); Powell, G. 11; Puttnam, D.P. 38(5); Rawcliffe, P. –(1); Schofield, J.D. 41(1); Scott, K. 1(5); Sims, S.F. 5; Smith, N. 9(3); Smith, P.M. 45(1); Stant, P.R. 4; Stoutt, S.P. 15(10); Wallington, F.M. 23; Ward, P. 9; Warren, L.A. 2(1); West, D. 1; West, G. 3; Wilson, D.G. 3.

League Goals (50): Lormor 12, Puttnam 6, Smith P 6, Casey 4, Nicholson 4 (3 pens), Alexander 3, Lee 3, Schofield 3, Carmichael 2, Davis 2, Brown 1, Dobson 1, Stoutt 1, Warren 1, West D 1.

Rumbelows Cup (1): Davis 1.

FA Cup (1): Lormor 1.

Ground: Sincil Bank, Lincoln LN5 8LD (0522–22224 and 510263)

Nearest Station: Lincoln Central and St Mark's

Manager: Steve Thompson **Secretary:** G.R. Davey

Colours: Red and white striped shorts; black shorts

Record home gate: 23,196 v Derby, November 1967 (League Cup)

Honours – Champions: Division 3 North: 1931–2, 1947–8, 1951–2; Division 4: 1975–6

LIVERPOOL — DIV. 1

Ablett, Gary I.
Barnes, John C.B.
Beardsley, Peter A.
Burrows, David
Carter, James W.C.
Collins, David D.
Cousins, Anthony J.
Gillespie, Gary T.
Godfrey, Warren
Grobbelaar, Bruce D.
Harkness, Steven
Hollis, Stephen J.
Hooper, Michael D.
Houghton, Raymond J.
Hutchison, Donald
Hysen, Glenn I.
Johnston, Craig P.
Jones, Barry
Kenny, Marc V.
Lampkin, Kevin
McMahon, Stephen
McManaman, Steven
Marsh, Michael A.
Molby, Jan
Nicol, Stephen
Payne, Russell
Redknapp, Jamie F.
Robinson, Jamie
Rosenthal, Ronny
Rush, Ian J.
Speedie, David R.
Staunton, Stephen
Tanner, Nicholas
Venison, Barry
Whelan, Ronald A.

League Appearances: Ablett, G.I. 23; Barnes, J.C.B. 35; Beardsley, P.A. 24(3); Burrows, D. 34(1); Carter, J.W.C. 2(3); Gillespie, G.T. 30; Grobbelaar, B.D. 31; Hooper, M.D. 7; Houghton, R.J. 31(1); Hysen, G.I. 32; McMahon, S. 22; McManaman, S. –(2); Marsh, M.A. 1(1); Molby, J. 22(3); Nicol, S. 35; Rosenthal, R. 4(12); Rush, I.J. 37; Speedie, D.R. 8(4); Staunton, S. 20(4); Venison, B. 6; Whelan, R.A. 14.

League Goals (77): Barnes 16 (1 pen), Rush 16, Beardsley 11, Molby 9 (8 pens), Houghton 7, Speedie 6, Rosenthal 5, Nichol 3, Gillespie 1, Whelan 1, own goals 2.

Rumbelows Cup (10): Rush 5, Houghton 2, Gillespie 1, McMahon 1, Staunton 1.

FA Cup (13): Rush 5, Beardsley 3, McMahon 2, Barnes 1, Houghton 1, Staunton 1, own goal 1.

Ground: Anfield Road, Liverpool L4 0TH (051–263 2361)

Nearest Station: All stations Liverpool

Manager: Graeme Souness **Chief Executive/Secretary:** P.B. Robinson

Colours: All red

Record home gate: 61,905 v Wolverhampton, February 1952 (FA Cup)
Honours – Champions: Division 1: 1900–1, 1905–6, 1921–2, 1922–3, 1946–7, 1963–4, 1965–6, 1972–3, 1975–6, 1976–7, 1978–9, 1979–80, 1981–2, 1982–3, 1983–4, 1985–6, 1987–8, 1989–90 (record 18 titles); Division 2: 1893–4, 1895–6, 1904–5, 1961–2
FA Cup winners: 1964–5, 1973–4, 1985–6, 1988–9
Football League Cup winners: 1980–81, 1981–2, 1982–3, 1983–4
European Cup winners: 1976–7, 1977–8, 1980–81, 1983–4
UEFA Cup winners: 1972–3, 1975–6
Super Cup winners: 1977

LUTON TOWN — DIV. 1

Allpress, Timothy J.
Beaumont, David A.
Black, Kingsley
Chamberlain, Alec F.R.
Dreyer, John B.
Elstrup, Lars
Farrell, Sean P.
Gillard, Kenneth J.
Gormley, David P.
Harvey, Richard G.
Holsgrove, Paul
Hughes, Ceri M.
Jackson, Matthew
James, Julian C.
Johnson, Marvin A.
McDonough, Darren K.
Nogan, Kurt
O'Brien, Michael T.
Pembridge, Mark A.
Petterson, Andrew K.
Preece, David W.
Rees, Jason
Rodger, Graham
Salton, Darren B.
Shanley, Kevin J.
Telfer, Paul N.
Tighe, Aaron P.

League Appearances: Beaumont, D.A. 29(4); Black, K. 37; Breacker, T.S. 8; Chamberlain, A.F.R. 38; Dowie, I. 26(3); Dreyer, J.B. 38; Elstrup, L. 37; Farrell, S.P. 11(9); Harvey, R.G. 26(3); Holsgrove, P. –(1); Hughes, C.M. 17; James, J.C. 10(7); Johnson, M.A. 24(2); McDonough, D.K. 21(5); Nogan, K. 1(8); Pembridge, M.A. 18; Preece, D.W. 37; Rees, J. 11(10); Rodger, G. 14; Telfer, P.N. –(1); Williams, S.C. 15(1).
League Goals (42): Elstrup 15, Black 7, Dowie 7, Dreyer 3 (3 pens), Rodger 2, Farrell 1, Hughes 1, James 1, Pembridge 1, Preece 1, own goals 3.
Rumbelows Cup (2): Black 1, Harvey 1.
FA Cup (4): Elstrup 2, Black 1, Farrell 1.
Ground: Kenilworth Road Stadium, Luton LU1 1DH (0582–411622)
Nearest Station: Luton
Manager: David Pleat **General-Manager-Secretary:** William J. Tomlins
Colours: White shirts with navy V-neck; navy shorts
Record home gate: 30,069 v Blackpool, March 1959 (FA cup)
Honours – Champions: Division 2: 1981–2; Division 4: 1967–8
League Cup winners: 1987–8

MAIDSTONE UNITED — DIV. 4

Davis, Darren
Gall, Mark I.
Golley, Mark A.
Haylock, Paul
Henry, Liburd
Johns, Nicholas P.
Lillis, Jason W.
Madden, David J.
Osborne, Lawrence W.
Oxbrow, Darren W.
Roast, Jesse
Rumble, Paul
Sandeman, Bradley R.
Sorrell, Anthony C.
Stebbing, Gary S.

League Appearances: Beeney, M. 17; Berry, L.D. 25; Bromage, R. 3; Brown, R.A. 3; Butler, S. 32; Charlery, K. 22(7); Cooper, G. 22(5); Davis, D. 11; Elsey, K.W. 26(2); Gall, M.I. 29(5); Gilbert, W.A. 2(2); Golley, M.A. 32(4); Haylock, P. 16; Henry, L. 25(5); Johns, N.P. 29; Kevan, D.J. 3; Lillis, J.W. 10(9); Madden, D.J. 10; Moore, G. –(5); Osborne, L.W. 33(4); Oxbrow, D.W. 29(1); Pritchard, H.K. 8(1); Pullan, C.J. –(1); Roast, J. 16; Rumble, P. 26(1); Sandeman, B. 20; Sorrell, A.C. 25(2); Stebbing, G.S. 30(3); Wimbleton, P.P. 2.
League Goals (66): Butler 20 (1 pen), Gall 11 (2 pens), Charlery 9, Sorrell 5, Osborne 4, Cooper 3 (1 pen), Berry 2, Henry 2, Pritchard 2, Elsey 1, Moore 1, Oxbrow 1, Rumble 1, Sandeman 1, Stebbing 1, Wimbleton 1, own goal 1.
Rumbelows Cup (3): Butler 2, Charlery 1.
FA Cup (5): Butler 2, Gall 2, Osborne 1.
Ground: Watling Street, Dartford, Kent DA2 6EN (0622) 754403
Nearest Station: Dartford
Manager: Graham Carr **Secretary:** W.T. Williams
Colours: Amber shirts, black shorts
Record home gate: (at The Stadium, London Road, Madstone) 10,591 v Charlton, January 1979 (FA Cup)
Honours: Nil

MANCHESTER CITY DIV. 1

Allen, Clive
Beckford, Jason N
Brennan, Mark R.
Brightwell, David J
Brightwell, Ian
Clarke, Wayne
Cotton, Anthony P.
Dibble, Andrew G.
Harkin, Sean C.
Harper, Alan
Heath, Adrian P.
Hendry, Edward C.J.
Hill, Andrew R.
Hughes, Michael E.
Kelly, Paul
Lake, Paul A.
Lomas, Stephen M.
Margetson, Martyn W.
Megson, Gary J.
Peters, Mark
Pointon, Neil
Quigley, Michael A.
Quinn, Niall
Redmond, Stephen
Reid, Peter
Sheron, Michael N.
Sliney, Gary S.
Wallace, Michael
Ward, Ashley S.
Ward, Mark W.
White, David

League Appearances: Allen, C. 8(12); Beckford, J.N. –(2); Brennan, M.R. 12(4); Brightwell, I. 30(3); Clarke, W. 3(4); Coton, A.P. 33; Dibble, A. 3; Harper, A. 25(4); Heath, A.P. 31(4); Hendry, E.C.J. 32; Hill, A.R. 7(1); Hughes, M.E. –(1); Lake, P.A. 3; Margetson, M.W. 2; Megson, G.J. 19; Pointon, N. 35; Quinn, N. 38; Redmond, S. 35(2); Reid, P. 28(2); Ward, M.W. 36; White, D. 38.
League Goals (64): Quinn 20, White 16, Ward 11 (9 pens), Allen 4 (1 pen), Brennan 3, Redmond 3, Clarke 1, Harper 1, Heath 1, Hendry 1, Hill 1, Megson 1, Pointon 1.
Rumbelows Cup (5): Allen 2, Beckford 1, Harper 1, Hendry 1.
FA Cup (3): Allen 1, Hendry 1, Quinn 1.
Ground: Maine Road, Moss Side, Manchester M14 7WN (061–226 1191/2)
Nearest Station: Manchester Piccadilly
Manager: Peter Reid **Secretary:** J.B. Halford
Colours: Sky blue shirts; white shorts
Record home gate: 84,569 v Stoke City, March 1934 (FA Cup)
Honours – Champions: Division 1: 1936–7, 1967–8; Division 2: 1898–9, 1902–3, 1909–10, 1927–8, 1946–7, 1965–6

FA Cup winners: 1903–4, 1933–4, 1955–6, 1968–9
League Cup winners: 1969–70, 1975–6
European Cup Winners' Cup winners: 1969–70

MANCHESTER UNITED DIV. 1

Beardsmore, Russell P.
Blackmore, Clayton G.
Brazil, Derek M.
Bruce, Stephen R.
Carey, Brian P.
Doherty, Adrian J.
Donaghy, Malachy M.
Ferguson, Darren
Gibbs, Ryan J.
Graham, Deiniol W.T.
Hughes, Leslie M.
Ince, Paul E.C.
Irwin, Denis J.
Lawton, Craig T.
Leighton, James
Lydiate, Jason L.
McAuley, Sean
McClair, Brian J.
Maiorana, Giuliano
Martin, Lee A.
Pallister, Gary A.
Phelan, Michael C.
Robins, Mark G.
Robson, Bryan
Sealey, Leslie J.
Sharpe, Lee S.
Sixsmith, Paul
Toal, Kieran M.
Wallace, David L.
Walsh, Gary
Webb, Neil J.
Whitworth, Neil A.
Wratten, Paul.

League Appearances: Anderson, V.A. 1; Beardsmore, R.P. 5(7); Blackmore, C.G. 35; Bosnich, M.J. 2; Bruce, S.R. 31; Donaghy, M.M. 17(8); Ferguson, D. 2(3); Giggs, R.J. 1(1); Hughes, L.M. 29(2); Ince, P.E.C. 31; Irwin, D.J. 33(1); Kontchelskis, A. 1; McClair, B.J. 34(2); Martin, L.A. 7(7); Pallister, G.A. 36; Phelan, M.C. 30(3); Robins, M.G. 7(12); Robson, B. 15(2); Sealey, L.J. 31; Sharpe, L.S. 20(3); Wallace, D.L. 13(6); Walsh, G. 5; Webb, N.J. 31(1); Whitworth, N.A. 1; Wratten, P. –(2).
League Goals (58): Bruce 13 (7 pens), McClair 13, Hughes 10, Blackmore 4 (1 pen), Robins 4, Ince 3, Wallace 3, Webb 3, Sharpe 2, Giggs 1, Phelan 1, Robson 1.
Rumbelows Cup (21): Hughes 6, Sharpe 6, Blackmore 2, Bruce (2 pens), McClair 2, Anderson 1, Wallace 1, Webb 1.
FA Cup (4): Hughes 2 McClair 2.
Ground: Old Trafford M16 0RA (061–872 1661)
Nearest Stations: All stations Manchester
Manager: Alex Ferguson **Secretary:** K.R. Merrett
Colours: Red shirts; white shorts
Record home gate: 76,962 FA Cup semi-final (Wolverhampton v Grimsby Town), March 1939; **club:** 70,504 v Aston Villa, December 1920 (League)
Honours Champions: Division 1: 1907–8, 1910–11, 1951–2, 1955–6, 1956–7, 1964–5, 1966–7; Division 2: 1935–6, 1974–5
FA Cup winners: 1908–9, 1947–8, 1962–3, 1976–7, 1982–3, 1984–5, 1989–90
European Cup Winners' Cup winners: 1990–1
European Cup winners: 1967–8

MANSFIELD TOWN DIV. 4

Beasley, Andrew
Casteldine, Gary J.
Chambers, Stephen
Charles, Stephen
Clark, Martin J.
Davidson, Wayne
Fairclough, Wayne R.
Fee, Gregory P.
Ford, Gary
Foster, George W.
Gary, Kevin J.
Murray, Malcolm
Pearcey, Jason
Spooner, Stephen A.
Stringfellow, Ian R.
Wilkinson, Stephen J.
Withe, Christopher

League Appearances: Beasley, A. 42; Chambers, S. 30(2); Chapman, G.A. 6; Charles, S. 36(3); Christie, T. 33(2); Clark, M.J. 24; Fairclough, W.R. 41; Fee, G.P. 10; Ford, G. 12; Foster, G.W. 34; Gray, K.J. 28(3); Hathaway, I.A. 6(4); Hodges, D. –(2); Holland, P. 1; Kearney, M.J. 20; Kent, K.J. 27; Leishman, G. 1(10); Ling, M. 3; Lowery, A.W. 5(2); Murray, M. 28(2), Pearcey, J. 4; Prindiville, S. 4(2); Smalley, M.A. 21; Smith, M.A. 6(1); Spooner, S.A. 12; Stringfellow, I.R. 15(9); Wilkinson, S.J. 36(3); Withe, C. 21.

League Goals (42): Wilkinson 11, Christie 10, Fairclough 6, Charles 4, Kent 4, Stringfellow 2, Ford 1, Gray 1, Leishman 1, Smalley 1, own goal 1.

Rumbelows Cup (1): Charles 1.

FA Cup (3): Charles 1, Kearney 1, Wilkinson 1.

Ground: Field Mill, Quarry Lane, Mansfield, Nottingham NG18 5DA (0624–23567)

Nearest Station: Mansfield, Alfreton Parkway

Manager: George Foster **Secretary:** J.D. Eaton

Colours: Amber shirts; blue shorts

Record home gate: 24,467 v Nottingham Forest, January 1953 (FA Cup)

Honours – Champions: Division 3: 1976–7; Division 4: 1974–5

Associate Members Cup winners: 1986–7.

MIDDLESBROUGH — DIV. 2

Arnold, Ian
Baird, Ian J.
Coleman, Simon
Cooper, Colin T.
Crosby, Lee D.
Hamilton, Gary J.
Hanford, Paul A.
Hendrie, John G.
Holmes, Daniel G.
Kernaghan, Alan N.
Lake, Robert M.
McGee, owen E.
Mohan, Nicholas
Mowbray, Anthony M.
Mustoe, Robbie
Parkinson, Gary A.
Pears, Stephen
Phillips, James N.
Poole, Kevin
Proctor, Mark G.
Putney, Trevor A.
Ripley, Stuart E.
Russell, Martin
Slaven, Bernard
Wark, John

League Appearances: Arnold, I. (2); Baird, I.J. 41(3); Coleman, S. 18(1); Cooper, C.T. 32; Dibble, A.G. 19; Hendrie, J.G. 40(1); Kernaghan, A.N. 23(1); Kerr, P. 20(4); McGee, O.E. 6(2); Mowbray, A.M. 40; Mustoe, R. 39(2), Parkinson, G.A. 10; Pears, S. 27; Phillips, J.N. 44, Pollock, J. –(1); Proctor, M.G. 13(5); Putney, T.A. 20(3); Ripley, S.E. 22(17); Russell, M. 10(1); Slaven, B. 41(5); Walsh, C.D. 10(3); Wark, J. 31(1).

League Goals (66): Slaven 16, Baird 14 (2 pens), Kerr 6, Ripley 6, Mustoe 4, Hendrie 3, Mowbray 3, Phillips 2, Russell 2, Wark 2, Coleman 1, McGee 1, Parkinson 1 (pen), Putney 1, Walsh 1, own goals 3.

Rumbelows Cup (9): Mustoe 3, Slaven 3, Hendrie 1, Kerr 1, Mowbray 1.

FA Cup (2): Baird 1, Kerr 1.

Ground: Ayresome Park, Middlesbrough TS1 4PB (0642–819659)

Nearest Station: Middlesbrough

Manager: Lennie Lawrence **Secretary;** Tom Hughes

Colours: Red shirts; white shorts

Record home gate: 53,596 v Newcastle United, December 1949 (League)

Honours – Champions: Division 2: 1926–7, 1928–9, 1973–4

Amateur Cup: 1895, 1898

Anglo-Scottish Cup: 1975–6

MILLWALL DIV. 2

Allen, Malcolm
Branagan, Keith G.
Briley, Leslie
Cunningham, Kenneth E.
Dawes, Ian R.
Devine, Sean T.
Donegan, John
Emberson, Carl W.
Foran, Mark J.
Goodman, Jonathan
Horne, Brian S.
Humphrey, John M.
Kerr, Paul
McCarthy, Michael J.
McGinlay, John
McGlashan, John
McLeary, Alan T.
Morgan, Darren J.
Rae, Alexander S.
Sheringham, Edward P.
Stephenson, Paul
Stephens, Keith H.
Thompson, David
Waddock, Gary P.
Wood, Stephen A.

League Appearances: Allen, M. 18(3); Branagan, K.G. 18; Briley, L. 21; Carter, J.W.C. 23(1); Cunningham, K.E. 21(2); Dawes, I.R. 40; Dowson, A.P. 1; Fillery, M.C. 1; Goddard, P. 4(2); Goodman, J. 20(3); Horne, B.S. 28; Kerr, P. 10; McCarthy, M.J. 11(1); McGinlay, J. 2; McGlashan, J. 4(4); McLeary, A.T. 41(1); Morgan, D.J. 7(1); O'Callaghan, K. 9(11); Rae, A. 37(2); Sheringham, E.P. 46; Stephenson, P. 25(5); Stevens, K.H. 42; Thompson, D. 16(1); Waddock, G.P. 37(3); Wood, S.A. 24(1).

League Goals (70): Sheringham 33 (3 pens), Rae 10, Allen 7, Goodman 5, Carter 3, Thompson 3, Kerr 2, O'Callaghan 2, Waddock 2, Briley 1, Stephenson 1, Stevens 1.

Rumbelows Cup (2): Sheringham 2.

FA Cup (6): Rae 2, Sheringham 2, Stephenson 2.

Ground: The Den, Cold Blow Lane, London SE14 5RH (071-639 3143/4)

Nearest Stations: New Cross or New Cross Gate (SR and Metropolitan line)

Manager: Bruce Rioch **Secretary:** G.I.S. Hortop

Colours: Royal blue shirts; white shorts

Record home gate: 48,672 v Derby County, February 1937 (FA Cup)

Honours – Champions: Division 2: 1987–8; Division 3 South: 1927–8, 1937–8; Division 4: 1961–2

Football League Trophy: 1982–3

NEWCASTLE UNITED DIV. 2

Aitken, Robert S.
Anderson, John
Appleby, Matthew W.
Askew, William
Bradshaw, Darren S.
Brock, Kevin S.
Clark, Lee R.
Cole, Anthony R.
Elliott, Robert J.
Gallacher, John
Gourlay, Archibald M.
Howey, Stephen N.
Hunt, Andrew
Kristensen, Bjorn
Makel, Lee R.
Mason, Philip
Neilson, Alan B.
O'Brien, Liam F.
Parkinson, Michael
Peacock, Gavin
Quinn, Michael
Ranson, Raymond
Robinson, David J.
Roche, David
Scott, Kevin W.
Simpson, Neil
Sloan, Scott
Srnicek, Pavel
Stimson, Mark
Thompson, Alan
Watson, Stephen C.
Wright, Thomas J.

League Appearances: Aitken, R.S. 32; Anderson, J. 27; Appleby, M.W. 1; Askew, W. 1(1); Bradshaw, D.S. 6(1); Brock, K.S. 36(2); Burridge, J. 39; Clark, L.R. 13(6); Dillon, K. 19; Elliot, R.J. 5(1); Fereday, W. 6(2); Gallacher, J. 1; Gaynor, T. 4; Gourlay, A.M. 2; Howey, S.N. 3(8); Hunt, A. 13(3); Kristensen, B. 39(1); McGhee,

M. 17(4); Makel, L.R. 1(2); Mitchell, D.S. 2; Moran, P. 1; Neilson, A.B. 2(1); O'Brien, L.F. 23(10); Peacock, G. 27; Quinn, M. 43; Ranson, R. 24(3); Robinson, D.J. –(3); Roche, D. 5(3); Scott, K.W. 42; Simpson, N. 1(3); Sloan, S. 11(5); Srnicek, R. 7; Stimson, M. 23; Sweeney, P. 8(1); Watson, J.I. –(1); Watson, S.C. 22(2).
League Goals (49): Quinn 18 (2 pens), Peacock 7, Brock, 5, McGhee 5, O'Brien 3, Clark 2, Hunt 2, Anderson 1, Gaynor 1, Kristensen 1, Mitchell 1, Sloan 1, Stimson 1, own goal 1.
Rumbelows Cup (1): Anderson 1.
FA Cup (4): Quinn 2, McGhee 1, Stimson 1.
Ground: St James' Park, Newcastle-upon-Tyne NE1 4ST (Tyneside 091–2328361)
Nearest Stations: Newcastle Central (BR) or St James' Park (Metro)
Manager: Ossie Ardiles **Secretary:** R. Cushing
Colours: Black and white vertically striped shirts; black shorts
Record home gate: 68,386 v Chelsea, September 1930 (League)
Honours – Champions: Division 1: 1904–5, 1906–7, 1908–9, 1926–7; Division 2: 1964–5
FA Cup winners: 1909–10, 1923–4, 1931–2, 1950–1, 1951–2, 1954–5
European Fairs Cup winners: 1968–9
Anglo-Italian Cup winners: 1973

NORTHAMPTON TOWN DIV. 4

Adcock, Anthony C.
Angus, Terence N.
Barnes, David O.
Beavon, Michael S.
Bell, Michael
Brown, Steven F.
Campbell, Gregory
Chard, Philip J.
Gernon, Frederick A.J.
Gleasure, Peter
Johnson, David
Quow, Trevor S.
Scope, David F.
Terry, Steven
Thorpe, Adrian
Wilkin, Kevin
Wilson, Paul A.
Wood, Darren

League Appearances: Adcock, A.C. 20(1); Angus, T.N. 42; Barnes, D.O. 42(1); Beavon, M.S. 41; Bell, M. 22(6); Beresford, M. 13; Berry, S.A. 20(7); Brown, S.F. 37(3); Campbell, G. 20(5); Chard, P.J. 43; Collins, D. 3(5); Evans, G.J. 2; Fee, G.P. 1; Gernon, F.A.J. 8; Gleasure, P. 16; Hitchcock, K. 17; Johnson, D. 8(17); Quow, T.S. 12(1); Sandeman, B.R. –(5); Scope, D.F. 3(4); Scully, P. 15; Terry, S. 46; Thorpe, A. 12(15); Wilkin, K. 7(2); Williams, W. 10(4); Wilson, P.A. 44; Wood, D. 2.
League Goals (57): Barnes 13 (1 pen), Beavon 10 (7 pens), Chard 7, Terry 6, Campbell 4, Adcock 3, Wilson 3, Angus 2, Berry 2, Brown 2, Wilkin 2, Collins 1, Thorpe 1, Wood 1.
Rumbelows Cup (4): Wilkin 2, Barnes 1 (pen), Brown 1.
FA Cup (4): Barnes 2, Beavon 1, Campbell 1.
Ground: County Ground, Abington Avenue, Northampton NN1 4PS (0604–234100)
Nearest Station: Northampton
Manager: Theo Foley **Secretary:** Philip Mark Hough
Colours: Yellow shirts claret trim, yellow shorts
Record home gate: 24,523 v Fulham, April 1966 (League)
Honours – Champions: Division 3: 1962–3; Division 4: 1986–7

NORWICH CITY DIV. 1

Ball, Stephen J.
Blades, Paul A.
Bowen, Mark, R.
Butterworth, Ian S.
Coney, Dean H.
Crook, Ian B.
Culverhouse, Ian B.
Fleck, Robert
Fox, Ruel A.
Gordon, Dale, A.
Goss, Jeremy
Gunn, Bryan
Minett, Jason K.
Mortensen, Henrick
Pennock, Adrian B.
Phillips, David O.
Polston, John D.
Power, Lee M.
Sheffield, Jonathan
Sherwood, Timothy A.
Smith, David C.
Sutch, Daryl
Ullathorne, Robert
Walton, Mark
Woodthorpe, Colin.

League Appearances: Blades, P.A. 21; Bowen, M.R. 37; Butterworth, I.S. 31; Crook, I.S. 31(1); Culverhouse, I.B. 34; Fleck, R. 23(6); Fox, R.A. 23(5); Gordon, D.A. 35(1); Goss, J. 14(5); Gunn, B. 34; Minett, J.K. –(2); Mortensen, H. –(3); Phillips, D.O. 38; Polston, J.D. 27; Power, L.M. 13(3); Rosario, R.M. 9; Sherwood, T.A. 37; Smith, D.C. 2(1); Sutch, D. 2(2); Sutton, C.R. –(2); Ullathorne, R. 2; Walton, M. 4; Woodthorpe, C. 1.
League Goals (41): Gordon 7, Sherwood 7, Fleck 5, Fox 4, Phillips 4, Polston 4, Crook 3, Power 3, Bowen 1, Goss 1, own goals 2
Rumbelows Cup (5): Goss 2, Crook 1, Fleck 1, Sheerwood 1.
FA Cup (7): Fleck 3, Gordon 2, Mortensen 1, Rosario 1.
Ground: Carrow Road Stadium, Norwich NR1 1JE (0603–612131)
Nearest Station: Norwich Thorpe
Manager: Dave Stringer **Secretary:** A.R.W. Neville
Colours: Yellow shirts with green trim; green shorts with yellow trim
Record home gate: 43,984 v Leicester, March 1963 (FA Cup)
Honours Champions: Division 2: 1971–2, 1985–6; Division 3 South: 1933–4
League Cup winners: 1961–2, 1984–5

NOTTINGHAM FOREST DIV. 1

Barry, Thomas D.
Bell, Steven
Broadman, Craig G.
Bowyer, Gary D.
Byrne, Raymond
Carr, Franz A.
Cash, Stuart P.
Charles, Gary A.
Chettle, Stephen
Clough, Nigel H.
Crosby, Gary
Crossley, Mark G.
Fancutt, Martin S.
Gaynor, Thomas
Gemmill, Scott
Gilchrist, Phillip
Glover, Edward L.
Hawkes, Leigh
Hodge, Stephen B.
Hope, Christopher J.
Howe, Stephen R.
Jemson, Nigel B.
Keane, Roy M.
Kilford, Ian A.
Laws, Brian
Loughlan, Anthony J.
Lyne, Neil G.F.
Mahood, Alan S.
Marriott, Andrew
Noble, Barrett J.
Orlygsson, Thorvaldur
Parker, Garry S.
Pearce, Dale
Pearce, Stuart
Rice, Brian
Smith, Mark
Smith, Mark A.
Starbuck, Phillip M.
Stone, Steven B.
Sutton, Stephen J.
Telford, Mark
Walker, Desmond S.
Wassall, Darrent P.
Williams, Brett
Wilson, Terry
Woan, Ian S.
Yates, Luke

League Appearances: Carr, F.A. 13; Charles, G.A. 9(1); Chettle, S. 37; Clough, N.H. 37; Crosby, G. 27(2); Crossley, M.G. 38; Gaynor, T. 9(2); Gemmill, S. 2(2); Glover, E.L. 8; Hodge, S.B. 12(2); Jemson, N.B. 22(1); Keane, R.M. 35; Laws, B. 30(2); Loughlan, A.J. 2; Parker, G.S. 35(1); Pearce, S. 33; Rice, B. –(1); Starbuck, P.M. 3(9); Walker, D.S. 37; Wassall, D.P. 3(4); Williams, B. 4; Wilson, T. 13(2); Woan, I.S. 9(3).
League Goals (65): Clough 14 (1 pen), Pearce 11, Jemson 8 (2 pens), Keane 8, Gaynor 3, Hodge 3, Parker 3, Wilson 3, Woan 3, Carr 2, Chettle 2, Crosby 2, Glover 1, Loughlan 1, own goal 1.
Rumbelows Cup (11): Clough 3, Jemson 2, Parker 2, Chettle 1, Crosby 1, Keane 1, Pearce 1.
FA Cup (20): Pearce 4, Jemson 3 (1 pen), Parker 3, Clough 2, Crosby 2, Hodge 2, Keane 2, Charles 1, Wilson 1.
Ground: City Ground, Pavilion Road, Nottingham NG2 5FJ (0602–822202)
Nearest Station: Nottingham Midland
Manager: Brian Clough OBE **Secretary:** P. White
Colours: Red shirts: white shorts
Record home gate: 49,945 v Manchester United, October, 1967 (League)
Honours – Champions: Division 1: 1977–8; Division 2: 1906–7, 1921–2; Division 3 South: 1950–1
FA Cup winners: 1897–8, 1958–9
FA Cup winners: 1977–8, 1978–9, 1988–9, 1989–90
Full Members Cup winners: 1988–9, 1989–90
Super Cup winners: 1979–80
European Cup winners: 1978–9, 1979–80
Anglo-Scottish Cup winners: 1976–7

NOTTS COUNTY — DIV. 1

Aldridge, Stephen P.
Bartlett, Kevin F.
Browne, Shaun M.K.
Chapman, Gary A.
Cherry, Steven R.
Cox, Paul R.
Dolan, Kenneth P.
Draper, Mark A.
Finch, Craig B.
Harding, Paul
Hodder, Steven J.
Johnson, Thomas
Lund, Gary J.
Norton, David W.
O'Riordan, Donald J.
Palmer, Charles A.
Paris, Alan D.
Platnauer, Nicholas R.
Regis, David R.
Robinson, Philip J.
Short, Christian M.
Short, Jonathan C.
Snook, Edward K.G.
Thomas, Dean R.
Thompson, John A.
Turner, Philip
Walker, Richard N.
Wells, Mark A.
Yates, Dean R.

League Appearances: Bartlett, K.F. 37(3); Brook, G. –(1); Chapman, G.A. –(6); Cherry, S.R. 46; Davis, S. –(2); Draper, M.A. 41(4); Harding, P. 20(4); Johnson, T. 29(8); Lund, G.J. 16; Nelson, G.P. –(2); Norton, D.W. 3(1); O'Riordan, D.J. 31; Palmer, C.A. 39(1); Paris, A.D. 13(2); Platnauer, N.R. 13; Regis, D. 26(11); Robinson, P.J. 18(1); Short, C.M. 11(4); Short, J.C. 43; Thomas, D.R. 44; Turner, P. 35(3); Yates, D.R. 41.
League Goals (76): Johnson 16 (2 pens), Regis 15 (1 pen), Bartlett 13, Draper 9 (3 pens), Yates 4, Lund 3, Robinson 3, Thomas 3, O'Riordan 1, Palmer 1, Paris 1, Platnauer 1, Short Chris 1, Turner 1 own goals 4.
Rumbelows Cup (5): Johnson 3 (1 pen), Bartlett 1, Robinson 1.

FA Cup (9): Lund 2, O.Riordan 2, Turner 2, Bartlett 1, Short Craig 1 own goal 1.
Ground: Meadow Lane, Nottingham NG2 3HJ (0602–861155)
Nearest Station: Nottingham
Manager: Neil Warnock **Chief Executive:** N.E. Hook
Colours: Black and white striped shirts; black shorts
Record home gate: 47,310 v York, March 1955 (FA Cup)
Honours – Champions: Division 2: 1896–7, 1913–14, 1922–3; Division 3 South: 1930–31, 1949–50; Division 4: 1970–71
FA Cup winners: 1893–4

OLDHAM ATHLETIC DIV. 1

Adams, Neil J.
Barlow, Andrew J.
Barrett, Earl D.
Bunn, Frankie S.
Currie, David N.
Donachie, William
Fillery, Michael C.
Halle, Gunnar
Halworth, Jonathan G.
Henry, Nicholas I.
Heseltine, Wayne A.
Holden, Andrew I.
Holden, Richard W.
Jobson, Richard I.
Kane, Paul
Keeley, John H.
Marshall, Ian P.
Moulden, Paul
Palmer, Roger N.
Redfearn, Neil D.
Ritchie, Andrew T.
Thompstone, Ian P.
Warhurst, Paul

League Appearances: Adams, N.J. 21(10); Barlow, A.J. 46; Barrett, E.D. 46; Bernard, P.R.J. 2; Brazil, D.M. 1; Currie, D.N. 16(11); Donachie, W. 12(5); Fillery, M.C. 1(1); Halle, G. 17; Hallworth, J.G. 46; Henry, N.I. 43; Holden, A.I. 2; Holden, R.W. 42; Jobson, R.I. 43(1); Kane, P. 12(5); Marshall, I.P. 25(1); Moulden, P. 11(13); Palmer, R.N. 20(9); Redfearn, N.D. 41(4); Ritchie, A.T. 29(2); Warhurst, P. 30(3); Williams, G.A. –(2).
League Goals (83): Marshall 17, Ritchie 15 (3 pens), Redfearn 14 (3 pens), Palmer 9, Adams 6, Holden R 5, Henry 4, Barrett 3, Moulden 3, Currie 2, Bernard 1, Johnson 1, Warhurst 1, own goals 2.
Rumbelows Cup (5): Currie 2, Holden R 1, Moulden 1, Redfearn 1 (pen).
FA Cup (3): Redfearn 2 (2 pens), Adams 1.
Ground: Boundary Park, Oldham OL1 2PA (061–624 4972)
Nearest Stations: Oldham, Werneth and Oldham Mumps
Manager: Joe Royle **Secretary:** Terry Cale
Colours: All blue
Record home gate: 47,671 v Sheffield Wednesday, January 1930 (FA Cup)
Honours Champions: Division 2: 1990–1; Division 3 North: 1952–3; Division 3: 1973–4

OXFORD UNITED DIV. 2

Allen, Christopher A.
Beauchamp, Joseph D.
Byrne, Paul P.
Durnin, John
Evans, Ceri L.
Evans, Paul
Fisher, Stuart M.
Ford, Michael P.
Foster, Stephen B.
Foyle, Martin J.
Harwood, Paul D.A.
Jackson, Darren W.
Kee, Paul V.
Keeble, Matthew E.
Lewis, Michael
McClaren, Stephen
McDonnell, Matthew T.
Magilton, James

Melville, Andrew R.	Phillips, Leslie M.	Stein, Earl M.S.
Muttock, Jonathon L.	Robinson, Leslie	Veysey, Kenneth J.
Nogan, Lee M.	Simpson, Paul D.	
Penney, David M.	Smart, Garry	

League Appearances: Beauchamp, J.D. 4; Byrne, P.P. 2; Durnin, J. 20(6); Evans, C.L. 17(1); Ford, M.P. 27(1); Foster, S.B. 38; Foyle, M.J. 36; Gardner, L. 2(5); Jackson, D.W. 4(1); Judge, A.G. 6; Kee, P.V. 13; Lewis, M. 34; McClaren, S. 6(1); Magilton, J. 37; Melville, A.R. 46; Nogan, L.M. 29(3); Penney, D.M. 3(6); Phillips, L.M. 24(1); Robinson, L. 43; Simpson, P.D. 46; Smart, G. 14(1); Stein, E.M.S. 28(6); Veysey, K.J. 25; Walker, I.M. 2.

League Goals (69): Simpson 17 (1 pen), Foyle 10, Durnin 9, Stein 8, Magilton 6 (1 pen), Nogan 5, Foster 3, Melville 3, Evans 1, Ford 1, Lewis 1, Penney 1, Phillips 1, own goals 3.

Rumbelows Cup (8): Foyle 3, Foster, Magilton 1, Melville 1, Simpson 1.

FA Cup (5): Foyle 2, Durnin 1, Magilton 1, Nogan 1.

Ground: Manor Ground, Beech Road, Headington, Oxford OX3 7RS (0865–61503)

Nearest Station: Oxford

Manager: Brian Horton **Secretary:** John Clinkard

Colours: Gold shirts with navy blue sleeves; navy shorts

Record home gate: 22,750 v Preston, February 1964 (FA Cup)

Honours – Champions: Division 2: 1984–5; Division 3: 1967–8, 1983–4

League Cup winners: 1985–6

PETERBOROUGH UNITED DIV. 3

Bremner, Kevin J.	Crosby, Philip A.	Robinson, David A.
Butterworth, Garry J.	Gavin, Patrick J.	Sterling, Worrell R.
Charlery, Kenneth L.	Halsall, Michael	Swailes, Christopher W.
Cooper, Gary	Luke, Noel E.	
Costello, Peter	Riley, David	

League Appearances: Berry, G.F. 28(4); Bradshaw, P.W. 39; Bremner, K.J. 13(4); Butterworth, G.J. 46; Charlery, K.L. 2(2); Clayton, G. 4; Cooper, G. 2(4); Costello, P. 3(2); Crosby, P.A. 45; Culpin, P. 21(7); Danzey, M.J. –(1); Dearden, K.C. 7; Gavin, P.J. 10(1); Halsall, M. 45; Hill, P.J. 1; Hine, M. 33; Luke, N.E. 45; McElhinney, G.M.A. 20; Morgan, D. 5; Oakes, K.B. 27; Osborne, S.C. 3(16); Pope, N. 1(1); Riley, D. 35(6); Robinson, D.A. 6; Robinson, D.J. 7; Russell, K.J. 7; Sterling, W.R. 46; Watkins, D.A. 5(4).

League Goals (67): Culpin 10, Sterling 9, Riley 7, Berry 6 (3 pens), Halsall 6, Gavin 5, Hine 4, Bremner 3 (2 pens), Oakes 3, Robinson DJ 3, Russell 3, Luke 2, Robinson DA 2, Cooper 1, Osborne 1, own goals 2.

Rumbelows Cup (6): Bremner 3, Culpin 1, Sterling 1, own goal 1.

FA Cup (7): Culpin 2, Halsall 2, Riley 2, Sterling 1.

Ground: London Road Ground, Peterborough PE2 8AL (0733–63947)

Nearest Station: Peterborough

Manager: Chris Turner **Secretary:** A.V. Blades

Colours: Royal blue shirts; white shorts

Record home gate: 30,096 v Swansea, February 1965 (FA Cup)

Honours – Champions: Division 4: 1960–1, 1973–4

PLYMOUTH ARGYLE DIV. 2

Adcock, Paul M.
Barlow, Martin D.
Brown, Kenneth J.
Burrows, Adrian M.
Clement, Andrew D.
Clode, Mark J.
Cross, Ryan
Damerell, Mark A.
Edworthy, Marc
Evans, Michael J.
Fiore, Mark J.
Garner, Darren J.
Hodges, Kevin
King, Adam
Marker, Nicholas R.T.
Maxwell, Paul J.
Morgan, Stephen A.
Morrison, Andrew C.
Pickard, Owen
Robinson, Paul
Rowbotham, Jason
Salman, Danis M.M.
Turner, Robert P.
Walter, David W.
Wilmot, Rhys J.

League Appearances: Adcock, P.M. 9(3); Ampadu, K. 6; Barlow, M.D. 25(5); Brown, K.J. 43; Burrows, A.M. 45; Byrne, D.S. 11(3); Clement, A.D. 8(8); Cooper, D.A. –(3); Cross, R. 6(1); Damerell, M.A. –(4); Edwards, K. 3; Evans, M.J. 1(3); Fiore, M.J. 38; Garner, D.J. 5; Hodges, K. 40(2); King, A. 4(4); McAllister, B. 7(1); Marker, N.R.T. 39; Meade, R. 2(3); Morgan, S.A. 40; Morrison, A.C. 27(5); Pickard, O. 4(3); Robinson, P. 7(4); Salman, D.M.M. 35; Summerfield, K. 1; Tallon, D.J.B. 1; Thomas, A.M. 14; Turner, R.P. 39; Walter, D.W. 10; Wilmot, R.J. 36.
League Goals (54): Turner 14, Thomas 6, Burrows 4, Brown 3 (1 pen), Fiore 3, Hodges 3, Morgan 3, Robinson 3, Salman 3, Marker 2 (1 pen), Morrison 2, Ampadu 1, Barlow 1, Edwards 1, Garner 1, Pickard 1, own goals 3.
Rumbelows Cup (4): Thomas 2, Fiore 1, Salman 1.
FA Cup (1): Marker (1 pen),
Ground: Home Park, Plymouth Devon PL2 3DQ (0752–565261)
Nearest Station: Plymouth North Road
Manager: David Kemp **Secretary:** Graham Little
Colours: Green shirts; black shorts
Record home gate: 43,596 v Aston Villa, October 1936 (League)
Honours – Champions: Division 3 South: 1929–30, 1951–2; Division 3: 1958–9

PORTSMOUTH DIV. 2

Anderton, Darren R.
Aspinall, Warren
Awford, Andrew T.
Beresford, John
Black, Kenneth G.
Burns, Christopher
Butters, Guy
Chamberlain, Mark V.
Clarke, Colin J.
Daniel, Raymond C.
Doling, Stuart J.
Gale, Shaun M.
Gosney, Andrew R.
Gough, Alan T.
Hogg, Graeme J.
Kelly, Mark J.
Knight, Alan E.
Kuhl, Martin
McFarlane, Andrew A.
Maguire, Gavin T.
Murray, Shaun
Neill. Warren A.
Powell, Darryl A.
Ross, Michael P.
Russell, Lee
Stevens, Gary A.
Symons, Christopher J.
Whittingham, Guy
Wigley, Steven

League Appearances: Anderton, D.R. 13(7); Aspinall, W. 32(1); Awford, A.T. 8(6); Beresford, J. 39(3); Black, K.G. 14(7); Butters, G. 23; Chamberlain, M.V. 22(3); Clarke, C.J. 38(4); Daniel, R.C. 13(1); Fillery, M.C. 3; Gale, S.M. 2(1); Gosney, A.R. 24; Hogg, G.J. 20; Kelly, M.J. 2(3); Knight, A.E. 22; Kuhl, M. 41; Maguire, G.T. 22(1); Murray, S. 17(8); Neill, W.A. 30; Powell, D.A. –(8); Russell, L. 16(3); Stevens, G.A. 31; Symons, C.J. 1; Whittingham, G. 34(3); Wigley, S. 39(2).

League Goals (58): Clarke 13 (1 pen), Kuhl 13 (8 pens), Whittingham 12, Wigley 5, Aspinall 4 (1 pen), Beresford 2, Chamberlain 2, Stevens 2, Black 1, Kelly 1, Murray 1, Russell 1, own goal 1.
Rumbelows Cup (6): Clarke 2, Aspinall 1, Chamberlain 1, Neill 1, Whittingham 1.
FA Cup (11): Whittingham 7, Clarke 2, Aspinall 1, Chamberlain 1.
Ground: Fratton Park, Frogmore Road, Portsmouth PO4 8RA (0705–731204)
Nearest Stations: Fratton, Portsmouth and Southsea
Manager: Jim Smith **Secretary:** P. Weld
Colours: Blue shirts; white shorts
Record home gate: 51,385 v Derby County, February 1949 (FA Cup)
Honours – Champions: Division: 1948–9, 1949–50; Division 3 South: 1923–4; Division 3: 1961–2, 1982–3
FA Cup winners: 1938–9

PORT VALE — DIV. 2

Aspin, Neil
Beckford, Darren
Cross, Nicholas J.R.
Earle, Robert
Glover, Dean V.
Grew, Mark I.
Hughes, Darren J.
Jeffers, John J.
Kent, Kevin J.
Kidd, Ryan A.
McInstry, Gary
Millar, Paul W.
Mills, Brian
Mills, Simon
Parkin, Timothy J.
Porter, Andrew M.
Van Der Laan, Robertus P.
Walker, Raymond
Webb, Alan R.
West, Gary
West, Paul D.
Wood, Trevor J.

League Appearances: Agboola, R.O.F. 9; Aspin, N. 40(1); Beckford, D. 43; Cross, N.J.R. 14(5); Earle, R. 34)1); Ford, G. 22(8); Gibson, C.J. 5(1); Glover, D.V. 41; Grew, M.S. 14; Hughes, D.J. 16(1); Jeffers, J.J. 29(2); Jepson, R.F. 11(4); Kent, K. 11; Millar, P.W. 8(9); Mills, B. 1(1); Mills, S. 39(2); Parkin, T.J. 28(1); Platnauer, N.R. 14; Porter, A.M. 36(4); Van der Laan, R.P. 10(8); Walker, R. 45; Webb, A.R. 4; Wood, T.J. 32.
League Goals (56): Beckford 22 (2 pens), Earle 11, Walker 6 (4 pens), Van der Laan 4, Cross 2, Ford 2, Gibson 2, Jeffers 2, Mills B 2, Aspin 1, Glover 1, Millar 1.
Rumbelows Cup (0).
FA Cup (3): Beckford 2, Walker 1 (pen)
Ground: Vale Park, Hamil Road, Burslem, Stoke-on-Trent ST6 1AW (0782–814134)
Nearest Stations: Longport, and Stoke-on-Trent
Manager: John Rudge **Secretary:** D.E. Barber J.P. AMITD
Colours: White shirts with black trim; black shorts
Record home gate: 50,000 v Aston Villa, February 1960 (FA Cup)
Honours – Champions: Division 3 North: 1929–30, 1953–4; Division 4: 1958–9

PRESTON NORTH END — DIV. 3

Atkins, Robert G.
Bogie, Ian
Farnworth, Simon
Flynn, Michael A.
Greenwood, Nigel P.
Hughes, Adrian F.S.
James, Martin J.
Jepson, Ronald F.
Joyce, Warren G.
Kelly, Alan T.
Lambert, Matthew R.
Peel, Nathan J.

Senior, Stephen
Shaw, Graham P.
Swann, Gary
Thompson, David S.
Williams, Neill J.F.
Wrighton, Jeffrey G.

League Appearances: Ashcroft, L. 6(8); Bogie, I. 28(3); Cartwright, L. 13(1); Easter, G.P. 1; Eaves, D.M.C. 1(2); Farnworth, S. 23; Fee, G.P. 15; Flynn, M.A. 33(2); Greaves, S.R. 2; Greenwood, N.P. 3(2); Harper, S.J. 27(9); Hughes, A.F.S. 25(1); Jackson, M. 3(1); James, M.J. 34(3); Jepson, R.F. 13(1); Joyce, W.G. 42; Kelly, A.T. 23; Kerfoot, J.J.T. –(1); Lambert, M.R. 4(1); Mooney, B.J. 9; Peel, N.J. 1(9); Rathbone, M.J. 11(2); Senior, S. 38; Shaw, G.P. 44; Swann, G. 30; Thomas, J.W. 5; Thompson, D.S. 21; Williams, N.J.F. 11(2); Wrightson, J.G. 40.
League Goals (54): Shaw 10, Joyce 9 (1 pen), Bogie 8 (1 pen), Swann 5, Jepson 3, Wrightson 3, James 2, Mooney 2, Senior 2, Thompson 2, Ashcroft 1, Cartwright 1, Flynn 1, Greenwood 1, Hughes 1, Peel 1, Rathbone 1, Thomas 1 (pen).
Rumbelows Cup (3) Swann 2, Shaw 1.
FA Cup (0).
Ground: Deepdale, Preston PR1 6RU (0772–795919)
Nearest Station: Preston
Manager: Les Chapman **Secretary:** D.J. Allen
Colours: All white
Record home gate: 42.684 v Arsenal April 1938 (League)
Honours – Champions: Division 1: 1888–9, 1889–9; Division 2: 1903–4, 1912–3, 1950–1; Division 1970–1
FA Cup winners: 1888–9, 1937–8

QUEENS PARK RANGERS — DIV. 1

Allen, Bradley J.
Bardsley, David J.
Barker, Simon
Brevett, Rufus E.
Caldwell, Peter J.
Channing, Justin A.
Doyle, Maurice
Falco, Mark P.
Ferdinand, Leslie
Herrera, Roberto
Impey, Andrew R.
Iorfa, Dominic
Law, Brian J.
McCarthy, Alan J.
McDonald, Alan
McEnroe, David J.
Macciochi, David A.
Maddix, Daniel S.
Meaker, Michael J.
Parker, Paul A.
Peacock, Darren
Ready, Karl
Roberts, Anthony M.
Rutherford, Michael A.
Sinton, Andrew
Stejskal, Jan
Tillson, Andrew
Vowles, Paul
Wegerle, Roy C.
Wilkins, Raymond C.
Wilson, Clive

League Appearances: Allen, B.J. 4(6); Bardsley, D.J. 38; Brevett, R.E. 10; Barker, S. 31(4); Caesar, G.C. 5; Channing, J.A. 3(2); Falco, M.P. 17(3); Ferdinand, L. 15(3); Herrera, R. 3; Iorfa, D. 1(5); Law, B.J. 3; McCarthy, A.J. 1(1); McDonald, A. 17; Maddix, D.S. 32; Meaker, M.J. –(8); Parker, P.A. 13(4); Peacock, D. 19; Roberts, A.M. 12; Sansom, K.G. 28; Sinton, A. 38; Stejskal, J. 26; Tillson, A. 18(1); Wegerle, R.C. 35; Wilkins, R.C. 38; Wilson, C. 11(2).
League Goals (44): Wegerle 18 (8 pens), Ferdinand 8, Falco 5, Sinton 3, Allen 2, Tillson 2, Wilkins 2, Barker 1, Maddix 1, Parker 1, Wilson 1.
Rumbelows Cup (6): Ferdinand 2, Barker 1, Falco 1, Maddix 1, Wegerle 1.
FA Cup (1): Maddix 1.
Ground: Rangers Stadium, South Africa Road, Shepherds Bush, W12 7PA (081-743 0262)

Nearest Stations: Shepherds Bush (Metropolitan and Central lines); White City (Central line)
Manager: Gerry Francis **Secretary:** Miss S.F. Marson
Colours: Blue and white hooped shirts; white shorts
Record home gate: 35,353 v Leeds United, April 1974 (League)
Honours – Champions: Division 2: 1982–3; Division 3 South: 1947–8; Division 3: 1966–7.
League Cup winners: 1966–7

READING DIV. 3

Bailey, Daniel S.
Conroy, Michael K.
Francis, Stephen S.
Gilkes, Michael E.
Gooding, Michael C.
Hicks, Martin
Jones, Linden
Leworthy, David J.
Lovell, Stuart A.
McPherson, Keith A.
Maskell, Craig D.
Richardson, Steven E.
Senior, Trevor J.
Seymour, Christopher D.
Streete, Floyd A.
Taylor, Scott D.
Williams, Adrian

League Appearances: Bailey, D.S. 26; Brooke, G.J. 1(3); Burns, P.M. 12; Conroy, M.K. 29(4); Edwards, M. 6(2); Francis, S.S. 34; Friel, G.P. 8(5); Gilkes, M.E. 19(2); Gooding, M.C. 44; Hicks, M. 44; Jones, L. 27; Knight, K. 1; Leworthy, D.J. 4(6); Lovell, S.A. 22(8); McPherson, K.A. 46; Maskell, C.D. 31(7); Moran, S.J. 21(5); Morrow, S.J. 10; Richardson, S.E. 32; Senior, T.J. 35(5); Seymour, C.D. 7(2); Smith, M. 3; Statham, B. 8; Streete, F.A. 4; Taylor, S.D. 25(7); Williams, A. 7.
League Goals (53): Senior 15, Maskell 10 (1 pen), Moran 8, Gooding 7, McPherson 3, Bailey 2, Jones 2, Lovell 2, Conroy 1, Friel 1, Gilkes 1, Taylor 1.
Rumbelows Cup (1): Hicks 1.
FA Cup (1): Hicks 1.
Ground: Elm Park, Norfolk Road, Reading RG3 2EF (0734–507878)
Nearest Station: Reading
Manager: Mark McGhee **Secretary:**
Colours: Sky blue with white centre panel; sky blue shorts
Record home gate: 33,042 v Brentford, February 1927 (FA Cup)
Honours – Champions: Division 3: 1985–6; Division 3 South: 1925–6; Division 4: 1978–9
Full Members Cup winners: 1987–8

ROCHDALE DIV. 4

Brown, Antony J.
Chapman, Vincent J.
Doyle, Stephen C.
Graham, James
Gray, Gareth
Hilditch, Mark
Hughes, Zacari D.
Milner, Andrew J.
Morgan, Stephen J.
O'Shaughnessy, Stephen
Ward, Peter
Welch, Keith J.

League Appearances: Anders, J.S. –(2); Blundell, C.K. 10(4); Brown, A.J. 24(2); Burns, W. 26(2); Butler, P.J. –(2); Chapman, V.J. 19(1); Cole, D.A. 32(9); Colleton, A. –(1); Costello, P. 31(3); Dawson, J. 12(16); Doyle, S.C. 31; Duggan, A.J. 1; Elliott, S.B. 27(3); Goodison, C.W. 33(1); Graham, J. 26(2); Herring, P.J. –(1);

Hilditch, M. 12(2); Hill, J.W. 3(8); Holmes, M.A. 14(2); Lee, C. 24(2); Lockett, P.B. 1(1); McInerney, I.D. 4; Milner, A.J. 30(5); Morgan, S.J. 11; Norton, D.W. 9; O'Shaughnessy, S. 36(2); Rose, K.P. 3; Ward, P. 44; Welch, K.J. 43.
League Goals (50): Costello 10, Dawson 5, Holmes 5 (3 pens), Milner 5, Ward 5, Elliott 3, Morgan 3, Cole 2, Hilditch 2, Lee 2, O'Shaughnessy 2, Burns 1 (pen), Chapman 1, Graham 1, Hill 1, McInerney 1, own goal 1.
Rumbelows Cup (7): Milner 2, Costello 1, Elliott 1, Goodison 1 (pen); Lee 1, O'Shaughnessy 1.
FA Cup (2): Costello 2.
Ground: Spotland, Sandy Lane, Rochdale OL11 5DS (0706–44648/9)
Nearest Station: Rochdale
Manager: Dave Sutton **Secretary:** Bill Kenyon JP
Colours: All royal blue
Record home gate: 24,231 v Notts County, December 1949 (FA Cup)
Honours: Nil

ROTHERHAM UNITED DIV. 4

Barrick, Dean
Evans, Stewart J.
Goater, Leonard S.
Goodwin, Shaun L.
Hathaway, Ian A.
Hazel, Desmond L.
Hodges, Mark
Howard, Jonathan
Johnson, Nigel M.
Law, Nicholas
Mendonca, Clive P.
Mercer, William
O'Hanlon, Kelham G.
Pickering, Albert G.
Richardson, Neil T.
Robinson, Ronald
Thompson, Simon L.
Watts, Julian

League Appearances: Barnsley, A. 19; Barrick, D. 19; Buckley, J.W. 2(1); Cullen, A. 3; Dempsey, M.J. 25(1); Duffield, P. 17; Evans, S.J. 14(6); Forrest, G. 32(2); Goater, L.S. 13(9); Goodwin, S.L. 33(1); Hathaway, I.A. 3(2); Hazel, D.L. 36(3); Hodges, M. 3(1); Howard, J. –(1); Jenkinson, L. 5(2); Johnson, N.M. 17; Law, N. 30(2); Mendonca, C.P. 32(2); Mercer, W. 13; O'Hanlon, K.G. 33; Pearson, J.S. 11; Pickering, A.G. 1; Richardson, N.T. 16; Robinson, R. 38; Russell, W.M. 25(1); Scott, M. 13; Spooner, S.A. 15(4); Stancliffe, P.I. 5; Taylor, A. 5; Thompson, S.L. 9(7); Watts, J. 10; Williamson, R. 9.
League Goals (50): Mendonca 10 (1 pen), Pearson 5, Duffield 4 (1 pen), Evans 4, Dempsey 3 (1 pen), Goodwin 3, Hazel 3, Williamson 3 (1 pen), Barrick 2, Goater 2, Law 2, Richardson 2, Buckley 1, Cullen 1, Hathaway 1, Johnson 1, Scott 1, Spooner 1, own goal 1.
Rumbelows Cup (9): Williamson 3 (1 pen), Hazel 2, Dempsey 1, Goodwin 1, own goals 2
FA Cup (8): Dempsey 2, Goater 2, Mendonca 2, Evans 1, Johnson 1.
Ground: Millmoor, Rotherham S60 1HR (0709–562434)
Nearest Station: Rotherham
Manager: Billy McEwan **Secretary:** N. Darnill
Colours: Red shirts; white shorts
Record home gate: 25,000 v Sheffield United December 1952 and Sheffield Wednesday, January 1952 (League)
Honours – Champions: Division 3; 1980–1; Division 3 North: 1950–1; Division 4: 1988–9.

SCARBOROUGH DIV. 4

Ash, Mark C.
Carter, Stephen G.
Eshelby, Paul
Fletcher, Andrew M.
Foreman, Darren
Himsworth, Gary P.
Hirst, Lee
Ironside, Ian
Kamara, Alan
Lee, Christopher
Logan, David
Matthews, Michael
Meyer, Adrian M.
Mockler, Andrew J.
Mooney, Thomas J.
Mudd, Paul A.
Richards, Stephen C.

League Appearances: Ash, M.C. 9; Brook, G. 8; Carter, S.G. 31(3); Clarke, M.D. 1; Cook, M. 9; Dobson, P. 2(4); Eshelby, P. 2(1); Fletcher, A.M. 1(5); Foreman, D. 14; Himsworth, G.P. 23; Hirst, L. 32; Ironside, I. 40; Kamara, A. 40(1); Lee, C. 8(1); Lee, R. 2(8); Logan, D. 33(1); MacDonald, J. 10(1); Matthews, M. 43(2); Meyer, A.M. 17; Mockler, A.J. 32(2); Mooney, T.J. 17(10); Mudd, P.A. 21(3); Oghani, G.W. 30(6); Reed, J.P. 14; Richards, S.C. 45; Richardson, B. 6; Wilson, P. 16(3).
League Goals (59): Oghani 14 (7 pens), Mooney 13, Reed 5, Foreman 5, Mockler 5 (1 pen), Carter 3, Richards 3, Dobson 2, Hirst 2, Cook (1 pen), Fletcher 1, Himsworth 1, Logan 1, MacDonald 1, Meyer 1, Wilson 1.
Rumbelows Cup (3): Oghani 2 (2 pens), Matthews 1.
FA Cup (0).
Ground: The Athletic Ground, Seamer Road, Scarborough YO12 4HF (0723–375094)
Nearest Station: Scarborough
Manager: Ray McHale **General Manager/Secretary:** G.J. Alston
Colours: All red
Record home gate: 11,130 v Luton T., January 1938 (FA Cup)
Honours: Nil

SCUNTHORPE UNITED DIV. 4

Alexander, Graham
Daws, Anthony
Flounders, Andrew J.
Hamilton, Ian R.
Hicks, Stuart R.
Hine, Mark
Humphries, Glenn
Joyce, Joseph P.
Lillis, Mark A.
Lister, Stephen H.
Longden, David P.
Miller, Ian
Musselwhite, Paul S.
Stevenson, Andrew J.

League Appearances: Alexander, G. –(1); Bramhall, J. 11; Cotton, P. 10(5); Cowling, D.R. 18; Cox, N.J. 17; Daws, A. 32(2); Flounders, A.J. 44(2); Hall, R.A. 21; Hamilton, I.R. 31(3); Hicks, S.J. 46; Hill, D.M. 8(1); Hine, M. 12; Humphries, G. 10; Joyce, J.P. 21; Lillis, M.A. 35(4); Lister, S.H. 7; Litchfield, P. 8; Longden, D.P. 46; Marshall, G. 7; Miller, I. 8(4); Musselwhite, P.S. 38; Powell, G. 3(1); Smalley, P.T. 2(1); Stevenson, A.J. 4(5); Taylor, K. 38(4); Ward, P.T. 29(1).
League Goals (71): Flounders 23 (7 pens), Daws 14, Lillis 10, Taylor 4, Cowling 3, Hall 3, Hamilton 2, Hine 2, Ward 2, Cotton 1, Cox 1, Hicks 1, Hill 1, Humphries 1, Powell 1, own goals 2.
Rumbelows Cup (1): Lillis 1.
FA Cup (8): Flounders 3 (1 pen), Lillis 2, Bramhall 1, Hicks 1, Ward 1.
Ground: Glanford Park, Scunthorpe DN15 7RH (0724–848077)
Nearest Station: Scunthorpe

Manager: Bill Green **Secretary:** A.D. Rowing
Colours: All claret and blue
Record home gate: 28,775 v Rotherham U, May 1989 (League)
Honours – Champions: Division 3 North: 1957–8

SHEFFIELD UNITED DIV. 1

Agana, Patrick A.O.
Barnes, David
Beesley, Paul
Booker, Robert
Bradshaw, Carl
Bryson, James I.C.
Deane, Brian C.
Duffield, Peter
Gannon, John S.
Hill, Colin F.
Hodges, Glyn P.
Hoyland, Jamie W.
Jones, Vincent
Kite, Phillip D.
Lake, Michael C.
Lucas, Richard
Marwood, Brian
Morris, Mark J.
Pemberton, John M.
Powell, Christopher G.
Reed, John P.
Smith, Brian
Todd, Mark K.
Tracey, Simon P.
Ward, Mitchum D.
Whitehouse, Dane L.
Wilder, Christopher J.
Winter, Julian
Wood, Paul A.

League Appearances: Agana, P.A.O. 11(5); Barnes, D. 28; Beesley, P. 37; Booker, R. 19(10); Bradshaw, C. 24(3); Bryson, J.I.C. 25(4); Deane, B.C. 38; Duffield, P. –(2); Gannon, J.S. 19(3); Hill, C.F. 24; Hodges, G.P. 12; Hoyland, J.W. 17(4); Jones, V. 31; Kite, P.D. 7; Lake, M.C. 3(4); Lucas, R. 8(1); Marwood, B. 13(4); Morris, M.J. 12(2); Pemberton, J.M. 21; Rostron, J.W. 9(1); Sayer, A.C. –(3); Stancliffe, P.I. 3; Todd, M.K. 2(1); Tracey, S.P. 31; Ward, M.D. 3(1); Whitehouse, D.L. 1(3); Whitehurst, W. 3(5); Wilder, C.J. 16; Wood, P.A. 1(6).
League Goals (36): Deane 13 (1 pen), Bryson 7, Hodges 4, Booker 3, Agana 2, Jones 2, Marwood 2, Barnes 1, Beesley 1, Bradshaw 1.
Rumbelows Cup (5): Deane 3, Agana 1, Bradshaw 1.
FA Cup (1): Bradshaw 1.
Ground: Bramall Lane, Sheffield S2 4SU (0742–738955)
Nearest Station: Sheffield
Manager: Dave Bassett **Secretary:** D. Capper
Colours: Red and white striped shirts; black shorts
Record home gate: 68,287 v Leeds, February 1936 (FA Cup)
Honours – Champions: Division 1: 1897–8; Division 2: 1952–3; Division 4: 1981–2
FA Cup winners: 1898–9, 1901–2, 1914–15, 1924–5

SHEFFIELD WEDNESDAY DIV. 1

Anderson, Vivian A.
Beresford, Marlon
Cam, Scott H.
Francis, Trevor J.
Harkes, John A.
Hirst, David E.
Hyde, Graham
Johnson, David A.
Key, Lance
King, Phillip G.
McCall, Stephen H.
Mackenzie, Stephen
Newsome, Jon
Nilsson, Nils L.R.
Palmer, Carlton L.
Pearson, Nigel G.
Pressman, Kevin P.
Sheridan, John J.
Shirtliff, Peter A.
Sowden, Shaun
Taylor, Robert M.
Turner, Christopher R.
Watson, Gordon
Wetherall, David

Williams, Michael A.
Williams, Paul A.
Wilson, Daniel J.
Wood, Darren T.
Worthington, Nigel

League Appearances: Anderson, V.A. 21(1); Francis, T.J. 18(20); Harkes, J.A. 22(1); Hirst, D.E. 39(2); King, P.G. 43; MacKenzie, S. 5(7); McCall, S.H. 13(6); Madden, L.D. 1(4); Newsome, J. 1; Nilsson, N.L.R. 22; Palmer, C.L. 45; Pearson, N.G. 39; Pressman, K.P. 23; Sheridan, J.J. 45(1); Shirtliff, P.A. 39; Turner, C.R. 23; Watson, G. 1(4); Whitton, S.P. –(1); Williams, P.A. 40(6); Wilson, D.J. 35(1); Worthington, N. 31(2).
League Goals (80): Hirst 24, Williams 15, Sheridan 10 (5 pens), Pearson 6, Wilson 6, Francis 4, Anderson 2, Harkes 2, McCall 2, MacKenzie 2, Palmer 2, Shirtliff 2, Worthington 1, own goals 2.
Rumbelows Cup (15): Pearson 5, Hirst 3, Williams 2, Francis 1, Harkes 1, Sheridan 1, Shirtliff 1, Wilson 1.
FA Cup (8): Hirst 2, Anderson 1, Francis 1, Palmer 1, Pearson 1, Sheridan 1 (pen), Shirtliff 1.
Ground: Hillsborough, Sheffield S6 1SW (0742–343122)
Nearest Station: Sheffield
Manager: Trevor Francis **Secretary:** G.H. Mackrell FCCA
Colours: Blue and white striped shirts; black shorts
Record home gate: 72,841 v Manchester City, February 1934 (FA Cup)
Honours – Champions: Division 1: 1902–3, 1903–4, 1928–9, 1929–30; Division 2: 1899–1900, 1925–6, 1951–2, 1955–6, 1958–9
FA Cup winners: 1895–6, 1906–7, 1934–5
League Cup winners: 1990–1

SHREWSBURY TOWN DIV. 3

Blake, Mark C.
Brown, Michael A.
Gorman, Paul A.
Griffiths, Carl B.
Heathcote, Michael
Hughes, Kenneth D.
Kelly, Anthony G.
Lynch, Thomas M.
O'Toole, Christopher P.
Parrish, Sean
Perks, Stephen J.
Ryan, Darren T.
Spink, Dean P.
Summerfield, Kevin
Weir, William
Wimbleton, Paul P.
Worsley, Graeme

League Appearances: Askew, W. 5; Blake, M.C. 46; Brown, M.A. 43; Burton, M.J. 3(3); Clarke, W. 7; Clements, K.H. 19(1); Coughlin, R.J. 4(1); Gorman, P.A. 27(3); Griffiths, C.B. 14(5); Hartford, R.A. 8; Heathcote, M. 38(1); Hughes, K.D. 36; Kelly, A.G. 38; Lynch, T.M. 34(5); Lyne, N.G.F. 16; Moore, J. 7(1); Naughton, W.B.S. 3(3); O'Toole, C.P. 11; Parrish, S. 1; Perks, S.J. 10; Ryan, D.T. 1(1); Shaw, G.R. 20(2); Spink, D.P. 30(13); Summerfield, K. 30(2); Taylor, R.M. 19; Weir, W. –(8); Wimbleton, P.P. 9(9); Worsley, G. 27(4).
League Goals (61): Clarke 6 (1 pen), Heathcote 6, Lyne 6, Spink 6, Kelly 5, Shaw 5, Summerfield 5, Griffiths 4, Blake 2, Lynch 2, Taylor 2, Brown 1, Moore 1, Naughton 1, Weir 1, Wimbleton 1, Worsley 1, own goals 6.
Rumbelows Cup (3): Griffiths 1, Kelly, Moore 1.
FA Cup (8): Shaw 5, Brown 1, Kelly (pen), Spink 1.
Ground: Gay Meadow, Shrewsbury SY2 6AB (0743–60111)
Nearest Station: Shrewsbury
Manager: John Bond **Secretary:** M.J. Starkey

Colours: White shirts with blue trim; blue shorts
Record home gate: 18,917 v Walsall, April 1961 (League)
Honours – Champions: Division 3: 1978–9

SOUTHAMPTON DIV. 1

Adams, Michael R.
Andrews. Ian E.
Banger, Nicholas L.
Benali, Francis V.
Bound, Matthew T.
Case, James R.
Cherednik, Alexsey
Cockerill, Glenn
Cook, Andrew C.
Davis, Stephen M.
Dodd, Jason R.
Flowers, Timothy D.
Gittens, Jon
Gotsmanov, Sergei A.
Hall, Richard A.
Horne, Barry
Kenna, Jeffrey J.
Le Tissier, Matthew P.
Luscombe, Lee J.
McLoughlin, Alan F.
Maddison, Neil S.
Osman, Russell C.
Powell, Lee
Rideout, Paul D.
Roast, Stephen
Ruddock, Neil
Shearer, Alan
Wallace, Raymond G.
Wallace, Rodney S.
Widdrington, Thomas

League Appearances: Adams, M.R. 29(1); Andrews, I.E. 1; Banger, N.L. –(6); Benali, F.V. 9(3); Case, J.R. 24(1); Cherednik, A. 12(3); Cockerill, G. 28(4); Cook, A.C. 5(2); Davis, S.M. 1(1); Dodd, J.R. 16(3); Flowers, T.D. 37; Gittens, J. 7(1); Gotsmanov, S.A. 2(6); Hall, R.A. –(1); Horne, B. 38; Kenna, J.J. 1(1); Le Tissier, M.P. 34(1); McLoughlin, A.F. 22; Maddison, N.S. 1(3); Moore, K.T. 19; Osman, R.C. 17(3); Rideout, P.D. 14(2); Ruddock, N. 32(3); Shearer, A. 34(2); Wallace, R.S. 35(2).
League Goals (58): Le Tissier 19 (5 pens), Wallace Rod 14, Rideout 6, Shearer 4, Ruddock 3, Cockerill 2, Case 1, Horne 1, McLoughlin 1, Moore 1, Osman 1, own goals 5.
Rumbelows Cup (15): Shearer 6 (1 pen), Banger 3, Le Tissier 2, Wallace Rod 2, Horne 1, Ruddock 1.
FA Cup (8): Le Tissier 2, Shearer 2 (1 pen), Wallace Rod 2, Case 1, Ruddock 1.
Ground: The Dell, Milton Road, Southampton SO9 4XX (0703–220505)
Nearest Station: Southampton
Manager: Ian Branfoot **Secretary:** B.P. Truscott
Colours: Red and white striped shirts; black shorts
Record home gate: 31,044 v Manchester United October, 1969 (League)
Honours – Champions: Division 3 South 1921–2; Division 3: 1959–60
FA Cup winners: 1975–6

SOUTHEND UNITED DIV. 2

Angell, Brett
Ansah, Andrew
Austin, Dean B.
Benjamin, Ian
Butler, Peter J.
Clark, Paul P.
Cornwell, John A.
Edwards, Andrew D.
Heffer, Steven P.
Hyslop, Christian
Ling, Martin
Locke, Adam S.
Martin, David
Powell, Christopher G.
Prior, Spencer J.
Sansome, Paul E.
Scott, Morrys J.
Scully, Patrick J.
Smith, Paul W.
Tilson, Stephen B.

League Appearances: Angell, B. 37(5); Ansah, A. 37(3); Austin, D.B. 44; Benjamin, I. 46; Butler, P.J. 42; Cawley, P. 6(1); Clark, P.P. 40; Cook, J.P. –(1); Cornwell, J.A. 13(6); Edwards, A.D. 2; Hyslop, C. 10(1); Ling, M. 1(2); Locke, A.S. 18(10); Martin, D. 40(1); Moran, P. 1; Powell, C.G. 43(2); Prior, S.J. 19; Sansome, P.E. 46; Scully, P.J. 21; Smith, P.W. 2; Tilson, S.B. 38.

League Goals (67): Angell 15, Benjamin 13, Martin 11 (2 pens), Ansah 9, Tilson 8, Locke 4, Butler 2, Cornwell 2, Crawley 1, Edwards 1, Powell 1.

Rumbelows Cup (5): Angell 2, Austin 1, Butler 1, Martin 1.

FA Cup (2): Angell 2.

Ground: Roots Hall Football Ground, Victoria Avenue, Southend SS2 6NQ (0702 340707)

Nearest Stations: Pittlewell or Southend Central

Manager: David Webb **Secretary:** J.W. Adams

Colours: Blue shirts; yellow shorts with blue trim

Record home gate: 31,090 v Liverpool January 1979 (FA Cup)

Honours – Champions: Division 4: 1980–81

STOCKPORT COUNTY DIV. 3

Barras, Anthony
Beaumont, Christopher P.
Brown, Malcolm
Cooper, Paul D.
Finley, Alan
Frain, David
Francis, Kevin
Gannon, James P.
Kilner, Andrew W.
Knowles, Darren T.
Matthews, Neil
Pennock, Anthony
Redfern, David
Thorpe, Andrew
Todd, Lee
Williams, Paul R.C.
Williams, William R.

League Appearances: Alexander, K. 9(2); Barras, A. 37(3); Beaumont, C.P. 45; Brabin, G. –(1); Brown, M. 34; Bullock, S. 29(1); Cooper, P.D. 22; Finley, A. 19; Frain, D. 43; Francis, K. 11(2); Gannon, J.P. 41; Kilner, A.W. 21(3); Knowles, D.T. 6(6); Lee, J.B. 2; McInerney, I. 1(1); Maguire, P. –(2); Matthews, N. 22(7); Payne, M.R.C. 24(7); Redfern, D. 24; Robertson, P. 1; Thorpe, A. 39(1); Todd, L. 12(2); Williams, P. 24; Williams, P.R.C. 23(1); Williams, W.R. 17(1).

League Goals (84): Beaumont 15, Matthews 14, Williams PA 14, Kilner 11 (1 pen), Payne 9 (2 pens), Gannon 6, Francis 5, Finley 3, Frain 3, Williams PR 2, Brown 1 (pen), Williams B 1.

Rumbelows Cup (1): Williams PA 1.

FA Cup (0)

Ground: Edgeley Park, Stockport SK3 9DD (061–480 8888)

Nearest Station: Stockport

Manager: Danny Bergara **Secretary:** J.D. Simpson

Colours: White shirts: royal blue shorts

Record home gate: 27,833 v Liverpool, February 1950 (FA Cup)

Honours – Champions: Division 3 North: 1921–2, 1936–7; Division 4: 1966–7

STOKE CITY DIV. 3

Baines, Paul
Barnes, Paul L.
Beeston, Carl F.
Biggins, Wayne
Blake, Noel L.G.
Boughey, Darren J.

Butler, John E.
Cranson, Ian
Devlin, Mark A.
Ellis, Anthony J.
Fowler, Lee E.
Fox, Peter D.
Gallimore, Anthony M.
Kelly, Anthony
Kennedy, Michael F.
Kevan, David J.
Male, Christopher
Percival, Jason C.
Rennie, Paul A.
Sandford, Lee R.
Scott, Ian
Ware, Paul D.
Wright, Ian M.

League Appearances: Baines, P. 1(1); Barnes, P.L. 3(3); Beeston, C.F. 37; Biggins, W. 36(2); Blake, N.L.G. 44; Bright, D.J. –(1); Butler, J.E. 31; Carr, C.P. 15(5); Clarke, W. 9; Cranson, I. 7(2); Devlin, M.A. 18(3); Ellis, A.J. 33(5); Evans, G.J. 5; Fowler, L.E. 14(3); Fox, P.D. 44; Gallimore, A.M. 4(3); Hilaire, V.M. 10; Kelly, A. 16(13); Kennedy, M.F. 32; Kevan, D.J. 4(1); Noble, D.W.T. 2; Rennie, P.A. 3; Rice, B. 18; Sandford, L.R. 32; Scott, I. 1(1); Statham, D.J. 22; Thomas, M.R. 32(6); Ware, P.D. 29(5); Whitehurst, W. 3; Wright, I.M. 1.

League Goals (55): Biggins 12, Ellis 9, Thomas 7, Blake 3, Clarke 3, Kelly 3, Kennedy 3 (2 pens), Beeston 2, Butler 2, Devlin 2, Hilaire 2, Sandford 2, Ware 2, Evans 1, Statham 1, own goal 1

Rumbelows Cup (2): Evans 1, Kelly 1.

FA Cup (1): Sandford 1.

Ground: Victoria Ground, Stoke-on-Trent ST4 4EG (0782–413511)

Nearest Station: Stoke-on-Trent

Manager: Lou Macari **Secretary:** M.J. Potts

Colours: Red and white striped shirts; white shorts

Record home gate: 51,380 v Arsenal, March 1937 (League)

Honours – Champions: Division 2: 1932–3, 1962–3; Division 3 North: 1926–7

League Cup winners: 1971–2

SUNDERLAND DIV. 2

Agboola, Reuben O.F.
Armstrong, Gordon I.
Atkinson, Brian
Ball, Kevin A.
Bennett, Gary E.
Bracewell, Paul W.
Brady, Kieron
Carter, Timothy D.
Cornforth, John M.
Cullen, Anthony
Davenport, Peter
Gabbiadini, Marco
Gaughan, Steven E.
Gray, Martin
Guthrie, Simon
Hardyman, Paul G.
Hauser, Thomas
Hawke, Warren R.
Kay, John
Mooney, Brian J.
Norman, Anthony J.
Ord, Richard J.
Owers, Gary
Pascoe, Colin J.
Rush, David
Sampson, Ian
Smith, Anthony
Trigg, Jonathan M.
Walls, Wayne M.
Williams, Paul L.

League Appearances: Agboola, R.O.F. 5; Armstrong, G.I. 35; Atkinson, B. 4(2); Ball, K.A. 33; Bennett, G.E. 37; Bracewell, P.W. 37; Brady, K. 4(10); Carter, T.D. 1; Cornforth, J.M. 1(1); Cullen, A. 2(3); Davenport, P. 27(2); Gabbiadini, M. 30(1); Hardyman, P.G. 30(2); Hauser, T. 5(5); Hawke, W.R. 3(4); Kay, J. 28(2); MacPhail, J. 1; Mooney, B.J. 5(1); Norman, A.J. 37; Ord, R.J. 12(2); Owers, G. 38; Pascoe, C.J. 25; Rush, D. 8(3); Smith, A. 9; Williams, P.L. 1.

League Goals (38): Gabbiadini 9, Davenport 7 (1 pen), Armstrong 6, Pascoe 5, Ball 3 (2 pens), Bennett 2, Brady 2, Rush 2, Hauser 1, Owers 1.

Rumbelows Cup (6): Gabbiadini 2, Ball 1, Cullen 1, Hauser 1, Owers 1.

FA Cup (1): Own goal 1.

Ground: Roker Park, Grantham Road, Sunderland SR6 9SW (091-5140332)
Nearest Stations: Sunderland or Seaburn
Manager: Denis Smith **Secretary:** G. Davidson F.C.A.
Colours: Red and white striped shirts; black shorts
Record home gate: 75,118 v Derby, March 1933 (FA Cup)
Honours – Champions: Division 1: 1891–2, 1892–3, 1894–5, 1901–2, 1912–13, 1935–6; Division 2: 1975–6; Division 3: 1987–8.
FA Cup winners: 1972–3

SWANSEA CITY DIV. 3

Bowen, Jason
Bracey, Lee M.I.
Chalmers, Paul
Coleman, Christopher P.
Connor, Terence F.
Coughlin, Russell J.
Davey, Simon
Davies, Alan
Freeman, Clive R.
Gilligan, James M.
Harris, Mark A.
Heeps, James A.
Hough, David J.
Jenkins, Stephen J.
Kendall, Mark
Legg, Andrew
Miller, Paul R.
Raynor, Paul J.
Thornber, Stephen J.
Trick, Desmond
Walker, Keith C.
Watson, Andrew A.

League Appearances: Bowen, J. 1(2); Bracey, L.M.I. 35; Chalmers, P. 12(9); Coleman, C.P. 41; Connor, T.F. 33; Coughlin, R.J. 29; D'Auria, D. 12(8); Davey, S. 11(7); Davies, A. 35; Freeman, C.R. 2; Gilligan, J.M. 36(1); Harris, M.A. 41; Honor, C.R. 2; Hough, D.J. 39(2); Hutchison, T. 6(3); Jenkins, S. –(1); Kendall, M. 11; Legg, A. 37(2); Miller, P.R. 8(4); Penney, D.M. 12; Raynor, P.J. 36(7); Thornber, S.J. 11(8); Trick, D. 14(1); Walker, K.C. 21(3); Watson, A.A. 9(5); Williams, P.L. 12.
League Goals (49): Gilligan 16, Connor 5, Legg 5, Raynor 5 (2 pens), D'Auria 4, Davies 3, Penney 3 (1 pen), Chalmers 2, Davey 2, Harris 1, Watson 1, own goals 2.
Rumbelows Cup (0).
FA Cup (7): Connor 2, Gilligan 2 (2 pens), Legg 2, Thornber 1.
Ground: Vetch Field, Swansea SA1 3SU (0792–474114)
Nearest Station: Swansea
Manager: Frank Burrows **Secretary:** George Taylor
Colours: All white
Record home gate: 32,796 v Arsenal, February 1968 (FA Cup)
Honours – Champions: Division 3 South: 1924–5, 1948–9

SWINDON TOWN DIV. 2

Bennett, David
Calderwood, Colin
Close, Shaun C.
Digby, Fraser C.
Foley, Steven
Green, Richard E.
Hammond, Nicholas D.
Hazard, Michael
Hunt, Paul C.
Jones, Tom
Kerslake, David
Lorenzo, Nestor G.
MacLaren, Ross
Shearer, Duncan N.
Simpson, Fitzroy
Spalding, Lee A.
Summerbee, Nicholas J.
Trollope, Paul J.
Viveash, Adrian L.
White, Stephen J.

League Appearances: Bennett, D. 1; Bodin, P.J. 31; Buttigieg, J. 2(1); Calderwood, C. 22(1); Close, S.C. 4(10); Digby, F.C. 41; Finnigan, A. 2(1); Foley, S. 42(2); Gittens, J. 28; Hammond, N.D. 5; Hazard, M. 31(3); Hockaday, D. 1(2); Hunt, P.C. –(2); Jones, T. 42(1); Kerslake, D. 37; Ling, M. –(1); Lorenzo, N.G. 18(2); MacLaren, R. 45; McLoughlin, A.F. 15(2); Murray, E.J. –(1); Rideout, P. 9; Shearer, D.N. 44; Simpson, F. 27(11); Summerbee, N.J. 1(6); Tanner, N. 7; Viveash, A.L. 23(2); White, S.J. 28(7).

League Goals (65): Shearer 22, White 9, Hazard 8 (3 pens), Foley 7, McLaughlin 4, Simpson, 3, Bodin, 2; Calderwood, 2, Lorenzo 2, Gittens 1, MacLaren 1, Rideout 1, Viveash 1, own goals 2.

Rumbelows Cup (4): Close 1, McLoughlin 1, Simpson 1, own goal 1.

FA Cup (3): White 2, Shearer 1.

Ground: County Ground, Swindon SN1 2ED (0793–22118 and 36170)

Nearest Station: Swindon

Manager: Glenn Hoddle **Secretary:** Lisa Maberly

Colours: All red

Record home gate: 32,000 v Arsenal, January 1972 (FA Cup)

Honours – Champions: Division 4: 1985–6

League Cup winners: 1968–9

Anglo-Italian Cup winners: 1970

TORQUAY UNITED DIV. 3

Bastow, Ian J.
Curran, Christopher
Edwards, Dean S.
Elliott, Matthew S.
Hall, Paul A.
Hodges, David
Holmes, Michael A.
Holmes, Paul
Howells, Gareth
Joyce, Sean W.
Lloyd, Phillip R.
Loram, Mark J.
Myers, Christopher
Rowland, Andrew J.
Saunders, Wesley
Smith, Paul
Tynan, Thomas E.
Uzzell, John E.
Whiston, Peter M.

League Appearances: Cookson, S.J. –(2); Curran, C. 11(2); Edwards, D.S. 35(4); Elliott, M.S. 45; Evans, S.J. 15; Hall, P.A. 9(8); Hay, A.B. 2; Hodges, D. 5(5); Holmes, M.A. 16(6); Holmes, P. 28(5); Howells, G. 45; Joyce, S.W. 23(2); Lloyd, P.R. 19; Loram, M.J. 34(7); Musker, R. 20(1); Myers, C. 24(5); Rowland, A.J. 4(5); Saunders, W. 37; Smith, P. 26(3); Tynan, T.E. 34(1); Uzzell, J.E. 46; Veysey, K.J. 1; Whiston, P.M. 27(1).

League Goals 64): Edwards 15 (1 pen), Tynan 13 (3 pens), Loran 7, Elliott 6, Evans 5, Smith 5, Joyce 3, Saunders 3, Holmes M 2, Myers 2, Holmes P 1, Musker 1, own goal 1.

Rumbelows Cup (3): Saunders 1, Tynan 1, Whiston 1.

FA Cup (1): Tynan 1.

Ground: Plainmoor, Torquay, Devon TQ1 3PS (0803–328666/7)

Nearest Stations: Torquay or Torre

Manager: John Impey **Secretary:** D. F. Turner

Colours: All white with yellow and blue trim

Record home gate: 21,908 v Huddersfield, January 1955 (FA Cup)

Honours: Nil

TOTTENHAM HOTSPUR DIV. 1

Allen, Paul K.
Amar, Mohamed A.
Barmby, Nicholas J.
Bergsson, Gudni
Dearden, Kevin C.
Edinburgh, Justin V.
Edwards, Matthew D.
Fenwick, Terrence W.
Garland, Peter J.
Gascoigne, Paul J.
Gilzean, Ian R.
Gray, Philip
Hendon, Ian M.
Hendry, John
Houghton, Scott A.
Howells, David
Lineker, Gary W.
McDonald, David H.
Mabbutt, Gary V.
Moncur, John F.
Moran, Paul
Polston, Andy A.
Robson, Mark A.
Samways, Vincent
Sedgley, Steven P.
Smith, Kevin
Smith, Neil J.
Statham, Brian
Stewart, Paul A.
Thomas, Mitchell A.
Thorsverdt, Erik
Tuttle, David
Van Den Hauwe, Patrick W.R.
Walker, Ian M.
Walsh, Paul A.

League Appearances: Allen, P.K. 34(2); Amar, M.A. (Nayim) 32(1); Bergsson, G. 9(3); Edinburgh, J.V. 14(2); Fenwick, T.W. 4; Garland, P.J. –(1); Gascoigne, P.J. 26; Gray, P. 3(3); Hendon, I.M. –(2); Hendry, J. 2(2); Howells, D. 29; Lineker, G.W. 32; Mabbutt, G.V. 35; Moncur, J.F. 4(5); Moran, P. –(1); Samways, V. 14(9); Sedgley, S.P. 33(1); Stewart, P.A. 35; Thomas, M.A. 23(8); Thorstvedt, E. 37; Tuttle, D. 4(2); Van Den Hauwe, P.W.R. 31(1); Walker, I.M. 1; Walsh, P.A. 16(13).
League Goals (51): Lineker 15 (3 pens), Gascoigne 7, Walsh 7, Nayim 5, Howells 4, Allen 3, Stewart 3, Hendry 2, Mabbutt 2, Bergsson 1, Edinburgh 1, Samways 1.
Rumbelows Cup (11): Gascoigne 6 (1 pen), Stewart 4, Lineker 1.
FA Cup (14): Gascoigne 6, Lineker 3, Stewart 2, Mabbutt 1, own goals 2.
Ground: White Hart Lane, 748 High Road, Tottenham N17 0AP (081-808 8080)
Nearest Stations: White Hart Lane (BR), Northumberland Park (BR), or Seven Sisters (Victoria Lane) thence by bus
Team manager: Peter Shreeves **Secretary:** Peter Barnes
Colours: White shirts; navy blue shorts
Record home gate: 75,038 v Sunderland, March 1938 (FA Cup)
Honours – Champions: Division 1: 1950–51, 1960–61; Division 2: 1919–20, 1949–50
FA Cup winners: 1900–1, 1920–21, 1960–61, 1961–62, 1966–7, 1980–81, 1981–2, 1990–1 (eight wins record)
League Cup winners: 1970–71, 1972–3
European Cup Winners' Cup winners: 1962–3
UEFA Cup winners: 1971–2, 1983–4

TRANMERE ROVERS DIV. 2

Brannon, Gerard D.
Collings, Paul W.
Cooper, Stephen B.
Foster, Michael G.
Garnett, Shaun M.
Harvey, James
Higgins, David A.
Hughes, Mark
Irons, Kenneth
McGreal, John
McNab, Neil
Malkin, Christopher G.
Martindale, David
Morrissey, John J.
Muir, Ian J.
Mungall, Steven H.
Nixon, Eric W.
Steel, William J.
Thomas, Tony
Vickers, Stephen H.

League Appearances: Bishop, E.M. 5(3); Brannan, G.D. 14(4); Collings, P.W. 3; Cooper, S.B. 9(8); Garnett, S.M. 16; Harvey, J. 35(4); Higgins, D.A. 33; Hughes, M.

42; Irons, K. 26(6); McCarrick, M.B. 11; McNab, N. 39(1); Malkin, C.G. 12(13); Martindale, D. 2(9); Morrissey, J.J. 33(7); Muir, I.J. 33(2); Mungall, S.H. 32(1); Nixon, E.W. 43; Steel, W.J. 43(1); Thomas, T. 33; Vickers, S.H. 42.
League Goals (64): Muir 13 (3 pens), Morrissey 9, Irons 6 (1 pen), Steel 6, Malkin 4, Bishop 3, Harvey 3, McNab 3, Thomas 3, Cooper 2, Higgins 2, Hughes 2, McCarrick 2, Brannan 1, Garnett 1, Mungall 1, Vickers 1, own goals 2.
Rumbelows Cup (2): Steel 1, Vickers 1.
FA Cup (4): Irons 1, Morrisey 1, Steel 1, Vickers 1
Ground: Prenton Park, Birkenhead, L42 9PN (051–608 4194)
Nearest Stations: Central Station Birkenhead and Rock Ferry
Manager: John King **Secretary:** C.N. Wilson F.A.A.I.
Colours: All white
Record home gate: 24,424 v Stoke, February 1972 (FA Cup)
Honours – Champions: Division 3 North: 1937–8
Associate Members Cup – Winners: 1989–90

WALSALL DIV. 4

Barber, Frederick
Cecere, Michele J.
Goldsmith, Martin
Grealish, Anthony P.
Jackson, Robert G.
McDonald, Rodney
Marsh, Christopher J.
Methven, Colin J.
Ntamark, Charles
O'Hara, Stephen
Singleton, Martin D.
Smith, Dean

League Appearances: Barber, F. 2; Barnett, D.K.G. 4(1); Bodak, P.J. 3(1); Bryant, M. 13; Cecere, M.J. 26(6); Goldsmith, M. 2(2); Gordon, C.K. 6; Grealish, A.P. 29(2); Green, R.R. 44; Hutchings, C. 40; Jackson, R.G. 1; Kelly, J. 12(1); Littlejohn, A.S. 15(18); Lowery, A.W. 6; McDonald, R. 31(5); McParland, I. 11; Marsh, C.J. 16(7); Methven, C.J. 32; Mower, K.M. 16(1); Naughton, W.B.S. 15(1); Ntamark, C. 40(2); O'Hara, S. 18(2); Rimmer, S.A. 27; Singleton, M.D. 20(8); Skipper, P.D. 41; Smith, D. 32(1); Thompson, C.D. 3; Whitehouse, P. 1(2).
League Goals (48): Rimmer 13 (4 pens), Cecere 6, McParland 6 (1 pen), McDonald 5, Ntamark 3, Goldsmith 2, Jackson 2, Marsh 2, Bodak 1, Gordon 1 Grealish 1, Littlejohn 1, Methven 1, Naughton 1 (pen), Singleton 1, Skipper 1, own goal 1.
Rumbelows Cup (6): Rimmer 4 (1 pen), Goldsmith 1, Hutchings 1.
FA Cup (2): Hutchings 1, McDonald 1.
Ground: Bescot Stadium, Bescot Crescent, Walsall WS1 4SA (0922–22791)
Nearest Stations: Walsall or Bescott then 15 min walk
Manager: Ken Hibbitt **Secretary:** K.R. Whalley
Colours: Red shirts; white shorts
Record home gate: 25,453 v Newcastle, August 1961 (League)
Honours – Champions: Division 4: 1959–60

WATFORD DIV. 2

Alsford, Julian
Ashby, Barry J.
Bazeley, Darren S.
Butler, Steven
Byrne, David S.
Denton, Edward J.
Devonshire, Alan E.
Drysdale, Jason
Dublin, Keith B.L.

Falconer, William
Gallen, Joseph M.
Gavin, Mark W.
Gibbs, Nigel J.
Holdsworth, David G.
Inglethorpe, Alex M.
James, David
Kennedy, Andrew J.
McLaughlin, Joseph
Meara, James S.
Nicholas, Peter
Porter, Gary M.
Roeder, Glenn V.
Sheppard, Simon
Soloman, Jason R.
Thomas, Roderick C.
Waugh, Keith
Wilkinson, Paul
Williams, Gary

League Appearances: Ashby, B.J. 20(3); Bazeley, D.S. 1(6); Butler, S. 10; Byrne, D.S. 16(1); Callaghan, N. 6(6); Denton, E.J. –(2); Devonshire, A.E. 23(1); Drysdale, J. 25(5); Dublin, K.B.L. 43; Falconer, W. 32(3); Gavin, M.W. 8(5); Gibbs, N.J. 34; Harrison, G.R. 4(2); Holdsworth, D.G. 15; Inglethorpe, A.M. 1; James, D. 46; Kennedy, A.J. 13(5); McLaughlin, J. 24; Nicholas, P. 15; Penrice, G.K. 12(2); Porter, G.M. 40(5); Pullan, C.J. 1(1); Roeder, G.V. 30(3); Soloman, J.R. 5(3); Thomas, R.C. 15(9); Wilkinson, P. 46; Williams, G. 21(3).
League Goals (45): Wilkinson 18, Penrice 5, Falconer 4, Porter 4 (1 pen), Kennedy 3, Byrne 2, Holdsworth 2, Butler 1, Callaghan 1, Devonshire 1, McLaughlin 1, Roeder 1, Thomas 1, own goal 1.
Rumbelows Cup (0).
FA Cup (1): Falconer 1.
Ground: Vicarage Road Stadium, Watford WD1 8ER (0923 30933)
Nearest Stations: Watford Junction, Watford High Street or Watford Stadium Halt
Manager: Steve Perryman **Chief Executive:** E. Plumley F.A.A.I.
Colours: Yellow shirts with black and red trim; black shorts
Record home gate: 34,099 v Manchester United, February 1969 (FA Cup)
Honours –Champions: Division 3: 1968–9; Division 4: 1977–8:

WEST BROMWICH ALBION — DIV. 3

Bannister, Gary
Bradley, Darren M.
Burgess, Daryl
Cartwright, Neil A.
Dobbins, Lionel W.
Ford, Tony
Foster, Adrian M.
Goodman, Donald R.
Hackett, Gary S.
Harbey, Graham K.
Hodson, Simeon P.
McNally, Bernard A.
Naylor, Stuart
Palmer, Leslie J.
Parkin, Stephen
Piggott, Gary D.
Pritchard, David M.
Raven, Paul D.
Rees, Melvyn J.
Roberts, Graham P.
Robson, Gary
Rogers, Darren
Shakespeare, Craig R.
Strodder, Gary J.
West, Colin
White, Eric W.
Williams, Paul A.

League Appearances: Ampadu, K. 3(4); Anderson, C.R. 22(1); Bannister, G. 38(6); Bradley, D.M. 38(1); Burgess, D. 24(1); Dobbins, L.W. 5(3); Ehiogu, U. –2(2); Ford, T. 46; Foster, A.M. 2(3); Goodman, D.R. 16(6); Hackett, G.S. –(5); Harbey, G.K. 21; Hawker, P. 1; Hodson, S.P. 26(4); McNally, B.A. 20(5); Naylor, S. 28; Palmer, L.J. 5(2); Parkin, S. 22(3); Raven, P.D. 11(2); Rees, M.J. 18; Roberts, G.P. 27; Robson, G. 30(1); Rogers, D. 3(1); Shakespeare, C.R. 32(4); Strodder, G.J. 30(4); West, C. 24(4); White, E.W. 4(2); Williams, P.A. 10.
League Goals (52): Bannister 13, Goodman 8, West 8 (2 pens), Ford 5, Roberts 4 (3 pens), Anderson 2, Robson 2, Ampadu 1, Bradley 1, Harbey 1, McNally 1, Palmer 1, Parkin 1 Shakespeare 1, Strodder 1, White 1, own goal 1.
Rumbelows Cup (2): Bannister 1, Hackett 1.

FA Cup (2): Bradley 1, West 1.
Ground: The Hawthorns West Bromwich B71 4LF (021–525 8888)
Nearest Stations: Smethwick Rolfe Street or Birmingham New Street
Manager: Bobby Gould **Secretary:** Dr J.J. Evans
Colours: Navy blue and white striped shirts; navy blue shorts
Record home gate: 64,815 v Arsenal, March 1937 (FA Cup)
Honours – Champions: Division 1: 1919–20; Division 2: 1901–2, 1910–11
FA Cup winners: 1887–8, 1891–2, 1930–31, 1953–4, 1967–8
League Cup winners: 1965–6

WEST HAM UNITED DIV. 1

Allen, Martin J.
Banks, Steven
Bishop, Ian W.
Breacker, Timothy S.
Clarke, Simon N.
Dicks, Julian A.
Dowie, Iain
Foster, Colin J.
Gale, Anthony P.
Houghton, Christopher W.G.
Keen, Kevin I.
Livett, Simon R.
McAvennie, Francis
Martin, Alvin E.
Miklosko, Ludek
Morley, Trevor W.
Parris, George M.R.
Potts, Steven J.
Quinn, James M.
Rosenior, Leroy D.G.
Rush, Matthew J.
Slater, Stuart I.

League Appearances: Allen, M.J. 28(12); Bishop, I.W. 40; Breacker, T.S. 23(1); Carr, F. 1(2); Clarke, S.N. –(1); Dicks, J.A. 13; Dowie, I. 12; Foster, C.J. 36; Gale, A.P. 23(1); Hughton, C.W.G. 32; Keen, K.I. 36(4); Livett, S.R. 1; McAvennie, F. 24(10); Martin, A.E. 20; Miklosko, L. 46; Morley, T.W. 38; Parris, G.M.R. 37(7); Potts, S.J. 36(1); Quinn, J.M. 16(10); Robson, S.I. –(1); Rosenior, L.D.G. –(2); Rush, M.J. 2(3); Slater, S.I. 37(3); Stewart, R.S. 5.
League Goals (60): Morley 12, McAvennie 10, Quinn 6, Parris 5, Bishop 4 (1 pen), Dicks 4 (2 pens), Dowie 4, Allen 3, Foster 3, Slater 3, Breacker 1, Gale 1, Martin 1, Potts 1, own goals 2.
Rumbelows Cup (6): Allen 2, Dicks 1 (pen), Keen 1, Morley 1, Quinn 1.
FA Cup (15): Morley 4, Parris 3, Bishop 2, Quinn 2, Slater 2, Foster 1, McAvennie 1.
Ground: Boleyn Ground, Green Street, Upton Park E13 9AZ (081-472 2740)
Nearest Station: Upton Park (District line)
Manager: Billy Bonds **Chief Executive Secretary:** T.M. Finn
Colours: Claret shirts with blue trim; white shorts
Record home gate: 42,322 v Tottenham, H, October 1970 (League)
Honours – Champions: Division 2: 1957–8, 1980–81
FA Cup winners: 1963–4, 1974–5, 1979–80
European Cup Winners' Cup winners: 1964–5

WIGAN ATHLETIC DIV. 3

Adkins, Nigel H.
Appleton, Stephen
Atherton, Peter
Carberry, James
Daley, Phillip
Griffiths, Bryan
Johnson, Alan K.
Jones, Philip A.
Langley, Kevin J.

Page, Donald R.
Paladino, Giuseppe
Parkinson, Joseph S.
Pattterson, Daren J.
Pilling, Andrew J.
Rimmer, Neill
Tankard, Allen J.
Worthington, Gary

League Appearances: Adkins, N.H. 18, Appleton, S. 3(7); Atherton, P. 46; Boughey, D.J. 2; Carberry, J. 14(14); Daley, P. 41; Fairclough, D. 4(3); Griffiths, B. 38(5); Griffiths, I.J. 6(5); Hildersley, R. 4; Hughes, P. 19; Johnson, A.K. 40(3); Jones, P.A. 19(1); Langley, K.J. 38(1); Nugent, S. –(1); Page, D.R. 31(3); Paladino, G. 7; Parkinson, J.S. 25; Patterson, D.J. 18(10); Pennock, A. 2; Pilling, A.J. 8(5); Powell, G. 13(1); Rimmer, N. 34; Rogerson, L.A. –(1); Tankard, A.J. 46; Woods, R.G. 20; Worthington, G. 10(2).

League Goals (71): Page 13, Griffiths B 12 (5 pens), Daley 10, Johnson 5, Worthington 5, Patterson 4, Powell 4, Carberry 3, Pilling 3, Woods 3, Boughey 2, Langley 2, Rimmer 2, Fairclough 1, Jones 1, Tankard 1.

Rumbelows Cup (1): Page 1.

FA Cup (8): Griffiths B, 3, Rimmer 2, Page 1, Patterson 1, Woods 1.

Ground: Springfield Park, Wigan WN6 7BA (0942–44433)

Nearest Stations: Wigan Wallgate and Wigan North West

Manager: Bryan Hamilton **Secretary:** Mark A. Blackbourne

Colours: Blue shirts; white shorts

Record home gate: 27,500 v Hereford United, December 1953 (FA Cup)

Honours: Nil

Associate Members Cup winners: 1984–5

WIMBLEDON DIV. 1

Anthrobus, Stephen A.
Barton, Warren
Bennett, Michael R.
Blackwell, Dean R.
Clarke, Andrew W.
Cork, Alan G.
Cotterill, Stephen
Curle, Keith
Dobbs, Gerald F.
Elkins, Gary
Fairweather, Carlton
Fashanu, John
Fitzgerald, Scott
Gibson, Terence B.
Joseph, Roger A.
Kruszynski, Zbigniew
McAllister, Brian
McGee, Paul
Miller, Paul A.
Newhouse, Aidan
Phelan, Terry M.
Quamina, Mark E.
Ryan, Vaughan W.
Sanchez, Lawrence P.
Scales, John R.
Segers, Johannes C.A.
Sullivan, Neil

League Appearances: Anthrobus, S.A. 3; Ardley, N.C. 1; Barton, W. 37; Bennett, M.R. 1(5); Blackwell, D.R. 31(4); Clarke, A.W. 7(5); Cork, A.G. 9(16); Cotterill, S. 4; Curle, K. 37; Elkins, G. 10; Fairweather, C. 3(2); Fashanu, J. 34(1); Gayle, J. 7; Gibson, T.B. 18(1); Joseph, R.A. 38; Kruszynski, Z. 25(2); McGee, P. 26(1); Miller, P.A. 1; Newhouse, A. 1(7); Phelan, T.M. 29; Ryan, V.W. 1(1); Sanchez, L.P. 21(8); Scales, J.R. 36; Segers, J.C.A. 37; Sullivan, N. 1.

League Goals (53): Fashanu 20 (1 pen), McGee 6, Cork 5, Gibson 5, Barton 3, Clarke 3, Krusynski 2, Scales 2, Cotterill 1, Curle 1, Fairweather 1, Gayle 1, Newhouse 1 own goals 2.

Rumbelows Cup (0).

FA Cup (2): Cork 1, McGee 1.

Ground: Selhurst Park, South Norwood, London SE25 (081-771 2233)

Nearest Stations: Selhurst, Norwood Junction or Thornton Heath

Manager: Ray Harford **Secretary:** Adrian Cook

Colours: All blue with yellow trim
Record home gate: 18,000 v HMS Victory, 1934–5 (FA Amateur Cup)
Honours – Champions: Division 4: 1982–3
FA Cup winners: 1987–8

WOLVERHAMPTON WANDERERS DIV. 2

Ashley, Kevin M.
Bartram, Vincent L.
Bellamy, Gary
Bennett, Thomas M.
Birch, Paul
Bull, Stephen G.
Burke, Mark S.
Clarke, Nicholas J.
Cooke, Paul A.
Dennison, Robert
Downing, Keith G.
Hindmarch, Robert
Lange, Anthony S.
Leeding, Stuart
McLoughlin, Paul B.
Mutch, Andrew
Paskin, William J.
Roberts, Brian
Smith, Darren L.
Steele, Timothy W.
Stowell, Michael
Taylor, Colin D.
Thompson, Andrew R.
Venus, Mark
Westley, Shane L.M.

League Appearances: Ashley, K.M. 15(1); Bartram, V.L. 4; Bellamy, G. 26; Birch, P. 20; Bennett, T.M. 24(2); Blake, M.A. 2; Bull, S.G. 43; Burke, M. 3(3); Clarke, N.J. 10(4); Cook, P.A. 42; Dennison, R. 41(1); Downing, K.G. 31; Hindmarch, R. 40; Jones, P.A. –(1); Lange, A.S. 3; McLoughlin, P.B. 2(4); Mutch, A. 29; Paskin, W.J. 10(5); Roberts, B. 17(4); Stancliffe, P.I. 17; Steele, T.W. 22(6); Stowell, M. 39; Taylor, C.D. 6(9); Thompson, A.R. 43(1); Todd, M.K. 6(1); Venus, M. 6; Westley, S.L.M. 5(1).
League Goals (63): Bull 26, Mutch 8, Cook 6 (1 pen), Dennison 5, Bellamy 3, Thompson 3, Birch 2, Hindmarch 2, Steele 2, Taylor 2, Downing 1, Paskin 1, Westley 1, own goal 1.
Rumbelows Cup (1): Steele 1.
FA Cup (0)
Ground: Molineux Grounds, Wolverhampton WV1 4QR (0902–712181)
Nearest Station: Wolverhampton
Manager: Graham Turner **Secretary:** K.D. Pearson A.C.I.S.
Colours: Gold shirts; black shorts
Record home gate: 61,315 v Liverpool, February 1939 (FA Cup)
Honours – Champions: Division 1: 1953–4, 1957–8, 1958–9; Division 2: 1931–32, 1976–7; Division 3 North: 1923–4; Division 3: 1988–9; Division 4: 1987–8
FA Cup winners: 1892–3, 1907–8, 1948–9, 1959–60.
League Cup winners: 1973–4, 1979–80
Associate Members Cup winners: 1987–8

WREXHAM DIV. 4

Armstrong, Christopher P.
Beaumont, Nigel
Bowden, Jon L.
Flynn, Brian
Griffiths, Ian J.
Hardy, Phillip
Jones, Joseph P.
Morris, Mark
O'Keefe, Vincent J.
Owen, Gareth
Phillips, Wayne
Preece, Andrew P.
Reck, Sean M.
Sertori, Mark A.
Thackeray, Andrew J.
Watkin, Stephen
Williams, Michael

League Appearances: Armstrong, C. 30(8); Barnes, R.A. –(1); Beaumont, N. 36(1); Bowden, J.L. 39(1); Carey, B.P. 3; Cooper, G. 5(4); Flynn, B. 10(1); Griffiths, I.J. 11; Hardy, P. 32; Hunter, G. 22(2); Jones, J.P. 21; Jones, P.L. 13(5); Jones, R.S. 5(1); Kelly, J. 2(10); Kennedy, A.P. 9; Lunt, R.J. 1(7); Morris, M. 40; Murray, J. 11; O'Gorman, D.J. 8(9); O'Keefe, V.J. 6; Owen, G. 24(3); Phillips, W. 24(4); Preece, A.P. 31(3); Reck, S.M. 13; Sertori, M.A. 27(2); Thackeray, A.J. 41; Ward, A.S. 4; Watkin, S. 9; Worthington, G.L. 29(1).
League Goals (48): Armstrong 10, Worthington 6, Bowden 5 (3 pens), Jones L 5, Preece 4, Hunter 3, Cooper 2, Jones J 2, Owen 2, Thackeray 2, Ward 2, Beaumont 1, Flynn 1, Jones R 1, Reck 1, Watkin 1.
Rumbelows Cup (3): Worthington 2 (1 pen), Preece 1.
FA Cup (2): Preece 2.
Ground: The Racecourse, Mold Road, Wrexham LL1 2AN (0978–262129)
Nearest Station: Wrexham General
Manager: Brian Flynn **Secretary:** D.L. Rhodes
Colours: Red shirts; white shorts
Record home gate: 34,445 v Manchester United, January 1957 (FA Cup)
Honours – Champions: Division 4. 1977–8

YORK CITY — DIV. 4

Barratt, Anthony
Blackstone, Ian K.
Bushell, Stephen P.
Canham, Anthony
Hall, Wayne
Helliwell, Ian
Kiely, Dean
McCarthy, Jonathan D.
McMillan, Lyndon A.
Marples, Christopher
Naylor, Glenn
Pepper, Nigel
Reid, Shaun
Tutill, Stephen A.
Waburton, Ray

League Appearances: Barratt, A. 27(2); Blackstone, I.K. 20(8); Bradshaw, M. –(1); Bushell, S.P. 10(5); Canham, A. 39(2); Cook, M.J. 3(3); Cooper, G. 2; Crossley, R.M. 5; Curtis, A. 2(3); Dunn, I.G.W. 18(15); Grayson, N. –(1); Hall, W. 46; Hart, N. 1; Helliwell, I. 41; Himsworth, G.P. 1(1); Howlett, G.P. 15(2); Kiely, D. 17; Lister, S.H. 4; Longhurst, D.J. 2; McCarthy, J.D. 26(1); McMillan, L.A. 45; Marples, C. 29; Naylor, G. 17(3); Pepper, N. 38(1); Reid, S. 28(1); Tutill, S.A. 42; Warburton, R. 22; Weatherhead, S. 6(2); Wood, M. –(1).
League Goals (45): Helliwell 7, Blackstone 6, Canham 5, Naylor 5, Warburton 4, Dunn 3, Howlett 3 (1 pen), Pepper 3 (2 pens), McCarthy 2, Barratt 1, Hall 1, Lister 1, McMillan 1, own goals 3.
Rumbelows Cup (0)
FA Cup (3): Canham 2, Pepper 1.
Ground: Bootham Crescent, York YO3 7AQ (0904–624447)
Nearest Station: York
Manager: John Bird **Secretary:** Keith Usher
Colours: Red shirts, navy blue shorts
Record home gate: 28,123 v Huddersfield T, March 1938 (FA Cup)
Honours – Champions: Division 4: 1983–4

LIST OF REFEREES FOR SEASON 1991–92

Paul Alcock (S. Merstham, Surrey)
David Allison (Lancaster)
Gerald Ashby, (Worcester)
David Axcell, (Southend)
Mike Bailey, (Impington, Cambridge)
Keren Barrett, (Coventry)
Steven Bell, (Huddersfield)
Alan Bennett, (Sheffield)
Ray Bigger, (Croydon)
Martin Bodenham, (Looe, Cornwall)
Jim Borrett, (Harleston, Norfolk)
John Brandwood, (Lichfield, Staffs.)
Kevin Breen, (Liverpool)
Alf Buksh, (London)
Keith Burge, (Tonypandy)
Billy Burns, (Scarborough)
Vic Callow, (Solihull)
John Carter, (Christchurch)
Brian Coddington, (Sheffield)
Keith Cooper, (Pontypridd)
Keith Cooper, (Swindon)
George Courtney, (Spennymoor)
Ian Cruikshanks, (Hartlepool)
Paul Danson, (Leicester)
Alan Dawson, (Jarrowe)
John Deakin, (Llantwit Major, S. Glam.)
Roger Dilkes, (Mossley, Lancs.)
Phil Don, (Hanworth Park, Middlesex)
Paul Durkin, (Portland, Dorset)
David Elleray, (Harrow)
Tom Fitzharris, (Bolton)
Alan Flood, (Stockport)
Peter Foakes, (Clacton-on-Sea)
David Frampton, (Poole, Dorset)
Dermot Gallagher, (Banbury, Oxon.)
Rodger Gifford, (Llanbradach, Mid. Glam.)
Ron Groves, (Weston-Super-Mare)
Allan Gunn, (South Chailey, Sussex)
Keith Hackett, (Sheffield)
Bob Hamer, (Bristol)
Paul Harrison, (Oldham)
Robert Hart, (Darlington)
Ian Hemley, (Ampthill, Beds.)
Ian Hendrick, (Preston)
Brian Hill, (Kettering)
Terry Holbrook, (Walsall)
Mike James, (Horsham)
Peter Jones, (Loughborough)
John Key, (Sheffield)
Howard King, (Merthyr Tydfil)
John Kirby, (Sheffield)
Ray Lewis, (Gt. Bookham, Surrey)
John Lloyd, (Wrexham)
Stephen Lodge, (Barnsley)
Terry Lunt, (Ashton-in-Makerfield, Lancs)
Ken Lupton, (Stockton-on-Tees)
John Martin, (Nr. Alton, Hants.)
Neil Midgley, (Bolton)
Roger Milford, (Bristol)
Kelvin Morton, (Bury St. Edmunds)
John Moules, (Erith, Kent)
Bob Nixon, (West Kirkby, Wirrall)
Jim Parker, (Preston)
Roger Pawley, (Cambridge)
Mike Peck, (Kendal)
David Phillips, (Barnsley)
Michael Pierce, (Portsmouth)
Graham Poll, (Berkhamsted)
Graham Pooley, (Bishops Stortford)
Richard Poulain, (Huddersfield)
Ken Redfern, (Whitley Bay)
Mike Reed, (Birmingham)
Jim Rushton, (Stoke-on-Trent)
Paul Scoble, (Portsmouth)
Dave Shadwell, (Bromsgrove)
Lester Shapter, (Torquay)
Ray Shepherd, (Leeds)
Gurnam Singh, (Wolverhampton)
Arthur Smith, (Rubery, Birmingham)
Jeff Smith, (Stafford)
Paul Taylor, (Waltham Cross, Herts.)
Colin Trussell, (Liverpool)
Paul Vanes, (Warley, West Midlands)
Tony Ward, (London)
John Watson, (Whitley Bay)
Trevor West, (Hull)
Clive Wilkes, (Gloucester)
Alan Wilkie, (Chester-le-Street)
Gary Willard, (Worthing, W. Sussex)
Roger Wiseman (Borehamwood, Herts.)
Joe Worrall, (Warrington)
Philip Wright, (Northwich)

FOOTBALL LEAGUE REVIEW

Arsenal won their 10th League Championship title in what proved to be rather anti-climactic circumstances. On 4 May Arsenal were three points ahead of Liverpool and had a superior goal difference. That afternoon Liverpool lost 4-2 at Chelsea. Arsenal kicked off after the full programme of games had been played and in front of the TV cameras drew 0-0 at Sunderland. Two days later, Liverpool lost 2-1 in the afternoon at Nottingham Forest, again on the small screen, and handed the title to Arsenal who then celebrated in the evening by beating Manchester United 3-1.

Thus the two points which had been deducted from Arsenal's total for their part in the fracas which had occurred at Old Trafford against Manchester United on 20 October – United lost one point – did not materially affect the outcome.

For the first time this century the team winning the championship conceded only one match. Defensively Arsenal looked to be well on course at one time to beat the record for fewest goals conceded. In the end they let in only 18 and much credit must be given to the defence for this situation.

Goalkeeper David Seaman in his first term at Highbury following his transfer from Queens Park Rangers was outstanding. At one stage Bob Wilson the TV commentator and former Arsenal goalkeeper reckoned that he had been at fault with only two of the goals let in by the team. Full-backs Lee Dixon and Nigel Winterburn were also ever present in the side as was Steve Bould at centre-back who enjoyed his best season.

Up front the unselfish Alan Smith still managed to finish leading goalscorer in the First Division with 23 goals and late in the season a more regular berth alongside him was found for Kevin Campbell, an Arsenal discovery of some promise. Swedish international Anders Limpar also did well in his debut term.

Liverpool had lost 3-0 to Arsenal at Highbury on 2 December and that might have been the moment when the prospect of the championship remaining at Anfield began to fade, if only slightly. Later Kenny Dalglish resigned as manager and Ronnie Moran took over in a caretaker capacity until Graeme Souness was appointed after his successes with Rangers. Naturally none of these changes helped towards continuity.

Increased promotional opportunities from the Second Division, with four teams moving up and only two coming down from the top, helped to swell interest in the latter stages of the competition as a whole. For the fifth successive season there was an increase in attendances, if only slight, but in the recessional climate existing in the country, this was most satisfying. Certainly the play-off system which has been in existence since the 1986–87 season has given fresh impetus to the League fare.

THE LEAGUE – DIVISION I

HOME TEAM	Arsenal	Aston Villa	Chelsea	Coventry C.	Crystal Palace	Derby Co.	Everton	Leeds U.
Arsenal	—	5–0	4–1	6–1	4–0	3–0	1–0	2–0
Aston Villa	0–0	—	2–2	2–1	2–0	3–2	2–2	0–0
Chelsea	2–1	1–0	—	2–1	2–1	2–1	1–2	1–2
Coventry C.	0–2	2–1	1–0	—	3–1	3–0	3–1	1–1
Crystal Palace	0–0	0–0	2–1	2–1	—	2–1	0–0	1–1
Derby Co.	0–2	0–2	4–6	1–1	0–2	—	2–3	0–1
Everton	1–1	1–0	2–2	1–0	0–0	2–0	—	2–3
Leeds U.	2–2	5–2	4–1	2–0	1–2	3–0	2–0	—
Liverpool	0–1	2–1	2–0	1–1	3–0	2–0	3–1	3–0
Luton T.	1–1	2–0	2–0	1–0	1–1	2–0	1–1	1–0
Manchester C.	0–1	2–1	2–1	2–0	0–2	2–1	1–0	2–3
Manchester U.	0–1	1–1	2–3	2–0	2–0	3–1	0–2	1–1
Norwich C.	0–0	2–0	1–3	2–2	0–3	2–1	1–0	2–0
Nottingham F.	0–2	2–2	7–0	3–0	0–1	1–0	3–1	4–3
Q.P.R.	1–3	2–1	1–0	1–0	1–2	1–1	1–1	2–0
Sheffield U.	0–2	2–1	1–0	0–1	0–1	1–0	0–0	0–2
Southampton	1–1	1–1	3–3	2–1	2–3	0–1	3–4	2–0
Sunderland	0–0	1–3	1–0	0–0	2–1	1–2	2–2	0–1
Tottenham H.	0–0	2–1	1–1	2–2	1–1	3–0	3–3	0–0
Wimbledon	0–3	0–0	2–1	1–0	0–3	3–1	2–1	0–1

1990–91 RESULTS

Liverpool	Luton T.	Manchester C.	Manchester U.	Norwich C.	Nottingham F.	Q.P.R.	Sheffield U.	Southampton	Sunderland	Tottenham H.	Wimbledon
3–0	2–1	2–2	3–1	2–0	1–1	2–0	4–1	4–0	1–0	0–0	2–2
0–0	1–2	1–5	1–1	2–1	1–1	2–2	2–1	1–1	3–0	3–2	1–2
4–2	3–3	1–1	3–2	1–1	0–0	2–0	2–2	0–2	3–2	3–2	0–0
0–1	2–1	3–1	2–2	2–0	2–2	3–1	0–0	1–2	0–0	2–0	0–0
1–0	1–0	1–3	3–0	1–3	2–2	0–0	1–0	2–1	2–1	1–0	4–3
1–7	2–1	1–1	0–0	0–0	2–1	1–1	1–1	6–2	3–3	0–1	1–1
2–3	1–0	2–0	0–1	1–0	0–0	3–0	1–2	3–0	2–0	1–1	1–2
4–5	2–1	1–2	0–0	3–0	3–1	2–3	2–1	2–1	5–0	0–2	3–0
—	4–0	2–2	4–0	3–0	2–0	1–3	2–0	3–2	2–1	2–0	1–1
3–1	—	2–2	0–1	0–1	1–0	1–2	0–1	3–4	1–2	0–0	0–1
0–3	3–0	—	3–3	2–1	3–1	2–1	2–0	3–3	3–2	2–1	1–1
1–1	4–1	1–0	—	3–1	0–1	3–1	2–0	3–2	3–0	1–1	2–1
1–1	1–3	1–2	0–3	—	2–6	1–0	3–0	3–1	3–2	2–1	0–4
2–1	2–2	1–3	1–1	5–0	—	1–1	2–0	3–1	2–0	1–2	2–1
1–1	6–1	1–0	1–1	1–3	1–2	—	1–2	2–1	3–2	0–0	0–1
1–3	2–1	1–1	2–1	2–1	3–2	1–0	—	4–1	0–2	2–2	1–2
1–0	1–2	2–1	1–1	1–0	1–1	3–1	2–0	—	3–1	3–0	1–1
0–1	2–0	1–1	2–1	1–2	1–0	0–1	0–1	1–0	—	0–0	0–0
1–3	2–1	3–1	1–2	2–1	1–1	0–0	4–0	2–0	3–3	—	4–2
1–2	2–0	1–1	1–3	0–0	3–1	3–0	1–1	1–1	2–2	5–1	—

THE LEAGUE – DIVISION II

HOME TEAM	Barnsley	Blackburn R.	Brighton & H.A.	Bristol C.	Bristol R.	Charlton Ath.	Hull C.	Ipswich T.	Leicester C.
Barnsley	—	0–1	2–1	2–0	1–0	1–1	3–1	5–1	0–0
Blackburn R.	1–2	—	1–2	0–1	2–2	2–2	2–1	0–1	4–1
Brighton & H.A.	1–0	1–0	—	0–1	0–1	3–2	3–1	2–1	3–0
Bristol C.	1–0	4–2	3–1	—	1–0	0–1	4–1	4–2	1–0
Bristol R.	2–1	1–2	1–3	3–2	—	2–1	1–1	1–0	0–0
Charlton Ath.	2–1	0–0	1–2	2–1	2–2	—	2–1	1–1	1–2
Hull C.	1–2	3–1	0–1	1–2	2–0	2–2	—	3–3	5–2
Ipswich T.	2–0	2–1	1–3	1–1	2–1	4–4	2–0	—	3–2
Leicester C.	2–1	1–3	3–0	0–3	3–2	1–2	0–1	1–2	—
Middlesbrough	1–0	0–1	2–0	2–1	1–2	1–2	3–0	1–1	6–0
Millwall	4–1	2–1	3–0	1–2	1–1	3–1	3–3	1–1	2–1
Newcastle U.	0–0	1–0	0–0	0–0	0–2	1–3	1–2	2–2	2–1
Notts Co.	2–3	4–1	2–1	3–2	3–2	2–2	2–1	3–1	0–2
Oldham Ath.	2–0	1–1	6–1	2–1	2–0	1–1	1–2	2–0	2–0
Oxford U.	2–0	0–0	3–0	3–1	3–1	1–1	1–0	2–1	2–2
Plymouth Arg.	1–1	4–1	2–0	1–0	2–2	2–0	4–1	0–0	2–0
Portsmouth	0–0	3–2	1–0	4–1	3–1	0–1	5–1	1–1	3–1
Port Vale	0–1	3–0	0–1	3–2	3–2	1–1	0–0	1–2	2–0
Sheffield W.	3–1	3–1	1–1	3–1	2–1	0–0	5–1	2–2	0–0
Swindon T.	1–2	1–1	1–3	0–1	0–2	1–1	3–1	1–0	5–2
Watford	0–0	0–3	0–1	2–3	1–1	2–1	0–1	1–1	1–0
W.B.A.	1–1	2–0	1–1	2–1	3–1	1–0	1–1	1–2	2–1
West Ham U.	3–2	1–0	2–1	1–0	1–0	2–1	7–1	3–1	1–0
Wolverhampton W.	0–5	2–3	2–3	4–0	1–1	3–0	0–0	2–2	2–1

1990–91 RESULTS

Middlesbrough	Millwall	Newcastle U.	Notts Co.	Oldham Ath.	Oxford U.	Plymouth Arg.	Portsmouth	Port Vale	Sheffield W.	Swindon T.	Watford	W.B.A.	West Ham U.	Wolverhampton W.
1–0	1–2	1–1	1–0	0–1	3–0	1–0	4–0	1–1	1–1	5–1	2–1	1–1	1–0	1–1
1–0	1–0	0–1	0–1	2–0	1–3	0–0	1–1	1–1	1–0	2–1	0–2	0–3	3–1	1–1
2–4	0–0	4–2	0–0	1–2	0–3	3–2	3–2	1–2	0–4	3–3	3–0	2–0	1–0	1–1
3–0	1–4	1–0	3–2	1–2	3–1	1–1	4–1	1–1	1–1	0–4	3–2	2–0	1–1	1–1
2–0	1–0	1–1	1–1	2–0	1–0	0–0	1–2	2–0	0–1	2–1	3–1	1–1	0–1	1–1
0–1	0–0	1–0	3–1	1–1	3–3	0–1	2–1	0–1	0–1	1–2	1–2	2–0	1–1	1–0
0–0	1–1	2–1	1–2	2–2	3–3	2–0	0–2	3–2	0–1	1–1	1–1	1–1	0–0	1–2
0–1	0–3	2–1	0–0	1–2	1–1	3–1	2–2	3–0	0–2	1–1	1–1	1–0	0–1	0–0
4–3	1–2	5–4	2–1	0–0	1–0	3–1	2–1	1–1	2–4	2–2	0–0	2–1	1–2	1–0
—	2–1	3–0	1–0	0–1	0–0	0–0	1–2	4–0	0–2	2–0	1–2	3–2	0–0	2–0
2–2	—	0–1	1–2	0–0	1–2	4–1	2–0	1–2	4–2	1–0	0–2	4–1	1–1	2–1
0–0	1–2	—	0–2	3–2	2–2	2–0	2–1	2–0	1–0	1–1	1–0	1–1	1–1	0–0
3–2	0–1	3–0	—	2–0	3–1	4–0	2–1	1–1	0–2	0–0	1–0	4–3	0–1	1–1
2–0	1–1	1–1	2–1	—	3–0	5–3	3–1	2–0	3–2	3–2	4–1	2–1	1–1	4–1
2–5	0–0	0–0	3–3	5–1	—	0–0	1–0	5–2	2–2	2–4	0–1	1–3	2–1	1–1
1–1	3–2	0–1	0–0	1–2	2–2	—	1–1	2–0	1–1	3–3	1–1	2–0	0–1	1–0
0–3	0–0	0–1	2–1	1–4	1–1	3–1	—	2–4	2–0	2–1	0–1	1–1	0–1	0–0
3–1	0–2	0–1	0–1	1–0	1–0	5–1	3–2	—	1–1	3–1	0–0	1–2	0–1	1–2
2–0	2–1	2–2	2–2	2–2	0–2	3–0	2–1	1–1	—	2–1	2–0	1–0	1–1	2–2
1–3	0–0	3–2	1–2	2–2	0–0	1–1	3–0	1–2	2–1	—	1–2	2–1	0–1	1–0
0–3	1–2	1–2	1–3	1–1	1–1	2–0	0–1	2–1	2–2	2–2	—	1–1	0–1	3–1
0–1	0–1	1–1	2–2	0–0	2–0	1–2	0–0	1–1	1–2	2–1	1–1	—	0–0	1–1
0–0	3–1	1–1	1–2	2–0	2–0	2–2	1–1	0–0	1–3	2–0	1–0	3–1	—	1–1
1–0	4–1	2–1	0–2	2–3	3–3	3–1	3–1	3–1	3–2	1–2	0–0	2–2	2–1	—

THE LEAGUE – DIVISION III

HOME TEAM	Birmingham C.	Bolton W.	Bournemouth	Bradford C.	Brentford	Bury	Cambridge U.	Chester C.	Crewe Alex.
Birmingham C.	—	1–3	0–0	1–1	0–2	1–0	0–3	1–0	0–2
Bolton W.	3–1	—	4–1	0–1	1–0	1–3	2–2	1–0	3–2
Bournemouth	1–2	1–0	—	3–1	2–0	1–1	0–1	1–0	1–1
Bradford C.	2–0	1–1	3–0	—	0–1	3–1	0–1	2–1	2–0
Brentford	2–2	4–2	0–0	6–1	—	3–2	0–3	0–1	1–0
Bury	0–1	2–2	2–4	0–0	1–1	—	3–1	2–1	1–3
Cambridge U.	0–1	2–1	4–0	2–1	0–0	2–2	—	1–1	3–4
Chester C.	0–1	0–2	0–0	4–2	1–2	1–0	0–2	—	3–1
Crewe Alex.	1–1	1–3	0–2	0–0	3–3	2–2	3–1	1–3	—
Exeter C.	0–2	2–1	2–0	2–2	1–1	2–0	0–1	1–1	3–0
Fulham	2–2	0–1	1–1	0–0	0–1	2–0	0–2	4–1	2–1
Grimsby T.	0–0	0–1	5–0	1–1	2–0	0–1	1–0	2–0	0–1
Huddersfield T.	0–1	4–0	1–3	1–2	1–2	2–1	3–1	1–1	3–1
Leyton Orient	1–1	0–1	2–0	2–1	1–2	1–0	0–3	1–0	3–2
Mansfield T.	1–2	4–0	1–1	0–1	0–2	0–1	2–2	1–0	1–3
Preston N.E.	2–0	1–2	0–0	0–3	1–1	1–1	0–2	0–0	5–1
Reading	2–2	0–1	2–1	1–2	1–2	1–0	2–2	2–2	2–1
Rotherham U.	1–1	2–2	1–1	0–2	2–2	0–3	3–2	2–1	1–1
Shrewsbury T.	4–1	0–1	3–1	1–0	1–1	1–1	1–2	1–0	1–0
Southend U.	2–1	1–1	2–1	1–1	0–1	2–1	0–0	1–1	3–2
Stoke C.	0–1	2–2	1–3	2–1	2–2	2–2	1–1	2–3	1–0
Swansea C.	2–0	1–2	1–2	0–2	2–2	1–2	0–0	1–0	3–1
Tranmere R.	1–0	1–1	1–0	2–1	2–1	1–2	2–0	1–2	2–0
Wigan Ath.	1–1	2–1	2–0	3–0	1–0	1–2	0–1	2–0	1–0

1990–91 RESULTS

Exeter C.	Fulham	Grimsby T.	Huddersfield T.	Leyton Orient	Mansfield T.	Preston N.E	Reading	Rotherham U.	Shrewsbury T.	Southend U.	Stoke C.	Swansea C.	Tranmere R.	Wigan Ath.
1–1	2–0	0–0	1–2	3–1	0–0	1–1	1–1	2–1	0–1	1–1	2–1	2–0	1–0	0–0
1–0	3–0	0–0	1–1	1–0	1–1	1–2	3–1	0–0	1–0	1–0	0–1	1–0	2–1	2–1
2–1	3–0	2–1	3–1	2–2	0–0	0–0	2–0	4–2	3–2	3–1	1–1	1–0	1–0	0–3
3–0	0–0	0–2	2–2	4–0	1–0	2–1	2–1	1–0	2–4	2–1	1–2	0–1	1–2	2–1
1–0	1–2	1–0	1–0	1–0	0–0	2–0	1–0	1–2	3–0	0–1	0–4	2–0	0–2	1–0
3–1	1–1	3–2	2–1	1–0	1–0	3–1	2–1	3–1	2–1	0–1	1–1	1–0	3–0	2–2
1–0	1–0	1–0	0–0	1–0	2–1	1–1	3–0	4–1	3–1	1–4	3–0	2–0	3–1	2–3
1–2	1–0	1–2	1–2	2–0	1–0	1–1	1–0	1–2	3–2	1–0	1–1	2–1	0–2	1–2
1–1	1–1	1–2	1–1	3–3	3–0	2–2	1–0	3–1	1–2	0–2	1–2	3–0	2–3	1–0
—	0–1	0–0	2–2	2–0	2–0	4–0	1–3	2–0	3–0	1–2	2–0	2–0	0–0	1–0
3–2	—	0–0	0–0	1–1	1–0	1–0	1–1	2–0	4–0	0–3	0–1	1–1	1–2	1–2
2–1	3–0	—	4–0	2–2	2–0	4–1	3–0	2–1	1–0	1–0	2–0	1–0	0–1	4–3
1–0	1–0	1–1	—	1–0	2–2	1–0	0–2	4–0	2–1	1–2	3–0	1–2	2–1	1–0
1–0	1–0	0–2	1–0	—	2–1	1–0	4–0	3–0	3–2	0–1	0–2	3–0	4–0	1–1
0–2	1–1	1–1	0–0	3–3	—	0–1	2–0	1–2	2–1	0–1	0–0	2–0	0–2	1–1
1–0	1–0	1–3	1–1	2–1	3–1	—	1–2	1–2	4–3	2–1	2–0	2–0	0–4	2–1
1–0	1–0	2–0	1–2	1–2	2–1	3–3	—	2–0	1–2	2–4	1–0	0–0	1–0	3–1
2–4	3–1	1–4	1–3	0–0	1–1	1–0	0–2	—	2–2	0–1	0–0	2–3	1–1	5–1
2–2	2–2	1–2	0–0	3–0	0–3	0–1	5–1	0–0	—	0–1	2–0	1–2	0–1	0–0
2–1	1–1	2–0	0–1	1–1	2–1	3–2	1–2	2–1	2–1	—	1–0	4–1	1–0	0–2
2–1	2–1	0–0	2–0	1–2	3–1	0–1	0–1	3–1	1–3	4–0	—	2–2	1–1	2–0
0–3	2–2	0–0	1–0	0–0	1–2	3–1	3–1	5–0	0–1	1–4	2–1	—	1–1	1–6
1–0	1–1	1–2	2–0	3–0	6–2	2–1	0–0	1–2	1–1	3–1	1–2	2–1	—	1–1
4–1	2–0	2–0	1–1	1–2	0–2	2–1	1–0	2–0	2–2	4–1	4–0	2–4	0–1	—

THE LEAGUE – DIVISION IV

HOME TEAM	Aldershot	Blackpool	Burnley	Cardiff C.	Carlisle U.	Chesterfield	Darlington	Doncaster R.	Gillingham
Aldershot	—	1–4	1–2	0–0	3–0	1–0	0–2	1–1	1–0
Blackpool	4–2	—	1–2	3–0	6–0	3–0	1–2	2–0	2–0
Burnley	3–0	2–0	—	2–0	2–1	0–1	3–1	1–0	2–2
Cardiff C.	1–3	1–1	3–0	—	3–1	2–1	0–1	0–2	2–0
Carlisle U.	1–2	1–0	1–1	3–2	—	1–0	0–2	2–3	0–4
Chesterfield	1–0	2–2	2–1	0–0	4–1	—	2–2	2–1	1–1
Darlington	3–1	1–1	3–1	4–1	3–1	1–0	—	1–1	1–1
Doncaster R.	3–0	1–0	2–1	1–1	4–0	0–1	0–1	—	1–1
Gillingham	1–1	2–2	3–2	4–0	2–1	0–1	1–0	2–0	—
Halifax T.	3–0	5–3	1–2	1–2	1–1	2–1	0–0	0–1	1–2
Hartlepool U.	1–0	1–2	0–0	0–1	4–1	2–0	0–0	1–1	1–0
Hereford U.	1–0	1–1	3–0	1–1	4–2	2–3	1–1	1–1	1–1
Lincoln C.	2–2	0–1	1–0	0–0	6–2	1–1	0–3	0–0	1–1
Maidstone U.	1–1	1–1	1–0	3–0	0–0	1–0	2–3	0–1	3–1
Northampton T.	2–1	1–0	0–0	0–0	1–1	2–0	0–3	0–0	2–1
Peterborough U.	3–2	2–0	3–2	3–0	1–1	2–1	2–2	1–1	2–0
Rochdale	4–0	2–1	0–0	0–0	0–1	3–0	1–1	0–3	1–3
Scarborough	2–0	0–1	0–1	1–2	1–1	1–0	1–1	2–1	2–1
Scunthorpe U.	6–2	2–0	1–3	0–2	2–0	3–0	2–1	1–1	1–0
Stockport Co.	3–2	0–0	2–2	1–1	3–1	3–1	3–1	0–0	1–1
Torquay U.	5–0	2–1	2–0	2–1	3–0	2–0	2–1	1–0	3–1
Walsall	2–2	2–0	1–0	0–0	1–1	3–0	2–2	1–0	0–0
Wrexham	4–2	0–1	2–4	1–0	3–0	1–1	1–1	2–1	3–0
York C.	2–0	0–1	2–0	1–2	2–0	0–2	0–1	3–1	1–1

1990–91 RESULTS

Halifax Town	Hartlepool U.	Hereford U.	Lincoln C.	Maidstone U.	Northampton T.	Peterborough U.	Rochdale	Scarborough	Scunthorpe U.	Stockport Co.	Torquay U.	Walsall	Wrexham	York C.
2–2	1–5	1–0	0–3	4–3	3–3	5–0	2–2	2–2	3–2	2–2	2–3	0–4	3–2	0–1
2–0	2–0	3–0	5–0	2–2	2–1	1–1	0–0	3–1	3–1	3–2	1–0	1–2	4–1	1–0
2–1	4–0	2–1	2–2	2–1	3–0	4–1	1–0	2–1	1–1	3–2	1–1	2–0	2–0	0–0
1–0	1–0	0–2	0–1	0–0	1–0	1–1	0–1	0–0	1–0	3–3	3–3	0–2	1–0	2–1
0–2	1–0	0–1	0–0	1–0	4–1	3–2	1–1	4–1	0–3	1–0	3–1	0–3	2–0	1–0
2–1	2–3	1–0	1–1	1–2	0–0	2–2	1–1	0–1	1–0	1–1	1–1	2–2	2–1	2–2
3–0	0–1	3–1	1–1	1–1	1–1	0–1	2–0	2–1	0–0	1–0	3–0	1–0	1–0	0–0
1–2	2–2	3–1	1–0	3–0	2–1	0–2	1–0	0–2	2–3	1–0	1–1	2–0	3–1	2–2
1–0	3–0	2–1	2–2	0–2	0–0	2–3	2–2	1–1	1–1	1–3	2–2	1–0	2–3	0–0
—	1–2	0–4	1–1	3–2	2–1	1–1	2–0	1–2	0–0	0–0	0–1	5–2	2–0	2–1
2–1	—	2–1	2–0	1–0	3–1	2–0	2–2	2–0	2–0	3–1	0–0	2–1	2–1	0–1
1–0	1–3	—	0–1	4–0	1–2	0–0	2–0	3–3	2–0	0–0	0–0	0–0	1–0	2–0
1–0	3–1	1–1	—	2–1	3–1	0–2	1–2	2–0	1–2	0–3	3–2	2–1	0–0	2–1
5–1	1–4	1–1	4–1	—	1–3	2–0	0–1	0–1	6–1	2–3	2–2	1–3	0–2	5–4
1–0	3–2	3–0	1–1	2–0	—	1–2	3–2	0–2	2–1	1–0	1–4	5–0	1–0	2–1
2–0	1–1	3–0	2–0	2–0	1–0	—	1–1	2–0	0–0	0–0	1–2	0–0	2–2	2–0
1–1	0–0	2–1	0–0	3–2	1–1	0–3	—	1–1	2–1	1–0	0–0	3–2	2–0	2–1
4–1	2–0	2–1	3–0	0–2	1–1	3–1	0–0	—	3–1	0–2	1–0	1–0	4–2	2–2
4–4	2–1	3–0	2–1	2–2	3–0	1–1	2–1	3–0	—	3–0	3–0	1–0	2–0	2–1
5–1	1–3	4–2	4–0	1–0	2–0	2–1	3–0	2–2	5–0	—	2–1	3–0	2–0	2–0
3–1	0–1	1–1	0–1	1–1	0–0	0–0	3–1	2–0	1–1	1–1	—	0–0	1–0	2–1
3–1	0–1	0–0	0–0	0–0	3–3	0–1	0–1	0–0	3–0	0–2	2–2	—	1–0	1–1
1–2	2–2	1–2	2–2	2–2	0–2	0–0	2–1	1–2	1–0	1–3	2–1	1–1	—	0–4
3–3	0–0	1–0	1–0	0–1	0–1	0–4	0–2	2–0	2–2	0–2	0–0	1–0	0–0	—

BARCLAYS LEAGUE FINAL TABLES 1990–91

First Division		Home			Goals		Away			Goals			
	P	*W*	*D*	*L*	*F*	*A*	*W*	*D*	*L*	*F*	*A*	*Pts*	*GD*
*1 Arsenal	38	15	4	0	51	10	9	9	1	23	8	83	+56
2 Liverpool	38	14	3	2	42	13	9	4	6	35	27	76	+37
3 Crystal Palace	38	11	6	2	26	17	9	3	7	24	24	69	+9
4 Leeds U	38	12	2	5	46	23	7	5	7	19	24	64	+18
5 Manchester C	38	12	3	4	35	25	5	8	6	29	28	62	+11
*6 Manchester U	38	11	4	4	34	17	5	8	6	24	28	59	+13
7 Wimbledon	38	8	6	5	28	22	6	8	5	25	24	56	+7
8 Nottingham F	38	11	4	4	42	21	3	8	8	23	29	54	+15
9 Everton	38	9	5	5	26	15	4	7	8	24	31	51	+4
10 Tottenham H	38	8	9	2	35	22	3	7	9	16	28	49	+1
11 Chelsea	38	10	6	3	33	25	3	4	12	25	44	49	−11
12 QPR	38	8	5	6	27	22	4	5	10	17	31	46	−9
13 Sheffield U	38	9	3	7	23	23	4	4	11	13	32	46	−19
14 Southampton	38	9	6	4	33	22	3	3	13	25	47	45	−11
15 Norwich C	38	9	3	7	27	32	4	3	12	14	32	45	−23
16 Coventry C	38	10	6	3	30	16	1	5	13	12	33	44	−7
17 Aston Villa	38	7	9	3	29	25	2	5	12	17	33	41	−12
18 Luton T	38	7	5	7	22	18	3	2	14	20	43	37	−19
19 Sunderland	38	6	6	7	15	16	2	4	13	23	44	34	−22
20 Derby Co	38	3	8	8	25	36	2	1	16	12	39	24	−38

*Arsenal 2 points deducted.
*Manchester U 1 point deducted.

LEADING GOALSCORERS 1990–91

DIVISION 1	*League*	*FA Cup*	*Rumbelows League Cup*	*Other Cups*	*Total*
Lee Chapman *(Leeds United)*	21	3	4	3	**31**
Alan Smith *(Arsenal)*	23	2	3	0	**28**
Ian Rush *(Liverpool)*	16	5	5	0	**26**
Ian Wright *(Crystal Palace)*	15	1	3	6	**25**
David Platt *(Aston Villa)*	19	0	3	2	**24**
Tony Cottee *(Everton)*	10	2	4	8	**24**
Matthew Le Tissier *(Southampton)*	19	2	2	0	**23**
Niall Quinn *(Manchester City)*	20	1	0	1	**22**
Dean Saunders *(Derby County)*	17	0	3	1	**21**
Mark Hughes *(Manchester United)*	10	2	6	3	**21**
Brian McClair *(Manchester United)*	13	2	2	4	**21**
Nigel Clough *(Nottingham Forest)*	14	2	3	1	**20**
John Fashanu *(Wimbledon)*	20	0	0	0	**20**
Roy Wegerle *(Queens Park Rangers)*	18	0	1	0	**19**
Paul Gascoigne *(Tottenham Hotspur)*	7	6	6	0	**19**
Gary Lineker *(Tottenham Hotspur)*	15	3	1	0	**19**
Steve Bruce *(Manchester United)*	13	0	2	4	**19**
Rodney Wallace *(Southampton)*	14	2	2	1	**19**

NB. Other Cups: European Cup-Winners' Cup, UEFA Cup, Zenith Data Systems Cup and Leyland Daf Cup.

Second Division

		Home			Goals		Away			Goals			
	P	W	D	L	F	A	W	D	L	F	A	Pts	GD
1 Oldham Ath	46	17	5	1	55	21	8	8	7	28	32	88	+30
2 West Ham U	46	15	6	2	41	18	9	9	5	19	16	87	+26
3 Sheffield W	46	12	10	1	43	23	10	6	7	37	28	82	+29
4 Notts Co	46	14	4	5	45	28	9	7	7	31	27	80	+21
5 Millwall	46	11	6	6	43	28	9	7	7	27	23	73	+19
6 Brighton & HA	46	12	4	7	37	31	9	3	11	26	38	70	−6
7 Middlesbrough	46	12	4	7	36	17	8	5	10	30	30	69	+19
8 Barnsley	46	13	7	3	39	16	6	5	12	24	32	69	+15
9 Bristol C	46	14	5	4	44	28	6	2	15	24	43	67	−3
10 Oxford U	46	10	9	4	41	29	4	10	9	28	37	61	+3
11 Newcastle U	46	8	10	5	24	22	6	7	10	25	34	59	−7
12 Wolverhampton W	46	11	6	6	45	35	2	13	8	18	28	58	0
13 Bristol R	46	11	7	5	29	20	4	6	13	27	39	58	−3
14 Ipswich T	46	9	8	6	32	28	4	10	9	28	40	57	−8
15 Port Vale	46	10	4	9	32	24	5	8	10	24	40	57	−8
16 Charlton Ath	46	8	7	8	27	25	5	10	8	30	36	56	−4
17 Portsmouth	46	10	6	7	34	27	4	5	14	24	43	53	−12
18 Plymouth Arg	46	10	10	3	36	20	2	7	14	18	48	53	−14
19 Blackburn R	46	8	6	9	26	27	6	4	13	25	39	52	−15
20 Watford	46	5	8	10	24	32	7	7	9	21	27	51	−14
21 Swindon T	46	8	6	9	31	30	4	8	11	34	43	50	−8
22 Leicester C	46	12	4	7	41	33	2	4	17	19	50	50	−23
23 WBA	46	7	11	5	26	21	3	7	13	26	40	48	−9
24 Hull C	46	6	10	7	35	32	4	5	14	22	53	45	−28

DIVISION 2	League	FA Cup	Rumbelows League Cup	Other Cups	Total
Teddy Sheringham *(Millwall)*	33	2	2	1	**38**
David Hirst *(Sheffield Wednesday)*	24	2	3	3	**32**
Steve Bull *(Wolverhampton Wanderers)*	26	0	0	1	**27**
Steve Butler *(Watford) (Including 25 for Maidstone United)*	21	2	2	1	**26**
Andy Payton *(Hull City)*	25	0	0	0	**25**
Darren Beckford *(Port Vale)*	22	2	0	0	**24**
Duncan Shearer *(Swindon Town)*	22	1	0	0	**23**
Mike Small *(Brighton & Hove Albion)*	15	2	1	2	**20**
Bernie Slaven *(Middlesbrough)*	16	0	3	1	**20**
Guy Whittingham *(Portsmouth)*	12	7	1	0	**20**
Mick Quinn *(Newcastle United)*	18	2	0	0	**20**
Stuart Rimmer *(Barnsley) (Including 18 for Walsall)*	14	0	4	1	**19**
Tommy Johnson *(Notts County)*	16	0	3	0	**19**
Paul Wilkinson *(Watford)*	18	0	0	1	**19**
Paul Simpson *(Oxford United)*	17	0	1	0	**18**
Ian Marshall *(Oldham Athletic)*	17	0	0	1	**18**

NB. Other Cups: European Cup-Winners' Cup, UEFA Cup, Zenith Data Systems Cup and Leyland Daf Cup.

Third Division

		Home			Goals		Away			Goals			
	P	W	D	L	F	A	W	D	L	F	A	Pts	GD
1 Cambridge U	46	14	5	4	42	22	11	6	6	33	23	86	+30
2 Southend U	46	13	6	4	34	23	13	1	9	33	28	85	+16
3 Grimsby T	46	16	3	4	42	13	8	8	7	24	21	83	+32
4 Bolton W	46	14	5	4	33	18	10	6	7	31	32	83	+14
5 Tranmere R	46	13	5	5	38	21	10	4	9	26	25	78	+18
6 Brentford	46	12	4	7	30	22	9	9	5	29	25	76	+12
7 Bury	46	13	6	4	39	26	7	7	9	28	30	73	+11
8 Bradford C	46	13	3	7	36	22	7	7	9	26	32	70	+8
9 Bournemouth	46	14	6	3	37	20	5	7	11	21	38	70	0
10 Wigan Ath	46	14	3	6	40	20	6	6	11	31	34	69	+17
11 Huddersfield T	46	13	3	7	37	23	5	10	8	20	28	67	+6
12 Birmingham C	46	8	9	6	21	21	8	8	7	24	28	65	−4
13 Leyton Orient	46	15	2	6	35	19	3	8	12	20	39	64	−3
14 Stoke C	46	9	7	7	36	29	7	5	11	19	30	60	−4
15 Reading	46	11	5	7	34	28	6	3	14	19	38	59	−13
16 Exeter C	46	12	6	5	35	16	4	3	16	23	36	57	+6
17 Preston NE	46	11	5	7	33	29	4	6	13	21	38	56	−13
18 Shrewsbury T	46	8	7	8	29	22	6	3	14	32	46	52	−7
19 Chester C	46	10	3	10	27	27	4	6	13	19	31	51	−12
20 Swansea C	46	8	6	9	31	33	5	3	15	18	39	48	−23
21 Fulham	46	8	8	7	27	22	2	8	13	14	34	46	−15
22 Crewe Alex	46	6	9	8	35	35	5	2	16	27	45	44	−18
23 Rotherham U	46	5	10	8	31	38	5	2	16	19	49	42	−37
24 Mansfield T	46	5	8	10	23	27	3	6	14	19	36	38	−21

DIVISION 3	League	FA Cup	Rumbelows League Cup	Other Cups	Total
Tony Philliskirk *(Bolton Wanderers)*	19	2	5	0	**26**
Brett Angell *(Southend United)*	15	2	2	7	**26**
Dion Dublin *(Cambridge United)*	16	4	1	2	**23**
Luther Blissett *(Bournemouth)*	19	0	2	0	**21**
Ian Muir *(Tranmere Rovers)*	13	0	0	8	**21**
John Taylor *(Cambridge United)*	14	5	0	1	**20**
Jimmy Gilligan *(Swansea City)*	16	2	0	2	**20**
Don Page *(Wigan Athletic)*	13	1	1	3	**18**
Steve Castle *(Leyton Orient)*	12	3	3	0	**18**
Bryan Griffiths *(Wigan Athletic)*	12	3	0	2	**17**
Sean McCarthy *(Bradford City)*	13	0	2	1	**16**
Andy Sussex *(Crewe Alexandra)*	11	1	4	0	**16**
Ian Benjamin *(Southend United)*	13	0	0	3	**16**
Graham Shaw *(Preston North End)*	10	0	1	5	**16**
Gary Blissett *(Brentford)*	10	2	0	3	**15**
David Lee *(Bury)*	15	0	0	0	**15**
Carl Dale *(Chester City)*	10	4	0	1	**15**
Craig Hignett *(Crewe Alexandra)*	13	2	0	0	**15**
Trevor Senior *(Reading)*	15	0	0	0	**15**

NB. Other Cups: European Cup-Winners' Cup, UEFA Cup, Zenith Data Systems Cup and Leyland Daf Cup.

Fourth Division

		Home			Goals		Away			Goals			
	P	W	D	L	F	A	W	D	L	F	A	Pts	GD
1 Darlington	46	13	8	2	36	14	9	9	5	32	24	83	+30
2 Stockport Co	46	16	6	1	54	19	7	7	9	30	28	82	+37
3 Hartlepool U	46	15	5	3	35	15	9	5	9	32	33	82	+19
4 Peterborough U	46	13	9	1	38	15	8	8	7	29	30	80	+22
5 Blackpool	46	17	3	3	55	17	6	7	10	23	30	79	+31
6 Burnley	46	17	5	1	46	16	6	5	12	24	35	79	+19
7 Torquay U	46	14	7	2	37	13	4	11	8	27	34	72	+17
8 Scunthorpe U	46	17	4	2	51	20	3	7	13	20	42	71	+9
9 Scarborough	46	13	5	5	36	21	6	7	10	23	35	69	+3
10 Northampton T	46	14	5	4	34	21	4	8	11	23	37	67	−1
11 Doncaster R	46	12	5	6	36	22	5	9	9	20	24	65	+10
12 Rochdale	46	10	9	4	29	22	5	8	10	21	31	62	−3
13 Cardiff C	46	10	6	7	26	23	5	9	9	17	31	60	−11
14 Lincoln C	46	10	7	6	32	27	4	10	9	18	34	59	−11
15 Gillingham	46	9	9	5	35	27	3	9	11	22	33	54	−3
16 Walsall	46	7	12	4	25	17	5	5	13	23	34	53	−3
17 Hereford U	46	9	10	4	32	19	4	4	15	21	39	53	−5
18 Chesterfield	46	8	12	3	33	26	5	2	16	14	36	53	−15
19 Maidstone U	46	9	5	9	42	34	4	7	12	24	37	51	−5
20 Carlisle U	46	12	3	8	30	30	1	6	16	17	59	48	−42
21 York C	46	8	6	9	21	23	3	7	13	24	34	46	−12
22 Halifax T	46	9	6	8	34	29	3	4	16	25	50	46	−20
23 Aldershot	46	8	7	8	38	43	2	4	17	23	58	41	−40
24 Wrexham	46	8	7	8	33	34	2	3	18	15	40	40	−26

DIVISION 4	*League*	*FA Cup*	*Rumbelows League Cup*	*Other Cups*	*Total*
Steve Norris *(Halifax Town) (Including 2 for Carlisle United)*	32	2	0	1	**35**
Joe Allon *(Hartlepool United)*	28	3	2	2	**35**
Andy Flounders *(Scunthorpe United)*	23	3	0	1	**27**
David Puckett *(Aldershot)*	21	2	3	0	**26**
Steve Lovell *(Gillingham)*	19	0	1	1	**21**
Ron Futcher *(Burnley)*	18	0	1	1	**20**
Tommy Tynan *(Torquay United)*	13	1	1	4	**19**
Dave Bamber *(Blackpool) (Including 2 for Hull City)*	19	0	0	0	**19**
John Francis *(Burnley)*	14	1	0	1	**16**
Bobby Barnes *(Northampton Town)*	13	2	1	0	**16**
George Oghani *(Scarborough)*	14	0	2	0	**16**
Dean Edwards *(Torquay United)*	15	0	0	1	**16**
Charlie Henry *(Aldershot)*	13	2	0	0	**15**
Cohen Griffith *(Cardiff City)*	9	0	5	1	**15**
Chris Pike *(Cardiff City)*	14	0	1	0	**15**
John Muir *(Doncaster Rovers)*	13	0	1	1	**15**
Mark Lillis *(Scunthorpe United)*	10	2	1	2	**15**
Chris Beaumont *(Stockport County)*	15	0	0	0	**15**

NB. Other Cups: European Cup-Winners' Cup, UEFA Cup, Zenith Data Systems Cup and Leyland Daf Cup.

DIVISION ONE LEAGUE POSITIONS 1965–66 TO 1989–90

	1989–90	1988–89	1987–88	1986–87	1985–86	1984–85	1983–84	1982–83	1981–82	1980–81	1979–80	1978–79	1977–78
Arsenal	4	1	6	4	7	7	6	10	5	3	4	7	5
Aston Villa	2	17	–	22	16	10	10	6	11	1	7	8	8
Birmingham C	–	–	–	–	21	–	20	17	16	13	–	21	11
Blackburn R	–	–	–	–	–	–	–	–	–	–	–	–	–
Blackpool	–	–	–	–	–	–	–	–	–	–	–	–	–
Bolton W	–	–	–	–	–	–	–	–	–	–	22	17	–
Brighton & HA	–	–	–	–	–	–	–	22	13	19	16	–	–
Bristol C	–	–	–	–	–	–	–	–	–	–	20	13	17
Burnley	–	–	–	–	–	–	–	–	–	–	–	–	–
Carlisle U	–	–	–	–	–	–	–	–	–	–	–	–	–
Charlton Ath	19	14	17	19	–	–	–	–	–	–	–	–	–
Chelsea	5	–	18	14	6	6	–	–	–	–	–	22	16
Coventry C	12	7	10	10	17	18	19	19	14	16	15	10	7
Crystal Palace	15	–	–	–	–	–	–	–	–	22	13	–	–
Derby Co	16	5	15	–	–	–	–	–	–	–	21	19	12
Everton	6	8	4	1	2	1	7	7	8	15	19	4	3
Fulham	–	–	–	–	–	–	–	–	–	–	–	–	–
Huddersfield T	–	–	–	–	–	–	–	–	–	–	–	–	–
Ipswich T	–	–	–	–	20	17	12	9	2	2	3	6	18
Leeds U	–	–	–	–	–	–	–	–	20	9	11	5	9
Leicester C	–	–	–	20	19	15	15	–	–	21	–	–	22
Liverpool	1	2	1	2	1	2	1	1	1	5	1	1	2
Luton T	17	16	9	7	9	13	16	18	–	–	–	–	–
Manchester C	14	–	–	21	15	–	–	20	10	12	17	15	4
Manchester U	13	11	2	11	4	4	4	3	3	8	2	9	10
Middlesbrough	–	18	–	–	–	–	–	–	22	14	9	12	14
Millwall	20	10	–	–	–	–	–	–	–	–	–	–	–
Newcastle U	–	20	8	17	11	14	–	–	–	–	–	–	21
Northampton T	–	–	–	–	–	–	–	–	–	–	–	–	–
Norwich C	10	4	14	5	–	20	14	14	–	20	12	16	13
Nottingham F	9	3	3	8	8	9	3	5	12	7	5	2	1
Notts Co	–	–	–	–	–	–	21	15	15	–	–	–	–
Oxford U	–	–	21	18	18	–	–	–	–	–	–	–	–
Portsmouth	–	–	19	–	–	–	–	–	–	–	–	–	–
QPR	11	9	5	16	13	19	5	–	–	–	–	20	19
Sheffield U	–	–	–	–	–	–	–	–	–	–	–	–	–
Sheffield W	18	15	11	13	5	8	–	–	–	–	–	–	–
Southampton	7	13	12	12	14	5	2	12	7	6	8	14	–
Stoke C	–	–	–	–	–	22	18	13	18	11	18	–	–
Sunderland	–	–	–	–	–	21	13	16	19	17	–	–	–
Swansea City	–	–	–	–	–	–	–	21	6	–	–	–	–
Tottenham H	3	6	13	3	10	3	8	4	4	10	14	11	–
Watford	–	–	20	9	12	11	11	2	–	–	–	–	–
WBA	–	–	–	–	22	12	17	11	17	4	10	3	6
West Ham U	–	19	16	15	3	16	9	8	9	–	–	–	20
Wimbledon	8	12	7	6	–	–	–	–	–	–	–	–	–
W'hampton W	–	–	–	–	–	–	22	–	21	18	6	18	15

1976–77	1975–76	1974–75	1973–74	1972–73	1971–72	1970–71	1969–70	1968–69	1967–68	1966–67	1965–66	
8	17	16	10	2	5	1	12	4	9	7	14	Arsenal
4	16	–	–	–	–	–	–	–	–	21	16	Aston Villa
13	19	17	19	10	–	–	–	–	–	–	–	Birmingham C
–	–	–	–	–	–	–	–	–	–	–	22	Blackburn R
–	–	–	–	–	–	22	–	–	–	22	13	Blackpool
–	–	–	–	–	–	–	–	–	–	–	–	Bolton
–	–	–	–	–	–	–	–	–	–	–	–	Brighton & HA
18	–	–	–	–	–	–	–	–	–	–	–	Bristol C
–	21	10	6	–	–	21	14	14	14	14	3	Burnley
–	–	22			–	–	–	–	–	–	–	Carlisle
–	–	–	–	–	–	–	–	–	–	–	–	Charlton Ath
–	–	21	17	12	7	6	3	5	6	9	5	Chelsea
19	14	14	16	19	18	10	6	20	20	–		Coventry C
	–	–	–	21	20	18	20	–	–	–	–	Crystal Palace
15	4	1	3	7	1	9	4	–	–	–	–	Derby Co
9	11	4	7	17	15	14	1	3	5	6	11	Everton
–	–	–	–	–	–	–	–		22	18	20	Fulham
–		–	–	–	22	15	–	–	–	–	–	Huddersfield T
3	6	3	4	4	13	19	18	12	–	–	–	Ipswich T
10	5	9	1	3	2	2	2	1	4	4	2	Leeds U
11	7	18	9	16	12	–	–	21	13	8	7	Leicester C
1	1	2	2	1	3	5	5	2	3	5	1	Liverpool
–	–	20	–	–	–	–	–	–	–	–	–	Luton T
2	8	8	14	11	4	11	10	13	1	15	–	Manchester C
6	3	–	21	18	8	8	8	11	2	1	4	Manchester U
12	13	7	–	–	–	–	–	–	–	–	–	Middlesbrough
–	–	–	–	–	–	–	–	–	–	–	–	Millwall
5	15	15	15	9	11	12	7	9	10	20	15	Newcastle U
–	–	–	–	–	–	–	–	–	–	–	21	Northampton T
16	10	–	22	20	–	–	–	–	–	–	–	Norwich C
–	–	–	–	–	21	16	15	18	11	2	18	Nottingham F
–	–	–	–	–	–	–	–	–	–	–	–	Notts Co
–	–	–	–	–	–	–	–	–	–	–	–	Oxford U
–	–	–	–	–	–	–	–	–	–	–	–	Portsmouth
14	2	11	8	–	–	–	–	22	–	–	–	QPR
–	22	6	13	14	10	–	–	–	21	10	9	Sheffield U
–	–	–	–	–	–	–	22	15	19	11	17	Sheffield W
–	–	–	20	13	19	7	19	7	16	19	–	Southampton
21	12	5	5	15	17	13	9	19	18	12	10	Stoke C
20	–	–	–	–	–	–	21	17	15	17	19	Sunderland
–	–	–	–	–	–	–	–	–	–	–	–	Swansea City
22	9	19	11	8	6	3	11	6	7	3	8	Tottenham H
–	–	–	–	–	–	–	–	–	–	–	–	Watford
7	–	–	–	22	16	17	16	10	8	13	6	WBA
17	18	13	18	6	14	20	17	8	12	16	12	West Ham U
–	–	–	–	–	–	–	–	–	–	–	–	Wimbledon
–	20	12	12	5	9	4	13	16	17	–	–	W'hampton W

DIVISION TWO LEAGUE POSITIONS 1965–66 TO 1989–90

	1989–90	1988–89	1987–88	1986–87	1985–86	1984–85	1983–84	1982–83	1981–82	1980–81	1979–80	1978–79	1977–78
Aston Villa	–	–	2	–	–	–	–	–	–	–	–	–	–
Barnsley	19	7	14	11	12	11	14	10	6	–	–	–	–
Birmingham C	–	23	19	19	–	2	–	–	–	–	3	–	–
Blackburn R	5	5	5	12	19	5	6	11	10	4	–	22	5
Blackpool	–	–	–	–	–	–	–	–	–	–	–	–	20
Bolton W	–	–	–	–	–	–	–	22	19	18	–	–	1
Bournemouth	22	12	17	–	–	–	–	–	–	–	–	–	–
Bradford C	23	14	4	10	13	–	–	–	–	–	–	–	–
Brighton & HA	18	19	–	22	11	6	9	–	–	–	–	2	4
Bristol C	–	–	–	–	–	–	–	–	–	21	–	–	–
Bristol R	–	–	–	–	–	–	–	–	–	22	19	16	18
Burnley	–	–	–	–	–	–	–	21	–	–	21	13	11
Bury	–	–	–	–	–	–	–	–	–	–	–	–	–
Cambridge U	–	–	–	–	–	–	22	12	14	13	8	12	–
Cardiff C	–	–	–	–	–	21	15	–	20	19	15	9	19
Carlisle U	–	–	–	–	20	16	7	14	–	–	–	–	–
Charlton Ath	–	–	–	–	2	17	13	17	13	–	22	19	17
Chelsea	–	1	–	–	–	–	1	18	12	12	4	–	–
Coventry C	–	–	–	–	–	–	–	–	–	–	–	–	–
Crystal Palace	–	3	6	6	5	15	18	15	5	–	–	1	9
Derby Co	–	–	–	1	–	–	20	13	16	6	–	–	–
Fulham	–	–	–	–	22	9	11	4	–	–	20	10	10
Grimsby T	–	–	–	21	15	10	5	19	17	7	–	–	–
Hereford U	–	–	–	–	–	–	–	–	–	–	–	–	–
Huddersfield T	–	–	23	17	16	13	12	–	–	–	–	–	–
Hull C	14	21	15	14	6	–	–	–	–	–	–	–	22
Ipswich T	9	8	8	5	–	–	–	–	–	–	–	–	–
Leeds U	1	10	7	4	14	7	10	8	–	–	–	–	–
Leicester C	13	15	13	–	–	–	–	3	8	–	1	17	–
Leyton Orient	–	–	–	–	–	–	–	–	22	17	14	11	14
Luton T	–	–	–	–	–	–	–	–	1	5	6	18	13
Manchester C	–	2	9	–	–	3	4	–	–	–	–	–	–
Manchester U	–	–	–	–	–	–	–	–	–	–	–	–	–
Mansfield T	–	–	–	–	–	–	–	–	–	–	–	–	21
Middlesbrough	21	–	3	–	21	19	17	16	–	–	–	–	–
Millwall	–	–	1	16	9	–	–	–	–	–	–	21	16
Newcastle U	3	–	–	–	–	–	3	5	9	11	9	8	–
Northampton T	–	–	–	–	–	–	–	–	–	–	–	–	–
Norwich C	–	–	–	–	1	–	–	–	3	–	–	–	–
Nottingham F	–	–	–	–	–	–	–	–	–	–	–	–	–
Notts Co	–	–	–	–	–	20	–	–	–	2	17	6	15
Oldham Ath	8	16	10	3	8	14	19	7	11	15	11	14	8
Oxford U	17	17	–	–	–	1	–	–	–	–	–	–	–
Plymouth Arg	16	18	16	7	–	–	–	–	–	–	–	–	–
Port Vale	11	–	–	–	–	–	–	–	–	–	–	–	–
Portsmouth	12	20	–	2	4	4	16	–	–	–	–	–	–
Preston NE	–	–	–	–	–	–	–	–	–	20	10	7	–

1976–77	1975–76	1974–75	1973–74	1972–73	1971–72	1970–71	1969–70	1968–69	1967–68	1966–67	1965–66	
–	–	2	14	3	–	–	21	18	16	–	–	Aston Villa
–	–	–	–	–	–	–	–	–	–	–	–	Barnsley
–	–	–	–	–	2	9	18	7	4	10	10	Birmingham C
12	15	–	–	–	–	21	8	19	8	4	–	Blackburn R
5	10	7	5	7	6	–	2	8	3	–	–	Blackpool
4	4	10	11	–	–	22	16	17	12	9	9	Bolton W
–	–	–	–	–	–	–	–	–	–	–	–	Bournemouth
–	–	–	–	–	–	–	–	–	–	–	–	Bradford C
–	–	–	–	22	–	–	–	–	–	–	–	Brighton & HA
–	2	5	16	5	8	19	14	16	19	15	5	Bristol C
15	18	19	–	–	–	–	–	–	–	–	–	Bristol R
16	–	–	–	1	7	–	–	–	–	–	–	Burnley
–	–	–	–	–	–	–	–	21	–	22	19	Bury
–	–	–	–	–	–	–	–	–	–	–	–	Cambridge U
18	–	21	17	20	19	3	7	5	13	20	20	Cardiff C
20	19	–	3	18	10	4	12	12	10	3	14	Carlisle U
7	9	–	–	–	21	20	20	3	15	19	16	Charlton Ath
2	11	–	–	–	–	–	–	–	–	–	–	Chelsea
–	–	–	–	–	–	–	–	–	–	1	3	Coventry C
–	–	–	20	–	–	–	–	2	11	7	11	Crystal Palace
–	–	–	–	–	–	–	–	1	18	17	8	Derby Co
17	12	9	13	9	20	–	–	22	–	–	–	Fulham
–	–	–	–	–	–	–	–	–	–	–	–	Grimsby T
22	–	–	–	–	–	–	–	–	–	–	–	Hereford U
–	–	–	–	21	–	–	1	6	14	6	4	Huddersfield T
14	14	8	9	13	12	5	13	11	17	12	–	Hull C
–	–	–	–	–	–	–	–	–	1	5	15	Ipswich T
–	–	–	–	–	–	–	–	–	–	–	–	Leeds U
–	–	–	–	–	–	1	3	–	–	–	–	Leicester C
19	13	12	4	15	17	17	–	–	–	–	22	Leyton Orient
6	7	–	2	12	13	6	–	–	–	–	–	Luton T
–	–	–	–	–	–	–	–	–	–	–	1	Manchester C
–	–	1	–	–	–	–	–	–	–	–	–	Manchester U
–	–	–	–	–	–	–	–	–	–	–	–	Mansfield T
–	–	–	1	4	9	7	4	4	6	–	21	Middlesbrough
10	–	20	12	11	3	8	10	10	7	8	–	Millwall
–	–	–	–	–	–	–	–	–	–	–	–	Newcastle U
–	–	–	–	–	–	–	–	–	–	21	–	Northampton T
–	–	3	–	–	1	10	11	13	9	11	13	Norwich C
3	8	16	7	14	–	–	–	–	–	–	–	Nottingham F
8	5	14	10	–	–	–	–	–	–	–	–	Notts Co
13	17	18	–	–	–	–	–	–	–	–	–	Oldham Ath
–	20	11	18	8	15	14	15	20	–	–	–	Oxford U
21	16	–	–	–	–	–	–	–	22	16	18	Plymouth Arg
–	–	–	–	–	–	–	–	–	–	–	–	Port Vale
–	22	17	15	17	16	16	17	15	5	14	12	Portsmouth
–	–	–	21	19	18	–	22	14	20	13	17	Preston NE

DIVISION TWO LEAGUE POSITIONS 1965–66 TO 1989–90

	1989–90	1988–89	1987–88	1986–87	1985–86	1984–85	1983–84	1982–83	1981–82	1980–81	1979–80	1978–79	1977–78
QPR	–	–	–	–	–	–	–	1	5	8	5	–	–
Reading	–	–	22	13	–	–	–	–	–	–	–	–	–
Rotherham U	–	–	–	–	–	–	–	20	7	–	–	–	–
Sheffield U	2	–	21	9	7	18	–	–	–	–	–	20	12
Sheffield W	–	–	–	–	–	–	2	6	4	10	–	–	–
Shrewsbury T	–	22	18	18	17	8	8	9	18	14	13	–	–
Southampton	–	–	–	–	–	–	–	–	–	–	–	–	2
Stoke C	24	13	11	8	10	–	–	–	–	–	–	3	7
Sunderland	6	11	–	20	18	–	–	–	–	–	2	4	6
Swansea C	–	–	–	–	–	–	21	–	–	3	12	–	–
Swindon T	4	6	12	–	–	–	–	–	–	–	–	–	–
Tottenham H	–	–	–	–	–	–	–	–	–	–	–	–	3
Walsall	–	24	–	–	–	–	–	–	–	–	–	–	–
Watford	15	4	–	–	–	–	–	–	2	9	18	–	–
WBA	20	9	20	15	–	–	–	–	–	–	–	–	–
West Ham U	7	–	–	–	–	–	–	–	–	1	7	5	–
Wimbledon	–	–	–	–	3	12	–	–	–	–	–	–	–
Wolv'hampton W	10	–	–	–	–	22	–	2	–	–	–	–	–
Wrexham	–	–	–	–	–	–	–	–	21	16	16	15	–
York C	–	–	–	–	–	–	–	–	–	–	–	–	–

LEAGUE TITLE WINS

League Division I–18–Liverpool; 10–Arsenal, Everton; 7–Aston Villa, Manchester U; 6–Sunderland; 4–Newcastle, Sheffield Wednesday; 3–Huddersfield, Wolves; 2–Blackburn R, Burnley, Derby Co, Leeds, Manchester C, Portsmouth, Preston NE, Tottenham; 1–Chelsea, Ipswich, Nottingham F, Sheffield U, West Bromwich Albion.

League Division II–6–Manchester C, Leicester C; 5–Sheffield Wednesday; 4–*Birmingham, Derby C, Liverpool; 3–Middlesbrough, Notts Co, Preston; 2–Aston Villa, Bolton, Burnley, Chelsea, Grimsby, Ipswich, Leeds, Manchester U, Norwich C, Nottingham F, Stoke, Tottenham, West Bromwich, West Ham U, Wolverhampton W; 1–Blackburn R, Blackpool, Bradford C, Brentford, Bristol C, Bury, Coventry, Crystal P, Everton, Fulham, Huddersfield, Leeds U, Luton, Millwall, Newcastle, Oldham Ath, Oxford U, QPR, Sheffield U, Sunderland.
**Once as Small Heath.*

League Division III–2–Oxford U, Portsmouth; 1–Aston Villa, Blackburn R, Bolton, Bournemouth, Bradford C, Bristol R, Burnley, Bury, Cambridge U, Carlisle, Coventry, Grimsby T, Hereford U, Hull, Mansfield, Northampton, Oldham Ath,

1976–77	1975–76	1974–75	1973–74	1972–73	1971–72	1970–71	1969–70	1968–69	1967–68	1966–67	1965–66	
–	–	–	–	2	4	11	9	–	2	–	–	QPR
–	–	–	–	–	–	–	–	–	–	–	–	Reading
–	–	–	–	–	–	–	–	–	21	18	7	Rotherham U
11	–	–	–	–	–	2	6	9	–	–	–	Sheffield U
–	–	22	19	10	14	15	–	–	–	–	–	Sheffield W
–	–	–	–	–	–	–	–	–	–	–	–	Shrewsbury T
9	6	13	–	–	–	–	–	–	–	–	2	Southampton
–	–	–	–	–	–	–	–	–	–	–	–	Stoke C
–	1	4	6	6	5	13	–	–	–	–	–	Sunderland
–	–	–	–	–	–	–	–	–	–	–	–	Swansea C
–	–	–	22	16	11	12	5	–	–	–	–	Swindon T
–	–	–	–	–	–	–	–	–	–	–	–	Tottenham H
–	–	–	–	–	–	–	–	–	–	–	–	Walsall
–	–	–	–	–	22	18	19	–	–	–	–	Watford
–	3	6	8	–	–	–	–	–	–	–	–	WBA
–	–	–	–	–	–	–	–	–	–	–	–	West Ham U
–	–	–	–	–	–	–	–	–	–	–	–	Wimbledon
1	–	–	–	–	–	–	–	–	–	2	6	Wolv'hampton W
–	–	–	–	–	–	–	–	–	–	–	–	Wrexham
–	21	15	–	–	–	–	–	–	–	–	–	York C

Orient, Plymouth, Preston NE, Queen's Park Rangers, Reading, Rotherham U, Shrewsbury T, Southampton, Sunderland, Watford, Wolverhampton W, Wrexham.

League Division IV–2–Chesterfield, Doncaster R, Peterborough U; 1–Brentford, Brighton, Cambridge, Darlington, Exeter C, Gillingham, Grimsby, Huddersfield T, Lincoln C, Luton, Mansfield T, Millwall, Northampton T, Notts Co, Port Vale, Reading, Rotherham U, Sheffield U, Southend U, Southport, Swindon T, Walsall, Watford, Wimbledon, Wolverhampton W, York C.

To 1957–58
Division III (South): Bristol C; 2 Charlton, Ipswich, Millwall, Notts Co, Plymouth, Swansea; 1 Brentford, Brighton, Bristol R, Cardiff, Coventry, Crystal P, Fulham, Leyton Orient, Luton, Newport, Nottingham F, Norwich, Portsmouth, Queen's Park Rangers, Reading, Southampton.
Division III (North): 3 Barnsley, Doncaster, Lincoln; 2 Chesterfield, Grimsby, Hull, Port Vale, Stockport; 1 Bradford, Bradford C, Darlington, Derby, Nelson, Oldham, Rotherham, Scunthorpe, Stoke, Tranmere, Wolverhampton.

DIVISION THREE LEAGUE POSITIONS 1965–66 TO 1989–90

	1989–90	1988–89	1987–88	1986–87	1985–86	1984–85	1983–84	1982–83	1981–82	1980–81	1979–80	1978–79	1977–78	1976–77	1975–76	1974–75	1973–74	1972–73	1971–72	1970–71	1969–70	1968–69	1967–68	1966–67	1965–66	
Aldershot	–	24	20	–	–	–	–	–	–	–	–	–	–	–	21	20	8	–	–	–	–	–	–	–	–	Aldershot
Aston Villa	–	–	–	–	–	–	–	–	–	–	–	–	–	–	–	–	–	–	1	4	–	–	–	–	–	Aston Villa
Barnsley	–	–	–	–	–	–	–	–	–	2	11	–	–	–	–	–	–	–	22	12	7	10	–	–	–	Barnsley
Barrow	–	–	–	–	–	–	–	–	–	–	–	–	–	–	–	–	–	–	–	–	23	19	8	–	–	Barrow
Birmingham C	7	–	–	–	–	–	–	–	–	–	–	–	–	–	–	–	–	–	–	–	–	–	–	–	–	Birmingham C
Blackburn R	–	–	–	–	–	–	–	–	–	–	2	–	–	–	–	1	13	3	10	–	–	–	–	–	–	Blackburn R
Blackpool	23	19	10	9	12	–	–	–	–	23	18	12	–	–	–	–	–	–	–	–	–	–	–	–	–	Blackpool
Bolton W	6	10	–	21	18	17	10	–	–	–	–	–	–	–	–	–	–	1	7	–	–	–	–	–	–	Bolton W
Bournemouth	–	–	–	1	15	10	17	14	–	–	–	–	–	–	–	21	11	7	3	–	21	4	12	20	18	Bournemouth
Bradford C	–	–	–	–	–	1	7	12	–	–	–	–	22	–	–	–	–	–	24	19	10	–	–	–	–	Bradford C
Brentford	13	7	12	11	10	13	20	9	8	9	19	10	–	–	–	–	–	22	–	–	–	–	–	–	23	Brentford
Brighton & HA	–	–	2	–	–	–	–	–	–	–	–	–	–	2	4	19	19	–	2	14	5	12	10	19	15	Brighton & HA
Bristol C	2	11	5	6	9	5	–	–	23	–	–	–	–	–	–	–	–	–	–	–	–	–	–	–	–	Bristol C
Bristol R	1	5	8	19	16	6	5	7	15	–	–	–	–	–	–	–	2	5	6	6	3	16	15	5	16	Bristol R
Burnley	–	–	–	–	–	21	12	–	1	8	–	–	–	–	–	–	–	–	–	–	–	–	–	–	–	Burnley
Bury	5	13	14	16	20	–	–	–	–	–	21	19	15	7	13	14	–	–	–	22	19	–	2	–	–	Bury
Cambridge U	–	–	–	–	–	24	–	–	–	–	–	–	2	–	–	–	21	–	–	–	–	–	–	–	–	Cambridge U
Cardiff C	21	16	–	–	22	–	–	2	–	–	–	–	–	–	2	–	–	–	–	–	–	–	–	–	–	Cardiff C
Carlisle U	–	–	–	21	–	–	–	–	2	19	6	6	13	–	–	–	–	–	–	–	–	–	–	–	–	Carlisle U
Charlton Ath	–	–	–	–	–	–	–	–	–	3	–	–	–	–	–	3	14	11	–	–	–	–	–	–	–	Charlton Ath
Chester C	16	8	15	15	–	–	–	–	24	18	9	16	5	13	17	–	–	–	–	–	–	–	–	–	–	Chester C
Chesterfield	–	22	18	17	17	–	–	24	11	5	4	20	9	18	15	15	5	16	13	5	–	–	–	–	–	Chesterfield
Colchester U	–	–	–	–	–	–	–	–	–	22	5	7	8	–	22	11	–	–	–	–	–	–	22	13	–	Colchester U
Crewe Alex	12	–	–	–	–	–	–	–	–	–	–	–	–	–	–	–	–	–	–	–	–	23	–	–	–	Crewe Alex
Crystal Palace	–	–	–	–	–	–	–	–	–	–	–	–	–	3	5	5	–	–	–	–	–	–	–	–	–	Crystal Palace
Darlington	–	–	–	22	13	–	–	–	–	–	–	–	–	–	–	–	–	–	–	–	–	–	–	22	–	Darlington
Derby Co	–	–	–	–	3	7	–	–	–	–	–	–	–	–	–	–	–	–	–	–	–	–	–	–	–	Derby C
Doncaster R	–	–	24	13	11	14	–	23	19	–	–	–	–	–	–	–	–	–	–	23	11	–	–	23	–	Doncaster R
Exeter C	–	–	–	–	–	–	24	19	18	11	8	9	17	–	–	–	–	–	–	–	–	–	–	–	22	Exeter C

Fulham	20	4	9	18	–	–	–	–	3	13	–	–	–	–	–	–	–	–	–	2	4	–	–	–	–	Fulham
Gillingham	–	23	13	5	5	4	8	13	6	15	16	4	7	12	14	10	–	–	–	24	20	20	11	11	6	Gillingham
Grimsby T	–	–	22	–	–	–	–	–	–	–	1	–	–	23	18	16	6	9	–	–	–	–	21	17	11	Grimsby T
Halifax T	–	–	–	–	–	–	–	–	–	–	–	–	–	–	24	17	9	20	17	3	18	–	–	–	–	Halifax T
Hartlepool U	–	–	–	–	–	–	–	–	–	–	–	–	–	–	–	–	–	–	–	–	–	22	–	–	–	Hartlepool U
Hereford U	–	–	–	–	–	–	–	–	–	–	–	–	23	–	1	12	18	–	–	–	–	–	–	–	–	Hereford U
Huddersfield T	8	14	–	–	–	–	–	3	17	4	–	–	–	–	–	24	10	–	–	–	–	–	–	–	–	Huddersfield T
Hull C	–	–	–	–	–	3	4	–	–	24	20	8	–	–	–	–	–	–	–	–	–	–	–	–	1	Hull C
Leyton Orient	14	–	–	–	–	22	11	20	–	–	–	–	–	–	–	–	–	–	–	–	1	18	18	14	–	Leyton Orient
Lincoln C	–	–	–	–	21	19	14	6	4	–	–	24	16	9	–	–	–	–	–	–	–	–	–	–	–	Lincoln C
Luton T	–	–	–	–	–	–	–	–	–	–	–	–	–	–	–	–	–	–	–	–	2	3	–	–	–	Luton T
Mansfield T	15	15	19	10	–	–	–	–	–	–	23	18	–	1	11	–	–	–	21	7	6	15	20	9	19	Mansfield T
Middlesbrough	–	–	–	2	–	–	–	–	–	–	–	–	–	–	–	–	–	–	–	–	–	–	–	2	–	Middlesbrough
Millwall	–	–	–	–	–	2	9	17	9	16	14	–	–	–	3	–	–	–	–	–	–	–	–	–	2	Millwall
Newport Co	–	–	–	23	19	18	13	4	16	12	–	–	–	–	–	–	–	–	–	–	–	–	–	–	–	Newport Co
Northampton T	22	20	6	–	–	–	–	–	–	–	–	–	–	22	–	–	–	–	–	–	–	21	17	–	–	Northampton T
Notts Co	3	9	4	7	8	–	–	–	–	–	–	–	–	–	–	–	–	2	4	–	–	–	–	–	–	Notts C
Oldham Ath	–	–	–	–	–	–	–	–	–	–	–	–	–	–	–	–	1	4	11	–	–	24	16	10	20	Oldham Ath
Oxford U	–	–	–	–	–	–	1	5	5	14	17	11	18	17	–	–	–	–	–	–	–	–	1	16	14	Oxford U
Peterborough U	–	–	–	–	–	–	–	–	–	–	–	21	4	16	10	7	–	–	–	–	–	–	24	15	13	Peterborough U
Plymouth Arg	–	–	–	–	2	15	19	8	10	7	15	15	19	–	–	2	17	8	3	15	17	5	–	–	–	Plymouth Arg
Portsmouth	–	–	–	–	–	–	–	1	13	6	–	–	24	20	–	–	–	–	–	–	–	–	–	–	–	Portsmouth
Port Vale	–	3	11	12	–	–	23	–	–	–	–	–	21	19	12	6	20	6	15	17	–	–	–	–	–	Port Vale
Preston NE	19	6	16	–	–	23	16	16	14	–	–	–	3	6	8	9	–	–	–	1	–	–	–	–	–	Preston NE
QPR	–	–	–	–	–	–	–	–	–	–	–	–	–	–	–	–	–	–	–	–	–	–	–	1	3	QPR
Reading	10	18	–	–	1	9	–	21	12	10	7	–	–	21	–	–	–	–	–	21	8	14	5	4	8	Reading
Rochdale	–	–	–	–	–	–	–	–	–	–	–	–	–	–	–	–	24	13	[illegible]	16	9	–	–	–	–	Rochdale
Rotherham U	9	–	21	14	14	12	18	–	–	1	13	17	20	4	16	–	–	21	[illegible]	8	14	11	–	–	–	Rotherham U
Scunthorpe U	–	–	–	–	–	–	21	–	–	–	–	–	–	–	–	–	–	24	–	–	–	–	23	18	4	Scunthorpe U
Sheffield U	–	2	–	–	–	–	3	11	–	21	12	–	–	–	–	–	–	–	–	–	–	–	–	–	–	Sheffield U
Sheffield W	–	–	–	–	–	–	–	–	–	–	3	14	14	8	20	–	–	–	–	–	–	–	–	–	–	Sheffield W
Shrewsbury T	11	–	–	–	–	–	–	–	–	–	–	1	11	10	9	–	22	15	12	13	15	17	3	6	10	Shrewsbury T
Southend U	–	21	17	–	–	–	22	15	7	–	22	13	–	–	23	18	12	14	–	–	–	–	–	–	21	Southend U
Southport	–	–	–	–	–	–	–	–	–	–	–	–	–	–	–	–	23	–	–	–	22	8	14	–	–	Southport
Stockport Co	–	–	–	–	–	–	–	–	–	–	–	–	–	–	–	–	–	–	–	–	24	9	13	–	–	Stockport Co
Sunderland	–	–	1	–	–	–	–	–	–	–	–	–	–	–	–	–	–	–	–	–	–	–	–	–	–	Sunderland

DIVISION THREE LEAGUE POSITIONS 1965–66 TO 1989–90

	1989–90	1988–89	1987–88	1986–87	1985–86	1984–85	1983–84	1982–83	1981–82	1980–81	1979–80	1978–79	1977–78	1976–77	1975–76	1974–75	1973–74	1972–73	1971–72	1970–71	1969–70	1968–69	1967–68	1966–67	1965–66	
Swansea C	17	12	–	–	24	20	–	–	–	–	–	3	–	–	–	–	–	23	14	11	–	–	–	21	17	Swansea C
Swindon T	–	–	–	3	–	–	–	–	22	17	10	5	10	11	19	4	–	–	–	–	–	2	9	8	7	Swindon T
Torquay U	–	–	–	–	–	–	–	–	–	–	–	–	–	–	–	–	–	–	23	10	13	6	4	7	–	Torquay U
Tranmere R	4	–	–	–	–	–	–	–	–	–	–	23	12	14	–	22	16	10	20	18	16	7	19	–	–	Tranmere R
Walsall	24	–	3	8	6	11	6	10	20	20	–	22	6	15	7	8	15	17	9	20	12	13	7	12	9	Walsall
Watford	–	–	–	–	–	–	–	–	–	–	–	2	–	–	–	23	7	19	–	–	–	1	6	3	12	Watford
Wigan Ath	18	17	7	4	4	16	15	18	–	–	–	–	–	–	–	–	–	–	–	–	–	–	–	–	–	Wigan Ath
Wimbledon	–	–	–	–	–	–	2	–	21	–	24	–	–	–	–	–	–	–	–	–	–	–	–	–	–	Wimbledon
Wolv'hampton W	–	1	–	–	23	–	–	–	–	–	–	–	–	–	–	–	–	–	–	–	–	–	–	–	–	Wolv'hampton W
Workington	–	–	–	–	–	–	–	–	–	–	–	–	–	–	–	–	–	–	–	–	–	–	–	24	5	Workington
Wrexham	–	–	–	–	–	–	–	22	–	–	–	–	1	5	6	13	4	12	16	9	–	–	–	–	–	Wrexham
York City	–	–	23	20	7	8	–	–	–	–	–	–	–	24	–	–	3	18	19	–	–	–	–	–	24	York City

DIVISION FOUR LEAGUE POSITIONS
1965–66 TO 1989–90

	1989–90	1988–89	1987–88	1986–87	1985–86	1984–85	1983–84	1982–83	1981–82	1980–81	1979–80	1978–79	1977–78	1976–77	1975–76	1974–75	1973–74	1972–73	1971–72	1970–71	1969–70	1968–69	1967–68	1966–67	1965–66	
Aldershot	22	–	–	6	16	13	5	18	16	6	10	5	5	17	–	–	–	4	17	13	6	15	9	10	17	Aldershot
Barnsley	–	–	–	–	–	–	–	–	–	–	–	4	7	6	12	15	13	14	–	–	–	–	2	16	16	Barnsley
Barrow	–	–	–	–	–	–	–	–	–	–	–	–	–	–	–	–	–	–	22	24	–	–	–	3	12	Barrow
Blackpool	–	–	–	–	–	2	6	21	12	–	–	–	–	–	–	–	–	–	–	–	–	–	–	–	–	Blackpool
Bolton W	–	–	3	–	–	–	–	–	–	–	–	–	–	–	–	–	–	–	–	–	–	–	–	–	–	Bolton W
Bournemouth	–	–	–	–	–	–	–	–	4	13	11	18	17	13	6	–	–	–	–	2	–	–	–	–	–	Bournemouth
Bradford C	–	–	–	–	–	–	–	–	2	14	5	15	–	4	17	10	8	16	–	–	–	4	5	11	23	Bradford C
Bradford PA	–	–	–	–	–	–	–	–	–	–	–	–	–	–	–	–	–	–	–	–	24	24	24	23	11	Bradford PA
Brentford	–	–	–	–	–	–	–	–	–	–	–	–	4	15	18	8	19	–	3	14	5	11	14	9	–	Brentford
Bristol C	–	–	–	–	–	–	4	14	–	–	–	–	–	–	–	–	–	–	–	–	–	–	–	–	–	Bristol C
Burnley	16	16	10	22	14	–	–	–	–	–	–	–	–	–	–	–	–	–	–	–	–	–	–	–	–	Burnley
Bury	–	–	–	–	–	4	15	5	9	12	–	–	–	–	–	–	4	12	9	–	–	–	–	–	–	Bury
Cambridge U	6	8	15	11	22	–	–	–	–	–	–	–	–	1	13	6	–	3	10	20	–	–	–	–	–	Cambridge U
Cardiff C	–	–	2	13	–	–	–	–	–	–	–	–	–	–	–	–	–	–	–	–	–	–	–	–	–	Cardiff C
Carlisle U	8	12	23	–	–	–	–	–	–	–	–	–	–	–	–	–	–	–	–	–	–	–	–	–	–	Carlisle U
Chester C	–	–	–	–	2	16	24	13	–	–	–	–	–	–	–	4	7	15	20	5	11	14	22	19	7	Chester C
Chesterfield	7	–	–	–	–	1	13	–	–	–	–	–	–	–	–	–	–	–	–	–	1	20	7	15	20	Chesterfield
Colchester U	24	22	9	5	6	7	8	6	6	–	–	–	–	3	–	–	3	22	11	6	10	6	–	–	4	Colchester U
Crewe Alex	–	3	17	17	12	10	16	23	24	18	23	24	15	12	16	18	21	21	24	15	15	–	4	5	14	Crewe Alex
Darlington	–	24	13	–	–	3	14	17	13	8	22	21	19	11	20	21	20	24	19	12	22	5	16	–	2	Darlington
Doncaster R	20	23	–	–	–	–	2	–	–	3	12	22	12	3	10	17	22	17	12	–	–	1	10	–	1	Doncaster R
Exeter C	1	13	22	14	21	18	–	–	–	–	–	–	–	2	7	9	10	8	15	9	18	17	20	14	–	Exeter C
Gillingham	14	–	–	–	–	–	–	–	–	–	–	–	–	–	–	–	2	9	13	–	–	–	–	–	–	Gillingham
Grimsby T	2	9	–	–	–	–	–	–	–	–	–	2	6	–	–	–	–	–	1	19	16	23	–	–	–	Grimsby T
Halifax T	23	21	18	15	20	21	21	11	19	23	18	23	20	21	–	–	–	–	–	–	–	2	11	12	15	Halifax T
Hartlepool U	19	19	16	18	7	19	23	22	14	9	19	13	21	22	14	13	11	20	18	23	23	–	3	8	18	Hartlepool U
Hereford U	17	15	19	16	10	5	11	24	10	22	21	14	–	–	–	–	–	2	–	–	–	–	–	–	–	Hereford U
Huddersfield T	–	–	–	–	–	–	–	–	–	–	1	9	11	9	5	–	–	–	–	–	–	–	–	–	–	Huddersfield T

Hull C	–	–	–	–	–	–	–	2	8	–	–	–	–	–	–	–	–	–	–	–	–	–	–	–	–	Hull C
Leyton Orient	–	6	8	7	5	–	–	–	–	–	–	–	–	–	–	–	–	–	–	–	–	–	–	–	–	Leyton Orient
Lincoln C	10	10	–	24	–	–	–	–	–	2	7	–	–	–	1	5	12	10	5	21	8	8	13	24	22	Lincoln C
Luton T	–	–	–	–	–	–	–	–	–	–	–	–	–	–	–	–	–	–	–	–	–	–	1	17	6	Luton T
Maidstone U	5	–	–	–	–	–	–	–	–	–	–	–	–	–	–	–	–	–	–	–	–	–	–	–	–	Maidstone U
Mansfield T	–	–	–	–	3	14	19	10	20	7	–	–	–	–	–	1	17	6	–	–	–	–	–	–	–	Mansfield T
Newport Co	–	–	24	–	–	–	–	–	–	–	3	8	16	19	22	12	9	5	14	22	21	22	12	18	9	Newport C
Northampton T	–	–	–	1	8	23	18	15	22	10	13	19	10	–	2	16	5	23	21	7	14	–	–	–	–	Northampton T
Notts Co	–	–	–	–	–	–	–	–	–	–	–	–	–	–	–	–	–	–	–	1	7	19	17	20	8	Notts Co
Oldham Ath	–	–	–	–	–	–	–	–	–	–	–	–	–	–	–	–	–	–	–	3	19	–	–	–	–	Oldham Ath
Peterborough U	9	7	7	10	17	11	7	9	5	5	8	–	–	–	–	–	1	19	8	16	9	18	–	–	–	Peterborough U
Portsmouth	–	–	–	–	–	–	–	–	–	–	4	7	–	–	–	–	–	–	–	–	–	–	–	–	–	Portsmouth
Port Vale	–	–	–	–	4	12	–	3	7	19	20	16	–	–	–	–	–	–	–	–	4	13	18	13	19	Port Vale
Preston NE	–	–	–	2	23	–	–	–	–	–	–	–	–	–	–	–	–	–	–	–	–	–	–	–	–	Preston NE
Reading	–	–	–	–	–	–	3	–	–	–	–	1	8	–	3	7	6	7	16	–	–	–	–	–	–	Reading
Rochdale	12	18	21	21	18	17	22	20	21	15	24	20	24	18	15	19	–	–	–	–	–	3	19	21	21	Rochdale
Rotherham U	–	1	–	–	–	–	–	–	–	–	–	–	–	–	–	3	15	–	–	–	–	–	–	–	–	Rotherham U
Scarborough	18	5	12	–	–	–	–	–	–	–	–	–	–	–	–	–	–	–	–	–	–	–	–	–	–	Scarborough
Scunthorpe U	11	4	4	8	15	9	–	4	23	16	14	12	14	20	19	24	18	–	4	17	12	16	–	–	–	Scunthorpe U
Sheffield U	–	–	–	–	–	–	–	–	1	–	–	–	–	–	–	–	–	–	–	–	–	–	–	–	–	Sheffield U
Shrewsbury T	–	–	–	–	–	–	–	–	–	–	–	–	–	–	–	2	–	–	–	–	–	–	–	–	–	Shrewsbury T
Southend U	3	–	–	3	9	20	–	–	–	1	–	–	2	10	–	–	–	–	2	18	17	7	6	6	–	Southend U
Southport	–	–	–	–	–	–	–	–	–	–	–	–	23	23	23	11	–	1	7	8	–	–	–	2	10	Southport
Stockport Co	4	20	20	19	11	22	12	16	18	20	16	17	18	14	21	20	24	11	23	11	–	–	–	1	13	Stockport Co
Swansea C	–	–	6	12	–	–	–	–	–	–	–	–	3	5	11	22	14	–	–	–	3	10	15	–	–	Swansea C
Swindon T	–	–	–	–	1	8	17	8	–	–	–	–	–	–	–	–	–	–	–	–	–	–	–	–	–	Swindon T
Torquay U	15	14	5	23	24	24	9	12	15	17	9	11	9	16	9	14	16	18	–	–	–	–	–	–	3	Torquay U
Tranmere R	–	2	14	20	19	6	10	19	11	21	15	–	–	–	4	–	–	–	–	–	–	–	–	4	5	Tranmere R
Walsall	–	–	–	–	–	–	–	–	–	–	2	–	–	–	–	–	–	–	–	–	–	–	–	–	–	Walsall
Watford	–	–	–	–	–	–	–	–	–	–	–	–	1	7	8	–	–	–	–	–	–	–	–	–	–	Watford
Wigan Ath	–	–	–	–	–	–	–	–	3	11	6	6	–	–	–	–	–	–	–	–	–	–	–	–	–	Wigan Ath
Wimbledon	–	–	–	–	–	–	–	1	–	4	–	3	13	–	–	–	–	–	–	–	–	–	–	–	–	Wimbledon
Wolv'hampton W	–	–	1	4	–	–	–	–	–	–	–	–	–	–	–	–	–	–	–	–	–	–	–	–	–	Wolv'hampton W
Workington	–	–	–	–	–	–	–	–	–	–	–	–	–	24	24	23	23	13	6	10	20	12	23	–	–	Workington
Wrexham	21	7	11	9	13	15	20	–	–	–	–	–	–	–	–	–	–	–	–	–	2	9	8	7	24	Wrexham
York C	13	11	–	–	–	–	1	7	17	24	17	10	22	–	–	–	–	–	–	4	13	21	21	22	–	York C

LEAGUE CHAMPIONSHIP HONOURS

**Won on goal average. †won on goal difference.*
No championships during WWI and WWII.

First Division

	First	Pt	Second	Pt	Third	Pt
1888–9 *a*	Preston NE	40	Aston Villa	29	Wolverhampton W	28
1889–90	Preston NE	33	Everton	31	Blackburn R	27
1890–1	Everton	29	Preston NE	27	Wolverhampton Notts Co	26
1892–3 *c*	Sunderland	48	Preston NE	37	Everton	36
1893–4	Aston Villa	44	Sunderland	38	Derby Co	36
1894–5	Sunderland	47	Everton	42	Aston Villa	39
1895–6	Aston Villa	45	Derby Co	41	Everton	39
1896–7	Aston Villa	47	Sheffield U	36	Derby Co	36
1897–8	Sheffield U	42	Sunderland	37	Wolverhampton W	35
1898–9 *d*	Aston Villa	45	Liverpool	43	Burnley	39
1899–1900	Aston Villa	50	Sheffield U	48	Sunderland	41
1900–1	Liverpool	45	Sunderland	43	Notts Co	40
1901–2	Sunderland	44	Everton	41	Newcastle U	37
1902–3	The Wednesday	42	Aston Villa	41	Sunderland	41
1903–4	The Wednesday	47	Manchester C	44	Everton	43
1904–5	Newcastle U	48	Everton	47	Manchester C	46
1905–6 *e*	Liverpool	51	Preston NE	47	The Wednesday	44
1906–7	Newcastle U	51	Bristol C	48	Everton	45
1907–8	Manchester U	52	Aston Villa	43	Manchester C	43
1908–9	Newcastle U	53	Everton	46	Sunderland	44
1909–10	Aston Villa	53	Liverpool	48	Blackburn R	45
1910–11	Manchester U	52	Aston Villa	51	Sunderland	45
1911–12	Blackburn R	49	Everton	46	Newcastle U	44
1912–13	Sunderland	54	Aston Villa	50	Sheffield W	49
1913–14	Blackburn R	51	Aston Villa	44	Middlesbrough	43
1914–15	Everton	46	Oldham Ath	45	Blackburn R	43
1919–20*f*	WBA	60	Burnley	51	Chelsea	49
1920–1	Burnley	59	Manchester C	54	Bolton W	52
1921–2	Liverpool	57	Tottenham H	51	Burnley	49
1922–3	Liverpool	60	Sunderland	54	Huddersfield T	53
1923–4	*Huddersfield T	57	Cardiff C	57	Sunderland	53
1924–5	Huddersfield T	58	WBA	56	Bolton W	55
1925–6	Huddersfield T	57	Arsenal	52	Sunderland	48
1926–7	Newcastle U	56	Huddersfield T	51	Sunderland	49
1927–8	Everton	53	Huddersfield T	51	Leicester C	48
1928–9	Sheffield W	52	Leicester C	51	Aston Villa	50
1929–30	Sheffield W	60	Derby Co	50	Manchester C	47
1930–1	Arsenal	66	Aston Villa	59	Sheffield W	52
1931–2	Everton	56	Arsenal	54	Sheffield W	50
1932–3	Arsenal	58	Aston Villa	54	Sheffield W	51
1933–4	Arsenal	59	Huddersfield T	56	Tottenham H	49
1934–5	Arsenal	58	Sunderland	54	Sheffield W	49
1935–6	Sunderland	56	Derby Co	48	Huddersfield T	48
1936–7	Manchester C	57	Charlton Ath	54	Arsenal	52
1937–8	Arsenal	52	Wolverhampton W	51	Preston NE	49
1938–9	Everton	59	Wolverhampton W	55	Charlton Ath	50
1946–7	Liverpool	57	Manchester U	56	Wolverhampton W	56
1947–8	Arsenal	59	Manchester U	52	Burnley	52

1948–9	Portsmouth............58	Manchester U........53	Derby Co..................53
1949–50	*Portsmouth..........53	Wolverhampton W 53	Sunderland................52
1950–1	Tottenham H.........60	Manchester U........56	Blackpool..................50
1951–2	Manchester U........57	Tottenham H.........53	Arsenal......................53
1952–3	*Arsenal................54	Preston NE............54	Wolverhampton W 51
1953–4	Wolverhampton W 57	WBA.......................53	Huddersfield T..........51
1954–5	Chelsea..................52	Wolverhampton W 48	Portsmouth...............48
1955–6	Manchester U........60	Blackpool...............49	Wolverhampton W 49
1956–7	Manchester U........64	Tottenham H.........56	Preston NE................56
1957–8	Wolverhampton W 64	Preston NE............59	Tottenham H............51
1958–9	Wolverhampton W 61	Manchester U........55	Arsenal......................50
1959–60	Burnley..................55	Wolverhampton W 54	Tottenham H............53
1960–1	Tottenham H.........66	Sheffield W............58	Wolverhampton W 57
1961–2	Ipswich T...............56	Burnley..................53	Tottenham H............52
1962–3	Everton..................61	Tottenham H.........55	Burnley......................54
1963–4	Liverpool...............57	Manchester U........53	Everton......................52
1964–5	*Manchester U......61	Leeds U.................61	Chelsea......................56
1965–6	Liverpool...............61	Leeds U.................55	Burnley......................55
1966–7	Manchester U........60	Nottingham F........56	Tottenham H............56
1967–8	Manchester C........58	Manchester U........56	Liverpool...................55
1968–9	Leeds U.................67	Liverpool...............61	Everton......................57
1969–70	Everton..................66	Leeds U.................57	Chelsea......................55
1970–1	Arsenal..................65	Leeds U.................64	Tottenham H............52
1971–2	Derby Co...............58	Leeds U.................57	Liverpool...................57
1972–3	Liverpool...............60	Arsenal..................57	Leeds U......................53
1973–4	Leeds U.................62	Liverpool...............57	Derby Co..................48
1974–5	Derby Co...............53	Liverpool...............51	Ipswich T..................57
1975–6	Liverpool...............60	QPR.......................59	Manchester U...........56
1976–7	Liverpool...............57	Manchester C........56	Ipswich T..................52
1977–8	Nottingham F........64	Liverpool...............57	Everton......................55
1978–9	Liverpool...............68	Nottingham F........60	WBA.........................59
1979–80	Liverpool...............60	Manchester U........58	Ipswich T..................53
1980–1	Aston Villa............60	Ipswich T...............56	Arsenal......................53
1981–2 *g*	Liverpool...............87	Ipswich T...............83	Manchester U...........78
1982–3	Liverpool...............82	Watford.................71	Manchester U...........70
1983–4	Liverpool...............80	Southampton.........77	Nottingham F...........74
1984–5	Everton..................90	Liverpool...............77	Tottenham H............77
1985–6g	Liverpool...............88	Everton..................86	West Ham.................84
1986–7	Everton..................86	Liverpool...............77	Tottenham H............71
1987–8 *h*	Liverpool...............90	Manchester U........81	Nottingham F...........73
1988–9 *i*†	Arsenal..................76	Liverpool...............76	Nottingham F...........64
1989–90 *i*	Liverpool...............79	Aston Villa............70	Tottenham H............63
1990–91	Arsenal..................83	Liverpool...............76	Crystal Palace...........69

Maximum points: a 44; *b* 56; *c* 60; *d* 58; *e* 76; *f* 84; *g* 126; *h* 120; *i* 114.

Second Division

1892–3 *a*	Small Heath...........36	Sheffield U.............35	Darwen......................30
1893–4 *b*	Liverpool...............50	Small Heath...........42	Notts Co...................39
1894–5 *c*	Bury.......................48	Notts Co................39	Newton Heath...........38
1895–6	*Liverpool.............46	Manchester C........46	Grimsby T.................42
1896–7	Notts Co................42	Newton Heath.......39	Grimsby T.................38
1897–8	Burnley..................48	Newcastle U..........45	Manchester C............39
1898–9 *d*	Manchester C........52	Glossop NE...........46	Leicester Fosse..........45
1899–1900	The Wednesday.....54	Bolton W...............52	Small Heath..............46
1900–1	Grimsby T.............49	Small Heath...........48	Burnley......................44

1901–2	WBA	55	Middlesbrough	51	Preston NE	42
1902–3	Manchester C	54	Small Heath	51	Woolwich A	48
1903–4	Preston NE	50	Woolwich A	49	Manchester U	48
1904–5	Liverpool	58	Bolton W	56	Manchester U	53
1905–6 *e*	Bristol C	66	Manchester U	62	Chelsea	53
1906–7	Nottingham F	60	Chelsea	57	Leicester Fosse	48
1907–8	Bradford C	54	Leicester Fosse	52	Oldham Ath	50
1908–9	Bolton W	52	Tottenham H	51	WBA	51
1909–10	Manchester C	54	Oldham Ath	53	Hull C	53
1910–11	WBA	53	Bolton W	51	Chelsea	49
1911–12	*Derby Co	54	Chelsea	54	Burnley	52
1912–13	Preston NE	53	Burnley	50	Birmingham	46
1913–14	Notts Co	53	Bradford PA	49	Woolwich A	49
1914–15	Derby Co	53	Preston NE	50	Barnsley	47
1919–20*f*	Tottenham H	70	Huddersfield T	64	Birmingham	56
1920–1	*Birmingham	58	Cardiff C	58	Bristol C	51
1921–2	Nottingham F	56	Stoke C	52	Barnsley	52
1922–3	Notts Co	53	West Ham U	51	Leicester C	51
1923–4	Leeds U	54	Bury	51	Derby Co	51
1924–5	Leicester C	59	Manchester U	57	Derby Co	55
1925–6	Sheffield W	60	Derby Co	57	Chelsea	52
1926–7	Middlesbrough	62	Portsmouth	54	Manchester C	54
1927–8	Manchester C	59	Leeds U	57	Chelsea	54
1928–9	Middlesbrough	55	Grimsby T	53	Bradford	48
1929–30	Blackpool	58	Chelsea	55	Oldham Ath	53
1930–1	Everton	61	WBA	54	Tottenham H	51
1931–2	Wolverhampton W	56	Leeds U	54	Stoke C	52
1932–3	Stoke C	56	Tottenham H	55	Fulham	50
1933–4	Grimsby T	59	Preston NE	52	Bolton W	51
1934–5	Brentford	61	Bolton W	56	West Ham U	56
1935–6	Manchester U	56	Charlton Ath	55	Sheffield U	52
1936–7	Leicester C	56	Blackpool	55	Bury	52
1937–8	Aston Villa	57	Manchester U	53	Sheffield U	53
1938–9	Blackburn R	55	Sheffield U	54	Sheffield W	53
1946–7	Manchester C	62	Burnley	58	Birmingham C	55
1947–8	Birmingham C	59	Newcastle U	56	Southampton	52
1948–9	Fulham	57	WBA	56	Southampton	55
1949–50	Tottenham H	61	Sheffield W	52	Sheffield U	52
1950–1	Preston NE	57	Manchester C	52	Cardiff C	50
1951–2	Sheffield W	53	Cardiff C	51	Birmingham C	51
1952–3	Sheffield U	60	Huddersfield T	58	Luton T	52
1953–4	*Leicester C	56	Everton	56	Blackburn R	55
1954–5	*Birmingham C	54	Luton T	54	Rotherham U	54
1955–6	Sheffield W	55	Leeds U	52	Liverpool	48
1956–7	Leicester C	61	Nottingham F	54	Liverpool	53
1957–8	West Ham U	57	Blackburn R	56	Charlton Ath	55
1958–9	Sheffield W	62	Fulham	60	Sheffield U	53
1959–60	Aston Villa	59	Cardiff C	58	Liverpool	50
1960–1	Ipswich T	59	Sheffield U	58	Liverpool	52
1961–2	Liverpool	62	Leyton O	54	Sunderland	53
1962–3	Stoke C	53	Chelsea	52	Sunderland	52
1963–4	Leeds U	63	Sunderland	61	Preston NE	56
1964–5	Newcastle U	57	Northampton T	56	Bolton W	50
1965–6	Manchester C	59	Southampton	54	Coventry C	53
1966–7	Coventry C	59	Wolverhampton W	58	Carlisle U	52
1967–8	Ipswich T	59	QPR	58	Blackpool	58

1968–9	Derby Co.........63	Crystal Palace........56	Charlton Ath.........50
1969–70	Huddersfield T.......60	Blackpool.........53	Leicester C.........51
1970–1	Leicester C.........59	Sheffield U.........56	Cardiff C.........53
1971–2	Norwich C.........57	Birmingham C.......56	Millwall.........55
1972–3	Burnley.........62	QPR.........61	Aston Villa.........50
1973–4	Middlesbrough......65	Luton T.........50	Carlisle U.........49
1974–5	Manchester U........61	Aston Villa.........58	Norwich C.........53
1975–6	Sunderland.........56	Bristol C.........53	WBA.........53
1976–7	Wolverhampton W 57	Chelsea.........55	Nottingham F.........52
1977–8	Bolton W.........58	Southampton.........57	Tottenham H.........56
1978–9	Crystal Palace........57	Brighton.........56	Stoke C.........56
1979–80	Leicester C.........55	Sunderland.........54	Birmingham C.........53
1980–1	West Ham U.........66	Notts Co.........53	Swansea C.........50
1981–2 *g*	Luton T.........88	Watford.........80	Norwich C.........71
1982–3	QPR.........85	Wolverhampton W 75	Leicester C.........70
1983–4 †	Chelsea.........88	Sheffield W.........88	Newcastle U.........80
1984–5	Oxford U.........84	Birmingham C.......82	Manchester C.........74
1985–6	Norwich C.........84	Charlton Ath.........77	Wimbledon.........76
1986–7	Derby Co.........84	Portsmouth.........78	Oldham Ath.........75
1987–8 *h*	Millwall.........82	Aston Villa.........78	Middlesbrough.........78
1988–9 *i*	Chelsea.........99	Manchester C........82	Crystal Palace.........81
1989–90	Leeds U.........85	Sheffield U.........85	Newcastle U.........80
1990–91	Oldham Ath.........88	West Ham U.........87	Sheffield W.........82

Maximum points: *a*, 44; *b*, 56; *c*, 60; *d*, 58; *e*, 76; *f*, 84; *g*, 126; *h*, 132; *i*, 138

Third Division

1958–9 *a*	Plymouth Arg........62	Hull C.........61	Brentford.........57
1959–60	Southampton.........61	Norwich C.........59	Shrewsbury T.........52
1960–1	Bury.........68	Walsall.........62	QPR.........60
1961–2	Portsmouth.........65	Grimsby T.........62	Bournemouth.........59
1962–3	Northampton T.....62	Swindon T.........58	Port Vale.........54
1963–4	*Coventry C.........60	Crystal Palace........60	Watford.........58
1964–5	Carlisle U.........60	Bristol C.........59	Mansfield T.........59
1965–6	Hull C.........69	Millwall.........65	QPR.........57
1966–7	QPR.........67	Middlesbrough......55	Watford.........54
1967–8	Oxford U.........57	Bury.........56	Shrewsbury T.........55
1968–9	*Watford.........64	Swindon T.........64	Luton T.........61
1969–70	Orient.........62	Luton T.........60	Bristol R.........56
1970–1	Preston NE.........61	Fulham.........60	Halifax T.........56
1971–2	Aston Villa.........70	Brighton.........65	Bournemouth.........62
1972–3	Bolton W.........61	Notts Co.........57	Blackburn R.........55
1973–4	Oldham Ath.........62	Bristol R.........61	York C.........61
1974–5	Blackburn R.........60	Plymouth Arg........59	Charlton Ath.........55
1975–6	Hereford U.........63	Cardiff C.........57	Millwall.........56
1976–7	Mansfield T.........64	Brighton & HA.....61	Crystal Palace.........59
1977–8	Wrexham.........61	Cambridge U.........58	Preston NE.........56
1978–9	Shrewsbury T........61	Watford.........60	Swansea C.........60
1979–80	Grimsby T.........62	Blackburn R.........59	Sheffield W.........58
1980–1	Rotherham U........61	Barnsley.........59	Charlton Ath.........59
1981–2 *b*	Burnley.........80	Carlisle U.........80	Fulham.........78
1982–3	Portsmouth.........91	Cardiff C.........86	Huddersfield T.........82
1983–4	Oxford U.........95	Wimbledon.........87	Sheffield U.........83
1984–5	Bradford C.........94	Millwall.........90	Hull C.........87
1985–6	Reading.........94	Plymouth Arg........87	Derby Co.........84

Season	First	Second	Third
1986–7	Bournemouth 97	Middlesbrough 94	Swindon T 87
1987–8	Sunderland 93	Brighton & HA 84	Walsall 82
1988–9	Wolverhampton W 92	Sheffield U 84	Port Vale 84
1989–90	Bristol R 93	Bristol C 91	Notts Co 87
1990–91	Cambridge U 86	Southend U 85	Grimsby T 83

Maximum points: *a* 92; *b* 138

Third Division (Southern Section)

Season	First	Second	Third
1920–1 *a*	Crystal Palace 59	Southampton 54	QPR 53
1921–2	*Southampton 61	Plymouth Arg 61	Portsmouth 53
1922–3	Bristol C 59	Plymouth Arg 53	Swansea T 53
1923–4	Portsmouth 59	Plymouth Arg 55	Millwall 54
1924–5	Swansea T 57	Plymouth Arg 56	Bristol C 53
1925–6	Reading 57	Plymouth Arg 56	Millwall 53
1926–7	Bristol C 62	Plymouth Arg 60	Millwall 56
1927–8	Millwall 65	Northampton T 55	Plymouth Arg 53
1928–9	Charlton Ath 54	Crystal Palace 54	Northampton T 52
1929–30	Plymouth Arg 68	Brentford 61	QPR 51
1930–1	Notts Co 59	Crystal Palace 51	Brentford 50
1931–2	Fulham 57	Reading 55	Southend U 53
1932–3	Brentford 62	Exeter C 58	Norwich C 57
1933–4	Norwich C 61	Coventry C 54	Reading 54
1934–5	Charlton Ath 61	Reading 53	Coventry C 51
1935–6	Coventry C 57	Luton T 56	Reading 54
1936–7	Luton T 58	Notts Co 56	Brighton 53
1937–8	Millwall 56	Bristol C 55	QPR 53
1938–9	Newport Co 55	Crystal Palace 52	Brighton 49
1946–7	Cardiff C 66	QPR 57	Bristol C 51
1947–8	QPR 61	Bournemouth 57	Walsall 51
1948–9	Swansea T 62	Reading 55	Bournemouth 52
1949–50	Notts Co 58	Northampton T 51	Southend U 51
1950–1 *b*	Nottingham F 70	Norwich C 64	Reading 57
1951–2	Plymouth Arg 66	Reading 61	Norwich C 61
1952–3	Bristol R 64	Millwall 62	Northampton T 62
1953–4	Ipswich T 64	Brighton 61	Bristol C 56
1954–5	Bristol C 70	Leyton O 61	Southampton 59
1955–6	Leyton O 66	Brighton 65	Ipswich T 64
1956–7	*Ipswich T 59	Torquay U 59	Colchester U 58
1957–8	Brighton 60	Brentford 58	Plymouth Arg 58

Maximum points: *a* 84; *b* 76; *c* 80; *d* 92.

Third Division (Northern Section)

Season	First	Second	Third
1921–2 *a*	Stockport Co 56	Darlington 50	Grimsby T 50
1922–3	Nelson 51	Bradford PA 47	Walsall 46
1923–4 *b*	Wolverhampton W 63	Rochdale 62	Chesterfield 54
1924–5	Darlington 58	Nelson 53	New Brighton 53
1925–6	Grimsby T 61	Bradford PA 60	Rochdale 59
1926–7	Stoke C 63	Rochdale 58	Bradford PA 55
1927–8	Bradford PA 63	Lincoln C 55	Stockport Co 54
1928–9	Bradford C 63	Stockport Co 62	Wrexham 52
1929–30	Port Vale 67	Stockport Co 63	Darlington 50
1930–1	Chesterfield 58	Lincoln C 57	Wrexham 54
1931–2 *c*	*Lincoln C 57	Gateshead 57	Chester 50
1932–3 *b*	Hull C 59	Wrexham 57	Stockport Co 54

1933–4	Barnsley	62	Chesterfield	61	Stockport Co	59
1934–5	Doncaster R	57	Halifax T	55	Chester	54
1935–6	Chesterfield	60	Chester	55	Tranmere R	55
1936–7	Stockport Co	60	Lincoln C	57	Chester	53
1937–8	Tranmere R	56	Doncaster R	54	Hull C	53
1938–9	Barnsley	67	Doncaster R	56	Bradford C	52
1946–7	Doncaster R	72	Rotherham U	64	Chester	56
1947–8	Lincoln C	60	Rotherham U	59	Wrexham	50
1948–9	Hull C	65	Rotherham U	62	Doncaster R	50
1949–50	Doncaster R	55	Gateshead	53	Rochdale	51
1950–1 *d*	Rotherham U	71	Mansfield T	64	Carlisle U	62
1951–2	Lincoln C	69	Grimsby T	66	Stockport Co	59
1952–3	Oldham Ath	59	Port Vale	58	Wrexham	56
1953–4	Port Vale	69	Barnsley	58	Scunthorpe U	57
1954–5	Barnsley	65	Accrington S	61	Scunthorpe U	58
1955–6	Grimsby T	68	Derby Co	63	Accrington S	59
1956–7	Derby Co	63	Hartlepool U	59	Accrington S	58
1957–8	Scunthorpe U	66	Accrington S	59	Bradford C	57

Maximum points: *a*, 70; *b*, 84; *c*, 80; *d*, 90.

Division IV

1958–9 *a*	Port Vale	64	Coventry C	60	York C	60
1959–60	Walsall	65	Notts Co	60	Torquay U	
1960–1	Peterborough U	66	Crystal Palace	64	Northampton T	60
1961–2	Millwall	56	Colchester U	55	Wrexham	53
1962–3	Brentford	62	Oldham Ath	59	Crewe Alex	59
1963–4	*Gillingham	60	Carlisle U	60	Workington T	59
1964–5	Brighton	63	Millwall	62	York C	62
1965–6	*Doncaster R	59	Darlington	59	Torquay U	58
1966–7	Stockport Co	64	Southport	59	Barrow	59
1967–8	Luton T	66	Barnsley	61	Hartlepools U	60
1968–9	Doncaster R	59	Halifax T	57	Rochdale	56
1969–70	Chesterfield	64	Wrexham	61	Swansea C	60
1970–1	Notts Co	69	Bournemouth	60	Oldham Ath	59
1971–2	Grimsby T	63	Southend U	60	Brentford	59
1972–3	Southport	62	Hereford U	58	Cambridge U	57
1973–4	Peterborough U	65	Gillingham	62	Colchester U	59
1974–5	Mansfield T	68	Shrewsbury T	62	Rotherham U	59
1975–6	Lincoln C	74	Northampton T	68	Reading	60
1976–7	Cambridge U	65	Exeter C	62	Colchester U	59
1977–8	Watford	71	Southend U	60	Swansea C	56
1978–9	Reading	65	Grimsby T	61	Wimbledon	61
1979–80	Huddersfield T	66	Walsall	64	Newport Co	61
1980–1	Southend U	67	Lincoln C	65	Doncaster R	56
1981–2 *b*	Sheffield U	96	Bradford C	91	Wigan Ath	91
1982–3	Wimbledon	98	Hull C	90	Port Vale	88
1983–4	York C	101	Doncaster R	85	Reading	82
1984–5	Chesterfield	91	Blackpool	86	Darlington	85
1985–6	Swindon T	102	Chester C	84	Mansfield T	81
1986–7	Northampton T	99	Preston NE	90	Southend U	80
1987–8	Wolverhampton W	90	Cardiff C	85	Bolton W	78
1988–9	Rotherham U	82	Tranmere R	80	Crewe Alex	78
1989–90	Exeter C	89	Grimsby T	79	Southend U	75
1990–91	Darlington	83	†Stockport Co	82	Hartlepool U	82

Maximum points: 92; 138

RELEGATED CLUBS

(Since inception of automatic promotion and relegation in 1898–9)
**Relegated after play-offs*

Division II to Division III

1898–99 Bolton W and Sheffield W
1899–1900 Burnley and Glossop
1900–01 Preston NE and WBA
1901–02 Small Heath and Manchester C
1902–03 Grimsby T and Bolton W
1903–04 Liverpool and WBA
1904–05 League extended. Bury and Notts Co, two bottom clubs in First Division, re-elected.
1905–06 Nottingham F and Wolverhampton W
1906–07 Derby Co and Stoke C
1907–08 Bolton W and Birmingham C
1908–09 Manchester C and Leicester Fosse
1909–10 Bolton W and Chelsea
1910–11 Bristol C and Nottingham F
1911–12 Preston NE and Bury
1912–13 Notts Co and Woolwich Arsenal
1913–14 Preston NE and Derby Co
1914–15 Tottenham H and Chelsea*
1919–20 Notts Co and Sheffield W
1920–21 Derby Co and Bradford PA
1921–22 Bradford C and Manchester U
1922–23 Stoke C and Oldham Ath
1923–24 Chelsea and Middlesbrough
1924–25 Preston NE and Nottingham F
1925–26 Manchester C and Notts Co
1926–27 Leeds U and WBA
1927–28 Tottenham H and Middlesbrough
1928–29 Bury and Cardiff C
1929–30 Burnley and Everton
1930–31 Leeds U and Manchester U
1931–32 Grimsby T and West Ham U
1932–33 Bolton W and Blackpool
1933–34 Newcastle U and Sheffield U
1934–35 Leicester C and Tottenham H
1935–36 Aston Villa and Blackburn R
1936–37 Manchester U and Sheffield W
1937–38 Manchester C and WBA
1938–39 Birmingham C and Leicester C
1946–47 Brentford and Leeds U
1947–48 Blackburn R and Grimsby T
1948–49 Preston NE and Sheffield U
1949–50 Manchester C and Birmingham C
1950–51 Sheffield W and Everton
1951–52 Huddersfield and Fulham
1952–53 Stoke C and Derby Co
1953–54 Middlesbrough and Liverpool
1954–55 Leicester C and Sheffield W
1955–56 Huddersfield and Sheffield U
1956–57 Charlton Ath and Cardiff C
1957–58 Sheffield W and Sunderland
1958–59 Portsmouth and Aston Villa
1959–60 Luton T and Leeds U
1960–61 Preston NE and Newcastle U
1961–62 Chelsea and Cardiff C
1962–63 Manchester C and Leyton O
1963–64 Bolton W and Ipswich T
1964–65 Wolverhampton W and Birmingham C
1965–66 Northampton T and Blackburn R
1966–67 Aston Villa and Blackpool
1967–68 Fulham and Sheffield U
1968–69 Leicester C and QPR
1969–70 Sunderland and Sheffield W
1970–71 Burnley and Blackpool
1971–72 Huddersfield T and Nottingham F
1972–73 Crystal Palace and WBA
1973–74 Southampton, Manchester U, Norwich C
1974–75 Luton T, Chelsea, Carlisle U
1975–76 Wolverhampton W, Burnley, Sheffield U
1976–77 Sunderland, Stoke C, Tottenham H
1977–78 West Ham U, Newcastle U, Leicester C
1978–79 QPR, Birmingham C, Chelsea
1979–80 Bristol C, Derby Co, Bolton W
1980–81 Norwich C, Leicester C, Crystal Palace
1981–82 Leeds U, Wolverhampton W, Middlesbrough
1982–83 Manchester C, Swansea C, Brighton & HA

1983–84 Birmingham C, Notts Co, Wolverhampton W
1984–85 Norwich C, Sunderland, Stoke C
1985–86 Ipswich T, Birmingham C, WBA
1986–87 Leicester C, Manchester C, Aston Villa
1987–88 Chelsea**, Portsmouth, Watford, Oxford U
1988–89 Middlesbrough, West Ham U, Newcastle U
1989–90 Sheffield W, Charlton Ath, Millwall
1990–91 Sunderland and Derby Co

Division I to Division II

1920–21 Stockport Co
1921–22 Bradford and Bristol C
1922–23 Rotherham C and Wolverhampton W
1923–24 Nelson and Bristol C
1924–25 Crystal Palace and Coventry C
1925–26 Stoke C and Stockport Co
1926–27 Darlington and Bradford C
1927–28 Fulham and South Shields
1928–29 Port Vale and Clapton O
1929–30 Hull C and Notts Co
1930–31 Reading and Cardiff C
1931–32 Barnsley and Bristol C
1932–33 Chesterfield and Charlton Ath
1933–34 Millwall and Lincoln C
1934–35 Oldham Ath and Notts Co
1935–36 Port Vale and Hull C
1936–37 Doncaster R and Bradford C
1937–38 Barnsley and Stockport Co
1938–39 Norwich C and Tranmere R
1946–47 Swansea T and Newport Co
1947–48 Doncaster R and Millwall
1948–49 Nottingham F and Lincoln C
1949–50 Plymouth Arg and Bradford
1950–51 Grimsby T and Chesterfield
1951–52 Coventry C and QPR
1952–53 Southampton and Barnsley
1953–54 Brentford and Oldham Ath
1954–55 Ipswich T and Derby Co
1955–56 Plymouth Arg and Hull C
1956–57 Port Vale and Bury
1957–58 Doncaster R and Notts Co
1958–59 Barnsley and Grimsby T
1959–60 Bristol C and Hull C
1960–61 Lincoln C and Portsmouth
1961–62 Brighton & HA and Bristol R
1962–63 Walsall and Luton T
1963–64 Grimsby T and Scunthorpe U
1964–65 Swindon T and Swansea T
1965–66 Middlesbrough and Leyton O
1966–67 Northampton T and Bury
1967–68 Plymouth Arg and Rotherham U
1968–69 Fulham and Bury
1969–70 Preston NE and Aston Villa
1970–71 Blackburn R and Bolton W
1971–72 Charlton Ath and Watford
1972–73 Huddersfield T and Brighton & HA
1973–74 Crystal Palace, Preston NE, Swindon T
1974–75 Millwall, Cardiff C, Sheffield W
1975–76 Oxford U, York C, Portsmouth
1976–77 Carlisle U, Plymouth Arg, Hereford U
1977–78 Blackpool, Mansfield T, Hull C
1978–79 Sheffield U, Millwall, Blackburn R
1979–80 Fulham, Burnley, Charlton Ath
1980–81 Preston NE, Bristol C, Bristol R
1981–82 Cardiff C, Wrexham, Orient
1982–83 Rotherham U, Burnley, Bolton W
1983–84 Derby Co, Swansea C, Cambridge U
1984–85 Notts Co, Cardiff C, Wolverhampton W
1985–86 Carlisle U, Middlesbrough, Fulham
1986–87 Sunderland**, Grimsby T, Brighton & HA
1987–88 Huddersfield T, Reading, Sheffield U**
1988–89 Shrewsbury T, Birmingham C, Walsall
1989–90 Bournemouth, Bradford, Stoke C
1990–91 WBA and Hull C

Division III to Division IV

1958–59 Rochdale, Notts Co, Doncaster R and Stockport
1959–60 Accrington S, Wrexham, Mansfield T and York C
1960–61 Chesterfield, Colchester U, Bradford C and Tranmere R
1961–62 Newport Co, Brentford, Lincoln C and Torquay U
1962–63 Bradford PA, Brighton, Carlisle U and Halifax T
1963–64 Millwall, Crewe Alex, Wrexham and Notts Co
1964–65 Luton T, Port Vale, Colchester U and Barnsley
1965–66 Southend U, Exeter C, Brentford and York C
1966–67 Doncaster R, Workington, Darlington and Swansea T
1967–68 Scunthorpe U, Colchester U, Grimsby T and Peterborough U (demoted)
1968–69 Oldham Ath, Crewe Alex, Hartlepool and Northampton
1969–70 Bournemouth, Southport, Barrow, Stockport Co
1970–71 Reading, Bury, Doncaster R, Gillingham
1971–72 Mansfield T, Barnsley, Torquay U, Bradford C
1972–73 Rotherham U, Brentford, Swansea C, Scunthorpe U
1973–74 Cambridge U, Shrewsbury T, Southport, Rochdale
1974–75 AFC Bournemouth, Tranmere R, Watford, Huddersfield T

****Relegated after play-offs.*

1975–76 Aldershot, Colchester U, Southend U, Halifax T
1976–77 Reading, Northampton T, Grimsby T, York C
1977–78 Port Vale, Bradford C, Hereford U, Portsmouth
1978–79 Peterborough U, Walsall, Tranmere R, Lincoln C
1979–80 Bury, Southend U, Mansfield T, Wimbledon
1980–81 Sheffield U, Colchester U, Blackpool, Hull C
1981–82 Wimbledon, Swindon T, Bristol C, Chester
1982–83 Reading, Wrexham, Doncaster R, Chesterfield
1983–84 Scunthorpe U, Southend U, Port Vale, Exeter C
1984–85 Burnley, Orient, Preston NE, Cambridge U
1985–86 Lincoln C, Cardiff C, Wolverhampton W, Swansea C
1986–87 Bolton W**, Carlisle U, Darlington, Newport Co
1987–88 Doncaster R, York C, Grimbsy T, Rotherham U**
1988–89 Southend U, Chesterfield, Gillingham, Aldershot
1989–90 Cardiff C, Northampton T, Blackpool, Walsall
1990–91 Crewe Alex, Rotherham U, Mansfield T

APPLICATION FOR RE-ELECTION TO THIRD DIVISION UNTIL 1957—58

Seven: Walsall.
Six: Exeter C, Halifax T, Newport Co.
Five: Accrington S, Barrow, Gillingham, New Brighton, Southport.
Four: Rochdale, Norwich C.
Three: Crystal Palace, Crewe Alex, Darlington, Hartlepools U, Merthyr T, Swindon T.
Two: Aberdare Ath, Aldershot, Ashington, Bournemouth, Brentford, Chester, Colchester U, Durham C, Millwall, Nelson, QPR, Rotherham U, Southend U, Tranmere R, Watford, Workington.
One: Bradford C, Bradford PA, Brighton, Bristol R, Cardiff C, Carlisle U, Charlton Ath, Gateshead, Grimsby T, Mansfield T, Shrewsbury T, Torquay U, York C.

APPLICATIONS FOR RE-ELECTION FOURTH DIVISION UNTIL 1985–86

Eleven: Hartlepool U.
Seven: Crewe Alex.
Six: Barrow (lost League place to Hereford U 1972), Halifax T, Rochdale, Southport (lost League place to Wigan Ath 1978), York C.
Five: Chester C, Darlington, Lincoln C, Stockport Co, Workington (lost League place to Wimbledon 1977).
Four: Bradford PA (lost League place to Cambridge U 1970), Newport Co, Northampton T.
Three: Doncaster R, Hereford U.
Two: Bradford C, Exeter C, Oldham Ath, Scunthorpe U, Torquay U.
One: Aldershot, Colchester U, Gateshead (lost League place to Peterborough U 1960), Grimsby T, Swansea C, Tranmere R, Wrexham, Blackpool, Cambridge U, Preston NE.
Accrington S resigned and Oxford U were elected 1962.
Port Vale were forced to re-apply following expulsion in 1968.

Gateshead not re-elected, their place being taken by Peterborough in the 1960–1 season.
Accrington resigned March 1962, and Oxford U elected to replace them in 1962–3 season.
Bradford not re-elected, their place being taken by Cambridge U in the 1970–1 season.
Barrow not re-elected, their place being taken by Hereford U in tyhe 1972–3 season.
Workington not re-elected, their place being taken by Wimbledon in the 1977–8 season.
Southport not re-elected, their place being taken by Wigan in the 1978–9 season.

LEAGUE STATUS FROM 1986–87
1986–87 *Relegated:* Lincoln C *Promoted:* Scarborough
1987–88 *Relegated:* Newport Co *Promoted:* Lincoln C
1988–89 *Relegated:* Darlington *Promoted:* Maidstone U
1989–90 *Relegated:* Colchester U *Promoted:* Darlington
1990–91 *Relegated:* (no club) *Promoted:* Barnet

LEAGUE ATTENDANCES SINCE 1946–47

Season	*Matches*	*Total*	*Season*	*Matches*	*Total*
1946–47	1848	35,604,606	1968–69	2028	29,382,172
1947–48	1848	40,259,130	1969–70	2028	29,600,972
1948–49	1848	41,271,414	1970–71	2028	28,194,146
1949–50	1848	40,517,865	1971–72	2028	28,700,729
1950–51	2028	39,584,967	1972–73	2028	25,448,642
1951–52	2028	39,015,866	1973–74	2027	24,982,203
1952–53	2028	37,149,966	1974–75	2028	25,577,977
1953–54	2028	36,174,590	1975–76	2028	24,896,053
1954–55	2028	34,133,103	1976–77	2028	26,182,800
1955–56	2028	33,150,809	1977–78	2028	25,392,872
1956–57	2028	32,744,405	1978–79	2028	24,540,627
1957–58	2028	33,562,208	1979–80	2028	24,623,975
1958–59	2028	33,610,985	1980–81	2028	21,907,569
1959–60	2028	32,538,611	1981–82	2028	20,006,961
1960–61	2028	28,619,754	1982–83	2028	18,766,158
1961–62	2015	27,979,902	1983–84	2028	18,358,631
1962–63	2028	28,885,852	1984–85	2028	17,849,835
1963–64	2028	28,535,022	1985–86	2028	16,[illegible]
1964–65	2028	27,641,168	1986–87	2028	17,379,218
1965–66	2028	27,206,980	1987–88	2030	17,959,732
1966–67	2028	28,902,596	1988–89	2036	18,464,192
1967–68	2028	30,107,298	1989–90	2036	19,445,442
			1990–91	2036	19,508,202

This is the first time since the war that attendances have risen for five consecutive seasons.

	TOTAL ATTENDANCES	AVERAGE ATTENDANCES
DIVISION 1	8,618,709	22,680
DIVISION 2	6,285,068	11,385
DIVISION 3	2,835,759	5,137
DIVISION 4	1,768,666	3,204
TOTAL	19,508,202	9,581

BARCLAYS LEAGUE ATTENDANCES 1990–91

DIVISION ONE STATISTICS

	Average gate			*Season 1990/91*	
	1989/90	*1990/91*	*+/−%*	*Highest*	*Lowest*
Arsenal	33,713	36,864	+9.3	42,395	25,558
Aston Villa	25,544	25,663	+0.5	40,026	16,697
Chelsea	21,531	20,738	−3.7	33,478	9416
Coventry City	14,312	13,794	−3.6	22,549	8875
Crystal Palace	17,105	19,660	+14.9	28,131	14,439
Derby County	17,426	16,257	−6.7	31,115	11,680
Everton	26,280	25,028	−4.8	39,808	14,630
Leeds United	28,210	29,312	+3.9	33,699	25,802
Liverpool	36,589	36,038	−1.5	38,463	31,063
Luton Town	9886	10,325	+4.4	12,889	8219
Manchester City	27,975	27,874	−0.36	39,194	20,404
Manchester United	39,077	43,218	+10.6	47,485	32,776
Norwich City	16,737	15,468	−7.6	21,274	11,550
Nottingham Forest	20,606	22,137	+7.4	27,347	16,221
Queens Park Rangers	13,218	13,524	+2.3	21,405	9510
Sheffield United	16,989	21,461	+26.3	27,570	16,887
Southampton	16,463	15,413	−6.4	20,355	13,538
Sunderland	17,728	22,577	+27.4	31,133	17,899
Tottenham Hotspur	26,588	30,632	+15.2	35,003	21,675
Wimbledon	7756	7631	−1.6	13,776	3981

DIVISION TWO STATISTICS

	Average gate			*Season 1990/91*	
	1989/90	*1990/91*	+/−%	*Highest*	*Lowest*
Barnsley	9033	8937	−1.1	23,079	4921
Blackburn Rovers	9624	8126	−15.6	13,437	5969
Brighton & Hove A	8679	8386	−3.4	12,281	5354
Bristol City	11,544	13,495	+16.9	22,269	9346
Bristol Rovers	6202	5929	−4.4	7932	4563
Charlton Athletic	10,748	6548	−39.1	16,086	4455
Hull City	6518	6165	−5.4	10,907	3175
Ipswich Town	12,913	11,772	−8.8	20,451	7570
Leicester City	11,716	11,546	−1.5	19,011	8167
Middlesbrough	16,269	17,023	+4.6	22,869	13,844
Millwall	12,413	10,838	−12.7	20,598	6686
Newcastle United	21,590	16,835	−22.0	25,440	9628
Notts County	6151	8164	+32.7	12,835	5086
Oldham Athletic	9727	13,247	+36.2	18,809	11,296
Oxford United	5820	5780	−0.7	8474	4295
Plymouth Argyle	8749	6851	−21.7	11,490	5039
Portsmouth	8959	9689	+8.1	14,574	6902
Port Vale	8978	8092	−9.9	13,317	5820
Sheffield Wednesday	20,930	26,605	+27.1	34,845	20,431
Swindon Town	9394	9805	+4.4	14,093	7394
Watford	10,353	9576	−7.5	17,172	6361
West Bromwich Albion	11,308	11,993	+6.1	28,310	7657
West Ham United	20,311	22,551	+11.0	26,551	18,125
Wolverhampton Wanderers	17,045	15,837	−7.1	22,982	9313

DIVISION THREE STATISTICS

	Average gate			*Season 1990/91*	
	1989/90	*1990/91*	*+/−%*	*Highest*	*Lowest*
AFC Bournemouth	7454	6017	−19.3	7421	4662
Birmingham City	8558	7030	−17.9	10,123	4734
Bolton Wanderers	7286	7277	−0.1	12,826	3631
Bradford City	8777	6644	−24.3	9569	4776
Brentford	5662	6144	+8.5	8021	4812
Bury	3450	3572	+3.5	6318	2135
Cambridge United	3359	5503	+63.8	9023	3632
Chester City	2506	1564	−37.6	3759	631
Crewe Alexandra	4008	3748	−6.5	7195	2590
Exeter City	4859	4243	−12.7	6145	2763
Fulham	4484	4057	−9.5	6765	2750
Grimsby Town	5984	7237	+20.9	14,225	5162
Huddersfield Town	5630	5351	−5.0	9697	4052
Leyton Orient	4365	4194	−3.9	6369	2613
Mansfield Town	3129	2683	−14.3	4047	1919
Preston North End	6313	5214	−17.4	9845	3246
Reading	4060	4079	+0.5	6562	1934
Rotherham United	5612	4600	−18.0	8240	3190
Shrewsbury Town	3521	3442	−2.2	6210	2227
Southend United	3836	6174	+60.9	10,665	2982
Stoke City	12,449	11,565	−7.1	16,135	6994
Swansea City	4223	3665	−13.2	5938	2126
Tranmere Rovers	7449	6740	−9.5	11,079	4691
Wigan Athletic	2758	2889	+4.7	4726	1972

DIVISION FOUR STATISTICS

	Average gate			*Season 1990/91*	
	1989/90	*1990/91*	*+/−%*	*Highest*	*Lowest*
Aldershot	2022	2091	+3.4	3289	1398
Blackpool	4075	4059	−0.4	8590	2065
Burnley	6222	7882	+26.7	18,395	4723
Cardiff City	3642	2946	−19.1	4805	1629
Carlisle United	4740	3006	−36.6	5250	1762
Chesterfield	4181	3712	−11.2	8837	2222
Darlington	3588	4021	+12.1	9160	2882
Doncaster Rovers	2706	2831	+4.6	4244	1642
Gillingham	3887	3523	−9.4	8004	2319
Halifax Town	1895	1699	−10.3	4755	1002
Hartlepool United	2503	3180	+27.0	6957	1916
Hereford United	2676	2599	−2.9	5782	1438
Lincoln City	4071	2967	−27.1	5524	1974
Maidstone United	2427	1854	−23.6	3130	1020
Northampton Town	3187	3710	+16.4	5549	2544
Peterborough United	4804	5211	+8.5	8362	3082
Rochdale	2027	2238	+10.4	7344	1166
Scarborough	2325	1598	−31.3	2408	625
Scunthorpe United	3524	3114	−11.6	5769	2220
Stockport County	3899	3562	−8.6	6212	2569
Torquay United	2147	2986	+39.1	4337	2223
Walsall	4077	4149	+1.8	8051	2575
Wrexham	2368	1885	−20.4	3997	1029
York City	2615	2516	−3.8	4407	1490

TRANSFER TRAIL 1990–91
involving First Division Clubs
(*from May 1990 to May 1991*)

	From	*To*
May 1990		
25 Thompstone, Ian P.	Manchester City	Oldham Athletic
Temporary Transfers		
25 McKinnon, Robert	Hartlepool United	Manchester United
25 Short, Christian M.	Scarborough	Manchester United
June 1990		
7 Barton, Warren	Maidstone United	Wimbledon
5 Clarke, Colin J.	Queens Park Rangers	Portsmouth
27 Francis, Lee C.	Arsenal	Chesterfield
21 Hindmarch, Robert	Derby County	Wolverhampton Wanderers
18 Humphrey, John	Charlton Athletic	Crystal Palace
20 Irwin, Denis J.	Oldham Athletic	Manchester United
14 Lukic, Jovan	Arsenal	Leeds United
28 Stowell, Michael	Everton	Wolverhampton Wanderers
July 1990		
16 Ball, Kevin A.	Portsmouth	Sunderland
10 Beesley, Paul	Leyton Orient	Sheffield United
30 Benstead, Graham M.	Sheffield United	Brentford
18 Blades, Paul A.	Derby County	Norwich City
25 Brennan, Mark R.	Middlesbrough	Manchester City
27 Burke, David I.	Crystal Palace	Bolton Wanderers
20 Coton, Anthony P.	Watford	Manchester City
19 Davenport, Peter	Middlesbrough	Sunderland
30 Edinburgh, Justin C.	Southend United	Tottenham
10 Hayes, Martin	Arsenal	Celtic
12 Heathcote, Michael	Sunderland	Shrewsbury Town
5 Hendrie, John G.	Leeds United	Middlesbrough
31 Hendry, John	Dundee	Tottenham
17 Hinchcliffe, Andrew, G.	Manchester City	Everton
16 Hodges, Glyn P.	Watford	Crystal Palace
4 Hoyland, Jamie W.	Bury	Sheffield United
4 Linighan, Andrew	Norwich City	Arsenal
2 McAllister, Gary	Leicester City	Leeds United
27 Pemberton, John M.	Crystal Palace	Sheffield United
17 Pointon, Neil	Everton	Manchester City
24 Polston, John D.	Tottenham	Norwich City
5 Townsend, Andrew D.	Norwich City	Chelsea
4 Wilson, Clive	Chelsea	Queens Park Rangers
3 Wise, Dennis F.	Wimbledon	Chelsea
17 Woodthorpe, Colin	Chester City	Norwich City
August 1990		
10 Blake, Mark C.	Southampton	Shrewsbury Town
22 Clarke, Martin J.	Nottingham Forest	Mansfield Town
13 Cooper, Paul D	Manchester City	Stockport County

	From	To
23 Currie, David N.	Nottingham Forest	Oldham Athletic
20 Elkins, Gary	Fulham	Wimbledon
10 Kite, Philip D.	AFC Bournemouth	Sheffield United
24 Milligan, Michael	Oldham Athletic	Everton
1 O'Dowd, Anthony T.	Shelbourne	Leeds United
30 Powell, Christopher G.	Crystal Palace	Southend United
10 Thomas, Michael R.	Leeds United	Stoke City
3 West, Colin W.	Chelsea	Dundee
8 Wilson, Daniel J.	Luton Town	Sheffield Wednesday
15 Young, Eric	Wimbledon	Crystal Palace

Temporary Transfers

24 Dearden, Kevin C.	Tottenham	Peterborough United
17 Edwards, Neil R.	Leeds United	Huddersfield Town
23 Howells, Gareth	Tottenham	Torquay United
1 Parks, Anthony	Brentford	Queens Park Rangers
23 Scully, Patrick	Arsenal	Northampton Town
21 Sheffield, Jon	Norwich City	Aldershot
31 Walker, Ian M.	Tottenham	Oxford United
30 Watson, Alexander F.	Liverpool	Derby County
16 Webster, Simon P.	Sheffield United	Charlton Athletic
23 Wright, Mark A.	Everton	Blackpool

September 1990

28 Butters, Guy	Tottenham	Portsmouth
24 Howells, Gareth J.	Tottenham	Torquay United
13 Jones, Vincent	Leeds United	Sheffield United
21 Marwood, Brian	Arsenal	Sheffield United
14 Rammell, Andrew V.	Manchester United	Barnsley
24 Seagraves, Mark	Manchester City	Bolton Wanderers
13 Webster, Simon P.	Sheffield United	Charlton Athletic

Temporary Transfers

27 Callaghan, Nigel	Aston Villa	Derby County
18 Carr, Darren J.	Sheffield United	Crewe Alexandra
13 Cash, Stewart P.	Nottingham Forest	Brentford
27 Doyle, Maurice	Queens Park Rangers	Wolverhampton Wanderers
29 Dyer, Alexander C.	Crystal Palace	Charlton Athletic
27 Gibson, Colin J.	Manchester United	Port Vale
21 Hooper, Michael D.	Liverpool	Leicester City
6 Lemon, Paul A.	Sunderland	Chesterfield
27 McDonald, David H.	Tottenham	Gillingham
16 MacPhail, John	Sunderland	Hartlepool United
21 Muggleton, Carl D.	Leicester City	Liverpool
6 Powell, Gary	Everton	Lincoln City
10 Stancliffe, Paul I.	Sheffield United	Rotherham United
6 Starbuck, Philip M.	Nottingham Forest	Blackburn Rovers
28 Tanner, Nicholas	Liverpool	Swindon Town

October 1990

12 Breacker, Tim S.	Luton Town	West Ham United
18 Cousins, Anthony J.	Dundalk	Liverpool
3 Lee, Samuel	Southampton	Bolton Wanderers
3 Magilton, James	Liverpool	Oxford United

	From	To
Temporary Transfers		
31 Ampadu, Kwame	Arsenal	Plymouth Argyle
11 Beglin, James M.	Leeds United	Blackburn Rovers
17 Clarke, Wayne	Manchester City	Shrewsbury Town
8 Dearden, Kevin C.	Peterborough United	Tottenham (Tr. Back)
12 Dibble, Andrew G.	Manchester City	Aberdeen
25 Fenwick, Terence W.	Tottenham	Leicester City
19 Flower, John G.	Sheffield United	Aldershot
4 Gabbiadini, Ricardo	Sunderland	Crewe Alexandra
18 Kelly, Mark	Portsmouth	Tottenham
22 McGuinness, Paul E.	Manchester United	Brighton & Hove Albion
5 Pollitt, Michael F.	Manchester United	Oldham Athletic
12 Wilder, Christopher J.	Sheffield United	Charlton Athletic
November 1990		
16 Butcher, Terry I.	Rangers	Coventry City
30 Dyer, Alexander C.	Crystal Palace	Charlton Athletic
21 Gayle, John	Wimbledon	Birmingham City
27 Hutchison, Donald	Hartlepool United	Liverpool
8 Lemon, Paul A.	Sunderland	Chesterfield
15 Roberts, Graham P.	Chelsea	West Bromwich Albion
Temporary Transfers		
21 Agboola, Rueben	Sunderland	Port Vale
20 Brazil, Derek M.	Manchester United	Oldham Athletic
28 Caesar, Gus C.	Arsenal	Queens Park Rangers
15 Gallacher, Bernard	Aston Villa	Blackburn Rovers
22 Gaynor, Tommy	Nottingham Forest	Newcastle United
8 Gray, Philip	Tottenham	Fulham
1 Hughton, Christopher W. G.	Tottenham	West Ham United
22 Powell, Gary	Everton	Scunthorpe United
8 Stancliffe, Paul I.	Sheffield United	Wolverhampton Wanderers
16 Walker, Ian M.	Tottenham	Ipswich Town
1 Ward, Mitchum D.	Sheffield United	Crewe Alexandra
9 Whitehurst, William	Sheffield United	Stoke City
1 Wilson, David G.	Manchester United	Lincoln City
December 1990		
20 Carr, Darren	Sheffield United	Crewe Alexandra
21 Gibson, Colin J.	Manchester United	Leicester City
13 McLoughlin, Alan F.	Swindon Town	Southampton
13 MacPhail, John	Sunderland	Hartlepool United
31 Mimms, Robert A.	Tottenham	Blackburn Rovers
22 Peacock, Darren	Hereford United	Queens Park Rangers
17 Stancliffe, Paul I.	Sheffield United	Wolverhampton Wanderers
21 Tillson, Andrew	Grimsby Town	Queens Park Rangers
Temporary Transfers		
18 Ampadu, Kwame	Plymouth Argyle	Arsenal (Tr. Back)
4 Clarke, Wayne	Shrewsbury Town	Manchester City (Tr. Back)
7 Gray, Philip	Fulham	Tottenham (Tr. Back)

	From	To
21 Hill, Andrew R.	Bury	Manchester City
28 Hitchcock, Kevin	Chelsea	Northampton Town
17 Hooper, Michael D.	Leicester City	Liverpool (Tr. Back)
5 McAllister, Brian	Wimbledon	Plymouth Argyle
17 Muggleton, Carl D.	Liverpool	Leicester City (Tr. Back)
27 Smith, Mark	Nottingham Forest	Reading
28 Walker, Ian M.	Ipswich Town	Tottenham (Tr. Back)
20 Waugh, Keith	Coventry City	Watford

January 1991

10 Anderson, Vivian A.	Manchester United	Sheffield Wednesday
10 Carter, James W. C.	Millwall	Liverpool
17 Dobson, Anthony J.	Coventry City	Blackburn Rovers
19 Flower, Johannes G.	Sheffield United	Aldershot
4 Hughton, Christopher	Tottenham Hotspur	West Ham United
17 Livingstone, Stephen	Coventry City	Blackburn Rovers
15 Redknapp, Jamie F.	AFC Bournemouth	Liverpool
10 Rostron, John W.	Sheffield United	Brentford
18 Watson, Alexander F.	Liverpool	AFC Bournemouth
30 Woods, Raymond G.	Wigan Athletic	Coventry City

Temporary Transfers

17 Blake, Mark A.	Aston Villa	Wolverhampton Wanderers
17 Carey, Brian P.	Manchester United	Wrexham
29 Cullen, Anthony	Sunderland	Rotherham United
10 Dearden, Kevin C.	Tottenham Hotspur	Hull City
17 Doyle, Maurice	Queens Park Rangers	Crewe Alexandra
3 Edwards, Neil R.	Leeds United	Huddersfield Town
9 Gray, Martin D.	Sunderland	Aldershot
3 Heaney, Neil A.	Arsenal	Hartlepool United
17 Hodges, Glynn P.	Crystal Palace	Sheffield United
31 Jones, Philip A.	Everton	Wigan Athletic
3 McAllister, Brian	Wimbledon	Plymouth Argyle
8 Mitchell, David S.	Chelsea	Newcastle United
16 Morrow, Stephen J.	Arsenal	Reading
25 O'Dowd, Anthony T.	Leeds United	Kilkerry City
10 Reed, John P.	Sheffield United	Scarborough
8 Scully, Patrick J.	Arsenal	Southend United
10 Ward, Ashley S.	Manchester City	Wrexham
31 Wood, Paul A.	Sheffield United	AFC Bournemouth

February 1991

14 Barrick, Dean	Sheffield United	Rotherham United
1 Birch, Paul	Aston Villa	Wolverhampton Wanderers
15 Brevett, Rufus E.	Doncaster Rovers	Queens Park Rangers
12 Cox, Neil J.	Scunthorpe United	Aston Villa
21 Francis, Kevin	Derby County	Stockport County
13 Hall, Richard A.	Scunthorpe United	Southampton
7 Mooney, Brian J.	Preston North End	Sunderland
1 Speedie, David R.	Coventry City	Liverpool

Temporary Transfers

6 Carstairs, James W.	Arsenal	Brentford
20 Dibble, Andrew G.	Manchester City	Middlesbrough

	From	To
25 Gray, Martin D.	Aldershot	Sunderland (Tr. Back)
2 Jacobs, Giles W.	Chelsea	Aldershot
14 Moran, Paul	Tottenham Hotspur	Newcastle United
28 Pates, Colin	Arsenal	Brighton & Hove Albion
1 Rice, Brian	Nottingham Forest	Stoke City
1 Sutton, Stephen J.	Nottingham Forest	Coventry City
22 Whitehurst, William	Sheffield United	Doncaster Rovers

March 1991

20 Bodin, Paul	Swindon Town	Crystal Palace
9 Bullimore, Wayne A.	Manchester United	Barnsley
22 Dowie, Iain	Luton Town	West Ham United
28 Gittens, Jon	Swindon Town	Southampton
28 Goodyear, Clive	Wimbledon	Brentford
22 Hill, Andrew	Bury	Manchester City
6 Jones, Philip A.	Everton	Wigan Athletic
29 Mahood, Alan S.	Greenock Morton	Nottingham Forest
8 Nicholas, Peter	Chelsea	Watford
8 Penrice, Gary K.	Watford	Aston Villa
27 Rosario, Robert M.	Norwich City	Coventry City
14 Rowland, Andrew N.	Southampton	Torquay United
22 Sansom, Kenneth G.	Queens Park Rangers	Coventry City
28 Scully, Patrick J.	Arsenal	Southend United
21 Whitehurst, William	Sheffield United	Doncaster Rovers

Temporary Transfers

28 Ampadu, Kwame	Arsenal	West Bromwich Albion
14 Beckford, Jason	Manchester City	Blackburn Rovers
22 Brightwell, David	Manchester City	Chester City
18 Butler, Lee S.	Aston Villa	Hull City
9 Callaghan, Nigel	Aston Villa	Watford
11 Carr, Franz	Nottingham Forest	West Ham United
7 Clarke, Wayne	Manchester City	Stoke City
28 Davis, Stephen M.	Southampton	Notts County
28 Day, Mervyn	Leeds United	Coventry City
7 Duffield, Peter	Sheffield United	Rotherham United
28 Edwards, Mathew	Tottenham Hotspur	Reading
26 Houghton, Scott A.	Tottenham Hotspur	Ipswich Town
27 Jackson, Mathew	Luton Town	Preston North End
20 Leighton, James	Manchester United	Arsenal
14 Lyne, Neil G. F.	Nottingham Forest	Shrewsbury Town
28 MacDonald, Kevin	Coventry City	Cardiff City
21 Moran, Paul	Tottenham Hotspur	Southend United
28 O'Reilly, Gary M.	Crystal Palace	Birmingham City
28 Pearson, John S.	Leeds United	Rotherham United
10 Powell, Gary	Everton	Wigan Athletic
27 Quinlan, Philip E.	Everton	Huddersfield Town
28 Rideout, Paul	Southampton	Swindon Town
7 Robson, Stewart I.	West Ham United	Coventry City
26 Sayer, Andrew C.	Leyton Orient	Sheffield United
18 Sheffield, Johnathan	Norwich City	Cambridge United
28 Sheron, Michael	Manchester City	Bury
21 Smith, Mark A.	Nottingham Forest	Mansfield Town
28 Statham, Brian	Tottenham Hotspur	Reading
28 Taylor, Robert	Norwich City	Leyton Orient

	From	To
14 Todd, Mark K.	Sheffield United	Wolverhampton Wanderers
28 Williams, Paul L.	Sunderland	Swansea City
28 Wilson, David G.	Manchester United	Charlton Athletic
21 Wright, Mark A.	Everton	Huddersfield Town
April 1991		
16 Hodges, Glyn P	Crystal Palace	Sheffield United
Temporary Transfers		
4 Butler, Lee S	Hull City	Aston Villa (Tr. Back)
15 McIntosh, Martin	St Mirren	Sheffield United
May 1991		
30 Tiler, Carl	Barnsley	Nottingham Forest
Temporary Transfers		
15 Dryden, Richard A	Exeter City	Manchester City

FA CUP REVIEW

Tottenham Hotspur deservedly won the FA Cup at Wembley beating Nottingham Forest 2-1 after extra time. It was a match of some controversy. Within the first quarter-of-an-hour, Paul Gascoigne had committed two fouls, escaped a booking and been carried off the field with injury as a result of his second indiscretion.

Stuart Pearce took full advantage of the free-kick from the second offence to put Forest ahead, but this was achieved only because the wall was pulled apart before the moment of impact.

Yet with seemingly everything in their favour, Forest – one of the few truly attractive and entertaining teams in the First Division – failed to capitalize on the departure of the man who was largely responsible for Spurs reaching the final at all.

Indeed the result was the exact opposite. Spurs, who brought on Nayim, then took control of the game. They equalised in the 54th minute through the industrious Paul Stewart and took the lead in the 94th minute when Des Walker put through his own goal under pressure, for what proved to be the winning goal at 2-1.

It ended a season of some drama at White Hart Lane where off-the-field financial problems clearly had their effect on on-field events. Spurs had started their FA Cup programme with a 1-0 win at Blackpool, courtesy of Stewart who had embarked upon his professional career at Bloomfield Road.

The following day Nottingham Forest were involved in a goalless draw at Crystal Palace which was covered by the TV cameras. The replay also ended all square at 2-2 before Forest made more certain of matters in the third attempt when they won 3-0.

Gascoigne was on the mark twice in the 4-2 fourth round win over Oxford while Forest were again involved in a drawn affair, this time 2-2 at Newcastle United. Again Brian Clough's team won the replay by three clear goals. Again Gascoigne pulled Spurs out of trouble at Portsmouth in the fifth round, scoring twice late on for a 2-1 win. But for Forest yet another game had to be added to their programme following a 1-1 draw at Southampton. They won the replay 3-1.

In the sixth round, Forest won 1-0 at Norwich and that man Gascoigne rescued Spurs at the expense of Notts County with an 83rd minute winner at 2-1. Again both semi-finals were televised. Contrary to previous practice, one of the ties was staged at Wembley itself. Here Spurs beat Arsenal 3-1, while at Villa Park Forest beat ten man West Ham United 4-0 after Tony Gale was controversially dismissed for an alleged professional foul.

FA CUP 1990–91

FIRST ROUND

Aldershot (3) 6 Tiverton T (1) 2
Atherstone (1) 3 Fleetwood (0) 1
Aylesbury (0) 0 Walsall (1) 1
Barnet (2) 2 Chelmsford C (0) 2
Birmingham C (0) 1 Cheltenham T (0) 0
Bishop Auckland (0) 0 Barrow (0) 1
Blackpool (0) 2 Grimsby T (0) 0
Boston U (1) 1 Wycombe W (1) 1
Bournemouth (1) 2 Gillingham (0) 1
Bradford C (0) 0 Shrewsbury T (0) 0
Brentford (3) 5 Yeovil (0) 0
Cardiff C (0) 0 Hayes (0) 0
Chester C (1) 2 Doncaster R (0) 2
Chesterfield (3) 3 Spennymoor (1) 2
Chorley (2) 2 Bury (0) 1
Colchester U (0) 2 Reading (1) 1
Darlington (0) 1 York C (1) 1
Exeter C (0) 1 Cambridge U (1) 2
Fulham (1) 2 Farnborough (0) 1
Halesowen (1) 1 Tranmere R (1) 2
Halifax T (1) 3 Wrexham (1) 2
Hereford U (1) 1 Peterborough U (1) 1
Leyton Orient (0) 3 Southend U (0) 2
Lincoln C (1) 1 Crewe Alex (1) 4
Littlehampton (0) 0 Northampton T (2) 4
Maidstone U (2) 4 Torquay U (1) 1
Merthyr Tydfil (0) 1 Sutton U (0) 1
Preston NE (0) 0 Mansfield T (1) 1
Rochdale (0) 1 Scunthorpe U (0) 1
Rotherham U (0) 1 Stockport Co (0) 0
Runcorn (0) 0 Hartlepool U (1) 3
Scarborough (0) 0 Leek T (1) 2
Stafford R (0) 1 Burnley (3) 3
Swansea C (1) 5 Welling (2) 2
Tamworth (1) 4 Whitley Bay (2) 6
Telford U (0) 0 Stoke C (0) 0
Wigan Ath (3) 5 Carlisle U (0) 0
Witton A (0) 1 Bolton W (1) 2
Woking (0) 0 Kidderminster H (0) 0
Altrincham (1) 1 Huddersfield T (2) 2

FIRST ROUND REPLAYS

York C (1) 1 Darlington (0) 0
Doncaster R (0) 1 Chester C (0) 2
Peterborough U (2) 2 Hereford U (0) 1

Scunthorpe U (0) 2 Rochdale (1) 1 *aet*
Chelmsford C (0) 0 Barnet (0) 2
Hayes (0) 1 Cardiff C (0) 0
Kidderminster H (0) 1 Woking (0) 1 *aet*
Shrewsbury T (0) 2 Bradford C (1) 1
Stoke C (1) 1 Telford U (0) 0
Sutton U (0) 0 Merthyr Tydfil (1) 1
Wycombe W (1) 4 Boston U (0) 0

FIRST ROUND SECOND REPLAY
Kidderminster H (1) 1 Woking (0) 2

SECOND ROUND
Fulham (0) 0 Cambridge U (0) 0
Aldershot (1) 2 Maidstone U (1) 1
Barnet (0) 0 Northampton T (0) 0
Bournemouth (0) 1 Hayes (0) 0
Scunthorpe U (2) 3 Tranmere R (1) 2
Swansea C (2) 2 Walsall (1) 1
Wigan Ath (1) 2 Hartlepool U (0) 0
Woking (2) 5 Merthyr Tydfil (0) 1
Huddersfield T (0) 0 Blackpool (0) 2
Chesterfield (1) 3 Bolton W (2) 4
Rotherham U (1) 1 Halifax T (0) 1
Shrewsbury T (1) 1 Chorley (0) 0

SECOND ROUND REPLAY
Cambridge U (1) 2 Fulham (1) 1

SECOND ROUND
Birmingham C (0) 1 Brentford (2) 3
Burnley (0) 2 Stoke C (0) 0
Colchester U (0) 0 Leyton Orient (0) 0
Crewe Alex (1) 1 Atherstone (0) 0
Leek T (0) 1 Chester C (1) 1
Whitley Bay (0) 0 Barrow (0) 1
Wycombe W (0) 1 Peterborough U (0) 1

SECOND ROUND REPLAY
Northampton T (0) 0 Barnet (0) 1

SECOND ROUND
Mansfield T (1) 2 York C (0) 1

SECOND ROUND REPLAYS
Chester C (2) 4 Leek T (0) 0
Halifax T (0) 1 Rotherham U (2) 2
Leyton Orient (2) 4 Colchester U (1) 1
Peterborough U (2) 2 Wycombe W (0) 0

THIRD ROUND
Aldershot (0) 0 West Ham U (0) 0*
Arsenal (2) 2 Sunderland (0) 1
Aston Villa (0) 1 Wimbledon (1) 1
Barnet (0) 0 Portsmouth (2) 5
Blackburn R (0) 1 Liverpool (0) 1
Blackpool (0) 0 Tottenham H (0) 1
Bolton W (0) 1 Barrow (0) 0
Brighton & HA (2) 3 Scunthorpe U (1) 2
Bristol R (0) 0 Crewe Alex (1) 2
Charlton Ath (1) 1 Everton (1) 2
Chelsea (0) 1 Oxford U (1) 3
Chester C (0) 2 Bournemouth (2) 3
Coventry C (0) 1 Wigan Ath (0) 1
Hull C (1) 2 Notts Co (3) 5
Leyton Orient (0) 1 Swindon T (1) 1
Mansfield T (0) 0 Sheffield W (1) 2
Middlesbrough (0) 0 Plymouth Arg (0) 0
Millwall (0) 2 Leicester C (1) 1
Newcastle U (0) 2 Derby Co (0) 0
Norwich C (1) 2 Bristol C (1) 1
Oldham Ath (1) 3 Brentford (1) 1
Port Vale (1) 2 Peterborough U (1) 1
Sheffield U (0) 1 Luton T (0) 3
Shrewsbury T (1) 4 Watford (0) 1
Southampton (2) 3 Ipswich T (1) 2
Swansea C (0) 0 Rotherham U (0) 0
WBA (1) 2 Woking (0) 4
Wolverhampton W (0) 0 Cambridge U (0) 1
Barnsley (0) 1 Leeds U (0) 1
Burnley (0) 0 Manchester C (0) 1
Crystal Palace (0) 0 Nottingham F (0) 0
Manchester U (1) 2 QPR (1) 1

THIRD ROUND REPLAYS
Liverpool (2) 3 Blackburn R (0) 0
Leeds U (2) 4 Barnsley (0) 0
Wigan Ath (0) 0 Coventry C (1) 1
Wimbledon (0) 1 Aston Villa (0) 0 *aet*
Plymouth Arg (1) 1 Middlesbrough (1) 2
West Ham U (4) 6 Aldershot (1) 1
Nottingham F (0) 2 Crystal Palace (1) 2 *aet*
Rotherham U (0) 4 Swansea C (0) 0
Swindon T (0) 1 Leyton Orient (0) 0

FOURTH ROUND
Cambridge U (0) 2 Middlesbrough (0) 0
Coventry C (1) 1 Southampton (0) 1

Crewe Alex (1) 1 Rotherham U (0) 0
Liverpool (0) 2 Brighton & HA (0) 2
Luton T (0) 1 West Ham U (1) 1
Manchester U (0) 1 Bolton W (0) 0
Millwall (2) 4 Sheffield W (2) 4
Norwich C (0) 3 Swindon T (0) 1
Notts Co (1) 2 Oldham Ath (0) 0
Portsmouth (1) 5 Bournemouth (0) 1
Port Vale (1) 1 Manchester C (1) 2
Shrewsbury T (1) 1 Wimbledon (0) 0
Tottenham H (2) 4 Oxford U (1) 2
Arsenal (0) 0 Leeds U (0) 0
Woking (0) 0 Everton (0) 1†

THIRD ROUND SECOND REPLAY
Nottingham F (0) 3 Crystal Palace (0) 0

FOURTH ROUND REPLAYS
Southampton (1) 2 Coventry C (0) 0
Brighton & HA (1) 2 Liverpool (1) 3 *aet*
Leeds U (0) 1 Arsenal (0) 1 *aet*
Sheffield W (1) 2 Millwall (0) 0
West Ham U (1) 5 Luton T (0) 0

FOURTH ROUND
Newcastle U (2) 2 Nottingham F (0) 2

FOURTH ROUND SECOND REPLAY
Arsenal (0) 0 Leeds U (0) 0 *aet*

FOURTH ROUND THIRD REPLAY
Leeds U (0) 1 Arsenal (2) 2

FIFTH ROUND
Cambridge U (1) 4 Sheffield W (0) 0
Notts Co (0) 1 Manchester C (0) 0
Portsmouth (1) 1 Tottenham H (0) 2
West Ham U (0) 1 Crewe Alex (0) 0
Liverpool (0) 0 Everton (0) 0

FOURTH ROUND REPLAY
Nottingham F (1) 3 Newcastle U (0) 0

FIFTH ROUND
Norwich C (1) 2 Manchester U (1) 1

FIFTH ROUND REPLAY
Everton (0) 4 Liverpool (1) 4 *aet*

FIFTH ROUND
Southampton (1) 1 Nottingham F (0) 1
Shrewsbury T (0) 0 Arsenal (0) 1

FIFTH ROUND SECOND REPLAY
Everton (1) 1 Liverpool (0) 0

FIFTH ROUND REPLAY
Nottingham F (1) 3 Southampton (1) 1

SIXTH ROUND
Arsenal (1) 2 Cambridge U (0) 1
Norwich C (0) 0 Nottingham F (0) 1
Tottenham H (0) 2 Notts Co (1) 1
West Ham U (1) 2 Everton (0) 1

SEMI FINALS
Arsenal (1) 1 Tottenham H (2) 3
Nottingham F (0) 4 West Ham U (0) 0

FINAL at Wembley
18 MAY
Nottingham F (1) 1 *(Peurce)*
Tottenham H (0) 2 *(Stewart, Walker (og))* aet, 80,000

* *Played at West Ham.* † *Played at Everton*

PAST FA CUP FINALS

Details of some goalscorers are not available for the early years

Year	Winner	Score	Runner-up	Score
1872	The Wanderers	1	Royal Engineers	0
	Betts			
1873	The Wanderers	2	Oxford University	0
	Kinnaird, Wollaston			
1874	Oxford University	2	Royal Engineers	0
	Mackarness, Patton			
1875	Royal Engineers	1	Old Etonians	1*
	Unknown		*Bonsor*	
	Royal Engineers	2	Old Etonians	0
	Scorers in replay: Renny-Tailyour, Stafford			
1876	The Wanderers	1	Old Etonians	1*
	Edwards		*Bonsor*	
	The Wanderers	3	Old Etonians	0
	Wollaston, Hughes 2			
1877	The Wanderers	2	Oxford University	1*
	Kenrick, Heron		*Kinnaird (og)*	
1878	The Wanderers	3	Royal Engineers	1
	Kenrick 2, unknown		*Unknown*	
1879	Old Etonians	1	Clapham Rovers	0
	Clerke			
1880	Clapham Rovers	1	Oxford University	0
	Lloyd-Jones			
1881	Old Carthusians	3	Old Etonians	0
	Page, Wynard, Tod			
1882	Old Etonians	1	Blackburn Rovers	0
	Anderson			
1883	Blackburn Olympic	2	Old Etonians	1*
	Costley, Mathews		*Goodhart*	
1884	Blackburn Rovers	2	Queen's Park, Glasgow	1
	Forrest, Brown		*Christie*	
1885	Blackburn Rovers	2	Queen's Park, Glasgow	0
	Forrest, Brown			
1886	Blackburn Rovers	0	West Bromwich Albion	0
	Blackburn Rovers	2	West Bromwich Albion	0
	Brown, Sowerbutts			
1887	Aston Villa	2	West Bromwich Albion	0
	Hunter, Hodgetts			
1888	West Bromwich Albion	2	Preston NE	1
	Woodall, Bayliss		*Goodall*	
1889	Preston NE	3	Wolverhampton W	0
	Ross, Dewhurst, Thomson			
1890	Blackburn Rovers	6	Sheffield W	1
	Dewar, Lofthouse *John Southworth, Townley 3*		*Bennett*	
1891	Blackburn Rovers	3	Notts Co	1
	Dewar, John Southworth, Townley		*Oswald*	
1892	West Bromwich Albion	3	Aston Villa	0
	Reynolds, Nicholls, Geddes			
1893	Wolverhampton W	1	Everton	0
	Allen			
1894	Notts Co	4	Bolton W	1
	Watson, Logan 3		*Cassidy*	

1895	Aston Villa	1	West Bromwich Albion	0
	Chatt			
1896	Sheffield W	2	Wolverhampton W	1
	Spiksley		*Black*	
1897	Aston Villa	3	Everton	2
	Crabtree, Campell, Weldon		*Boyle, Bell*	
1898	Nottingham F	3	Derby Co	1
	McPherson, Capes 2		*Bloomer*	
1899	Sheffield U	4	Derby Co	1
	Bennett, Beers, Almond, Priest		*Boag*	
1900	Bury	4	Southampton	0
	Wood, McLuckie 2, Plant			
1901	Tottenham H	2	Sheffield U	2
	Brown		*Bennett, Priest*	
	Tottenham H	3	Sheffield U	1
	Cameron, Smith, Brown		*Priest*	
1902	Sheffield U	1	Southampton	1
	Common		*Wood*	
	Sheffield U	2	Southampton	1
	Hedley, Barnes		*Brown*	
1903	Bury	6	Derby Co	0
	Wood, Sagar, Ross, Plant, Leeming 2			
1904	Manchester C	1	Bolton W	0
	Meredith			
1905	Aston Villa	2	Newcastle U	0
	Hampton			
1906	Everton	1	Newcastle U	0
	Young			
1907	Sheffield W	2	Everton	1
	Stewart, Simpson		*Sharp*	
1908	Wolverhampton W	3	Newcastle U	1
	Hunt, Harrison, Hedley		*Howie*	
1909	Manchester U	1	Bristol C	0
	A. Turnbull			
1910	Newcastle U	1	Barnsley	1
	Rutherford		*Tuffnell*	
	Newcastle U	2	Barnsley	0
	Shepherd (1 pen)			
1911	Bradford C	0	Newcastle U	0
	Bradford C	1	Newcastle U	0
	Spiers			
1912	Barnsley	0	West Bromwich Albion	0
	Barnsley	1	West Bromwich Albion	0*
	Tuffnell			
1913	Aston Villa	1	Sunderland	0
	Barber			
1914	Burnley	1	Liverpool	0
	Freeman			
1915	Sheffield U	3	Chelsea	0
	Simmons, Fazackerley, Kitchen			
1920	Aston Villa	1	Huddersfield T	0*
	Kirton			
1921	Tottenham H	1	Wolverhampton W	0
	Dimmock			
1922	Huddersfield T	1	Preston NE	0
	Smith (pen)			

1923 Bolton W 2 — West Ham U 0
Jack, J.R. Smith

1924 Newcastle U 2 — Aston Villa 0
Harris, Seymour

1925 Sheffield U 1 — Cardiff C 0
Tunstall

1926 Bolton W 1 — Manchester C 0
Jack

1927 Cardiff C 1 — Arsenal 0
Ferguson

1928 Blackburn Rovers 3 — Huddersfield T 1
Roscamp 2, McLean — *A. Jackson*

1929 Bolton W 2 — Portsmouth 0
Butler, Blackmore

1930 Arsenal 2 — Huddersfield T 0
Lambert, James

1931 West Bromwich Albion 2 — Birmingham C 1
W.G. Richardson — *Bradford*

1932 Newcastle U 2 — Arsenal 1
Allen — *John*

1933 Everton 3 — Manchester C 0
Dunn, Dean, Stein

1934 Manchester C 2 — Portsmouth 1
Tilson — *Rutherford*

1935 Sheffield W 4 — West Bromwich Albion 2
Hooper, Palethorpe, Rimmer 2 — *Sandford, Boyes*

1936 Arsenal 1 — Sheffield U 0
Drake

1937 Sunderland 3 — Preston NE 1
Carter, Gurney, Burbanks — *F. O'Donnell*

1938 Preston NE 1 — Huddersfield T 0*
Mutch (pen)

1939 Portsmouth 4 — Wolverhampton W 1
Anderson, Barlow, Parker 2 — *Dorsett*

1946 Derby Co 4 — Charlton Ath 1*
H. Turner (og), Stamps 2, Doherty — *H. Turner*

1947 Charlton Ath 1 — Burnley 0*
Duffy

1948 Manchester U 4 — Blackpool 2
Anderson, Rowley 2, Pearson — *Shimwell (pen), Mortensen*

1949 Wolverhampton W 3 — Leicester C 1
Smyth, Pye 2 — *Griffiths*

1950 Arsenal 2 — Liverpool 0
Lewis

1951 Newcastle U 2 — Blackpool 0
Milburn

1952 Newcastle U 1 — Arsenal 0
G. Robledo

1953 Blackpool 4 — Bolton W 3
Mortensen 3, Perry — *Bell, Moir, Lofthouse*

1954 West Bromwich Albion 3 — Preston NE 2
Griffin, Allen 2 — *Wayman, Morrison*

1955 Newcastle U 3 — Manchester C 1
Milburn, Hannah, Mitchell — *Johnstone*

Year	Winners		Runners-up	
1956	Manchester C	3	Birmingham C	1
	Johnstone, Hayes, Dyson		*Kinsey*	
1957	Aston Villa	2	Manchester U	1
	McParland		*T. Taylor*	
1958	Bolton W	2	Manchester U	0
	Lofthouse			
1959	Nottingham F	2	Luton T	1
	Dwight, Wilson		*Pacey*	
1960	Wolverhampton W	3	Blackburn Rovers	0
	Deeley 2, McGrath (og)			
1961	Tottenham H	2	Leicester C	0
	Smith, Dyson			
1962	Tottenham H	3	Burnley	1
	Blanchflower (pen), Smith, Greaves		*Robson*	
1963	Manchester U	3	Leicester C	1
	Herd 2, Law		*Keyworth*	
1964	West Ham U	3	Preston NE	2
	Boyce, Hurst, Sissons		*Dawson, Holden*	
1965	Liverpool	2	Leeds U	1*
	Hunt, St John		*Bremner*	
1966	Everton	3	Sheffield W	2
	Trebilcock 2, Temple		*McCalliog, Ford*	
1967	Tottenham H	2	Chelsea	1
	Robertson, Saul		*Tambling*	
1968	West Bromwich Albion	1	Everton	0*
	Astle			
1969	Manchester C	1	Leicester C	0
	Young			
1970	Chelsea	2	Leeds U	2*
	Houseman, Hutchinson		*Charlton, Jones*	
	Chelsea	2	Leeds U	1*
	Webb, Osgood		*Jones*	
1971	Arsenal	2	Liverpool	1*
	Kelly, George		*Heighway*	
1972	Leeds U	1	Arsenal	0
	Clarke			
1973	Sunderland	1	Leeds U	0
	Porterfield			
1974	Liverpool	3	Newcastle U	0
	Keegan 2, Heighway			
1975	West Ham U	2	Fulham	0
	A. Taylor			
1976	Southampton	1	Manchester U	0
	Stokes			
1977	Manchester U	2	Liverpool	1
	Pearson, J. Greenhoff		*Case*	
1978	Ipswich T	1	Arsenal	0
	Osborne			
1979	Arsenal	3	Manchester U	2
	Talbot, Stapleton, Sunderland		*McQueen, McIlroy*	
1980	West Ham U	1	Arsenal	0
	Brooking			
1981	Tottenham H	1	Manchester C	1*
	Hutchison (og)		*Hutchison*	
	Tottenham H	3	Manchester C	2
	Crooks, Villa 2		*Mackenzie, Reeves (pen)*	

Year	Winner		Runner-up	
1982	Tottenham H	1	QPR	1*
	Hoddle		*Fenwick*	
	Tottenham H	1	QPR	0
	Hoddle (pen)			
1983	Manchester U	2	Brighton & HA	2*
	Stapleton, Wilkins		*Smith, Stevens*	
	Manchester U	4	Brighton & HA	0
	Robson 2, Whiteside, Muhren (pen)			
1984	Everton	2	Watford	0
	Sharp, Gray			
1985	Manchester U	1	Everton	0
	Whiteside			
1986	Liverpool	3	Everton	1
	Rush 2, Johnston		*Lineker*	
1987	Coventry C	3	Tottenham H	2*
	Bennett, Houchen, Mabbutt (og)		*C. Allen, Kilcline (og)*	
1988	Wimbledon	1	Liverpool	0
	Sanchez			
1989	Liverpool	3	Everton	2
	Aldridge, Rush 2		*McCall 2*	
1990	Manchester U	3	Crystal Palace	3
	Robson, Hughes 2		*O'Reilly, Wright 2*	
	Manchester U	1	Crystal P	0
	Martin			
1991	Tottenham H	2	Nottingham F	1*
	Stewart, Walker (og)		*Pearce*	

**After extra-time*

FA CUP WINNERS SINCE 1871

Tottenham Hotspur	8
Aston Villa	7
Manchester United	7
Blackburn Rovers	6
Newcastle United	6
Arsenal	5
Wanderers	5
West Bromwich Albion	5
Bolton Wanderers	4
Everton	4
Liverpool	4
Manchester City	4
Sheffield United	4
Wolverhampton Wanderers	4
Sheffield Wednesday	3
West Ham United	3
Bury	2
Nottingham Forest	2
Old Etonians	2
Preston North End	2
Sunderland	2
Barnsley	1
Blackburn Olympic	1
Blackpool	1
Bradford City	1
Burnley	1
Cardiff City	1
Charlton Athletic	1
Chelsea	1
Clapham Rovers	1
Coventry City	1
Derby County	1
Huddersfield Town	1
Ipswich Town	1
Leeds United	1
Notts County	1
Old Carthusians	1
Oxford University	1
Portmouth	1
Royal Engineers	1
Southampton	1
Wimbledon	1

APPEARANCES IN FA CUP FINAL

Arsenal	11
Everton	11
Manchester United	11
Newcastle United	11
West Bromwich Albion	10
Aston Villa	9
Liverpool	9
Tottenham Hotspur	9
Blackburn Rovers	8
Manchester City	8
Wolverhampton Wanderers	8
Bolton Wanderers	7
Preston North End	7
Old Etonians	6
Sheffield United	6
Huddersfield Town	5
Sheffield Wednesday	5
Wanderers	5
Derby Country	4
Leeds United	4
Leicester City	4
Oxford University	4
Royal Engineers	4
West Ham United	4
Blackpool	3
Burnley	3
Chelsea	3
Nottingham Forest	3
Portsmouth	3
Southampton	3
Sunderland	3
Barnsley	2
Birmingham City	2
Bury	2
Cardiff City	2
Charlton Athletic	2
Clapham Rovers	2
Notts County	2
Queen's Park (Glasgow)	2
Blackburn Olympic	1
Bradford City	1
Brighton & Hove Albion	1
Bristol City	1
Coventry City	1
Crystal Palace	1
Fulham	1
Ipswich Town	1
Luton Town	1
Old Carthusians	1
Queen's Park Rangers	1
Watford	1
Wimbledon	1

RUMBELOWS CUP

Sheffield Wednesday won the Rumbelows Cup at Wembley beating Manchester United 1-0, their goal coming from a fine shot driven in by John Sheridan on the edge of the penalty area after 37 minutes. Their victory was well deserved as United were never able to show any real consistency throughout the game, while Wednesday always appeared to be the more balanced side.

United had been hoping to take the Rumbelows as the first part of a hoped for cup double, their other objective having been the European Cup-Winners' Cup. In the first round they had beaten Fourth Division Halifax Town. Their opponents were struggling to find goals in the League at the time but had negotiated the first round safely. They did manage to score at home when United won 3-1 and again at Old Trafford when they were beaten 2-1.

Sheffield Wednesday began none too surely against Third Division Brentford. They needed two second-half goals to overturn a deficit in the opening 45 minutes in the home leg, but repeated the scoreline at Griffin Park.

In the third round, Manchester United produced their traditionally distinguished performance when facing Liverpool. They won 3-1 in some style at Old Trafford while Wednesday were again showing signs of nerves in being held to a goalless draw by Swindon Town at Hillsborough. However, they did manage a 1-0 win in Wiltshire.

Having disposed of Liverpool in such convincing fashion, United then took on the might of Arsenal at Highbury in the fourth round. At the time Arsenal were unbeaten in 14 League games but were still trailing League leaders Liverpool. Clayton Blackmore put United ahead in the first minute and in a devastating spell just on the interval, Mark Hughes and Lee Sharpe added further goals to give them a 3-0 lead. Arsenal did respond with two goals but Sharpe completed his hat-trick and Danny Wallace made it 6-2.

Meanwhile Sheffield Wednesday were finding Derby County a handful at Hillsborough and had to settle for a 1-1 draw, before winning the replay 2-1. Then it was United's turn to be involved in a replay after drawing their fifth round tie 1-1 at Southampton. Then a Mark Hughes hat-trick helped beat the Saints 3-2. Wednesday won with a Nigel Pearson goal at Coventry City.

In the semi-final, Leeds gave United a difficult game at Old Trafford before losing 2-1 and Sharpe's last minute strike at Elland Road sealed the tie 3-1 on aggregate. Wednesday won well at Chelsea 2-0 and equally effectively 3-1 at home.

The final itself saw Ron Atkinson in charge of Wednesday, having previously in his career led Manchester United. But if there was disappointment for Alex Ferguson in this match, there was ample reward for him and his team elsewhere.

RUMBELOWS LEAGUE CUP 1990–91

FIRST ROUND FIRST LEG

Stockport Co (0) 0 Burnley (1) 2
Birmingham C (0) 0 Bournemouth (1) 1
Brentford (1) 2 Hereford U (0) 0
Carlisle U (1) 1 Scunthorpe U (0) 0
Chesterfield (0) 1 Hartlepool U (1) 2
Darlington (0) 0 Blackpool (0) 0
Doncaster R (2) 2 Rotherham U (3) 6
Fulham (1) 1 Peterborough U (1) 2
Gillingham (0) 1 Shrewsbury T (0) 0
Grimsby T (0) 2 Crewe Alex (1) 1
Halifax T (0) 2 Lincoln C (0) 0
Mansfield T (0) 1 Cardiff C (1) 1
Middlesbrough (1) 1 Tranmere R (0) 1
Preston NE (0) 2 Chester C (0) 0
Reading (0) 0 Oxford U (0) 1
Rochdale (2) 4 Scarborough (0) 0
Southend U (0) 2 Aldershot (1) 1
Walsall (1) 4 Cambridge U (0) 2
Wigan Ath (0) 0 Barnsley (0) 1
York C (0) 0 Wrexham (0) 1
Bradford C (2) 2 Bury (0) 0
Brighton & HA (0) 0 Northampton T (1) 2
Bristol R (0) 1 Torquay U (0) 2
Exeter C (0) 1 Notts Co (1) 1
Huddersfield T (0) 0 Bolton W (2) 3
Maidstone U (0) 2 Leyton Orient (1) 2
Stoke C (0) 0 Swansea C (0) 0
WBA (1) 2 Bristol C (1) 2

FIRST ROUND SECOND LEG

Tranmere R (0) 1 Middlesbrough (0) 2
Aldershot (0) 2 Southend U (2) 2
Barnsley (0) 0 Wigan Ath (1) 1
Blackpool (1) 1 Darlington (0) 1
Bolton W (1) 2 Huddersfield T (1) 1
Bournemouth (1) 1 Birmingham C (0) 1
Burnley (0) 0 Stockport Co (1) 1
Bury (0) 3 Bradford C (0) 2 *aet*
Cambridge U (2) 2 Walsall (0) 1
Cardiff C (1) 3 Mansfield T (0) 0
Chester C (2) 5 Preston NE (0) 1 *aet*
Crewe Alex* (1) 1 Grimsby T (0) 0
Leyton Orient (3) 4 Maidstone U (0) 1
Northampton T (0) 1 Brighton & HA (0) 1

Notts Co (1) 1 Exeter C (0) 0
Peterborough U (1) 2 Fulham (0) 0
Rotherham U (1) 2 Doncaster R (0) 1
Scunthorpe U (0) 1 Carlisle U (1) 1
Shrewsbury T (2) 2 Gillingham (0) 0
Swansea C (0) 0 Stoke C (0) 1
Torquay U (1) 1 Bristol R (0) 1
Wrexham (1) 2 York C (0) 0
Bristol C (0) 1 WBA (0) 0 *aet*
Hereford U (1) 1 Brentford (0) 0
Lincoln C (1) 1 Halifax T (0) 0
Oxford U (0) 2 Reading (0) 1
Scarborough (1) 3 Rochdale (1) 3
Hartlepool U (0) 2 Chesterfield (2) 2

SECOND ROUND FIRST LEG
Port Vale (0) 0 Oxford U (0) 2
Bournemouth (0) 0 Millwall (0) 0
Cardiff C (0) 1 Portsmouth (1) 1
Carlisle U (1) 1 Derby Co (0) 1
Chester C (0) 0 Arsenal (0) 1
Crystal Palace (2) 8 Southend U (0) 0
Darlington (0) 3 Swindon T (0) 0
Hull C (0) 0 Wolverhampton W (0) 0
Liverpool (2) 5 Crewe Alex (1) 1
Luton T (1) 1 Bradford C (0) 1
Middlesbrough (1) 2 Newcastle U (0) 0
Northampton T (0) 0 Sheffield U (0) 1
Notts Co (0) 1 Oldham Ath (0) 0
Plymouth Arg (0) 1 Wimbledon (0) 0
Rochdale (0) 0 Southampton (0) 5
Rotherham U (0) 1 Blackburn R (1) 1
Shrewsbury T (1) 1 Ipswich T (1) 1
Sunderland (0) 0 Bristol C (1) 1
Wrexham (0) 0 Everton (2) 5
Aston Villa (0) 1 Barnsley (0) 0
Charlton Ath (1) 2 Leyton Orient (2) 2
Coventry C (1) (4) Bolton W (1) 2
Halifax T (1) 1 Manchester U (1) 3
Leicester C (1) 1 Leeds U (0) 0
Norwich C (1) 2 Watford (0) 0
Nottingham F (1) 4 Burnley (0) 1
QPR (0) 3 Peterborough U (0) 1
Sheffield W (0) 2 Brentford (1) 1
Torquay U (0) 0 Manchester C (2) 4
Tottenham H (2) 5 Hartlepool U (0) 0
Walsall (0) 0 Chelsea (3) 5
West Ham U (1) 3 Stoke C (0) 0

SECOND ROUND SECOND LEG

Arsenal (3) 5 Chester C (0) 0
Barnsley (0) 0 Aston Villa (1) 1
Blackburn R (0) 1 Rotherham U (0) 0
Bolton W (1) 2 Coventry C (1) 3
Brentford (1) 1 Sheffield W (2) 2
Bristol C (1) 1 Sunderland (2) 6
Crewe Alex (0) 1 Liverpool (2) 4
Everton (3) 6 Wrexham (0) 0
Hartlepool U (0) 1 Tottenham H (1) 2
Ipswich T (2) 3 Shrewsbury T (0) 0
Leyton Orient (0) 1 Charlton Ath (0) 0
Peterborough U (1) 1 QPR (0) 1
Portsmouth (1) 3 Cardiff C (0) 1 *aet*
Southampton (2) 3 Rochdale (0) 0
Southend U (0) 1 Crystal Palace (1) 2
Swindon T (3) 4 Darlington (0) 0
Watford (0) 0 Norwich C (1) 3
Wolverhampton W (1) 1 Hull C* (1) 1 *aet*
Bradford C (1) 1 Luton T (0) 1 *aet*
Bradford won 5–4 on penalties
Burnley (0) 0 Nottingham F (0) 1
Chelsea (2) 4 Walsall (0) 1
Derby Co (1) 1 Carlisle U (0) 0
Leeds U (0) 3 Leicester C (0) 0
Manchester C (0) 0 Torquay U (0) 0
Manchester U (1) 2 Halifax T (0) 1
Millwall (1) 2 Bournemouth (0) 1
Newcastle U (1) 1 Middlesbrough (0) 0
Oldham Ath (1) 5 Notts Co (1) 2 *aet*
Oxford U (0) 0 Port Vale (0) 0
Sheffield U (0) 2 Northampton T (0) 1
Stoke C (1) 1 West Ham U (0) 2
Wimbledon (0) 0 Plymouth Arg (1) 2

THIRD ROUND

Crystal Palace (0) 0 Leyton Orient (0) 0
Ipswich T (0) 0 Southampton (1) 2
Manchester C (0) 1 Arsenal (0) 2
Middlesbrough (2) 2 Norwich C (0) 0
Sheffield U (0) 2 Everton (0) 1
Tottenham H (2) 2 Bradford C (1) 1
Aston Villa (0) 2 Millwall (0) 0
Chelsea (0) 0 Portsmouth (0) 0
Coventry C (0) 3 Hull C (0) 0
Derby Co (4) 6 Sunderland (0) 0
Leeds U (2) 2 Oldham Ath (0) 0
Manchester U (2) 3 Liverpool (0) 1

Oxford U (1) 2 West Ham U (1) 1
Plymouth Arg (0) 1 Nottingham F (2) 2
QPR (2) 2 Blackburn R (1) 1
Sheffield W (0) 0 Swindon T (0) 0

THIRD ROUND REPLAYS
Portsmouth (1) 2 Chelsea (0) 3
Swindon T (0) 0 Sheffield W (1) 1
Leyton Orient (0) 0 Crystal Palace (0) 1

FOURTH ROUND
QPR (0) 0 Leeds U (3) 3
Sheffield U (0) 0 Tottenham H (0) 2
Southampton (1) 2 Crystal Palace (0) 0
Arsenal (0) 2 Manchester U (3) 6
Aston Villa (1) 3 Middlesbrough (0) 2
Coventry C (4) 5 Nottingham F (3) 4
Oxford U (1) 1 Chelsea (0) 2
Sheffield W (1) 1 Derby Co (1) 1

FOURTH ROUND REPLAY
Derby Co (0) 1 Sheffield W (1) 2

FIFTH ROUND
Chelsea (0) 0 Tottenham H (0) 0
Leeds U (1) 4 Aston Villa (0) 1
Southampton (0) 1 Manchester U (0) 1
Coventry C (0) 0 Sheffield W (1) 1

FIFTH ROUND REPLAYS
Manchester U (0) 3 Southampton (0) 2
Tottenham H (0) 0 Chelsea (1) 3

SEMI-FINALS FIRST LEG
Manchester U (0) 2 Leeds U (0) 1
Chelsea (0) 0 Sheffield W (0) 2

SEMI-FINALS SECOND LEG
Leeds U (0) 0 Manchester U (0) 1
Sheffield W (2) 3 Chelsea (0) 1

FINAL at Wembley
21 APR
Sheffield W (1) 1 *(Sheridan)*
Manchester U (0) 0, 80,000

** Won on away goals.*

PAST LEAGUE CUP FINALS

Played as two legs up to 1966

1961	Rotherham U *Webster, Kirkman*	2	Aston Villa	0
	Aston Villa *O'Neill, Burrows, McParland*	3	Rotherham U	0*
1962	Rochdale	0	Norwich C *Lythgoe 2, Punton*	3
	Norwich C *Hill*	1	Rochdale	0
1963	Birmingham C *Leek 2, Bloomfield*	3	Aston Villa *Thomson*	1
	Aston Villa	0	Birmingham C	0
1964	Stoke C *Bebbington*	1	Leicester C *Gibson*	1
	Leicester C *Stringfellow, Gibson, Riley*	3	Stoke C *Viollet, Kinnell*	2
1965	Chelsea *Tambling, Venables (pen), McCreadie*	3	Leicester C *Appleton, Goodfellow*	2
	Leicester C	0	Chelsea	0
1966	West Ham U *Moore, Byrne*	2	WBA *Astle*	1
	WBA *Kaye, Brown, Clark, Williams*	4	West Ham U *Peters*	1
1967	QPR *Morgan R., Marsh, Lazarus*	3	WBA *Clark C.*	2
1968	Leeds U *Cooper*	1	Arsenal	0
1969	Swindon T *Smart, Rogers 2*	3	Arsenal *Gould*	1
1970	Manchester C *Doyle, Pardoe*	2	WBA *Astle*	1
1971	Tottenham Hotspur *Chivers*	2	Aston Villa	0
1972	Chelsea *Osgood*	1	Stoke C *Conroy, Eastham*	2
1973	Tottenham Hotspur *Coates*	1	Norwich C	0
1974	Wolverhampton W *Hibbitt, Richards*	2	Manchester C *Bell*	1
1975	Aston Villa *Graydon*	1	Norwich C	0
1976	Manchester C *Barnes, Tueart*	2	Newcastle U *Gowling*	1
1977	Aston Villa	0	Everton	0
Replay	Aston Villa *Kenyon (og)*	1	Everton *Latchford*	1*
Replay	Aston Villa *Little 2, Nicholl*	3	Everton *Latchford, Lyons*	2*
1978	Nottingham F	0	Liverpool	0*
Replay	Nottingham F *Robertson (pen)*	1	Liverpool	0

1979	Nottingham F *Birtles 2, Woodcock*	3	Southampton *Peach, Holmes*	2
1980	Wolverhampton W *Gray*	1	Nottingham F	0
1981	Liverpool *Kennedy, A*	1	West Ham U *Stewart (pen)*	1*
Replay	Liverpool *Dalglish, Hansen*	2	West Ham U *Goddard*	1
1982	Liverpool *Whelan 2, Rush*	3	Tottenham *Archibald*	1*
1983	Liverpool *Kennedy, Whelan*	2	Manchester U *Whiteside*	1*
1984	Liverpool	0	Everton	0*
Replay	Liverpool *Souness*	1	Everton	0
1985	Norwich C *Chisholm (og)*	1	Sunderland	0
1986	Oxford U *Hebberd, Houghton, Charles*	3	QPR	0
1987	Arsenal *Nicholas*	2	Liverpool *Rush*	1
1988	Luton T *Stein, B. 2, Wilson*	3	Arsenal *Hayes, Smith*	2
1989	Nottingham F *Clough 2, Webb*	3	Luton T *Harford*	1
1990	Nottingham F *Jemson*	1	Oldham Ath	0

**After extra time*

LEYLAND DAF CUP 1990–91

PRELIMINARY ROUND
Halifax (0) 1 Rotherham U (0) 1
Bolton W (0) 1 Tranmere R (0) 0
Bournemouth (0) 0 Gillingham (0) 0
Burnley (1) 2 Crewe Alex (0) 1
Carlisle U (1) 1 Preston NE (1) 1
Chesterfield (1) 1 Doncaster R (0) 1
Grimsby T (0) 1 York C (2) 3
Peterborough U (0) 0 Cambridge U (0) 2
Southend U (5) 10 Aldershot (0) 1
Stoke C (0) 1 Northampton T (0) 1
Torquay U (0) 1 Swansea C (1) 1
Walsall (0) 0 Birmingham C (0) 1
Wigan Ath (3) 4 Chester C (0) 0
Bradford C (0) 1 Huddersfield T (1) 1
Leyton Orient (0) 0 Fulham (0) 2
Cardiff C (0) 0 Exeter C (1) 1
Aldershot (2) 3 Reading (0) 1
Birmingham C (2) 2 Lincoln C (0) 0
Chester C (1) 2 Bury (0) 0
Crewe Alex (0) 1 Stockport Co (0) 1
Doncaster R (0) 1 Scunthorpe U (0) 0
Fulham (0) 1 Brentford (1) 1
Gillingham (1) 4 Maidstone U (1) 1
Northampton T (0) 1 Mansfield T (0) 2
Preston NE (1) 3 Rochdale (0) 1
Rotherham U (1) 1 Scarborough (1) 1
Swansea C (0) 1 Shrewsbury T (1) 1
Tranmere R (1) 4 Blackpool (0) 0
Wrexham (2) 3 Peterborough U (2) 3
York C (2) 3 Darlington (1) 2
Exeter C (2) 2 Hereford U (2) 2
Huddersfield T (0) 1 Hartlepool U (1) 4
Reading (1) 1 Southend U (1) 4
Bury (0) 2 Wigan Ath (0) 1
Darlington (0) 3 Grimsby T (1) 1
Hereford U (1) 1 Cardiff C (0) 1
Maidstone U (2) 3 Bournemouth (0) 1
Lincoln C (1) 1 Walsall (0) 1
Blackpool (0) 3 Bolton W (0) 0
Cambridge U (1) 1 Wrexham (0) 0
Hartlepool U (0) 0 Bradford C (1) 4
Rochdale (1) 1 Carlisle U (0) 0
Scunthorpe U (0) 3 Chesterfield (1) 1
Shrewsbury T (0) 1 Torquay U (0) 1

Mansfield T (3) 3 Stoke C (0) 0
Stockport Co (1) 1 Burnley (1) 1
Scarborough (0) 1 Halifax T (1) 2
Brentford (2) 2 Leyton Orient (0) 0

PRELIMINARY ROUND REPLAYS
Shrewsbury T (1) 2 Torquay U (3) 6
Swansea C (4) 4 Shrewsbury T (2) 2
Torquay U (0) 2 Swansea C (0) 0

FIRST ROUND
Gillingham (0) 0 Hereford U (1) 1
Preston NE (1) 2 Darlington (1) 1 *aet*
Southend U (1) 2 Maidstone U (0) 0
Doncaster R (0) 0 Scunthorpe U (0) 0
aet: Scunthorpe U won 4–2 on penalties
Tranmere R (2) 3 Rotherham U (0) 0
Bradford C (1) 3 Hartlepool U (1) 2
Burnley (1) 3 Stockport Co (1) 2 *aet*
Halifax T (0) 0 Blackpool (1) 1
Wigan Ath (0) 2 Rochdale (0) 0
York C (1) 1 Bury (0) 2
Exeter C (1) 1 Aldershot (0) 0
Cambridge U (1) 1 Walsall (0) 0
Birmingham C (0) 0 Swansea C (0) 0
aet: Birmingham C won 4–2 on penalties
Mansfield T (2) 2 Fulham (0) 1
Torquay U (0) 2 Northampton T (0) 0
Brentford (0) 0 Wrexham (0) 0
aet: Brentford won 3–0 on penalties

QUARTER-FINALS
Northern Section
Bradford C (0) 0 Burnley (0) 1
Scunthorpe U (0) 1 Preston NE (3) 4
Tranmere R (0) 2 Blackpool (0) 0
Wigan Ath (0) 2 Bury (0) 0

Southern Section
Exeter C (0) 0 Cambridge U (1) 1
Birmingham C (1) 2 Mansfield T (0) 0
Southend U (0) 7 Torquay U (0) 0
Hereford U (0) 0 Brentford (1) 2

SEMI-FINALS
Northern Section
Preston NE (4) 6 Burnley (0) 1
Wigan Ath (0) 0 Tranmere R (1) 3

Southern Section
Birmingham C (2) 3 Cambridge U (0) 1
Southend U (0) 0 Brentford (2) 3

Northern Section Final First Leg
Tranmere R (2) 4 Preston NE (0) 0

Southern Section Final First Leg
Birmingham C (1) 2 Brentford (0) 1

Northern Section Final Second Leg
Preston NE (1) 1 Tranmere R (0) 0

Southern Section Final Second Leg
Brentford (0) 0 Birmingham C (0) 1

FINAL (at Wembley)
Birmingham C (2) 3 *(Sturridge, Gayle 2)*
Tranmere R (0) 2 *(Cooper, Steel)* 58,756

ZENITH DATA SYSTEMS CUP 1990–91

FIRST ROUND
Middlesbrough (0) 3 Hull C (0) 1 *aet*
Notts Co (1) 1 Port Vale (0) 0
Plymouth Arg (0) 0 Brighton & HA (0) 0
aet: Brighton & HA won 3–1 on penalties
Watford (0) 1 Bristol R (2) 2
Oxford U (0) 2 Bristol C (0) 2
aet: Oxford U won 3–2 on penalties
WBA (1) 3 Barnsley (2) 5
Leicester C (0) 0 Wolverhampton W (1) 1

SECOND ROUND
Southampton (3) 4 QPR (0) 0
Nottingham F (0) 2 Newcastle U (1) 1
Notts Co (1) 2 Sunderland (2) 2
aet: Sunderland won 3–1 on penalties
Sheffield U (2) 7 Oldham Ath (2) 2
Chelsea (0) 1 Swindon T (0) 0
Oxford U (1) 1 Portsmouth (0) 0
Wimbledon (0) 0 Ipswich T (1) 2
Blackburn R (0) 1 Everton (1) 4

Crystal Palace (1) 2 Bristol R (1) 1
Sheffield W (1) 3 Barnsley (0) 3
aet: Barnsley won 4–2 on penalties
Brighton & HA (1) 3 Charlton Ath (0) 1
Derby Co (0) 1 Coventry C (0) 0
Luton T (4) 5 West Ham U (0) 1
Manchester C (1) 2 Middlesbrough (0) 1
Norwich C (0) 1 Millwall (0) 1
aet: Norwich C won 6–5 on penalties
Wolverhampton W (0) 1 Leeds U (1) 2

NORTHERN QUARTER-FINALS
Everton (1) 4 Sunderland (0) 1
Leeds U (2) 2 Derby Co (0) 1
Sheffield U (0) 0 Manchester C (1) 2
Barnsley (1) 2 Nottingham F (1) 1

SOUTHERN QUARTER-FINALS
Ipswich T (1) 2 Oxford U (1) 1
Brighton & HA (0) 0 Crystal Palace (0) 2 *aet*
Chelsea (1) 1 Luton T (0) 1
aet: Luton T won 4–1 on penalties
Norwich C (2) 2 Southampton (1) 1

NORTHERN SEMI-FINALS
Leeds U (0) 2 Manchester C (0) 0
Barnsley (0) 0 Everton (1) 1

SOUTHERN SEMI-FINALS
Crystal Palace (2) 3 Luton T (1) 1
Norwich C (0) 2 Ipswich T (0) 0

SOUTHERN FINAL First Leg
Norwich C (1) 1 Crystal Palace (1) 1

SOUTHERN FINAL Second Leg
Crystal Palace (1) 2 Norwich C (0) 0

NORTHERN FINAL First Leg
Leeds U (2) 3 Everton (3) 3

NORTHERN FINAL Second Leg
Everton (0) 3 Leeds U (1) 1 *aet*

FINAL (at Wembley)
7 APR
Crystal Palace (0) 4 *(Thomas, Wright 2, Salako)*
Everton (0) 1 *(Warzycha) aet*, 52,460

FA CHARITY SHIELD WINNERS 1908–90

1908 Manchester U v QPR 4-0 after 1-1 draw
1909 Newcastle U v Northampton T 2-0
1910 Brighton v Aston Villa 1-0
1911 Manchester U v Swindon T 8-4
1912 Blackburn R v QPR 2-1
1913 Professionals v Amateurs 7-2
1919 WBA v Tottenham H 2-0
1920 Tottenham H v Burnley 2-0
1921 Huddersfield T v Liverpool 1-0
1922 Not played
1923 Professionals v Amateurs 2-0
1924 Professionals v Amateurs 3-1
1925 Amateurs v Professionals 6-1
1926 Amateurs v Professionals 6-3
1927 Cardiff C v Corinthians 2-1
1928 Everton v Blackburn R 2-1
1929 Professionals v Amateurs 3-0
1930 Arsenal v Sheffield W 2-1
1931 Arsenal v WBA 1-0
1932 Everton v Newcastle U 5-3
1933 Arsenal v Everton 3-0
1934 Arsenal v Manchester C 4-0
1935 Sheffield W v Arsenal 1-0
1936 Sunderland v Arsenal 2-1
1937 Manchester C v Sunderland 2-0
1938 Arsenal v Preston NE 2-1
1948 Arsenal v Manchester U 4-3
1949 Portsmouth v Wolverhampton W 1-1*
1950 World Cup Team v Canadian Touring Team 4-2
1951 Tottenham H v Newcastle U 2-1
1952 Manchester U v Newcastle U 4-2
1953 Arsenal v Blackpool 3-1
1954 Wolverhampton W v WBA 4-4*
1955 Chelsea v Newcastle U 3-0
1956 Manchester U v Manchester C 1-0
1957 Manchester U v Aston Villa 4-0
1958 Bolton W v Wolverhampton W 4-1
1959 Wolverhampton W v Nottingham F 3-1
1960 Burnley v Wolverhampton W 2-2*
1961 Tottenham H v FA XI 3-2
1962 Tottenham H v Ipswich T 5-1
1963 Everton v Manchester U 4-0
1964 Liverpool v West Ham U 2-2*
1965 Manchester U v Liverpool 2-2*
1966 Liverpool v Everton 1-0
1967 Manchester U v Tottenham H 3-3*
1968 Manchester C v WBA 6-1
1969 Leeds U v Manchester C 2-1
1970 Everton v Chelsea 2-1
1971 Leicester C v Liverpool 1-0
1972 Manchester C v Aston Villa 1-0
1973 Burnley v Manchester C 1-0
1974 Liverpool† v Leeds U 1-1

1975	Derby Co v West Ham U	2-0
1976	Liverpool v Southampton	1-0
1977	Liverpool v Manchester U	0-0*
1978	Nottingham F v Ipswich T	5-0
1979	Liverpool v Arsenal	3-1
1980	Liverpool v West Ham U	1-0
1981	Aston Villa v Tottenham H	2-2*
1982	Liverpool v Tottenham H	1-0
1983	Manchester U v Liverpool	2-0
1984	Everton v Liverpool	1-0
1985	Everton v Manchester U	2-0
1986	Everton v Liverpool	1-1*
1987	Everton v Coventry C	1-0
1988	Liverpool v Wimbledon	2-1
1989	Liverpool v Arsenal	1-0

* Each club retained shield for six months. † Won on penalties.

FA CHARITY SHIELD 1990

Liverpool (0) 1, Manchester U (1) 1
At Wembley, 18 August, 1990, attendance 66,558

Liverpool: Grobbelaar; Hysen, Burrows, Venison, Whelan, Ablett, Beardsley (Rosenthal), Houghton, Rush, Barnes, McMahon.

Scorer: Barnes (pen).

Manchester U: Sealey; Irwin, Donaghy, Bruce, Phelan, Pallister, Blackmore, Ince, McClair, Hughes, Wallace (Robins).

Scorer: Blackmore.

Referee: G. Courtney (Spennymoor).

SCOTTISH CLUBS

ABERDEEN — PREM. DIV.

Ground: Pittodrie Stadium, Aberdeen AB2 1QH (0224–632328)
Colours: All red with white trim.
Year formed: 1903. **Managers:** Alex Smith and Jocky Scott.
League appearances: Bett, J. 36; Booth, S. 8(11); Cameron, I. 3(7); Connor, R. 29; Dibble, A. 5; Gillhaus, H. 35; Grant, B. 32; Irvine, B. 29; Jess, E. 20(7); Mason, P. 25(1); McKimmie, S. 26; McLeish, A. 33; Robertson, C. 2(6); Robertson, D. 35; Robertson, I. (1); Snelders, T. 21; Van de Ven, P. 23(9); Van der Ark, W. 6(5); Watson, Gregg. 2(5); Watt, M. 10; Wright, S. 16(1).
Goals–League: (62): Gillhaus 14, Jess 13, Bett 7 (2 pens), Booth 6, Connor 6, Van der Ark 4, Mason 3, Grant 2, Irvine 2, Cameron 1, McKimmie 1, Robertson C 1, Robertson D 1, Wright 1.
Scottish Cup: (0).
Skol Cup: (9): Mason 3, Bett 2 (1 pen), Van de Ven 2, Irvine 1, Jess 1.

AIRDRIEONIANS — PREM. DIV.

Ground: Broomfield Park, Gartlea Road, Airdric ML6 9JL (0236–62067)
Colours: White shirts with red diamond, white shorts.
Year formed: 1878. **Manager:** Alex MacDonald
League appearances: Balfour, E. 32(1); Boyle, J. 6(5); Butler, J. 9(1); Conn, S. 18(3); Coyle, O. 24(4); Crainie, D. 19(9); Dawson, A. 9(1); Dick, J. (3); Gray, S. 13(2); Hendry, A. 2; Harvey, G. 24(3); Jack, P. 33(2); Kelly, J. 1; Kirkwood, D. 11(5); Lawrence, A. 38; MacDonald, I. 3(9); MacDonald, J. 10(4); McAdam, T. 9; McPhee, I. 36; Martin, J. 38; Scott, C. 1; Smith, A. 17(11); Smith, J. 28; Stewart, A. 18(7); Walsh, R. 1(1); Watson, J. 29(1);
Goals–League: (69): Coyle 20 (2 pen), Lawrence 13 (1 Pen), Harvey 11, Balfour 6, Watson 4, Butler 3 (1 pen), MacDonald J 3, Smith A 3, Conn 1, Crainie 1, Dawson 1, Gray 1 (pen), McPhee 1, Smith J 1.
Scottish Cup: (2): Jack 1, Watson 1.
Skol Cup: (1): Belfour 1.

ALBION ROVERS — DIV. 2

Ground: Cliftonhill Stadium, Main Street, Coatbridge ML5 9XX (0236–32350)
Colours: Yellow shirts with red and white trim, red shorts with yellow stripes.
Year formed: 1882. **Manager:** David Provan.
League appearances: Bettley, I. (3); Cadden, S. 32(1); Callaghan, W. 1; Clark, R. 37; Cormack, D. 4; Cougan, C. 7(11); Cousin, J. 14(1); Edgar, D. 12(8); Ferguson, W. 17(1); Green, J. 7(3); Henderson, J. 26(9); Kerr, B. 2; Lauchlan, G. 7(3); McAnenay, M. 35(1); McCulloch, R. 35; McDonald, D. 17(5); McFadzen, J. 2; McGuiness, B. 16(4); McKay, T. 1; McKeown, D. 39; McTeague, G. 15; Millar, G. 35; Quinn, S. 2; Richardson, A. 29(1); Smith, S. (1); Stalker, I. 13(6); Watson, E. 24(6).
Goals–League: (48): McAnenay 12, Clark 8 (8 pens), Cadden 5, Stalker 4, Ferguson 3, Richardson 3, Watson 3, Cougan 2, Henderson 2, Callaghan 1, Lauchlan 1, McKeown 1, own goals 3.
Scottish Cup: (0).
Skol Cup: (0).

ALLOA DIV. 2

Ground: Recreation Park, Alloa FK10 1RR (0259–722695)
Colours: Gold shirts with black trim, black shorts.
Year formed: 1883. **Manager:** Hugh McCann.
League appearances: Black, I. 18(8); Butter, J. 17; Campbell, C. 11; Feeney, M. 3; Gibson, J. 21; Grant, A. 24(3); Henry, S. 8(8); Irvine, J. 31(6); Lamont, P. (2); Lee, D. 5; Lee, R. 19; Lowrie, R. 22; McAvoy, N. 4(1); McCallum, M. 11(2); McCulloch, K. 39; McEntegart, T. 23(2); Moffat, B. 18(11); Newbigging, W. 38; Ormond, J. 11(16); Ramsay S. 26(5); Russell, G. (1); Smith, M. 25; Thomson, J. 21(2); Wilcox, D. 34.
Goals–League: (51): Irvine 11, Moffat 7, Newbigging 5 (2 pens), Black 4, Gibson 4, Grant 3, Henry 3, Smith 3, Wilcox 3, McEntergart 2, Ormond 2, Ramsay 2, McCallum 1, McCulloch1 .
Scottish Cup: (2): Irvine 1, Newbigging 1 (pen).
Skol Cup: (0).

ARBROATH DIV. 2

Ground: Gayfield Park, Arbroath DD11 1QB (0241–72157)
Colours: Maroon shirts, white shorts.
Year formed: 1878. **Manager:** Walter Borthwick.
League appearances: Balfour, D. 23; Bennett, M. 32; Brand, R. 6(4); Brown, S. 8; Bullock, S. 21(2); Campbell, I, 11; Carlin, G. 24; Dewar, G. 1(2); Farnan, C. 15; Florence, S. 19(3); Gallagher, J. 10(5); Gibson, I. 3; Glennie, R. 2; Hamilton, J. 30(4); Holmes, J. 37; Holmes W. 17(6); Jackson, D. 16; Kerr, G. 4; Malone, G. 4(3); Marshall, J. 8(2); Mitchell, B. 30(2); Morton, J. 18; Oliver, M. 13; Powell, D. 4(4); Roberts, P. 10; Smith, R. 7(8); Sorbie, S. 38; Stewart, I. 11(6); Thompson, G. 1; Thomson, B. 4(1); Tindall, K. 1; Young, J. 1.
Goals–League: (41): Bennett 10 (1 pen), Sorbie 10, Morton 5, Bulloch 4, Marshall 3, Hamilton 2, Mitchell 2, Carlin 1, Holmes W 1, Powell 1, Roberts 1, Thomson B 1.
Scottish Cup: (4): Bennett 1, Bulloch 1, Mitchell 1, Sorbie 1.
Skol Cup: (2): Mitchell 1, Morton 1 (pen).

AYR UNITED DIV. 1

Ground: Somerset Park, Ayr KA8 9NB (0292–263435)
Colours: White shirts with black trim, black shorts.
Year formed: 1910. **Manager:** George Burley.
League appearances: Brown, R. 3; Bryce, T. 34; Burley, G. 12; Cunningham, W. 2; Duncan, C. 11; Evans, S. 26(4); Fraser, A. 16; Furphy, W. 24; George, D. 9; Gillespie, A. 27(1); Graham, A. 38; Hughes, J. 7(3); Johnson, S. 24; Kennedy, D. 30(2); Love, J. 27(1); McAllister, I. 17(3); McCann, J. 6(1); McIntyre, S. 4(1); Purdie, D. 26; Ross, B. 3(1); Scott, R. 3; Shaw, G. 5(4); Smythe, D. 16; Templeton, H. 11(8); Walker, T. 18(8); Weir, P. 28(1); Willock, A. 2(2); Wilson, K. (1).
Goals–League: (47): Bryce 11 (2 pens), Johnston 9, Fraser 8, Graham 8, McAllister 3, Walker 3, Hughes 1, Kennedy 1, Scott 1, Weir 1 (pen), own goal 1
Scottish Cup: (6): Bryce 2, Fraser 2, Graham 1, Weir 1.
Skol Cup: (0).

BERWICK RANGERS DIV. 2

Ground: Shielfield Park, Berwick-on-Tweed TD15 2EF (0289–307424)
Colours: Black and gold striped shirts, black shorts.
Year formed: 1881. **Manager:**
League appearances: Ainslie, G. 6(1); Bickmore, S. 11(4); Callachan, R. 18(4); Cass, M. 19; Davidson, G. 25; Fraser, S. 22(6); Garner, W. 19(1); Graham, T. 30(6); Holden, D. 12(2); Kerr, N. 1; Leitch, G. 20(5); Locke, S. 4; Marshall, B. 16; McLaren, P. 6(2); Neil, M. 9(1); Neilson, D. 38; O'Donnell, J. 33; Ross, A. 9; Scally, D. 15(3); Smith, R. 24(2); Sokoluk, J. 28(6); Tait, G. 18(8); Thorpe, B. 12(5); Todd, K. 34.
Goals–League: (51): Todd 14, Graham 7, Sokoluk 7 (1 pen), Tait 5, Thorpe 5, Bickmore 4, Ross 3, Ainslee 2, Cass 1, Garner 1, Locke 1, Neil 1.
Scottish Cup: (4):Bickmore 1, Garner 1, Graham 1 (pen), Todd 1.
Skol Cup: (3): Graham 2, Todd 1.

BRECHIN CITY DIV. 2

Ground: Glebe Park, Brechin DD9 6BJ (03562–2856)
Colours: All red.
Year formed: 1906. **Manager:** John Ritchie.
League appearances: Baillie, R. 34; Brash, A. 8; Brown, R. 36; Candlish, C. 10(2); Conway, F. 16(2); Dow, R. 1; Duncan, R. (3); Fisher, D. 1; Hill, H. 32(4); Hutt, G. 5(2); Kenny, B. 4; Lawrie, D. 38; Lees, G. 20(5); Lennox, G. 12; McKillop, A. 28; Patterson, I. A. 8(10); Patterson, I. G. 23(1); Pryde, I. 23(5); Ritchie, P. 34(4); Scott, D. 30(3); Sexton, P. 21; Smart, B. 1; Thomson, N. 8(10); Thomson, S. 26(4); Wardell, S. 10(2).
Goals–League: (44): Ritchie 14, Pryde 7, Lees 6, Brown 4, Scott 3, Thomson S 3, Hill 2, Lennox 2, Wardell 2, Paterson IA 1.
Scottish Cup: (0).
Skol Cup: (0).

CELTIC PREM. DIV.

Ground: Celtic Park, Glasgow G40 3RE (041–554 2611)
Colours: Green and white hooped shirts, white shorts.
Year formed: 1888. **Manager:** Liam Brady.
League appearances: Baillie, L. 8(1); Bonner, P. 36; Britton, G. (2); Collins, J. 35; Coyne, T. 24(2); Creaney, G. 22(9); Dziekanowski, D. 11(4); Elliott, P. 27; Fulton, S. 19(2); Galloway, M. 3(3); Grant, P. 26(1); Hayes, M. 3(4); Hewitt, J. 1(3); Mathie, A. 2(2); McCarrison, D. (1); McLaughlin, P. 2(1); McNally, M. 17(2); McStay, P. 30; Miller, J. 24(6); Morris, C. 16(3); Nicholas, C. 12(2); Rogan, A. 25(2); Walker, A. 6(5); Wdowczyk, D. 23(1); Whyte, D. 24.
Goals–League: (52): Coyne 18 (1 pen), Miller 8, Creaney 7, Nicholas 6, Dziekanowski 2, Elliott 2, McStay 2, Whyte 2, Baillie 1, Collins 1, Galloway 1, Rogan 1, own goal 1.
Scottish Cup: (9): Creaney 2, Wdowczyk 2, Coyne 1, Miller 1, Rogan 1, own goals 2.
Skol Cup: (10): Dziekanowski 4, Elliott 3, Creaney 1, McStay 1, Miller 1.

CLYDE DIV. 2

Ground: Douglas Park, Hamilton ML3 0DF (Mon-Fri: 041-248 7953) (Match days: 0698 286103)
Colours: White shirts with red and black trim, black shorts.
Year formed: 1878. **Manager:** John Clark.
League appearances: Brogan, M. 10; Clark, G. 36(1); Clarke, S. 24; Devlin, J. 3(1); Gaughin, M. 11(3); Gilmore, J. 17(11); Halpin, J. 12(1); Knox, K. 32; Mallan, S. 30(5); McAulay, J. 5(6); McCoy, G. 7(12); McFarlane, B. 34; McVee, Graeme. 27; Mitchell, J. 22; Nolan, M. 3(1); O'Hanlon, S. 10; O'Hara, F. 2(1); Reid, W. 34; Ross, S. 29; Scott, M. 8(15); Speirs, C. 33; Thompson, D. 14; Wilson, K. 19; Wylde, G. 7(5).
Goals–League: (41): Mallan 8, Gilmour 6 (2 pens), Clark G 5 (1 pen), Scott 5, McCoy 4, Thompson 3, McAulay 2, Speirs 2, Clarke S 1, Knox 1, Mitchell 1, Reid 1, Wilson 1, own goal 1.
Scottish Cup: (0).
Skol Cup: (2): Gilmour 1, Scott 1.

CLYDEBANK DIV. 1

Ground: Kilbowie Park, Clydebank G81 2PB (041–952 2887)
Colours: White with red band, white shorts.
Year formed: 1965. **Manager:** John Steedman.
League appearances: Caffrey, H. 3(2); Coyle, T. 12(3); Crawford, D. 9; Davies, J. 14; Dickson, Joe. 20(1); Dickson, John. 13(13); Duncanson, J. 5(2); Eadie, K. 38; Ferguson, W. 3; Gallagher, J. 24; Harvey, P. 36; Henry, J. 2(1); Kelly, P. 17(3); Lamont, P. 5(2); Lansdowne, A. 14(2); Maher, J. 29; Mair, G. 7; Murdoch, S. 3; Roger, J. 26(1); Rossiter, B. 3; Rowe, G. 29; Sermanni, P. 19(10); Smith, B. 10(1); Spence, W. 15; Sweeney, S. 33; Templeton, H. 7(2); Traynor, J. 9(12); Wright, B. 21; Young, D. 3.
Goals–League: (65): Eadie 29 (4 pens), Kelly 9, Coyle 4 (1 pen), John Dickson 4, Sermanni 4, Harvey 2, Mair 2, Rodger 2, Rowe 2, Caffrey 1, Davies 1, Henry 1, Templeton 1, Wright 1, Young 1, own goal 1.
Scottish Cup: (0).
Skol Cup: (2): Eadie 1, Rowe 1.

COWDENBEATH DIV. 2

Ground: Central Park, Cowdenbeath KY4 9EY (0383–511205)
Colours: Royal blue shirts with white stripes, white shorts.
Year formed: 1881. **Manager:** John Brownlie.
League appearances: Abercrombie, W. 3(1); Archibald, E. 23(6); Bennett, W. 19; Buckley, G. 20(10); Dewar, G. 3(1); Dodds, J. 1; Douglas, H. 19(3); Duffy, D. (8); Hamill, K. 8(14); Houston, F. 2; Irvine, N. 23; Johnston, P. 1; Lamont, W. 32; MacKenzie, A. 28(5); Malone, G. 35(1); McGovern, D. 33(1); Patterson, C. (1); Robertson, A. 34(2); Ross, A. 28; Scott, C. 35(1); Smith, G. (2); Syme, W. 9; Thomson, C. 3; Thomson, K. 17(3); Watt, D. 21; Wilson, C. 1; Wright, J. 31(3).
Goals–League: (64): MacKenzie 15, Ross 13, Wright 9, Malone 8 (2 pens), Buckley 5, Hamill 3, Scott 3, Robertson 2, Syme 2, Douglas 1, Duffy 1, Irvine 1, own goal 1.
Scottish Cup: (4): MacKenzie 2, Buckley 1, Wright 1.
Skol Cup: (2): MacKenzie 1, Ross 1.

DUMBARTON DIV. 2

Ground: Boghead Park, Dumbarton G82 2JA (0389–62569 and 67864)
Colours: Gold with white band, black shorts.
Year formed: 1872. **Manager:** Billy Lamont.
League appearances: Boyd, J. 29(3); Chapman, J. 11; Dempsey, J. 35(1); Edgar, D. 4(2); Foster, A. 2; Gibson, C. 25(1); Gow, S. 31; Graham, P. 1; Hughes, J. 5(4); MacIver, S. 19(2); Marshall, S. 3(2); Marsland, J. 19(4); Martin, P. 14; McCracken, D. 12(1); McGarvey, M. 3(1); McGinley, J. 9(4); McGuire, W. 12(1); McKenzie, P. 18(1); McNair, C. 24(1); McQuade, J. 35(4); Meechan, J. 19(2); Melvin, M. 17; Millar, S. 10(16); Morrison, S. 32(5); Nolan, T. 1; Quinn, P. (10); Shearer, G. 1; Stevenson, H. 33; Strachan, H. B. 5.
Goals–League: (49): McQuade 14, Morrison 8 (3 pens), MacIver 6, Chapman 4, Gibson 4, Boyd 3 (1 pen), Edgar 2, McNair 2 (1 pen), Meechan 2, Dempsey 1, McGinley 1, McGuire 1, Martin 1.
Scottish Cup: (1): Morrison (1 pen).
Skol Cup: (2): MacIver 2.

DUNDEE DIV. 1

Ground: Dens Park, Dundee DD3 7JY (0382–826104)
Colours: Dark blue shirts with red and white trim, white shorts.
Year formed: 1893. **Manager:** Gordon Wallace.
League appearances: Bain, K. 7; Beedie, S. 8(1); Campbell, D. 10(6); Campbell, S. 3(3); Carson, T. 33; Chisholm, G. 34; Craib, M. 17(2); Craig, A. 3(9); Dinnie, A. 25; Dodds, W. 37; Forsyth, S. 18(3); Frail, S. 25(1); Fraser, C. 7; Holt, J. 4(4); Jamieson, W. 38; Mathers, P. 6; McBride, J. 4(10); McLeod, G. 23(1); McMartin, G. 15(4); McQuillan, J. 8(6); McSkimming, S. 15(1); Shannon, R. 37; West, C. 16(3); Wright, K. 36.
Goals–League: (59): Wright 18, Dodds 15 (3 pens), Chisholm 3, Craig 3, Dinnie 3, McSkimming 3, West 3, Jamieson 2, McBride 2, McLeod 2, Shannon 2 (1 pen), Campbell S 1, McMartin 1, McQuillan 1.
Scottish Cup: (4): Dodds 2, McMartin 1, West 1.
Skol Cup: (2) Chisholm 1, Forsyth 1.

DUNDEE UNITED PREM. DIV.

Ground: Tannadice Park, Dundee DD3 7JW (0382–833166)
Colours: Tangerine shirts with black trim, black shorts.
Year formed: 1909 as Dundee Hibernians, Dundee United from 1923.
League appearances: Bollan, G. 1(1); Bowman, D. 17(3); Clark, J. 17(1); Cleland, A. 16(4); Connolly, P. 7(3); Dailly, C. 16(2); Ferguson, D. 8(1); French, H. 16(3); Jackson, D. 30(3); Krivokapic, M. 24; Main, A. 31; Malpas, M. 36; McInally, J. 33; McKinlay, W. 29(5); McKinnon, R. 17; Narey, D. 4; O'Neil J. 11(4); O'Neill, M. 7(6); Paatelainen, M. 9(11); Preston, A. 1(2); Steinmann, G. 13(1); Thomson, W. 5; Van der Hoorn, F. 32; Welsh, B. 16(1).
Goals–League: (41): Jackson 12, Dailly 5, French 3, Clark 2, Cleland 2, Connolly 2, McKinlay 2, McKinnon 2, Bowman 1, Ferguson 1, McInally 1, Malpas 1 (pen), Paatelainen 1, Steinmann 1, Van der Hoorn 1, own goals 4.
Scottish Cup: (13): Ferguson 3, Clark 2, French 2, Jackson 2, Bowman 1, Connolly 1, McKinnon 1, O'Neil J 1.
Skol Cup: (8): Jackson 3, Dailly 2, McInally 1, Van der Hoorn 1, Welsh 1.

DUNFERMLINE ATHLETIC PREM. DIV.

Ground: East End Park, Dunfermline KY12 7RB (0383–724295)
Colours: Black and white striped shirts, black shorts.
Year formed: 1885. **Manager:** Iain Munro.
League appearances: Cunnington, E. 6(1); Davies, W. 26; Drizic, M. 5; Farningham, R. 6(4); Gallacher, S. 1; Gallagher E. 1(2); Haro, M. 2(6); Irons, D. 24(10); Jack, R. 28(5); Kelly, N. 1(1); Kozma, I. 32(2); Leitch, S. 8(5); McCall, I. 28(1); McAllister, P. (1); McCathie, N. 36; Moyes, D. 35; Nicholl, J. 7; O'Boyle, G. 15(1); O'Brien, P. (2); Rafferty, S. 12(2); Rhodes, A. 35; Sharp, R. 30(1); Sinclair, C. (3); Smith, P. 25(6); Westwater, I. 1; Williamson, A. 4(1); Wilson, T. 28.
Goals–League: (38): Jack 8 (1 pen), Moyes 7, O'Boyle 6, Irons 4, McCall 4, Leitch 3, Kozma 2, Smith 2, Drizic 1, McCathie 1.
Scottish Cup: (0).
Skol Cup: (5): Jack (2) (1 pen), Irons 1, O'Brien 1, Smith 1.

EAST FIFE DIV. 2

Ground: Bayview Park, Methil, Fife KY8 3AG (0333–26323)
Colours: Black and gold striped shirts, black shorts.
Year formed: 1903. **Manager:** Gavin Murray.
League appearances: Beaton, D. 12(1); Bell, G. 28(1); Brown, I. 18(10); Brown, W. 34; Charles, R. 13: Cowell, J. 14(4); Crolla, C. 30(2); Halliday, D. 3(2); Hamilton, R. 5(1); Hayton, G. 11(13); Hope, D. 13(11); Lennox, S. 22; Mitchell, A. 29(5); Moffat, J. 26: Prior, S. 32(1); Ritchie, I. (2); Rogerson, S. 16(1); Scott, R. 22(7); Taylor, P. 36; Taylor, P. H. 33; Wilson, S. 32(5).
Goals–League: (57): Brown W 10, Scott 10, Brown I 9 (1 pen), Mitchell 7, Beaton 3 (1 pen), Crolla 3, Hope 33, Lennox 3, Taylor P 2 (1 pen), Wilson 2, Bell 1, Hayton 1, Prior 1, own goals 2.
Scottish Cup: (8): Hope 3, Wilson 2, Cowell 1, Mitchell 1, Scott 1.
Skol Cup: (3): Mitchell 1, Scott 1, Wilson 1.

EAST STIRLING DIV. 2

Ground: Firs Park, Falkirk FK2 7AY (0324–23583)
Colours: White shirts with black band, white shorts.
Year formed: 1881. **Manager:** Dom Sullivan.
League appearances: Abercrombie, W. 5; Brannigan, K. 36; Byrne, W. 10(1); Clark, J. 15(2); Diver, D. 25(3); Erwin, H. 25(3); Gray, C. 6(1); Griffin, J. 3(1); Hamill, S. 4(1); Lawson, O. 7; Lytwyn, C. 26(1); Mackin, A. 1; McAleer, E. 10; McBride, M. 25(2); McCulley, R. 1(1); McDowell, P. 22(3); McKinnon, C. 9; McLaren, P. 2(5); McNab, C. 5(2); McNally, J. 6(6); O'Brien, P. 7(4); Rooney, J. 30(1); Ross, R. 6; Russell, G. 34(1); Walker, David, 15; Walker, Derek, 35(3); Watson, G. 32; Watson, P. 7(2); Wilson, C. 4(11); Workman, J. 16(1).
Goals–League: (36): Lytwyn 10 (1 pen), Derek Walker 10 (2 pens), Diver 6, McBride 2, McDowall 2, McNab 2, McNally 2, own goals 2.
Scottish Cup: (1): Derek Wakler 1.
Skol Cup: (2): Russell 1, Watson P 1.

FALKIRK PREM. DIV.

Ground: Brockville Park, Falkirk FK1 5AX (0324–24121 and 32487)
Colours: Dark blue shirts with white trim, white shorts.
Year formed: 1876. **Manager:** Jim Jefferies.
League appearances: Baptie, C. 25(1); Beaton, D. 9; Cody, S. 12(5); Corner, S. 1; Cowell, J. (3); Duffy, N. 20(5); Godfrey, P. 11; Hetherston, P. 22(4); Houston, P. 5(8); Hughes, J. 31(1); Logan, S. 1; Marshall, G. 39; McCoy, G. (1); McGivern, S. 28(2); McKinnon, C. 2(2); McNeill, W. 2(2); McQueen, T. 32; McWilliams, D. 29; May, E. 13; Melvin, M. 8(2); Mooney, M. 1(3); Nicol, A. 10(1); Robertson, J. 7; Rutherford, P. 3(3); Smith, G. 27(4); Stainrod, S. 37; Taylor, A. 29; Whittaker, B. 25.
Goals–League: (70): Stainrod 16 (4 pens), McGivern 15, McWilliams 10 (1 pen), May 6, Hetherston 4, Baptie 3, Rutherford 3, Duffy 2, Houston 2, Hughes 2, McQueen 2 (2 pens), Taylor 2, Beaton 1, Cody 1, Whittaker 1.
Scottish Cup: (6): McGivern 3, McWilliams 2, Taylor 1.
Skol Cup: (1): Houston 1.

FORFAR ATHLETIC DIV. 1

Ground: Station Park, Forfar, Angus DD8 3BT (0307–63576)
Colours: Sky blue shirts, navy shorts.
Year formed: 1885. **Manager:** Paul Hegarty.
League appearances: Adam, C. 17(1); Allan, R. 34; Brazil, A. 26(2); Brewster, C. 28(1); Byrne, J. 7; Campbell, A. 7(1); Clark, J. 15(12); Clinging, I. 4(9); Feeney, M. 3; Fotheringham, J. (1); Gardner, S. 2; Hamill, A. 37; Hegarty, P. 32; Holt, J. 14(1); Kennedy, S. 5; Leslie, A. 11(7); Lorimer, R. 26(3); Mearns, G. 5(2); McAulay, A. 1(4); McKenna, I. 4(2); McKenna, S. 1; Morris, R. 34; Paton, P. 17(1); Petrie, S. 32(4); Smith, P. 14(3); Whyte, G. 31(4); Winter, G. 22(4).
Goals–League: (50): Whyte 12 (2 pens), Brewster 11 (1 pen), Petrie 6, Paton 5, Clark 3, Adam 2, Brazil 2, Leslie 2, McKenna I 2, Campbell 1, Clinging 1, Winter 1, own goals 2.
Scottish Cup: (0).
Skol Cup: (1): Brewster 1 (pen).

HAMILTON ACADEMICAL DIV. 1

Ground: Douglas Park, Hamilton ML3 0DF (0698–286103)
Colours: Red and white hooped shirts, white shorts.
Year formed: 1875. **Manager:** Billy McLaren.
League appearances: Archer, S. 1(1); Burns, H. 22(1); Cramb, C. 2(1); Ferguson, A. 37; Harris, C. 24(3); Hillcoat, C. 5(4); Horne, J. 4(10); MacFarlane, I. 2; McCabe, G. 9(7); McDonald, P. 36(2); McGachie, J. (1); McGinley, M. 1(1); McCluskey, G. 35; McGuigan, R. 21(8); McKee, K. 38; McKenzie, P. 1(1); McNeil, N. (2); McQuilter, R. 9(5); Millen, A. 39; Miller, C. 37; Moore, S. 9(11); Napier, C. 39; O'Hara, A. 19(5); Weir, J. 39.
Goals–League: (50): McCluskey 14, Harris 7 (2 pens), McDonald 7 (2 pens), Burns 6, Napier 6, Cramb 2, McGuigan 2, Weir 2, Hillcoat 1, Horne 1, O'Hara 1 (pen), own goal.
Scottish Cup: (2): McCluskey 2, Moore 1.
Skol Cup: (2): Burns 1, McCluskey.

HEART OF MIDLOTHIAN PREM. DIV.

Ground: Tynecastle Park, Gorgie Road, Edinburgh EH11 2NL (031–337 6132)
Colours: Maroon shirts, white shorts.
Year formed: 1874. **Manager:** Joe Jordan.
League appearances: Bannon, E. 15(4); Berry, N. 18(1); Colquhoun, J. 36; Crabbe, S. 13(8); Ferguson, D. 25(3); Ferguson, I. 7(5); Foster, W. 21(7); Harrison, T. (3); Kidd, W. 1(3); Kirkwood, D. 8(1); Levein, C. 33; MacKay, G. 27(3); McCreery, D. 4(3); McKinlay, T. 31(2); McLaren, A. 18(5); McPherson, D. 34; Robertson, J. 31; Sandison, J. 24(1); Smith, H. 23; Walker, N. 13; Wright, G. 14(3).
Goals–League: (48): Robertson 12 (2 pens), Colquhoun 7, Levein 4, Crabbe 3, Mackay 3, Bannon 2, Ferguson D 2, Ferguson I 2, McKinlay 2, McPherson 2, Wright 2, Berry 1, Foster 1, Kirkwood 1, McLaren 1, Sandison 1, own goals 2.
Scottish Cup: (1): Mackay 1.
Skol Cup: (3): Bannon 1, Crabbe 1, Robertson 1.

HIBERNIAN PREM. DIV.

Ground: Easter Road Stadium, Edinburgh EH7 5QG (031–661 2159)
Colours: Green shirts with white sleeves and collar, white shorts.
Year formed: 1875. **Manager: Alex Miller.**
League appearances: Cooper, N. 11; Evans, G. 11(4); Farrell, D. 1(1); Fellenger, D. 8(4); Findlay, W. 21(5); Goram, A. 35; Hamilton, B. 25(1); Houchen, K. 17(4); Hunter, G. 20; Kane, P. 21; Lennon, D. 6; MacLeod, M. 25; McGinlay, P. 29(3); McGraw, M. 4(9); McIntyre, T. 9; Miller, W. 24(1); Milne, C. 21; Mitchell, G. 25(3); Nicholls, D. 1; Orr, N. 15(2); Reid, C. 1; Sneddon, A. 5(1); Tortolano , J. 13(5); Weir, M. 17(3); Wright, P. 31(2).
Goals–League: (24): Wright 6 (1 pen), Evans 2, Findlay 2, Hamilton 2, MacLeod 2, Fellinger 1, Houchen 1, Hunter 1, McGinlay 1, Miller 1, Orr 1, Tortolano 1, Weir 1, own goals 2.
Scottish Cup: (3): Hamilton 1, Houchen 1, Miller 1.
Skol Cup: (1): Houchen 1.

KILMARNOCK DIV. 1

Ground: Rugby Park, Kilmarnock KA1 2DP (0563–25184)
Colours: Blue and white striped shirts, blue shorts.
Year formed: 1869. **Manager:** Jim Fleeting.
League appearances: Agnew, G. 3(1); Brayshaw, A. 2(1); Burgess, S. 10(5); Burns, T. 37; Callaghan, T. 26(4); Campbell, C. 7; Curran, P. 1; Elliott, D. 14(7); Flexney, P. 33; Geddes, R, 38; Jenkins, E. 8(1); MacKinnon, D. 19(1); MacPherson, A. 12; McKellar, D. 1; McStay, W. 19(2); Montgomerie, R. 35(2); Reilly, R. 13(13); Shaw, G. 2(1); Sloane, T. 3(4); Sludden, J. 23(3); Smith, T. 8(4); Spence, T. 32(1); Stark, W. 21; Tait, T. 34(2); Watters, W. 5(4); Williamson, R. 23; Wylde, G. (1).
Goals–League: (58): Williamson 14, Burns 8, Sludden 8, Stark 6, Callaghan 4, Campbell 4, Tait 3, Flexney 2, Reilly 2, Watters 2, Elliott 1, Jenkins 1, Sloan 1, Smith 1, Spence 1.
Scottish Cup: (2): Sludden 2, Burns 1.
Skol Cup: **(3):**Callaghan 1, Spence 1, Stark 1.

MEADOWBANK THISTLE — DIV. 1

Ground: Meadowbank Stadium, Edinburgh EH7 6AE (031 661 5351)
Colours: Amber with black trim, black shorts.
Year formed: 1943 as Ferranti Thistle, Meadowbank Thistle from 1974.
Manager: Terry Christie.
League appearances: Armstrong, G. 39; Banks, A. 30(3); Boyd, W. 27(7); Bullen, L. (3); Cormack, P. 1; Forest, R. 18(8); Graham, T. 2(4); Grant, D. 39; Hendrie, T. 25(4); Irvine, N. 2(2); Irvine W. 31(3); Kane, K. 8(3); Little, I. 23(7); Logan, S. 32(1); McCormack, J. 11(1); McNaughton, B. 3(4); McQueen, J. 39; Neil, C. 2; Park, D. 2; Perry, J. 3; Prentice, A. 21(6); Roseburgh, D. 39; Sprott, A. 20; Whitehead, D. 1(1); Wiliamson, S. 11.
Goals–League: (56): Roseburgh 15 (1 pen), Irvine W 8, Little 8, Forrest 6, Boyd 5, Grant 3, Perry 3, Logan 2, Prentice 2, Sprott 2, Banks 1, Neil 1.
Scottish Cup: (6): Roseburgh 2 (1 pen), Boyd 1, Forrest 1, Irvine W 1, own goal 1.
Skol Cup: (0).

MONTROSE — DIV. 1

Ground: Links Park, Montrose DD10 8QD (0674–73200)
Colours: Blue with white trim, white shorts.
Year formed: 1879 **Manager:** Ian Stewart.
League appearances: Allan, M. 27(4); Brown, K. 3; Chalmers, C. 5; Den Bieman, I. 32(4); Dolan, A. 36; Dornan, A. 17; Feeney, M. 3; Fleming, J. 34; Fotheringham, J. 11(18); Kerr, B. 20; King, S. 31(1); Larter, D. 39; Lyons, A. 16(7); Mackay, H. 28(1); Maver, C. 24(9); Melville, D. 4; Morrison, B. 38; Murray, G. 19(14); Paterson, D. (1); Powell, D. 1; Price, R. 1; Rougvie, D. 29; Sheran, J. 3; Stephen, G. 7(6); Watt, D. 1.
Goals–League: (54): Murray 11 (2 pens), Dolan 8, Mackay 6, Den Bieman 5, Kerr 5, Allan 4, Fotheringham 4, Maver 4, Melville 2, Rougvie 2, King 1, Sheran 1, Stephen 1.
Scottish Cup: (4): Kerr 2 (1 pen), Allan 1, Murray 1.
Skol Cup: (1): Allan 1.

MORTON — DIV. 1

Ground: Cappielow Park, Greenock PA15 2TY (0475–23571)
Colours: Blue and white hooped shirts, white shorts.
Year formed: 1874. **Manager:** Allan McGraw.
League appearances: Alexander, R. 34; Boag, J. 20; Brown, C. (3); Collins, D. 36(1); Cowie, G. 10(9); Deeney, M. 4(10); Doak, M. 33; Fowler, J. 18(17); Gahagan, J. 34(1); Graham, P. 1; Hamilton, D. 2(2); Hopkin, D. 4(6); Hunter, J. 38; Kelly, G. 5; MacCabe, D. 35; Mahood, A. 4(4); McArthur, S. 2(2); McDonald, I. 34(2); McGoldrick, K. 1(5); McInnes, D. 24(7); McNeil, J. 3; Pickering, M. 30(1); Reid, B. 19; Wylie, D. 38.
Goals–League: (48): MacCabe 21, Alexander 6, Gahagan 6, McInnes 3, Boag 2, Collins 2, Fowler 2, Pickering 2, Deeney 1, Doak 1, Kelly 1, McDonald 1.
Scottish Cup: (5): Gahagan 2, MacCabe 2, Alexander 1.
Skol Cup: (3): Hopkin 2, Fowler 1.

MOTHERWELL — PREM. DIV.

Ground: Fir Park, Motherwell ML1 2QN (0698–61437/8)
Colours: Amber shirts with claret band, claret shorts.
Year formed: 1886. **Manager:** Tommy McLean.
League appearances: Angus, I. 14(6); Arnott, D. 26(3); Boyd, T. 30; Bryce, S. 1(3); Burley, G. 20; Cooper, D. 34; Cusack, N. 22(7); Dolan, J. 4(4); Ferguson, I. 13(2); Gahagan, J. 1; Griffin, J. 22(1); Kirk, S. 18(11); Mair, G. 2; Maxwell, A. 36; McCart; C. 36; McGrillen, P. (2); McLean, P. (1); McLeod, J. 10(12); Nijholt, L. 21(2); O'Donnell, P. 11(1); O'Neill, C. 21; Paterson, C. 28(4); Philliben, J. 11; Russell, R. 15(4).
Goals–League: (51): Arnott 14, Ferguson 8, Cooper 6, Cusack 4, Griffin 4, Angus 2, Boyd 2, Kirk 2, Paterson 2, Russell 2, Bryce 1, Dolan 1, McLeod 1, O'Neill 1, Philliben 1.
Scottish Cup: (14): Kirk 4, Arnott 2, Cusack 2, Angus 1, Boyd 1, Ferguson 1, McLeod 1, O'Donnell 1, O'Neill 1.
Skol Cup: (6): Cusack 2, O'Neill 2, Arnott 1, Burley 1.

PARTICK THISTLE — DIV. 1

Ground: Firhill Park, Glasgow G20 7AL (041-945 4811)
Colours: Amber shirts with red trim, red shorts.
Year formed: 1876. **Manager:** John Lambie.
League appearances: Buckley, J. 26; Campbell, C. 15(11); Charnley, C. 29(1); Craig, D. (3); Duffy, J. 34; Duncan, C. 20; Elliott, D. 37; English, I. 7(6); Flood, J. 7; Callagher, B. 3(2); Johnston, S. 8; Kennedy, A. 2; Law, R. 25(2); McConville, A. 1(1); McGlashan, C. 34(2); McGovern, P. 10(7); McLaughlin, P. 18; Murdoch, A. 18; Nelson, C. 1; Peebles, G. 26(7); Rae, G. 29(1); Roche, D. 8(3); Robertson, G. 34(1); Smith, T. (1); Tierney, G. 28; Wright, B. 9.
Goals–League: (56): Elliot 13, McGlashan 10, Charnley 7, Buckley 5, Campbell 4, McGovern 4, Peebles 3 (1 pen), Duffy 2 (2 pens), English 2, Flood 1, Gallagher 1, Johnston 1, Roche 1, Tierney 1, own goal 1.
Scottish Cup: (3): Duffy 1 (pen), McGlashan 1, Roche 1.
Skol Cup: (2): Charnley 1, Peebles 1.

QUEEN OF THE SOUTH — DIV. 2

Ground: Palmerston Park, Dumfries DG2 9BA (0387–54853)
Colours: Royal blue shirts, white shorts.
Year formed: 1919. **Manager:** Ally MacLeod.
League appearances: Adams, S. 8(2); Andrews, G. 2(5); Campbell, K. 2(3); Davidson, A. 32; Fraser, G. 22(6); Gordon, S. 32(4); Hetherington, K. 13(2); Johnston, G. 2; MacDonald, R. 8; McCafferty, T. 20(2); McCulloch, D. 2; McCulloch, D. 1; McFarlane, A. 26; McGarvey, F. 12(7); McGhie, W. 35(1); McGuire, J. 25(4); McKeown, B. 25: Mills, D, 12(2); Moffat, I. 2(4); Possee, M. (1); Rennie, A. 1; Robertson, J. 17(5); Thomson, A. 34(3); Thomson, I. 29; Thomson, M. 7; Sim, W. 24(6); Sloane, T. 11(1); Watters, W. 19; Wylde, G. 6.
Goals–League: (46): Thomson A 11, Gordon 7, McGuire 4, Roberston 4, Watters 4, Fraser 3, MacDonald 2, McGarvey 2, Sloan 2, Thomson I 2, Adams 1, Hetherington 1, McGhie 1, Sim 1, own goal 1.
Scottish Cup: (7): Watters 2, Gordon 1, McGhie 1, McGuire 1, Sim 1, Thomson A 1.
Skol Cup: (7): Thomson A 3, McGuire 2, Fraser 1, McGhie.

QUEEN'S PARK DIV. 2

Ground: Hampden Park, Glasgow G42 9BA (041 632 1275)
Colours: Black and white hooped shirts, white shorts.
Year formed: 1867. **Coach:** Eddie Hunter.
League appearances: Callan, D. 29; Caven, R. 39; Crooks, G. 2; Elder, G. 37; Greig, D. 19(14); Hendry, M. 38; Jack, S. 38; MacKenzie, K. 15(7); McEntegart, S. 33(5); McFadyen, James, (8); McFadyen, Joe. 2(11); McKay, M. 10; McKeever, R. 3; McNamee, P. 30(1); Millar, G. (1); Monaghan, M. 39; Morris, S. 1(2); Morton, C. 28(4); O'Brien, J. 31(1); Ogg, G. 33; Rodden, J. 2(3).
Goals–League: (48): Hendry 17 (2 pens), Caven 6, Elder 6, Greig 6, O'Brien 4, Ogg 3, Crooks 1, McEntegart 1, James McFadyen 1, Joe McFadyen 1, McNamee 1, Morton 1.
Scottish Cup: (1): own goal 1.
Skol Cup: (4): Hendry 2, McEntegart, O'Brien 1.

RAITH ROVERS DIV. 1

Ground: Stark's Park, Pratt Street, Kirkcaldy KY1 1SA (0592–263514)
Colours: Royal blue shirts, white shorts.
Year formed: 1883. **Manager:** Jimmy Nicholl.
League appearances: Arthur, G. 34; Banner, A. 5; Burn, P. 3(7); Coyle, R. 34(1); Dalziel, G. 39; Dennis, S. 35; Dunleavy, D. 15; Ferguson, I. 27(6); Fraser, C. 13; Henderson, N. 1; Logan, A. 17(12); MacDonald, K. 10(1); MacLeod, I. 26; McGeachie, G. 30(1); McStay, J. 36; Murray; D. 14(3); Nelson, M. 33; Nicholl, J. 10; Raeside, R. 12(2); Romaines, S. 8(5); Simpson, S. 11(3); Sinclair, D. 15(8); Strang, S. (4); Young, D. 1.
Goals–League: (54): Dalziel 25, Ferguson 8, Logan 4, Nelson 4, Dunleavy 2, MacDonald 2 (1 pen), Coyle 1, Dennis 1, MacLeod 1, McStay 1, Romaines 1, Simpson 1, Sinclair 1, own goals 2.
Scottish Cup: (0).
Skol Cup: (5): McGeachie 2, Coyle 1, Dalziel 1, own goal 1.

RANGERS PREM. DIV.

Ground: Ibrox Stadium, Glasgow G51 2XD (041–427 5232)
Colours: Royal blue shirts, white shorts.
Year formed: 1873. **Manager:** Walter Smith.
League appearances: Brown, J. 25(2); Butcher, T. 5; Cowan, T. 4(1); Dodds, D. 3; Durrant, I. 3(1); Ferguson, I. 10(1); Gough, R. 26; Hateley, M. 30(3); Huistra, P. 10(17); Hurlock, T. 29; Johnston, M. 29; Kuznetsov, O. 2; McCoist, A. 15(11); McSwegan, G. 1(2); Munro, S. 14; Nisbet, S. 15; Reid, B. 3; Robertson, A. 7(8); Spackman, N. 35; Spencer, J. 3(2); Steven, T. 19; Stevens, G. 36; Vinnicombe, C. 10; Walters, M. 26(4); Woods, 36.
Goals–League: (62): Walters 12 (2 pens), Johnston 11 (1 pen), McCoist 11 (1 pen), Hateley 10, Huistra 4, Stevens G 4, Hurlock 2, Steven T 2, Brown 1, Durrant 1, Ferguson 1, Robertson 1, Spencer 1, Vinnicombe 1.
Scottish Cup: (7): Hateley 2, Huistra 1, McCoist 1, Nisbet 1, Spackman 1, Walters 1 (pen).
Skol Cup: (15): Johnston 3, McCoist 3, Steven T 3, Hateley 2, Walters 2, Butcher 1, Gough 1.

ST JOHNSTONE — PREM. DIV.

Ground: McDiarmid Park, Crieff Road, Perth PH1 2SJ (0738–26961)
Colours: Royal blue shirts with white trim, blue shorts.
Year formed: 1884. **Manager:** Alex Totten.
League appearances: Balavage, J. 2; Baltacha, S. 34; Barron, 3(8); Bingham, D. 4(3); Cherry, P. 18(2); Curran, H. 35; Davies, J. 13(8); Deas, P. (1); Grant, R. 29(1); Hamilton, L. 34; Heddle, I. 2(5); Inglis, J. 31; Johnston, S. (1); Lee, I. 1(4); MacDonald, K. 5(6); Maskrey, S. 33(1); McGinnis, G. 32; McVicar, D. 18(5); Moore, A. 31; Nicholson, K. 5; Sweeney, P. 8, Treanor, M. 30; Turner, T. 27(1); Ward, K. 1(9).
Goals–League: (41): Curran 9, Grant 7, Maskrey 7, Moore 5, Treanor 4 (2 pens), Turner 3, Bingham 2, Davies 1, Inglis 1, McVicar 1, Ward 1.
Scottish Cup: (12): Moore 4, Grant 3, Maskrey 3, Curran 2.
Skol Cup: (0).

ST MIRREN — PREM. DIV.

Ground: St Mirren Park, Paisley PA3 2EJ (041–889 2558 and 041-840 1337)
Colours: White shirts with black vertical stripes, black shorts.
Year formed: 1877. **Manager:** David Hay.
League appearances: Archibald, S. 16; Black, T. 33(1); Broddle, J. 7(3); Dawson, R. 13(1); Fridge, L. 11; Godfrey, P. 14; Hutchinson, T. (2); Irvine, A. 8(3); Kinnaird, P. 18(5); Lambert, P. 30(1); Manley, R. 19; Martin, B. 31; McDowell, K. 11(12); McEwan, A. 1; McGill, D. 1(2); McGowne, K. 10; McIntyre, P. 4; McWalter, M. 16(6); McWhirter, N. 25; Money, C. 25; Shaw, G. 21(12); Stickroth, T. 26(5); Thiele, G. (1); Torfason, G. 18; Victor, (Munoz), 18; Winnie, D. 1; Wishart, F. 19(3).
Goals–League: (28): Kinnaird 4, McDowall 4, Torfason 4, McWalter 3, Archibald 2, Black 2, Lambert 2, Martin 2, McEwan 1, McIntyre 1, Shaw 1, Stickroth 1, Victor 1.
Scottish Cup: (5): Torfason 2, Kinnaird 1, McDowall 1, Victor 1.
Skol Cup: (1): Stickroth 1.

STENHOUSEMUIR — DIV. 2

Ground: Ochilview Park, Stenhousemuir FK5 5QL (0324–562992)
Colours: Maroon shirts with white trim, white shorts.
Year formed: 1884. **Manager:** Dennis Lawson.
League appearances: Aitken, N. 28; Anderson, P. 38; Bell, A. 10(11); Bullen, L. 14(7); Cairney, H. 39; Clouston, B. 30(2); Donald, G. 2; Elliott, T. (1); Gardiner, J. 1; Hallford, E. 38; Joyce, A. 1; Kelly, C. 38; Kemp, B. 33; McAvoy, M. 6(9); McCormick, S. 36(2); McGurn, J. (2); McNab, J. 1(3); Nelson, M. 10(6); Quinton, I. 9(15); Rennie, S. 3; Speirs, A. 32(7); Tracey, K. 22; Walker, C. 38.
Goals–League: (56): Speirs 17 (3 pens), McCormick 13 (1 pen), Bullen 4, McAvoy 4, Walker 4, Bell 3, Cairney 2, Quinton 2, Aitken 1, Anderson 1, Clouston 1, Donald 1, Elliott 1, Gardiner 1, Hallford 1.
Scottish Cup: (0).
Skol Cup: (0).

STIRLING ALBION DIV. 1

Ground: Annfield Park, Stirling FK8 2HE (0786–50399)
Colours: Red shirts with white sleeves, white shorts.
Year formed: 1945. **Manager:** John Brogan.
League appearances: Colquhoun, J. (1); Conway, M. 8(6); Docherty, R. 27(3); Hagart, L. 1; Hay, G. 36; Kerr, J. 38; Lawrie, D. 39; Lloyd, D. 34(1); Mailer, J. 6(3); McConville, R. 10(10); McGachie, J. 8(11); McGeown, M. 39; McInnes, I. 25(11); Mitchell, C. 38; Moore, V. 31(4); Pew, D. (1); Reid, J. 27(6); Robertson, S. 24(7); Shanks, D. 35; Watson, P. 3(1).
Goals–League: (62): Lloyd 14, Moore 13 (1 pen), Reid 11, McGachie 5, Docherty 4, Lawrie 4, McInnes 3, Conway 2, Shanks 2, Kerr 1, Mailer 1, Mitchell 1, Robertson 1.
Scottish Cup: (2): Docherty 1, Lloyd 1.
Skol Cup: (1): Reid 1.

STRANRAER DIV. 2

Ground: Stair Park, Stranraer DG9 8BS (0776 3271)
Colours: Royal blue shirts with amber band, blue shorts.
Year formed: 1870. **Manager:** Alex McAnespie.
League appearances: Atkins, D. 1; Cook, D. 18(17); Corrie, T. 5(1); Duffy, B. 30; Duncan, G. 28(5); Ewing, A. 1; Gallagher, A. 17(2), George, D. 28(2); Grant, A. 33(1); Harkness, C. 27(9); Henderson, D. 30(4); Holland, B. 8; Hughes, J. 7; Kyle, M. (1); Lindsay, C. 12(3); Lowe, L. 20; McCann, J. 7; McCutcheon, D. 10(6); McMillan, G. 18(6); McNiven, J. 37; Muir, W. (1); Scott, R. 10(3); Shirkie, S. 22; Spittal, I. 33(2); Thompson, H. 1(4); Tierney, M. 1(5); Walker, D. 25(2).
Goals–League: (61): Harkness 14 (2 pens), Cook 12, McMillan 6, Henderson 5, McNiven 5, Grant 4, George 3, Gallagher 2, McCutcheon 2 (1 pen), Spittal 2, Thompson 2, Duncan 1, Ewing 1, Shirkie 1, Walker 1 (pen).
Scottish Cup: (3): George 1, Grant 1, Henderson.
Skol Cup: (6): George 2, Cook 1, Henderson 1, McMillan 1, Spittal 1.

SCOTTISH REVIEW

Rangers won their 41st League championship title on the last day of the season beating nearest rivals Aberdeen 2-0 at Ibrox. Rangers had to win to take the flag as both teams were level on points with the Dons having the advantage of scoring more goals though both had the same goal difference.

There had seemed little danger to Rangers during the middle of the season. They had gone to the top for the first time on 6 October, ironically after a goalless draw at Aberdeen, before slipping to third following a run which included two 2-1 defeats at the hands of Dundee United.

However, Rangers had a successful sequence of 15 games without defeat which included seven successive wins. But Aberdeen took heart when they beat Rangers 1-0 with a Hans Gillhaus goal at Pittodrie on 2 March to put them six points behind with a game in hand.

The departure of Graeme Souness to Liverpool was a shock for Rangers but Walter Smith who had been a loyal and able No. 2 took over. But on 4 May the Ibrox team crashed 3-0 at Motherwell and with St Johnstone losing 2-1 at Aberdeen, the Dons moved to the top for the first time in the season, lining up the grandstand finish.

However, the League programme was affected by events during the season which saw a move by Falkirk gaining sufficient support for the promotion and relegation issues to be changed during the campaign. As a result, no teams were dropped from the Premier League, but two promoted from the First Division.

At the end of the season it was perhaps fortunate that Falkirk did manage to finish on top of the First Division and along with Airdrieonians win promotion.

In Europe it proved to be another disappointing season north of the border. Dundee United after a fairly unimpressive passage against their Icelandic opponents were humiliated by Vitesse the Arnhem based Dutch side. After losing 1-0 away, United crashed by four clear goals at Tannadice. Scotland's other UEFA Cup entrants Hearts returned from a trip to the USSR and a 1-1 draw with Dnepr. They completed the tie satisfactorily by winning 3-1 at home.

In the European Cup Rangers took four goals off Valletta in Malta and six at Ibrox. In the Cup-Winners' Cup Aberdeen won 2-0 in Famagusta and 3-0 at Pittodrie. But the second round ended all Scottish interest, Rangers losing to Red Star Belgrade 3-0 away and drawing 1-1 at home, Aberdeen being held goalless at home by Legia Warsaw and losing to a late goal in Poland and Hearts crashing out to Bologna despite winning their first leg. Taking a 3-1 lead to Italy might have seemed a sufficient advantage, but they conceded two goals in the last 17 minutes to lose the game 3-0 and 4-3 on aggregate.

SCOTTISH LEAGUE – PREMIER DIVISION RESULTS 1990–91

	Aberdeen	Celtic	Dundee U	Dunfermline Ath	Hearts	Hibernian	Motherwell	Rangers	St Johnstone	St Mirren
Aberdeen	—	3–0 1–0	1–1 0–1	3–2 0–0	3–0 5–0	2–0 2–0	1–1 3–0	0–0 1–0	0–0 2–1	2–1 1–0
Celtic	0–3 1–0	—	0–0 1–0	1–2 5–1	3–0 1–1	2–0 1–1	2–1 1–2	1–2 3–0	0–0 3–0	4–1 1–0
Dundee U	2–3 1–2	3–1 2–1	—	3–0 1–0	1–1 2–1	1–0 0–0	1–0 3–0	2–1 1–2	1–2 0–0	1–0 3–2
Dunfermline Ath	1–1 1–4	1–1 0–1	1–0 1–0	—	2–0 3–1	1–1 1–1	3–3 2–5	0–1 0–1	1–2 3–2	0–0 2–2
Hearts	1–0 1–4	1–0 0–1	1–0 2–1	1–1 4–1	—	1–1 3–1	3–2 2–1	1–3 0–1	2–3 2–1	1–1 2–0
Hibernian	1–1 2–4	0–3 0–2	0–0 1–0	1–1 3–0	0–3 1–4	—	1–0 1–1	0–0 0–2	1–0 0–1	1–0 4–3
Motherwell	0–0 0–2	2–0 1–1	0–2 1–0	2–0 1–0	1–1 1–3	4–1 1–0	—	2–4 3–0	3–0 2–2	1–1 3–1
Rangers	2–2 2–0	1–1 2–0	1–2 1–0	3–1 2–0	4–0 2–1	4–0 0–0	1–0 2–0	—	4–1 3–0	5–0 1–0
St Johnstone	5–0 0–1	3–2 2–3	1–3 0–1	3–2 0–1	2–1 0–2	1–1 0–0	2–1 1–4	0–0 1–1	—	0–1 2–1
St Mirren	0–4 0–1	2–3 0–2	1–1 0–1	0–1 2–2	2–1 0–0	1–0 1–0	1–0 2–2	0–3 0–1	2–2 0–[illegible]	—

SCOTTISH LEAGUE – DIVISION I RESULTS 1990–91

	Albion R	Alloa	Arbroath	Berwick R	Cowden	Dumbarton	East Fife	E Stirling	Montrose	Queen of S	Queen's P	Sten'muir	Stirling A	Stranraer
Albion R	—	3–1	1–1 1–3	1–1 4–2	3–1	3–2	0–2 3–1	4–0	0–3	1–0 2–2	1–0	1–4 0–0	2–2	0–1 1–4
Alloa	1–0 1–2	—	2–1 2–2	5–0 1–1	1–2	0–1 2–1	3–6	0–1	1–0 1–0	4–1	1–1	1–0 1–1	0–1	0–1
Arbroath	0–0	1–1	—	4–2 0–1	1–2	2–1 0–1	1–1 0–1	3–0 0–1	0–1	1–1	3–0	0–0 0–2	2–3 0–1	3–0 1–5
Berwick R	3–0	1–0	1–1	—	0–1 1–1	2–1	1–0	2–2 2–0	2–1 0-1	2–0 3–3	1–2 2–1	0–1	1–1 0–0	3–2
Cowdenbeath	2–0 2–2	1–1 1–0	0–1 4–2	0–1	—	4–2 1–3	2–0	2–1	0–1	2–1	0–1 2–1	3–3 1–1	0–2	2–3 2–0
Dumbarton	2–2 0–2	0–0	1–1	1–1 2–0	1–3	—	3–2 2–1	2–1	1–1 2–2	0–2 2–0	1–0 1–0	0–0 2–1	0–0	0–1
East Fife	2–2	2–2 1–3	2–0	4–1 0–1	1–1 0–5	2–1	—	1–1	1–3 2–2	2–0	2–1	2–1 1–0	1–1 2–2	1–2 1–2
East Stirling	0–3 1–1	0–0 1–6	1–1	0–4	1–3 0–0	2–1 2–0	3–1 5–1	—	1–0	1–0 1–1	1–3 1–1	2–2	0–1	0–2
Montrose	5–0 3–0	2–4	3–0 1–0	1–2	2–0 1–0	1–2	0–2	2–2 2–0	—	0–0	1–0	2–3	0–1 0–1	1–0 2–1
Queen of the S	1–1	1–3 0–0	1–0 6–1	2–0	2–4 2–2	1–2	3–0 1–3	1–2	2–1 0–3	—	3–2	3–2	0–0 0–0	1–1 1–2
Queen's Park	1–1 0–0	1–0 3–1	2–1 0–0	2–1	1–0	—	0–2 2–0	4–0	0–0 0–3	3–1 3–0	—	1–0	0–0	3–1
Stenhousemuir	3–2	1–0	2–0	2–1 1–1	1–4	1–1	2–0	4–1 0–0	0–1 0–1	2–1 0–1	1–2 4–1	—	2–2 2–1	3–2 2–0
Stirling A	2–0 3–0	2–0 1–2	3–1	4–1	5–1 0–0	2–0 0–1	1–2	3–0 4–0	3–0	0–0	0–1 2–0	1–1	—	3–1
Stranraer	2–1	2–0 0–0	1–1 2–3	1–2 4–1	1–3	2–1	2–2	1–2 2–0	1–0	4–1	2–1 1–3	1–2	1–4 0–0	—

SCOTTISH LEAGUE – DIVISION II RESULTS 1990–91

	Airdrie	Ayr U	Brechin C	Clyde	Clydebank	Dundee	Falkirk	Forfar Ath	Hamilton A	Kilmarnock	Meadowb'k	Morton	Partick Th	Raith R
Airdrieonians	—	4–0	3–0	2–2 1–1	2–2	0–1 0–1	1–3 0–3	1–1 2–1	2–1	2–0 2–0	0–0	4–0 3–0	0–0	1–5
Ayr U	2–2 0–1	—	4–1	4–1	1–1 0–1	2–4	1–1	1–1	2–2 1–2	1–2 1–0	1–1 2–0	1–0 1–1	0–1	2–0 5–3
Brechin C	1–2 1–1	1–2 2–2	—	0–2 2–0	3–2	1–3	0–2	2–1	0–1 2–2	0–2	1–3	0–1 1–3	2–2 1–2	0–4
Clyde	1–4	1–0 2–2	1–1	—	0–1 3–1	4–2 0–1	1–3	1–1 0–1	0–2	1–1 2–1	1–0	1–3 0–1	2–4 2–1	1–2
Clydebank	5–2 1–3	0–2	3–4 1–0	2–1	—	1–3 1–1	3–1 2–2	2–2	3–1 1–3	1–3 0–0	2–2	2–4	2–3 7–1	1–1
Dundee	0–1	1–0 4–0	1–2 0–1	3–1	1–0	—	2–2	4–1 1–0	3–2	1–1	1–2 4–0	1–0 1–0	1–1	2–1 2–0
Falkirk	1–1	1–2 4–1	3–0 2–1	2–0 1–0	5–1	1–0 0–0	—	1–0	0–1 3–0	1–1	2–2 4–2	2–1	0–2	7–1 0–2
Forfar Ath	1–4	3–1 1–1	0–0 4–1	1–3	0–3 2–2	1–1	1–2 0–0	—	0–0	2–2 1–1	3–2 2–0	5–1 2–2	0–1	3–1
Hamilton A	0–1 1–1	0–0	2–1	1–0 3–1	2–0	1–0 1–2	0–2	2–0 0–1	—	3–1	1–1 2–1	1–1	2–2 0–1	2–2 1–2
Kilmarnock	3–4	3–1	2–1 2–2	2–1	3–0	2–1 0–0	1–1 1–1	1–0	1–0 1–0	—	2–3	3–1 1–1	2–3 1–0	1–1
Meadowbank Th	2–4 0–1	1–0	6–1 1–1	0–2 1–1	0–3 2–3	0–1	1–1	2–2	1–1	1–0 1–8	—	1–1	1–1	1–1 4–1
Morton	1–0	2–1	3–3	0–0	2–0 2–2	0–1	0–0 0–1	1–1	0–2 0–4	3–0	0–3 1–1	—	4–0 1–1	4–0 1–2
Partick Th	1–1 0–2	0–0 2–0	3–3	2–0	0–1	1–3 1–0	2–0 1–1	3–2 2–0	0–[illegible]	2–0	1–1 2–4	2–2	—	0–3
Raith R	1–1 0–1	3–0	1–2 1–0	1–1 1–0	2–0 1–2	1–1	1–4	2–1 1–2	1–[illegible]	1–1 1–2	1–3	1–0	0–0 1–5	—

B & Q SCOTTISH LEAGUE FINAL TABLES 1990–91

Premier Division	P	Home W	D	L	Goals F	A	Away W	D	L	Goals F	A	GD	Pts
Rangers	36	14	3	1	40	8	10	4	4	22	15	+39	55
Aberdeen	36	12	5	1	30	7	10	4	4	32	20	+35	53
Celtic	36	10	4	4	30	14	7	3	8	22	24	+14	41
Dundee U	36	11	3	4	28	16	6	4	8	13	13	+12	41
Hearts	36	10	3	5	28	22	4	4	10	20	33	−7	35
Motherwell	36	9	5	4	28	18	3	4	11	23	32	+1	33
St Johnstone	36	6	4	8	23	25	5	5	8	18	29	−13	31
Dunfermline Ath	36	5	7	6	23	26	3	4	11	15	35	−23	27
Hibernian	36	6	5	7	17	25	0	8	10	7	26	−27	25
St Mirren	36	4	5	9	14	25	1	4	13	14	34	−31	19

First Division	P	Home W	D	L	Goals F	A	Away W	D	L	Goals F	A	GD	Pts
Falkirk	39	12	4	4	40	18	9	8	2	30	17	+35	54
Airdrieonians	39	9	5	5	32	21	12	6	2	37	22	+26	53
Dundee	39	12	3	4	33	15	10	5	5	26	18	+26	52
Partick T	39	7	6	6	25	24	9	7	4	31	29	+3	45
Kilmarnock	39	10	6	3	32	21	5	7	8	26	27	+10	43
Hamilton A	39	8	6	6	25	20	8	4	7	25	21	+9	42
Raith R	39	7	5	8	22	26	7	4	8	32	38	−10	37
Clydebank	39	6	6	8	40	39	7	4	8	25	31	−5	36
Morton	39	6	7	6	25	22	5	6	9	23	33	−7	35
Forfar Ath	39	6	9	5	32	28	3	6	10	18	29	−7	33
Meadowbank T	39	4	7	8	25	33	6	6	8	31	35	−12	33
Ayr U	39	7	7	6	32	24	3	5	11	15	35	−12	32
Clyde	39	6	4	10	24	32	3	5	11	17	29	−20	27
Brechin C	39	3	4	12	20	37	4	6	10	24	43	−36	24

Second Division	P	Home W	D	L	Goals F	A	Away W	D	L	Goals F	A	GD	Pts
Stirling Albion	39	12	3	4	39	11	8	11	1	23	13	+38	54
Montrose	39	10	2	7	29	18	10	4	6	25	16	+20	46
Cowdenbeath	39	9	4	7	31	26	9	5	5	33	24	+14	45
Stenhousemuir	39	11	4	5	32	20	5	8	6	24	22	+14	44
Queen's Park	39	11	6	2	27	12	6	2	12	21	30	+6	42
Stranraer	39	8	3	8	30	30	10	1	9	31	30	+1	40
Dumbarton	39	8	8	4	23	20	7	2	10	26	29	0	40
Berwick R	39	9	6	4	27	18	6	4	10	24	39	−6	40
Alloa	39	8	4	7	27	22	5	7	8	24	24	+5	37
East Fife	39	7	7	6	30	31	7	2	10	27	34	−8	37
Albion R	39	8	5	6	31	30	3	8	9	17	33	−15	35
Queen of the S	39	7	6	7	31	29	2	6	11	15	33	−16	30
East Stirling	39	5	7	8	22	32	4	4	11	14	39	−35	29
Arbroath	39	5	5	10	22	24	3	6	10	19	35	−18	27

Scottish League Leading Scorers 1990–91

Listed in order of total

Premier Division	*League*	*Scottish Cup*	*Skol Cup*	*Total*
Tommy Coyne (Celtic)	18	1	0	**19**
Doug Arnott (Motherwell)	14	2	1	**17**
Darren Jackson (Dundee U)	12	2	3	**17**
Mark Walters (Rangers)	12	1	2	**15**
Hans Gillhaus (Aberdeen)	14	0	0	**14**
Eoin Jess (Aberdeen)	13	0	1	**14**
Mo Johnston (Rangers)	11	0	3	**14**
First Division				
Ken Eadie (Clydebank)	29	0	1	**30**
Gordon Dalziel (Raith R)	25	0	1	**26**
Dave MacCabe (Morton)	21	2	0	**23**
Owen Coyle (Airdrieonians)	20	0	0	**20**
Keith Wright (Dundee)	18	0	0	**18**
Sam McGivern (Falkirk)	15	3	0	**18**
Second Division				
Mike Hendry (Queen's Park)	17	0	2	**19**
Alan MacKenzie (Cowdenbeath)	15	2	1	**18**
Tony Speirs (Stenhousemuir)	17	0	0	**17**
Kevin Todd (Berwick R)	14	1	1	**16**
David Lloyd (Stirling Alb)	14	1	0	**15**

Scottish League and Cup Honours

Championship wins

41 – Rangers (including one shared); 35 – Celtic; 4 – Aberdeen, Hearts, Hibernian; 2 – Dumbarton (including one shared); 1 – Dundee, Dundee U, Kilmarnock, Motherwell, Third Lanark.

Scottish FA Cup

29 – Celtic, Rangers; 10 – Queen's Park; 7 – Aberdeen; 5 – Hearts; 3 – Clyde, St Mirren, Vale of Leven; 2 – Dunfermline Ath, Falkirk, Hibernian, Kilmarnock, Motherwell, Renton, Third Lanark; 1 – Airdrieonians, Dumbarton, Dundee, East Fife, Morton, Partick Th, St Bernard's.

Scottish League/Skol Cup

16 – Rangers; 9 – Celtic; 5 – Aberdeen, Hearts; 3 – Dundee, East Fife; 2 – Dundee U; 1 – Hibernian, Motherwell, Partick Th.

SCOTTISH LEAGUE HONOURS LIST

Premier Division (maximum points: *a*, 72; *b*, 88)

	First	Pt	Second	Pt	Third	Pt
1975–76	Rangers	54	Celtic	48	Hibernian	43
1976–77*a*	Celtic	55	Rangers	46	Aberdeen	43
1977–78*a*	Rangers	55	Aberdeen	53	Dundee U	40
1978–79*a*	Celtic	48	Rangers	45	Dundee U	44
1979–80*a*	Aberdeen	48	Celtic	47	St Mirren	42
1980–81*a*	Celtic	56	Aberdeen	49	Rangers	44
1981–82*a*	Celtic	55	Aberdeen	53	Rangers	43
1982–83*a*	Dundee U	56	Celtic	55	Aberdeen	55
1983–84*a*	Aberdeen	57	Celtic	50	Dundee U	47
1984–85*a*	Aberdeen	59	Celtic	52	Dundee U	47
1985–86*a*	Celtic	50	Hearts	50	Dundee U	47
1986–87	Rangers	69	Celtic	63	Dundee U	60
1987–88	Celtic	72	Hearts	62	Rangers	60
1988–89*a*	Rangers	56	Aberdeen	50	Celtic	46
1989–90*a*	Rangers	51	Aberdeen	44	Hearts	44
1990–91*a*	Rangers	55	Aberdeen	53	*Celtic	41

First Division (Maximum points: *a*, 52; *b*, 78; *c*, 88)

	First	Pt	Second	Pt	Third	Pt
1975–76*a*	Partick T	41	Kilmarnock	35	Montrose	30
1976–77*b*	St Mirren	62	Clydebank	58	Dundee	51
1977–78*b*	*Morton	58	Hearts	58	Dundee	57
1978–79*b*	Dundee	55	*Kilmarnock	54	Clydebank	54
1979–80*b*	Hearts	53	Airdrieonians	51	Ayr U	44
1980–81*b*	Hibernian	57	Dundee	52	St Johnstone	51
1981–82*b*	Motherwell	61	Kilmarnock	51	Hearts	50
1982–83*b*	St Johnstone	55	Hearts	54	Clydebank	50
1983–84*b*	Morton	54	Dumbarton	51	Partick T	46
1984–85*b*	Motherwell	50	Clydebank	48	Falkirk	45
1985–86*b*	Hamilton A	56	Falkirk	45	Kilmarnock	44
1986–87*c*	Morton	57	Dunfermline Ath	56	Dumbarton	53
1987–88*c*	Hamilton A	56	Meadowbank T	52	Clydebank	49
1988–89*b*	Dunfermline Ath	54	Falkirk	52	Clydebank	48
1989–90*b*	St Johnstone	58	Airdrieonians	54	Clydebank	44
1990–91*b*	Falkirk	54	Airdrieonians	53	Dundee	52

Second Division (maximum points: *a*, 52; *b*, 78)

	First	Pt	Second	Pt	Third	Pt
1975–77*a*	*Clydebank	40	Raith R	40	Alloa	35
1976–77*b*	Stirling A	55	Alloa	51	Dunfermline Ath	50
1977–78*b*	*Clyde	53	Raith R	53	Dunfermline Ath	48
1978–79*b*	Berwick R	54	Dunfermline Ath	52	Falkirk	50
1979–80*b*	Falkirk	50	East Stirling	49	Forfar Ath	46
1980–81*b*	Queen's Park	50	Queen of the S	46	Cowdenbeath	45
1981–82*b*	Clyde	59	Alloa	50	Arbroath	50
1982–83*b*	Brechin C	55	Meadowbank T	54	Arbroath	49

1983–84*b*	Forfar Ath	63	East Fife	47	Berwick R	43
1984–85*b*	Montrose	53	Alloa	50	Dunfermline Ath	49
1985–86*b*	Dunfermline Ath	57	Queen of the S	55	Meadowbank T	49
1986–87*b*	Meadowbank T	55	*Raith R	52	Stirling A	52
1987–88*b*	Ayr U	61	St Johnstone	59	Queen's Park	51
1988–89*b*	Albion R	50	Alloa	45	Brechin C	43
1989–90*b*	Brechin C	49	Kilmarnock	48	Stirling A	47
1990–91*b*	Stirling A	54	Montrose	46	Cowdenbeath	45

First Division to 1974–75 (maximun points: *a*, 36; *b*, 44; *c*, 40; *d*, 52; *e*, 60; *f*, 68; *g*, 76; *h*, 84; *j*, 60)

	First	*Pt*	*Second*	*Pt*	*Third*	*Pt*
1890–91*a*	Dumbarton	29	Rangers	29	Celtic	24
1891–92*b*	Dumbarton	37	Celtic	35	Hearts	30
1892–93*a*	Celtic	29	Rangers	28	St Mirren	23
1893–94*a*	Celtic	29	Hearts	26	St Bernard's	22
1894–95	Hearts	31	Celtic	26	Rangers	21
1895–96	Celtic	30	Rangers	26	Hibernian	24
1896–97	Hearts	28	Hibernian	26	Rangers	25
1897–98	Celtic	33	Rangers	29	Hibernian	22
1898–99	Rangers	36	Hearts	26	Celtic	24
1899–1900	Rangers	32	Celtic	25	Hibernian	24
1900–01*c*	Rangers	35	Celtic	29	Hibernian	25
1901–02*a*	Rangers	28	Celtic	26	Hearts	22
1902–03*b*	Hibernian	37	Dundee	31	Rangers	29
1903–04	Third Lanark	43	Hearts	39	Rangers	38
1904–05*d*	Celtic	41	Rangers	41	Third Lanark	35
1905–06*e*	Celtic	49	Hearts	43	Airdrieonians	38
1906–07*f*	Celtic	55	Dundee	48	Rangers	45
1907–08	Celtic	55	Falkirk	51	Rangers	50
1908–09	Celtic	51	Dundee	50	Clyde	48
1909–10	Celtic	54	Falkirk	52	Rangers	46
1910–11	Rangers	52	Aberdeen	48	Falkirk	44
1911–12	Rangers	51	Celtic	45	Clyde	42
1912–13	Rangers	53	Celtic	49	Hearts	41
1913–14*g*	Celtic	65	Rangers	59	Hearts	54
1914–15*g*	Celtic	65	Hearts	61	Rangers	50
1915–16*g*	Celtic	67	Rangers	56	Morton	51
1916–17*g*	Celtic	64	Morton	54	Rangers	53
1917–18*f*	Rangers	56	Celtic	55	Kilmarnock	43
1918–19	Celtic	58	Rangers	57	Morton	47
1919–20*h*	Rangers	71	Celtic	68	Motherwell	57
1920–21	Rangers	76	Celtic	66	Hearts	56
1921–22	Celtic	67	Rangers	66	Raith R	56
1922–23*g*	Rangers	55	Airdrieonians	50	Celtic	46
1923–24	Rangers	59	Airdrieonians	50	Celtic	41
1924–25	Rangers	60	Airdrieonians	57	Hibernian	52
1925–26	Celtic	58	*Airdrieonians	50	Hearts	50

1926–27	Rangers	56	Motherwell	51	Celtic	49
1927–28	Rangers	60	*Celtic	55	Motherwell	55
1928–29	Rangers	67	Celtic	51	Motherwell	50
1929–30	Rangers	60	Motherwell	55	Aberdeen	53
1930–31	Rangers	60	Celtic	58	Motherwell	56
1931–32	Motherwell	66	Rangers	61	Celtic	48
1932–33	Rangers	62	Motherwell	59	Hearts	50
1933–34	Rangers	66	Motherwell	62	Celtic	47
1934–35	Rangers	55	Celtic	52	Hearts	50
1935–36	Celtic	66	*Rangers	61	Aberdeen	61
1936–37	Rangers	61	Aberdeen	54	Celtic	52
1937–38	Celtic	61	Hearts	58	Rangers	49
1938–39	Rangers	59	Celtic	48	Aberdeen	46
1946–47*f*	Rangers	46	Hibernian	44	Aberdeen	39
1947–48*j*	Hibernian	48	Rangers	46	Partick T	36
1948–49	Rangers	46	Dundee	45	Hibernian	39
1949–50	Rangers	50	Hibernian	49	Hearts	43
1950–51	Hibernian	48	Rangers	38	Dundee	38
1951–52	Hibernian	45	Rangers	41	East Fife	37
1952–53	*Rangers	43	Hibernian	43	East Fife	39
1953–54	Celtic	43	Hearts	38	Partick T	35
1954–55	Aberdeen	49	Celtic	46	Rangers	41
1955–56*f*	Rangers	52	Aberdeen	46	*Hearts	45
1956–57	Rangers	55	Hearts	53	Kilmarnock	42
1957–58	Hearts	62	Rangers	49	Celtic	46
1958–59	Rangers	50	Hearts	48	Motherwell	44
1959–60	Hearts	54	Kilmarnock	50	*Rangers	42
1960–61	Rangers	51	Kilmarnock	50	Third Lanark	42
1961–62	Dundee	54	Rangers	51	Celtic	46
1962–63	Rangers	57	Kilmarnock	48	Partick T	46
1963–64	Rangers	55	Kilmarnock	49	*Celtic	47
1964–65	*Kilmarnock	50	Hearts	50	Dunfermline Ath	49
1965–66	Celtic	57	Rangers	55	Kilmarnock	45
1966–67	Celtic	58	Rangers	55	Clyde	46
1967–68	Celtic	63	Rangers	61	Hibernian	45
1968–69	Celtic	54	Rangers	49	Dunfermline Ath	45
1969–70	Celtic	57	Rangers	45	Hibernian	44
1970–71	Celtic	56	Aberdeen	54	St Johnstone	44
1971–72	Celtic	60	Aberdeen	50	Rangers	44
1972–73	Celtic	57	Rangers	56	Hibernian	45
1973–74	Celtic	53	Hibernian	49	Rangers	48
1974–75	Rangers	56	Hibernian	49	Celtic	45

Second Division to 1974–75 from 1921–22 (maximum points: *a*, 76; *b*, 72; *c*, 68; *d*, 52; *e*, 60)

	First	*Pt*	*Second*	*Pt*	*Third*	*Pt*
1921–22*a*†	*Alloa	60	Cowdenbeath	47	Armadale	45
1922–23*a*	Queen's Park	57	Clydebank	**50	St Johnstone	**45

1923–24*a*	St Johnstone........56	Cowdenbeath.......55	Bathgate...............44
1924–25*a*	Dundee U............50	Clydebank............48	Clyde.....................47
1925–26*a*	Dunfermline Ath.59	Clyde.....................53	Ayr U 52
1926–27*a*	Bo'ness.................56	Raith R.................49	Clydebank............45
1927–28*a*	Ayr U 54	Third Lanark.......45	King's Park..........44
1928–29*b*	Dundee U............51	Morton 50	Arbroath..............47
1929–30*a*	*Leith Ath...........57	East Fife 57	Albion R..............54
1930–31*a*	Third Lanark.......61	Dundee U............50	Dunfermline Ath.47
1931–32*a*	*East Stirling.......55	St Johnstone........55	*Raith Rovers 46
1932–33*c*	Hibernian.............54	Queen of the S.....49	Dunfermline Ath.47
1933–34*c*	Albion R..............45	Dunfermline Ath.44	Arbroath..............44
1934–35*c*	Third Lanark.......52	Arbroath..............50	St Bernard's.........47
1935–36*c*	Falkirk.................59	St Mirren 52	Morton 48
1936–37*c*	Ayr U 54	Morton 51	St Bernard's.........48
1937–38*c*	*Raith R..............59	Albion R..............48	Airdrieonians.......47
1938–39*c*	Cowdenbeath.......60	*Alloa 48	East Fife..............48
1946–47*d*	Dundee 45	Airdrieonians.......42	East Fife 31
1947–48*e*	East Fife 53	Albion R..............42	Hamilton A 40
1948–49*e*	Raith R.................42	Stirling Albion.....42	*Airdrieonians.....41
1949–50*e*	Morton 47	Airdrieonians.......44	*St Johnstone 36
1950–51*e*	*Queen of the S...45	Stirling Albion.....45	*Ayr U 36
1951–52*e*	Clyde.....................44	Falkirk.................43	Ayr U 39
1952–53*e*	Stirling Albion.....44	Hamilton A 43	Queen's Park 37
1953–54*e*	Motherwell 45	Kilmarnock..........42	*Third Lanark.....36
1954–55*e*	Airdrieonians.......46	Dunfermline Ath.42	Hamilton A 39
1955–56*b*	Queen's Park 54	Ayr U 51	St Johnstone........49
1956–57*b*	Clyde.....................64	Third Lanark.......51	Cowdenbeath.......45
1957–58*b*	Stirling Albion.....55	Dunfermline Ath.53	Arbroath..............47
1958–59*b*	Ayr U 60	Arbroath..............51	Stenhousemuir.....40
1959–60*b*	St Johnstone........53	Dundee U............50	Queen of the S.....49
1960–61*b*	Stirling Albion.....55	Falkirk.................54	Stenhousemuir.....50
1961–62*b*	Clyde.....................54	Queen of the S.....53	Morton 44
1962–63*b*	St Johnstone........55	East Stirling.........49	Morton 48
1963–64*b*	Morton 67	Clyde.....................53	Arbroath..............46
1964–65*b*	Stirling Albion.....59	Hamilton A 50	Queen of the S.....45
1965–66*b*	Ayr U 53	Airdrieonians.......50	Queen of the S.....49
1966–67*b*	Morton 69	Raith R.................58	Arbroath..............57
1967–68*b*	St Mirren 62	Arbroath..............53	*East Fife 40
1968–69*b*	Motherwell 64	Ayr U 53	East Fife 47
1969–70*b*	Falkirk.................56	Cowdenbeath.......55	Queen of the S.....50
1970–71*b*	Partick T..............56	East Fife 51	Arbroath..............46
1971–72*b*	*Dumbarton 52	Arbroath..............52	Stirling Albion.....50
1972–73*b*	Clyde.....................56	Dumfermline Ath 52	*Raith R..............47
1973–74*b*	Airdrieonians.......60	Kilmarnock..........59	Hamilton A 55
1974–75*b*	Falkirk.................54	*Queen of the S...53	Montrose 53

**On goal average/difference. †Held jointly after indecisive play-off. ‡Won on deciding match. ‡‡Held jointly. **Two points deducted for fielding ineligible player. *†Only one club promoted. Competition suspended 1940–45.*

RELEGATED CLUBS

First Premier Division

1975–76 Dundee, St Johnstone
1976–77 Hearts, Kilmarnock
1977–78 Ayr U, Clydebank
1978–79 Hearts, Motherwell
1979–80 Dundee, Hibernian
1980–81 Kilmarnock, Hearts
1981–82 Partick T, Airdrieonians
1982–83 Morton, Kilmarnock
1983–84 St Johnstone, Motherwell
1984–85 Dumbarton, Morton
1985–86 *No relegation due to League reorganisation*
1986–87 Clydebank, Hamilton A
1987–88 Falkirk, Dunfermline Ath, Morton
1988–89 Hamilton A
1989–90 Dundee
1990–91 None

From First Division

1975–76 Dunfermline Ath, Clyde
1976–77 Raith R, Falkirk
1977–78 Alloa Ath, East Fife
1978–79 Montrose, Queen of the S
1979–80 Arbroath, Clyde
1980–81 Stirling A, Berwick R
1981–82 East Stirling, Queen of the S
1982–83 Dunfermline Ath, Queen's Park
1983–84 Raith R, Alloa
1984–85 Meadowbank T, St Johnstone
1985–86 Ayr U, Alloa
1986–87 Brechin C, Montrose
1987–88 East Fife, Dumbarton
1988–89 Kilmarnock, Queen of the S
1989–90 Albion R, Alloa
1990–91 Clyde, Brechin C

Relegated from First Division to 1973–74

1921–22 *Queen's Park, Dumbarton, Clydebank
1922–23 Albion R, Alloa Ath
1923–24 Clyde, Clydebank
1924–25 Third Lanark, Ayr U
1925–26 Raith R, Clydebank
1926–27 Morton, Dundee U
1927–28 Dunfermline Ath, Bo'ness
1928–29 Third Lanark, Raith R
1929–30 St Johnstone, Dundee U
1930–31 Hibernian, East Fife
1931–32 Dundee U, Leith Ath
1932–33 Morton, East Stirling
1933–34 Third Lanark, Cowdenbeath
1934–35 St Mirren, Falkirk
1935–36 Airdrieonians, Ayr U
1936–37 Dunfermline Ath, Albion R
1937–38 Dundee, Morton
1938–39 Queen's Park, Raith R
1946–47 Kilmarnock, Hamilton A
1947–48 Airdrieonians, Queen's Park
1948–49 Morton, Albion R
1949–50 Queen of the S, Stirling Albion
1950–51 Clyde, Falkirk
1951–52 Morton, Stirling Albion
1952–53 Motherwell, Third Lanark
1953–54 Airdrieonians, Hamilton A
1954–55 No clubs relegated
1955–56 Stirling Albion, Clyde
1956–57 Dunfermline Ath, Ayr U
1957–58 East Fife, Queen's Park
1958–59 Queen of the S, Falkirk
1959–60 Arbroath, Stirling Albion
1960–61 Ayr U, Clyde
1961–62 St Johnstone, Stirling Albion
1962–63 Clyde, Raith R
1963–64 Queen of the S, East Stirling
1964–65 Airdrieonians, Third Lanark
1965–66 Morton, Hamilton A
1966–67 St Mirren, Ayr U
1967–68 Motherwell, Stirling Albion
1968–69 Falkirk, Arbroath
1969–70 Raith R, Partick T
1970–71 St Mirren, Cowdenbeath
1971–72 Clyde, Dunfermline Ath
1972–73 Kilmarnock, Airdrieonians
1973–74 East Fife, Falkirk
1974–75 *League reorganised at end of season*

*Season 1921–22–only 1 club promoted, 3 clubs relegated.

SKOL CUP 1990–91

First Round
East Stirling 2, Dumbarton 2*
East Stirling won 4-1 on penalties
Queen's Park 3, East Fife 3*
Stenhousemuir 0, Cowdenbeath 2
Montrose 1, Queen of the S 2*
Stirling Albion 1, Arbroath 2
Stranraer 4, Berwick R 3*

Second Round
Airdrieonians 1, Stranraer 2
Alloa 0, Dundee U 3
Brechin C 0, Hamilton A 2
Dunfermline Ath 4, Albion R 0
Forfar Ath 1, Raith R 2
Kilmarnock 3, Clydebank 2
Motherwell 4, Morton 3
Queen of the S 2, Dundee 2*
Queen of the S won 4-1 on penalties
Queen's Park 1, Aberdeen 2
Rangers 5, East Stirling 0
St Johnstone 0, Clyde 2
Celtic 4, Ayr U 0
Cowdenbeath 0, Hearts 2
Falkirk 1, Partick T 1*
Partick T won 4-1 on penalties
Meadowbank T 0, Hibernian 1*
St Mirren 1, Arbroath 0

Third Round
Dunfermline Ath 1, Queen of the S 2
Motherwell 2, Clyde 0
Partick T 1, Dundee U 3
Rangers 1, Kilmarnock 0
Aberdeen 4, Stranraer 0
Hamilton A 0, Celtic 1
Raith R 1, Hibernian 0
St Mirren 0, Hearts 1

Quarter-finals
Dundee U 2, Motherwell 0
Rangers 6, Raith R 2
Aberdeen 3, Hearts 0
Celtic 2, Queen of the S 1

Semi-finals – at Hampden Park
Celtic 2, Dundee U 0
Aberdeen 0, Rangers 1

Final–at Hampden Park, att. 62,817
Rangers 2, Celtic 1*

**After extra time*

PAST SCOTTISH LEAGUE CUP FINALS

1946–47	Rangers	4	Aberdeen	0
1947–48	East Fife	0 4	Falkirk	0 1
1948–49	Rangers	2	Raith Rovers	0
1949–50	East Fife	3	Dunfermline	0
1950–51	Motherwell	3	Hibernian	0
1951–52	Dundee	3	Rangers	2
1952–53	Dundee	2	Kilmarnock	0
1953–54	East Fife	3	Partick Thistle	2
1954–55	Hearts	4	Motherwell	2
1955–56	Aberdeen	2	St Mirren	1
1956–57	Celtic	0 3	Partick Thistle	0 0
1957–58	Celtic	7	Rangers	1
1958–59	Hearts	5	Partick Thistle	1
1959–60	Hearts	2	Third Lanark	1
1960–61	Rangers	2	Kilmarnock	0
1961–62	Rangers	1 3	Hearts	1 1
1962–63	Hearts	1	Kilmarnock	0
1963–64	Rangers	5	Morton	0
1964–65	Rangers	2	Celtic	1
1965–66	Celtic	2	Rangers	1
1966–67	Celtic	1	Rangers	0
1967–68	Celtic	5	Dundee	3
1968–69	Celtic	6	Hibernian	2
1969–70	Celtic	1	St Johnstone	0
1970–71	Rangers	1	Celtic	0
1971–72	Partick Thistle	4	Celtic	1
1972–73	Hibernian	2	Celtic	1
1973–74	Dundee	1	Celtic	0
1974–75	Celtic	6	Hibernian	3
1975–76	Rangers	1	Celtic	0
1976–77	Aberdeen	2	Celtic	1
1977–78	Rangers	2	Celtic	1
1978–79	Rangers	2	Aberdeen	1
1979–80	Aberdeen	0 0	Dundee U.	0 3
1980–81	Dundee	0	Dundee U.	3
1981–82	Rangers	2	Dundee U.	1
1982–83	Celtic	2	Rangers	1
1983–84	Rangers	3	Celtic	2
1984–85	Rangers	1	Dundee U.	0
1985–86	Aberdeen	3	Hibernian	0
1986–87	Rangers	2	Celtic	1
1987–88	Rangers†	3	Aberdeen	3
1988–89	Aberdeen	2	Rangers	3
1989–90	Aberdeen	2	Rangers	1

†*Won on penalties*

B & Q CENTENARY CUP 1990–91

First Round
Airdrieonians 2, Partick T 1*
Alloa 3, Forfar Ath 0
Arbroath 2, Queen's Park 1*
Ayr U 3, Brechin C 0
Clydebank 1, East Fife 2
Cowdenbeath 2, Albion R 1
Falkirk 0, Raith R 3
Kilmarnock 4, Stirling Albion 1
Montrose 2, Berwick R 0
Stenhousemuir 0, Queen of the S 0*
Queen of the S won 4-3 on penalties
Clyde 4, Dumbarton 3
Meadowbank T 1, Morton 2*

Second Round
Airdrieonians 0, Clyde 2
Alloa 3, Dundee 5
East Fife 2, Stranraer 1
Kilmarnock 3, Arbroath 1
Montrose 2, Ayr U 3*
Morton 0, Cowdenbeath 0*
Cowdenbeath won 8-7 on penalties
Queen of the S 5, East Stirling 0
Raith R 3, Hamilton A 2

Quarter-finals
Ayr U 4, Queen of the S 1
Clyde 2, Cowdenbeath 1
East Fife 1, Kilmarnock 2
Raith R 0, Dundee 1

Semi-finals
Ayr U 2, Clyde 0
Kilmarnock 0, Dundee 2

Final – at Fir Park, att. 11,506
Dundee (0) 3 *(Dodds 3 (1 pen)*
Ayr U (1) 2 *(McAllister, Smyth)*

**After extra time*

SCOTTISH CUP 1990–91

FIRST ROUND
East Stirling (0) 1 Queen of the S (2) 3
Fraserburgh (1) 3 Vale of Leithen (1) 1
Ross County (1) 1 Alloa (1) 1
Montrose (0) 0 Dumbarton (0) 0
Threave Rovers (1) 1 Spartans (2) 2
Whitehill Welfare (0) 0 East Fife (2) 4

FIRST ROUND REPLAYS
Alloa 0 (1) Ross County (2) 3
Dumbarton (0) 1 Montrose (1) 4

SECOND ROUND
Berwick R (0) 1 Albion R (0) 0
Fraserburgh (0) 1 Cove Rangers (2) 4
Montrose (0) 0 Arbroath (1) 2
Queen's Park (0) 1 Stranraer (1) 2
Stirling Albion (0) 2 Stenhousemuir (0) 0
Inverness Thistle (1) 1 East Fife (1) 1
Spartans (0) 0 Cowdenbeath (0) 0
Ross County (1) 2 Queen of the S (1) 2

SECOND ROUND REPLAYS
East Fife (0) 1 Inverness Thistle (0) 0
Cowdenbeath (1) 2 Spartans (0) 0
Queen of the S (0) 2 Ross County (1) 6

THIRD ROUND
Aberdeen (0) 0 Motherwell (0) 1
Airdrieonians (0) 2 Hearts (1) 1
Clydebank (0) 0 Ayr U (0) 1
Cove Rangers (1) 1 Cowdenbeath (0) 2
Dundee (1) 1 Brechin C (0) 0
East Fife (1) 1 Dundee U (0) 1
Forfar Ath (0) 0 Celtic (2) 2
Kilmarnock (1) 3 Arbroath (1) 2
Partick T (0) 0 Falkirk (0) 0
Raith R (0) 0 Hamilton A (0) 1
St Johnstone (0) 0 Berwick R (0) 0
Stirling Albion (0) 0 Morton (0) 1
Stranraer (0) 1 St Mirren (2) 5
Clyde (0) 0 Hibernian (0) 2
Rangers (2) 2 Dunfermline Ath (0) 0
Ross County (0) 1 Meadowbank T (2) 6

THIRD ROUND REPLAYS
Dundee U (1) 2 East Fife (1) 1 *aet*
Berwick R (1) 3 St Johnstone (3) 4 *aet*
Falkirk (1) 4 Partick T (1) 3

FOURTH ROUND
Ayr U (0) 0 Hamilton A (0) 0
Dundee (2) 2 Kilmarnock (0) 0
Dundee U (0) 2 Airdrieonians (0) 0
Motherwell (1) 4 Falkirk (1) 2
Rangers (3) 5 Cowdenbeath (0) 0
St Johnstone (0) 2 Hibernian (1) 1
Celtic (3) 3 St Mirren (0) 0
Morton (3) 3 Meadowbank T (0) 0

FOURTH ROUND REPLAY
Hamilton A (1) 2 Ayr U (1) 3

QUARTER-FINALS
Dundee U (1) 3 Dundee (1) 1
Motherwell (0) 0 Morton (0) 0
St Johnstone (2) 5 Ayr U (0) 2
Celtic (2) 2 Rangers (0) 0

QUARTER-FINAL REPLAY
Morton (0) 1 Motherwell (1) 1
aet; Motherwell won 5-4 on penalties

SEMI-FINALS
Celtic (0) 0 Motherwell (0) 0
Dundee U (1) 2 St Johnstone (1) 1

SEMI-FINAL REPLAY
Celtic (2) 2 Motherwell (1) 4

FINAL
Motherwell (1) 4 (*Ferguson, O'Donnell, Angus, Kirk*)
Dundee U (0) 3 (*Bowman, O'Neil J, Jackson*) *aet*, 57,319

SCOTTISH CUP PAST FINALS

Year	Winner	Score	Runner-up	Score
1874	Queen's Park	2	Clydesdale	0
1875	Queen's Park	3	Renton	0
1876	Queen's Park	1 2	Third Lanark	1 0
1877	Vale of Leven	0 1 3	Rangers	0 1 2
1878	Vale of Leven	1	Third Lanark	0
1879	Vale of Leven	1	Rangers	1
	Vale of Leven awarded cup, Rangers did not appear for replay			
1880	Queen's Park	3	Thornlibank	0
1881	Queen's Park	2 3	Dumbarton	1 1
	Replayed because of protest			
1882	Queen's Park	2 4	Dumbarton	2 1
1883	Dumbarton	2 2	Vale of Leven	2 1
1884	*Queen's Park awarded cup when Vale of Leven did not appear for the final*			
1885	Renton	0 3	Vale of Leven	0 1
1886	Queen's Park	3	Renton	1
1887	Hibernian	2	Dumbarton	1
1888	Renton	6	Cambuslang	1
1889	Third Lanark	3 2	Celtic	0 1
	Replayed because of protest			
1890	Queen's Park	1 2	Vale of Leven	1 1
1891	Hearts	1	Dumbarton	0
1892	Celtic	1 5	Queen's Park	0 1
	Replayed because of protest			
1893	Queen's Park	2	Celtic	1
1894	Rangers	3	Celtic	1
1895	St Bernards	3	Renton	1
1896	Hearts	3	Hibernian	1
1897	Rangers	5	Dumbarton	1
1898	Rangers	2	Kilmarnock	0
1899	Celtic	2	Rangers	0
1900	Celtic	4	Queen's Park	3
1901	Hearts	4	Celtic	3
1902	Hibernian	1	Celtic	0
1903	Rangers	1 0 2	Hearts	1 0 0
1904	Celtic	3	Rangers	2
1905	Third Lanark	0 3	Rangers	0 1
1906	Hearts	1	Third Lanark	0
1907	Celtic	3	Hearts	0
1908	Celtic	5	St Mirren	1
1909	*After two drawn games between Celtic and Rangers, 2–2, 1–1, there was a riot and the cup was withheld*			
1910	Dundee	2 0 2	Clyde	2 0 1
1911	Celtic	0 2	Hamilton Acad	0 0
1912	Celtic	2	Clyde	0
1913	Falkirk	2	Raith R	0
1914	Celtic	0 4	Hibernian	0 1
1920	Kilmarnock	3	Albion R	2
1921	Partick Th	1	Rangers	0
1922	Morton	1	Rangers	0
1923	Celtic	1	Hibernian	0
1924	Airdrieonians	2	Hibernian	0
1925	Celtic	2	Dundee	1
1926	St Mirren	2	Celtic	0
1927	Celtic	3	East Fife	1
1928	Rangers	4	Celtic	0

1929	Kilmarnock	2	Rangers	0
1930	Rangers	0 2	Partick Th	0 1
1931	Celtic	2 4	Motherwell	2 2
1932	Rangers	1 3	Kilmarnock	1 0
1933	Celtic	1	Motherwell	0
1934	Rangers	5	St Mirren	0
1935	Rangers	2	Hamilton Acad	1
1936	Rangers	1	Third Lanark	0
1937	Celtic	2	Aberdeen	1
1938	East Fife	1 4	Kilmarnock	1 2
1939	Clyde	4	Motherwell	0
1947	Aberdeen	2	Hibernian	1
1948	Rangers	1 1	Morton	1 0
1949	Rangers	4	Clyde	1
1950	Rangers	3	East Fife	0
1951	Celtic	1	Motherwell	0
1952	Motherwell	4	Dundee	0
1953	Rangers	1 1	Aberdeen	1 0
1954	Celtic	2	Aberdeen	1
1955	Clyde	1 1	Celtic	1 0
1956	Hearts	3	Celtic	1
1957	Falkirk	1 2	Kilmarnock	1 1
1958	Clyde	1	Hibernian	0
1959	St Mirren	3	Aberdeen	1
1960	Rangers	2	Kilmarnock	0
1961	Dunfermline Ath	0 2	Celtic	0 0
1962	Rangers	2	St Mirren	0
1963	Rangers	1 3	Celtic	1 0
1964	Rangers	3	Dundee	1
1965	Celtic	3	Dunfermline Ath	2
1966	Rangers	0 1	Celtic	0 0
1967	Celtic	2	Aberdeen	0
1968	Dunfermline Ath	3	Hearts	1
1969	Celtic	4	Rangers	0
1970	Aberdeen	3	Celtic	1
1971	Celtic	1 2	Rangers	1 1
1972	Celtic	6	Hibernian	1
1973	Rangers	3	Celtic	2
1974	Celtic	3	Dundee U	0
1975	Celtic	3	Airdrieonians	1
1976	Rangers	3	Hearts	1
1977	Celtic	1	Rangers	0
1978	Rangers	2	Aberdeen	1
1979	Rangers	0 0 3	Hibernian	0 0 2
1980	Celtic	1	Rangers	0
1981	Rangers	0 4	Dundee U	0 1
1982	Aberdeen	4	Rangers	1 (aet)
1983	Aberdeen	1	Rangers	0 (aet)
1984	Aberdeen	2	Celtic	1 (aet)
1985	Celtic	2	Dundee U	1
1986	Aberdeen	3	Hearts	0
1987	St Mirren	1	Dundee U	0 (aet)
1988	Celtic	2	Dundee U	1
1989	Celtic	1	Rangers	0
1990	Aberdeen†	0	Celtic	0

†won on penalties

WELSH FOOTBALL 1990–91

THE ABACUS LEAGUE

National Division

	P	W	D	L	F	A	Pts
Abergavenny	30	21	6	3	68	23	69
Aberystwyth Town	30	18	5	7	68	35	59
Haverfordwest	30	16	6	8	56	34	54
Ton Pentre	30	15	8	7	51	30	53
Maesteg Park	30	15	5	10	50	41	50
Inter Cardiff	30	12	8	10	58	46	44
Briton Ferry Athletic	30	12	6	12	63	67	42
Brecon Corries	30	10	10	10	47	49	40
Cwmbran Town	30	11	6	13	63	58	39
Pembroke	30	10	9	11	49	51	39
Bridgend Town	30	11	6	13	50	56	39
Afan Lido	30	9	8	13	44	62	35
Ferndale	30	9	7	14	39	54	34
Llanelli	30	8	5	17	48	57	29
Port Talbot	30	8	5	17	31	56	29
Ammanford	30	2	6	22	20	86	12

Division One

	P	W	D	L	F	A	Pts
Morriston Town	32	16	12	4	58	37	60
Caldicot	32	17	9	6	50	30	60
Ebbw Vale	32	16	11	5	72	29	59
Llanwern	32	17	5	10	67	40	56
Aberaman	32	16	7	9	63	46	55
BP	32	13	5	14	55	61	44
Blaenrhondda	32	12	8	12	49	56	44
Seven Sisters	32	12	7	13	57	56	43
Newport YMCA	32	11	10	11	43	50	43
Garw	32	11	7	14	43	59	40
Ynysybwl	32	11	4	17	55	60	37
Caerleon	32	9	9	14	39	51	36
Merthyr Tydfil	32	10	6	16	53	67	36
Pontllanfraith	32	11	3	18	39	60	36
Cardiff Corries	32	9	8	15	44	57	35
Panteg	32	9	8	15	47	64	35
Milford*	32	8	9	15	51	62	22

*11 points deducted

Division Two

	P	W	D	L	F	A	Pts
Cardiff Civil Service	32	25	3	4	100	36	78
Risca Utd	32	24	3	5	77	34	75
Taffs Well	32	20	6	6	76	25	66
Caerau	32	17	6	9	41	30	57
Carmarthen	32	17	5	10	82	57	56
Treharris	32	16	3	13	65	68	51
Skewen	32	13	10	9	54	43	49
AFC Tondu	32	13	6	13	36	48	45

South Wales Police	32	12	5	15	48	55	41
Pontardawe	32	11	5	16	45	55	38
Blaenavon	32	9	9	14	56	58	36
Cardiff Institute	32	11	3	18	40	70	36
Tonyrefail	32	8	11	13	38	44	35
Pontyclun	32	9	5	18	35	62	32
Abercynon	32	7	9	16	43	74	30
Trelewis	32	7	8	17	42	64	29
Pontlottyn	32	2	5	25	32	87	11

IRISH FOOTBALL 1990–91

SMIRNOFF IRISH LEAGUE CHAMPIONSHIP FINAL TABLE

	P	W	D	L	F	A	Pts
Portadown	30	22	5	3	61	22	77
Bangor	30	19	4	7	52	29	61
Glentoran	30	18	6	6	50	32	60
Glenavon	30	17	6	7	63	38	57
Newry Town	30	15	5	10	50	42	50
Cliftonville	30	14	7	9	59	41	49
Linfield	30	12	10	8	40	34	46
Ballymena	30	12	8	10	49	46	44
Ards	30	12	7	11	47	40	43
Crusaders	30	11	9	10	53	46	42
Distillery	30	10	5	15	47	57	35
Omagh Town	30	10	4	16	48	66	34
Larne	30	8	6	16	41	59	30
Ballyclare	30	5	6	19	33	68	21
Carrick	30	4	5	21	30	58	17
Coleraine	30	2	5	23	25	70	11

REPUBLIC OF IRELAND

Final League Table 1990–91

	P	W	D	L	F	A	Pts
Dundalk	33	22	8	3	52	16	52
Cork City	33	19	12	2	45	17	50
St Patrick's Ath	33	17	10	6	46	21	44
Shelbourne	33	18	6	9	57	30	42
Sligo Rovers	33	13	12	8	34	22	38
Shamrock Rovers	33	14	9	10	51	37	37
Derry City	33	13	9	11	50	47	35
Galway United	33	9	5	20	35	61	23
Bohemians	33	7	8	18	26	41	22
Athlone Town	33	6	7	20	22	53	19
Limerick*	33	6	5	22	20	53	17
Waterford*	33	6	5	22	22	63	17

EUROPEAN CUPS REVIEW

Manchester United made it a splendid return to Europe for English clubs by winning the Cup-Winners' Cup in some style. Aston Villa managed to beat Banik Ostrava of Czechoslovakia in the first round of the UEFA Cup, but found Internazionale a much tougher obstacle in the next.

United began with a 2-0 win over Pecsi Munkas the Hungarian team while Villa were establishing a similar advantage after taking a 3-1 lead in their tie. Brian McClair ensured that United won 3-0 over the two legs and Villa also won by the odd goal in Ostrava thanks to an own goal by Ivo Stas at 2-1. Stas later became a Villa player.

Wrexham, who had earned a 1-0 win over Lyngby the Danish team in the first round, gave a plucky performance against Manchester United but lost 3-0 at Old Trafford and 2-0 at the Racecourse Ground. Then in beating Inter-Milan 2-0 at Villa Park, Aston Villa produced arguably their finest display in Europe since winning the European Cup. Alas in the return match they gave a naive exhibition and lost 3-0.

Despite the advantage of a first minute goal from McClair in the quarter-final against Montpellier, an own goal by Lee Martin in the seventh minute left United with a formidable task in France. But they came through impressively winning 2-0.

In the semi-final in Poland, they found Legia Warsaw a much poorer outfit than the record of a team which had knocked out Italian holders Sampdoria had suggested. They were full value for their 3-1 lead in Poland and the 1-1 scoreline at Old Trafford meant little enough.

In the final in Rotterdam, United deserved their 2-1 win over a disappointing Barcelona. In fact the scoreline did not reflect the territorial advantage enjoyed by Alex Ferguson's men. Mark Hughes scored twice in seven minutes in the second half and only a free-kick by Ronald Koeman with 11 minutes left reduced Barcelona's deficit and allowed an artificial climax.

The Champions Cup Final was a miserable affair and decided on penalty kicks following a goalless draw. Red Star Belgrade prevailed 5-3 on this lottery though the game deserved no better way of ending it. Again the UEFA Cup was an all-Italian Final with Inter-Milan taking the first leg 2-0 against Roma and holding on for an overall win despite losing 1-0 in the return game.

Alas the decision by UEFA to resurrect East German clubs robbed England of a possible extra place in the UEFA Cup for the 1991–92 season.

EUROPEAN CUP 1990–91

First Round, First Leg

Apoel	(1) 2	Bayern Munich	(0) 3
Akureyri	(1) 1	CSKA Sofia	(0) 0
Dinamo Bucharest	(3) 4	St Patrick's Athletic	(0) 0
Lech Poznan	(2) 3	Panathinaikos	(0) 0
Lillestrom	(0) 1	FC Brugge	(1) 1
Malmo	(1) 3	Besiktas	(0) 2
Marseille	(1) 5	Dinamo Tirana	(0) 1
Napoli	(0) 3	Ujpest Dozsa	(0) 0
Odense	(1) 1	Real Madrid	(2) 4
Porto	(3) 5	Portadown	(0) 0
Red Star Belgrade	(1) 1	Grasshoppers	(1) 1
Sparta Prague	(0) 0	Spartak Moscow	(1) 2
Tirol	(3) 5	Kuusysi	(0) 0
Union Luxembourg	(0) 0	Dynamo Dresden	(0) 0
Valetta	(0) 0	Rangers	(1) 4

AC Milan *bye*

First Round, Second Leg

Bayern Munich	(0) 4	Apoel	(0) 0
Besiktas	(2) 2	Malmo	(0) 2
FC Brugge	(1) 2	Lillestrom	(0) 0
CSKA Sofia	(1) 3	Akureyri	(0) 0
Dinamo Tirana	(0) 0	Marseille	(0) 0
Dynamo Dresden	(3) 3	Union Luxembourg	(0) 0
Grasshoppers	(0) 1	Red Star Belgrade	(1) 4
Kuusysi	(0) 1	Tirol	(1) 2
Panathinaikos	(1) 1	Lech Poznan	(0) 2
Portadown	(1) 1	Porto	(4) 8
Rangers	(4) 6	Valetta	(0) 0
Real Madrid	(2) 6	Odense	(0) 0
St Patrick's Athletic	(1) 1	Dinamo Bucharest	(0) 1
Spartak Moscow	(1) 2	Sparta Prague	(0) 0
Ujpest Dozsa	(0) 0	Napoli	(2) 2

Second Round, First Leg

Bayern Munich	(2) 4	CSKA Sofia	(0) 0
Dinamo Bucharest	(0) 0	Porto	(0) 0
Dynamo Dresden	(1) 1	Malmo	(1) 1
Lech Poznan	(2) 3	Marseille	(1) 2
AC Milan	(0) 0	FC Brugge	(0) 0
Napoli	(0) 0	Spartak Moscow	(0) 0
Real Madrid	(5) 9	Tirol	(1) 1
Red Star Belgrade	(1) 3	Rangers	(0) 0

Second Round, Second Leg

FC Brugge	(0) 0	AC Milan	(0) 1
CSKA Sofia	(0) 0	Bayern Munich	(1) 3
Malmo	(0) 1	Dynamo Dresden	(1) 1
(Dynamo Dresden won 5–4 on penalties)			
Marseille	(3) 6	Lech Poznan	(0) 1
Porto	(2) 4	Dinamo Bucharest	(0) 0
Rangers	(0) 1	Red Star Belgrade	(0) 1
Spartak Moscow	(0) 0	Napoli	(0) 0
(Spartak Moscow won 5–3 on penalties)			
Tirol	(1) 2	Real Madrid	(2) 2

Quarter-Finals, First Leg

Bayern Munich	(1) 1	Porto	(0) 1
AC Milan	(1) 1	Marseille	(1) 1
Red Star Belgrade	(2) 3	Dynamo Dresden	(0) 0
Spartak Moscow	(0) 0	Real Madrid	(0) 0

Quarter-Finals, Second Leg

Dynamo Dresden	(1) 1	Red Star Belgrade	(0) 2
Marseille	(0) 1	AC Milan	(0) 0
Porto	(0) 0	Bayern Munich	(1) 2
Real Madrid	(1) 1	Spartak Moscow	(2) 3

Semi-Finals, First Leg

Bayern Munich	(1) 1	Red Star Belgrade	(1) 2
Spartak Moscow	(0) 1	Marseille	(2) 3

Semi-Finals, Second Leg

Marseille	(1) 2	Spartak Moscow	(0) 1
Red Star Belgrade	(1) 2	Bayern Munich	(0) 2

Final: Red Star Belgrade (0) 0, Marseille (0) 0 *aet*
(Red Star Belgrade won 5-3 on penalties)
(in Bari, 29 May 1991, 56,000)

Red Star Belgrade: Stojanovic; Yugovic, Marovic, Sabanadzovic, Belodedic, Najdovski, Prosinecki, Mihajlovic, Pancev, Savicevic (Dodic 84), Binic.

Marseille: Olmeta; Amoros, Di Meco (Stojkovic 112), Boli, Mozer, Germain, Casoni, Waddle, Papin, Pele, Fournier (Vercruysse 75).

Referee: Lanese (Italy).

Penalty shoot-out: Red Star Belgrade: Prosinecki, Binic, Belodedic, Mihajlovic and Pancev scored; *Marseille:* Amoros (shot saved), Casoni, Papin and Mozer scored.

EUROPEAN CUP-WINNERS CUP 1990–91

Preliminary Round, First Leg

Bray Wanderers	(0) 1	Trabzonspor	(1) 1

Preliminary Round, Second Leg

Trabzonspor	(0) 2	Bray Wanderers	(0) 0

First Round, First Leg

Amadora	(1) 1	Neuchatel	(0) 1
Famagusta	(0) 0	Aberdeen	(0) 2
Fram	(0) 3	Djurgaarden	(0) 0
Glentoran	(0) 1	Steaua Bucharest	(0) 1
Kaiserslautern	(0) 1	Sampdoria	(0) 0
KuPS	(0) 2	Kiev Dynamo	(1) 2
Legia Warsaw	(0) 3	Hesperange	(0) 0
Manchester U	(2) 2	Pecsi Munkas	(0) 0
Montpellier	(0) 1	Eindhoven	(0) 0
Olympiakos	(2) 3	Flamurtari	(0) 1
Schwerin	(0) 0	FK Austria	(2) 2
Sliema Wanderers	(1) 1	Dukla Prague	(0) 2
Sliven	(0) 0	Juventus	(1) 2
Trabzonspor	(0) 1	Barcelona	(0) 0
Viking	(0) 0	Liege	(1) 2
Wrexham	(0) 0	Lyngby	(0) 0

First Round, Second Leg

Aberdeen	(2) 3	Famagusta	(0) 0
Barcelona	(5) 7	Trabzonspor	(1) 2
Djurgaarden	(0) 1	Fram	(1) 1
Dukla Prague	(0) 2	Sliema Wanderers	(0) 0
FK Austria	(0) 0	Schwerin	(0) 0
Flamurtari	(0) 0	Olympiakos	(0) 2
Hesperange	(0) 0	Legia Warsaw	(0) 3
Juventus	(3) 6	Sliven	(0) 1
Kiev Dynamo	(2) 4	KuPS	(0) 0
Liege	(2) 3	Viking	(0) 0
Lyngby	(0) 0	Wrexham	(1) 1
Neuchatel	(0) 1	Amadora	(0) 1
		(Amadora won 4–3 on penalties)	
Pecsi Munkas	(0) 0	Manchester U	(0) 1
PSV Eindhoven	(0) 0	Montpellier	(0) 0
Sampdoria	(1) 2	Kaiserslautern	(0) 0
Steaua	(3) 5	Glentoran	(0) 0

Second Round, First Leg

Aberdeen	(0) 0	Legia Warsaw	(0) 0
Fram	(0) 1	Barcelona	(1) 2
FK Austria	(0) 0	Juventus	(2) 4
Kiev Dynamo	(0) 1	Dukla Prague	(0) 0
Liege	(1) 2	Amadora	(0) 0
Manchester U	(2) 3	Wrexham	(0) 0
Montpellier	(1) 5	Steaua Bucharest	(0) 0
Olympiakos	(0) 0	Sampdoria	(0) 1

Second Round, Second Leg

Amadora	(1) 1	Liege	(0) 0
Barcelona	(2) 3	Fram	(0) 0
Dukla Prague	(0) 2	Kiev Dynamo	(1) 2
Juventus	(2) 4	FK Austria	(0) 0
Legia Warsaw	(0) 1	Aberdeen	(0) 0
Sampdoria	(2) 3	Olympiakos	(0) 1
Steaua Bucharest	(0) 0	Montpellier	(0) 3
Wrexham	(0) 0	Manchester U	(2) 2

Quarter-finals, First Leg

Kiev Dynamo	(1) 2	Barcelona	(2) 3
Legia Warsaw	(1) 1	Sampdoria	(0) 0
Liege	(0) 1	Juventus	(2) 3
Manchester U	(1) 1	Montpellier	(1) 1

Quarter-finals, Second Leg

Barcelona	(0) 1	Kiev Dynamo	(0) 1
Juventus	(3) 3	Liege	(0) 0
Montpellier	(0) 0	Manchester U	(1) 2
Sampdoria	(0) 2	Legia Warsaw	(1) 2

Semi-finals, First Leg

Barcelona	(0) 3	Juventus	(1) 1
Legia Warsaw	(1) 1	Manchester U	(1) 3

Semi-finals, Second Leg

Juventus	(0) 1	Barcelona	(0) 0
Manchester U	(1) 1	Legia Warsaw	(0) 1

Final: Manchester U (0) 2, Barcelona (0) 1

(in Rotterdam, 15 May 1991, 45,000)

Manchester U: Sealey; Irwin, Blackmore, Bruce, Phelan, Pallister, Robson, Ince, McClair, Hughes, Sharpe. *Scorer:* Hughes 68, 74.
Barcelona: Busquets; Nando, Alexanco (Pinilla 73), Koeman, Ferrer, Bakero, Goicoechea, Eusebio, Salinas, Laudrup, Beguiristain. *Scorer:* Koeman 80.
Referee: Karlsson (Sweden).

UEFA CUP 1990–91

First Round, First Leg

Anderlecht	(0) 2	Petrolul	(0) 0
Antwerp	(0) 0	Ferencvaros	(0) 0
Aston Villa	(1) 3	Banik Ostrava	(1) 1
Atalanta	(0) 0	Dinamo Zagreb	(0) 0
Avenir Beggen	(2) 2	Inter Bratislava	(1) 1
Bayer Leverkusen	(1) 1	Twente	(0) 0
Borussia Dortmund	(1) 2	Chemnitz	(0) 0
Brondby	(1) 5	Eintracht Frankfurt	(0) 0
Chernomorets Odessa	(1) 3	Rosenborg	(0) 1
Derry	(0) 0	Vitesse	(1) 1
Dnepr	(0) 1	Hearts	(1) 1
Fenerbahce	(2) 3	Guimaraes	(0) 0
Glenavon	(0) 0	Bordeaux	(0) 0
Hafnarfjordur	(1) 1	Dundee U	(1) 3
Hibernians Malta	(0) 0	Partizan Belgrade	(1) 3
Iraklis	(0) 0	Valencia	(0) 0
Katowice	(1) 3	Turun	(0) 0
Lausanne	(0) 3	Real Sociedad	(2) 2
Magdeburg	(0) 0	Rovanenmi	(0) 0
MTK VM	(1) 1	Lucerne	(1) 1
Norrkoping	(0) 0	Cologne	(0) 0
Partizani	(0) 0	Uni Craiova	(0) 1
Rapid	(0) 2	Internazionale	(1) 1
Roda	(1) 1	Monaco	(2) 3
Roma	(1) 1	Benfica	(0) 0
Seville	(0) 0	PAOK	(0) 0
Slavia Sofia	(1) 2	Omonia	(0) 1
Sporting Lisbon	(1) 1	Mechelen	(0) 0
Timisoara	(1) 2	Atletico Madrid	(0) 0
Torpedo Moscow	(4) 4	GAIS Gothenburg	(0) 1
Vejle	(0) 0	Admira Wacker	(0) 1
Zaglebie Lubin	(0) 0	Bologna	(0) 1

First Round, Second Leg

Admira Wacker	(3) 3	Vejle	(0) 0
Atletico Madrid	(0) 1	Timisoara	(0) 0
Banik Ostrava	(1) 1	Aston Villa	(0) 2
Benfica	(0) 0	Roma	(1) 1
Bologna	(0) 1	Zaglebie Lubin	(0) 0
Bordeaux	(2) 2	Glenavon	(0) 0
Chemnitz	(0) 0	Borussia Dortmund	(1) 2
Cologne	(0) 3	Norrkoping	(1) 1
Dinamo Zagreb	(0) 1	Atalanta	(0) 1

Dundee United	(0) 2	Hafnarfjordur	(2) 2
Eintracht Frankfurt	(3) 4	Brondby	(1) 1
Ferencvaros	(0) 3	Antwerp	(0) 1
GAIS Gothenburg	(0) 1	Torpedo Moscow	(1) 1
Guimaraes	(1) 2	Fenerbahce	(3) 3
Hearts	(3) 3	Dnepr	(1) 1
Internazionale	(2) 3	Rapid	(1) 1
Inter Bratislava	(2) 5	Avenir Beggen	(0) 0
Lucerne	(0) 2	MTK VM	(0) 1
Mechelen	(1) 2	Sporting Lisbon	(1) 2
Monaco	(1) 3	Roda	(0) 1
Omonia	(1) 4	Slavia Sofia	(1) 2
PAOK	(0) 0	Seville	(0) 0
	(Seville won 4–3 on penalties)		
Partizan Belgrade	(1) 2	Hibernians Malta	(0) 0
Petrolul	(0) 0	Anderlecht	(1) 2
Real Sociedad	(0) 1	Lausanne	(0) 0
Rovanenmi	(0) 0	Magdeburg	(1) 1
Rosenborg	(1) 2	Chernomorets Odessa	(1) 1
Turun	(0) 0	Katowice	(1) 1
Twente	(0) 1	Bayer Leverkusen	(0) 1
Uni Craiova	(0) 1	Partizani	(0) 0
Valencia	(0) 2	Iraklis	(0) 0
Vitesse	(0) 0	Derry	(0) 0

Second Round, First Leg

Aston Villa	(1) 2	Internazionale	(0) 0
Brondby	(1) 3	Ferencvaros	(0) 0
Chernomorets Odessa	(0) 0	Monaco	(0) 0
Cologne	(0) 0	Inter Bratislava	(0) 1
Fenerbahce	(0) 0	Atalanta	(1) 1
Hearts	(3) 3	Bologna	(0) 1
Katowice	(0) 1	Bayer Leverkusen	(1) 2
Lucerne	(0) 0	Admira Wacker	(0) 1
Magdeburg	(0) 0	Bordeaux	(1) 1
Omonia	(0) 1	Anderlecht	(0) 1
Real Sociedad	(0) 1	Partizan Belgrade	(0) 0
Sporting Lisbon	(2) 7	Timisoara	(0) 0
Torpedo Moscow	(0) 3	Seville	(0) 1
Uni Craiova	(0) 0	Borussia Dortmund	(0) 3
Valencia	(1) 1	Roma	(0) 1
Vitesse	(1) 1	Dundee U	(0) 0

Second Round, Second Leg

Admira Wacker	(0) 1	Lucerne	(0) 1
Anderlecht	(2) 3	Omonia	(0) 0
Atalanta	(1) 4	Fenerbahce	(0) 1

Bayer Leverkusen	(1) 4	Katowice	(0) 0
Bologna	(1) 3	Hearts	(0) 0
Bordeaux	(0) 1	Magdeburg	(0) 0
Borussia Dortmund	(1) 1	Uni Craiova	(0) 0
Dundee U	(0) 0	Vitesse	(2) 4
Ferencvaros	(0) 0	Brondby	(0) 1

(*Behind closed doors*)

Inter Bratislava	(0) 0	Cologne	(1) 2
Internazionale	(1) 3	Aston Villa	(0) 0
Monaco	(1) 1	Chernomorets Odessa	(0) 0
Partizan Belgrade	(0) 1	Real Sociedad	(0) 0

(*Partizan Belgrade won 5–4 on penalties*)

Roma	(1) 2	Valencia	(0) 1
Seville	(1) 2	Torpedo Moscow	(1) 1
Timisoara	(1) 2	Sporting Lisbon	(0) 0

Third Round, First Leg

Admira Wacker	(2) 3	Bologna	(0) 0
Anderlecht	(0) 1	Borussia Dortmund	(0) 0
Brondby	(1) 3	Bayer Leverkusen	(0) 0
Cologne	(0) 1	Atalanta	(0) 1
Internazionale	(1) 3	Partizan Belgrade	(0) 0
Roma	(2) 5	Bordeaux	(0) 0
Torpedo Moscow	(2) 2	Monaco	(0) 1
Vitesse	(0) 0	Sporting Lisbon	(2) 2

Third Round, Second Leg

Atalanta	(1) 1	Cologne	(0) 0
Bayer Leverkusen	(0) 0	Brondby	(0) 0
Bologna	(1) 3	Admira Wacker	(0) 0

(*Bologna won 6–5 on penalties*)

Bordeaux	(0) 0	Roma	(0) 2
Borussia Dortmund	(0) 2	Anderlecht	(1) 1
Monaco	(0) 1	Torpedo Moscow	(0) 2
Partizan Belgrade	(0) 1	Internazionale	(0) 1
Sporting Lisbon	(1) 2	Vitesse	(0) 1

Quarter-finals, First Leg

Atalanta	(0) 0	Internazionale	(0) 0
Bologna	(0) 1	Sporting Lisbon	(0) 1
Brondby	(0) 1	Torpedo Moscow	(0) 0
Roma	(1) 3	Anderlecht	(0) 0

Quarter-finals, Second Leg

Anderlecht	(0) 2	Roma	(1) 3
Internazionale	(0) 2	Atalanta	(0) 0

Sporting Lisbon	(1) 2	Bologna	(0) 0
Torpedo Moscow	(0) 1	Brondby	(0) 0

(*Brondby won 4–2 on penalties*)

Semi-finals, First Leg

Brondby	(0) 0	Roma	(0) 0
Sporting Lisbon	(0) 0	Internazionale	(0) 0

Semi-finals, Second Leg

Internazionale	(2) 2	Sporting Lisbon	(0) 0
Roma	(1) 2	Brondby	(0) 1

Final

First Leg: Internazionale (0) 2, Roma (0) 0
(in Milan, 8 May 1991, 68,887)

Internazionale: Zenga; Bergomi, Brehme, Battistini, Ferri, Paganin (Baresi 65), Bianchi, Berti, Matthaus, Klinsmann, Serena (Pizzi 90).
Scorers: Matthaus 55 pen, Berti 65.
Roma: Cervone; Tempestilli, Nela, Berthold, Aldair (Carboni 72), Comi (Muzzi 75), Gerolin, Di Mauro, Giannini, Voller, Rizzitelli.
Referee: Spirin (USSR).

Second Leg: Roma (0) 1 Internazionale (0) 0
(in Rome, 22 May 1991, 70,901)

Roma: Cervone; Tempestilli (Salsano 57), Aldair, Nela, Berthold, Gerolin, Desideri (Muzzi 69), Di Mauro, Giannini, Voller, Rizzitelli.
Scorer: Rizzitelli 81.
Internazionale: Zenga; Paganin, Bergomi, Ferri, Brehme, Battistini, Bianchi, Matthaus, Berti, Klinsmann, Pizzi (Mandorlini 67).
Referee: Quiniou (France).

UEFA CUP PAST FINALS

Year	Winner	Score	Runner-up	Score
1972	Tottenham H	2 1	Wolverhampton W	1 1
1973	Liverpool	3 0	Borussia Moenchengladbach	0 2
1974	Feyenoord	2 2	Tottenham H	2 0
1975	Borussia Moenchengladbach	0 5	Twente Enschede	0 1
1976	Liverpool	3 1	FC Bruges	2 1
1977	Juventus**	1 1	Athletic Bilbao	0 2
1978	PSV Eindhoven	0 3	SEC Bastia	0 0
1979	Borussia Moenchengladbach	1 1	Red Star Belgrade	1 0
1980	Borussia Moenchengladbach	3 0	Eintracht Frankfurt**	2 1
1981	Ipswich T	3 2	AZ 67 Alkmaar	0 4
1982	IFK Gothenburg	1 3	SV Hamburg	0 0
1983	RSC Anderlecht	1 1	Benfica	0 1
1984	Tottenham H†	1 1	RSC Anderlecht	1 1
1985	Real Madrid	3 0	Videoton	0 1
1986	Real Madrid	5 0	Cologne	1 2
1987	IFK Gothenburg	1 1	Dundee U	0 1
1988	Bayer Leverkusen†	0 3	Espanol	0 3
1989	Napoli	2 3	Stuttgart	1 3
1990	Juventus	3 0	Fiorentina	1 0

* *After extra time* ** *Won on away goals* †*Won on penalties* ‡*Aggregate score*

EUROPEAN CUP PAST FINALS

Year	Winner	Score	Runner-up	Score
1956	Real Madrid	4	Stade de Rheims	3
1957	Real Madrid	2	Fiorentina	0
1958	Real Madrid	3	AC Milan	2*
1959	Real Madrid	2	Stade de Rheims	0
1960	Real Madrid	7	Eintracht Frankfurt	3
1961	SL Benfica	3	Barcelona	2
1962	SL Benfica	5	Real Madrid	3
1963	AC Milan	2	SL Benfica	1
1964	Inter Milan	3	Real Madrid	1
1965	Inter Milan	1	SL Benfica	0
1966	Real Madrid	2	Partizan Belgrade	1
1967	Celtic	2	Inter Milan	1
1968	Manchester U	4	SL Benfica	1*
1969	AC Milan	4	Ajax Amsterdam	1
1970	Feyenoord	2	Celtic	1*
1971	Ajax Amsterdam	2	Panathinaikos	0
1972	Ajax Amsterdam	2	Inter Milan	0
1973	Ajax Amsterdam	1	Juventus	0
1974	Bayern Munich	1 4	Atletico Madrid	1 0
1975	Bayern Munich	2	Leeds U	0
1976	Bayern Munich	1	St Etienne	0
1977	Liverpool	3	Borussia Moenchengladbach	1
1978	Liverpool	1	FC Bruges	0
1979	Nottingham F	1	Malmö	0
1980	Nottingham F	1	SV Hamburg	0
1981	Liverpool	1	Real Madrid	0
1982	Aston Villa	1	Bayern Munich	0
1983	SV Hamburg	1	Juventus	0
1984	Liverpool†	1	AS Roma	1
1985	Juventus	1	Liverpool	0
1986	Steaua Bucharest†	0	Barcelona	0

1987	FC Porto	2	Bayern	1
1988	PSV Eindhoven†	0	Benfica	0
1989	AC Milan	4	Steaua Bucharest	0
1990	AC Milan	1	Benfica	0

EUROPEAN CUP-WINNERS' CUP PAST FINALS

1961	Fiorentina	4	Rangers	1†
1962	Atletico Madrid	1 3	Fiorentina	1 0
1963	Tottenham Hotspur	5	Atletico Madrid	1
1964	Sporting Lisbon	3 1	MTK Budapest	3 0
1965	West Ham U	2	Munich 1860	0
1966	Borussia Dortmund	2	Liverpool	1*
1967	Bayern Munich	1	Rangers	0*
1968	AC Milan	2	SV Hamburg	0
1969	Slovan Bratislava	3	Barcelona	2
1970	Manchester C	2	Gornik Zabrze	1
1971	Chelsea	1 2	Real Madrid	1 1*
1972	Rangers	3	Dynamo Moscow	2
1973	AC Milan	1	Leeds U	0
1974	Magdeburg	2	AC Milan	0
1975	Dynamo Kiev	3	Ferencvaros	0
1976	RSC Anderlecht	4	West Ham U	2
1977	SV Hamburg	2	Anderlecht	0
1978	RSC Anderlecht	4	Austria Vienna	0
1979	Barcelona	4	Fortuna Dusseldorf	3
1980	Valencia†	0	Arsenal	0
1981	Dynamo Tbilisi	2	Carl Zeiss Jena	1
1982	Barcelona	2	Standard Liege	1
1983	Aberdeen	2	Real Madrid	1
1984	Juventus	2	FC Porto	1
1985	Everton	3	Rapid Vienna	1
1986	Dynamo Kiev	3	Atletico Madrid	0
1987	Ajax Amsterdam	1	Lokomotiv Leipzig	0
1988	Mechelen	1	Ajax Amsterdam	0
1989	Barcelona	2	Sampdoria	0
1990	Sampdoria	2	Anderlecht	0

FAIRS CUP FINALS

1958	Barcelona	8	London	2‡
1960	Barcelona	4	Birmingham C	1‡
1961	AS Roma	4	Birmingham C	2‡
1962	Valencia	7	Barcelona	3‡
1963	Valencia	4	Dynamo Zagreb	1‡
1964	Real Zaragoza	2	Valencia	1
1965	Ferencvaros	1	Juventus	0
1966	Barcelona	4	Real Zaragoza	3‡
1967	Dynamo Zagreb	2	Leeds U	0‡
1968	Leeds U	1	Ferencvaros	0‡
1969	Newcastle U	6	Ujpest Dozsa	2‡
1970	Arsenal	4	Anderlecht	3‡
1971	Leeds U	3**	Juventus	3‡

EUROPEAN CHAMPIONSHIPS PAST FINALS

Paris, 10 July 1960 USSR 2, YUGOSLAVIA 1*
USSR: Yachin; Tchekeli, Kroutikov, Voinov, Maslenkin, Netto, Metreveli, Ivanov, Ponedelnik, Bubukin, Meshki. **Scorers:** Metreveli, Ponedelnik.
Yugoslavia: Vidinic; Durkovic, Jusufi, Zanetic, Miladinovic, Perusic, Sekularac, Jerkovic, Galic, Matus, Kostic. **Scorer:** Netto (og).

Madrid, 21 June 1964 SPAIN 2, USSR 1
Spain: Iribar; Rivilla, Calleja, Fuste, Olivella, Zoco, Amancio, Pereda, Marcellino, Suarez, Lapetra. **Scorers:** Pereda, Marcellino.
USSR: Yachin; Chustikov, Mudrik, Voronin, Shesternjev, Anitchkin, Chislenko, Ivanov, Ponedelnik, Kornaev, Khusainov. **Scorer:** Khusainov.

Rome, 8 June 1968 ITALY 1, YUGOSLAVIA 1
Italy: Zoff; Burgnich, Facchetti, Ferrini, Guarneri, Castano, Domenghini, Juliano, Anastasi, Lodetti, Prati. **Scorer:** Domenghini.
Yugoslavia: Pandelic; Fazlagic, Damjanovic, Pavlovic, Paunovic, Holcer, Petkovic, Acimovic, Musemic, Trivic, Dzajic. **Scorer:** Dzajic.

Replay: Rome, 10 June 1968 ITALY 2, YUGOSLAVIA 0
Italy: Zoff; Burgnich, Facchetti, Rosato, Guarneri, Salvadore, Domenghini, Mazzola, Anastasi, De Sista, Riva. **Scorers:** Riva, Anastasi.
Yugoslavia: Pantelic; Fazlagic, Damjanovic, Pavlovic, Paunovic, Holcer, Hosic, Acimovic, Meusemic, Trivic, Dzajic.

Brussels, 18 June 1972 WEST GERMANY 3, USSR 0
West Germany: Maier; Hottges, Schwarzenbeck, Beckenbauer, Breitner, Hoeness, Wimmer, Netzer, Heynckes, Muller, Kremers. **Scorers:** Muller 2, Wimmer.
USSR: Rudakov; Dzodzuashvili, Khurtsilava, Kaplichny, Istomin, Troshkin, Kolotov, Baidachni, Konkov (Dolmatov), Banishevski (Konzinkievits), Onishenko.

Belgrade, 20 June 1976 CZECHOSLOVAKIA 2, WEST GERMANY 2*
Czechoslovakia: Viktor; Dobias (Vesely, F.), Pivarnik, Ondrus, Capkovic, Gogh, Moder, Panenka, Svehlik (Jurkemik), Masny, Nehoda. **Scorers:** Svehlik, Dobias.
West Germany: Maier; Vogts, Beckenbauer, Schwarzenbeck, Dietz, Bonhof, Wimmer (Flohe), Müller, D., Beer (Bongartz), Hoeness, Holzenbein. **Scorers:** Müller, Holzenbein.
Czechoslovakia won 5-3 on penalties.

Rome, 22 June 1980 WEST GERMANY 2, BELGIUM 1
West Germany: Schumacher; Briegel, Forster, K., Dietz, Schuster, Rummenigge, Hrubesch, Müller, Allofs, Stielike, Kalz. **Scorer:** Hrubesch 2.
Belgium: Pfaff; Gerets, Millecamps, Meeuws, Renquin, Cools, Van der Eycken, Van Moer, Mommens, Van der Elst, Ceulemans. **Scorer:** Van der Eycken.

Paris, 27 June 1984 FRANCE 2, SPAIN 0
France: Bats; Battiston (Amoros), Le Roux, Bossis, Domergue, Giresse, Platini, Tigana, Fernandez, Lacombe (Genghini), Bellone. **Scorers:** Platini, Bellone.
Spain: Arconada; Urquiaga, Salva (Roberto), Gallego, Camacho, Francisco, Julio Alberto (Sarabia), Senor, Victor, Carrasco, Santilana.

Munich, 25 June 1988 HOLLAND 2, USSR 0
Holland: Van Breukelen; Van Aerle, Van Tiggelen, Wouters, Koeman, R., Rijkaard, Vanenburg, Gullit, Van Basten, Muhren, Koeman, E., **Scorers:** Gullit, Van Basten.
USSR: Dassayev; Khidiatulin, Aleinikov, Mikhailichenko, Litovchenko, Demianenko, Belanov, Gotsmanov (Baltacha), Protasov (Pasulko), Zavarov, Rats.

**After extra time*

EUROPEAN CHAMPIONSHIP 1990–92

Qualifying Tournament
Group 1
Reykjavik, 30 May 1990, 5250
Iceland (1) 2 *(Gudjohnsen 42, Edvaldsson 88)*
Albania (0) 0
Iceland: Kristinsson B; Thordarsson, Edvaldsson, Orlygsson T (Jonsson K 46), Gretarson, Jonsson Saevar, Berg, Ormslev, Torfarson (Orlyggson O 67), Petursson, Gudjohnsen.
Albania: Strakosha; Noga (Illiadhe 75), Lekbello, Kovi, Vapa, Jeri, Shehu (Arbete 46), Josa, Millo, Abazi, Demollari.

Reykjavik, 5 September 1990, 8388
Iceland (0) 1 *(Edvaldsson 85)*
France (1) 2 *(Papin 12, Cantona 74)*
Iceland: Sigurdsson; Thrainsson, Edvaldsson, Bergsson, Jonsson Saevar, Orlygsson T (Margeirsson 63), Gretarson, Thordarsson, Ormslev (Kristinsson 63), Gudjohnsen, Petursson.
France: Martini; Amoros, Boli, Sauzee, Casoni, Blanc (Durand 75), Pardo, Deschamps, Perez, Papin, Cantona (Fernandez 83).

Kosice, 26 September 1990, 30,184
Czechoslovakia (1) 1 *(Danek 43)*
Iceland (0) 0
Czechoslovakia: Stejskal; Kadlec, Kocian, Hipp, Hasek, Bilek (Weiss 67), Kubik, Kula, Moravcik, Skuhravy, Danek.
Iceland: Sigurdsson; Thrainsson, Bergsson, Edvaldsson, Jonsson Saevar, Kristinsson (Jonsson K 61), Gretarson, Thordarsson, Jonsson Siggi, Gudjohnsen, Margeirsson (Ormslev 76).

Seville, 10 October 1990, 18,399
Spain (0) 2 *(Butragueno 63, Munoz 66)*
Iceland (0) 1 *(Jonsson Siggi 66)*
Spain: Zubizarreta; Nando, Serna, Rafa Paz (Beguiristain 62), Sanchis, Fernando, Goicoechea, Michel, Butragueno, Martin Vazquez, Carlos (Valverde 71).
Iceland: Sigurdsson; Thrainsson, Edvaldsson, Jonsson K (Gregory 80), Gretarson, Jonsson Saevar, Bergsson, Jonsson Siggi (Ormslev 72), Gudjohnsen, Thordarsson, Margeirsson.

Paris, 13 October 1990, 38,249
France (0) 2 *(Papin 60, 83)*
Czechoslovakia (0) 1 *(Skuhravy 89)*
France: Martini; Boli, Blanc, Casoni, Angloma (Fernandez 52), Deschamps, Sauzee, Durand, Papin, Cantona, Vahirua (Silvestre 85).
Czechoslovakia: Stejskal; Kula, Kadlec, Kocian, Hipp, Moravcik, Chovanec, Kubik (Tittel 85), Bilek (Pecko 82), Skuhravy, Knoflicek.

Prague, 14 November 1990, 21,980
Czechoslovakia (1) 3 *(Danek 16, 67, Moravcik 77)*
Spain (1) 2 *(Roberto 30, Carlos 54)*
Czechoslovakia: Miklosko; Kocian, Kadlec, Hipp, Hasek, Tittel, Moravcik, Kula, Bilek (Bielik 80), Danek (Kuka 89), Skuhravy.
Spain: Zubizarreta; Quique, Sanchis, Nando, Serna, Michel (Amor 85), Martin Vazquez, Roberto, Goicoechea, Butragueno, Carlos (Bakero 62).

Tirana, 17 November 1990, 12,972

Albania (0) 0

France (1) 1 *(Boli 25)*

Albania: Arapi; Leskaj (Ferko 46), Stafa, Ibro, Hodja, Lekbello, Zmijani, Demollari, Josa, Kushta, Majaci (Kacasi 56).
France: Martini; Boli, Durand, Casoni, Blanc, Pardo, Deschamps, Sauzee, Tibeuf (Ginola 66), Ferreri, Vahirua (Angloma 82).

Seville, 19 December 1990, 12,625

Spain (4) 9 *(Amor 21, Carlos 24, 65, Butragueno 31, 57, 68, 88, Hierro 40, Bakero 76)*

Albania (0) 0

Spain: Zubizarreta; Sanchis, Alcorta, Goiceechea (Bakero 75), Amor, Hierro, Manolo, Michel (Quique 62), Butragueno, Martin Vazquez, Carlos.
Albania: Arapi; Ibro, Lekbello, Stafa, Kola (Demollari 39), Kushta, Millo, Zmijani, Ferko (Josa 55), Dema, Tahiri.

Paris, 20 February 1991, 45,000

France (1) 3 *(Sauzee 15, Papin 58, Blanc 77)*

Spain (1) 1 *(Bakero 11)*

France: Martini; Amoros, Boli, Casoni, Blanc, Pardo (Fernandez 50), Durand, Sauzee, Papin, Cantona, Vahirua (Deschamps 83).
Spain: Zubizarreta; Quique, Nando, Juanito, Sanchis, Michel, Amor, Vizcaino (Soler 61), Goicoechea, Bakero, Butragueno (Manolo 75).

Paris, 30 March 1991, 25,000

France (4) 5 *(Sauzee 1, 19, Papin 34 (pen), 43, Lekbello 79 (og))*

Albania (0) 0

France: Martini; Amoros, Boli, Blanc, Durand, Fernandez, Sauzee (Deschamps 73), Cocard, Cantona, Papin, Vahirua (Baills 57).
Albania: Nallbani; Zmijani, Lekbello, Vata, Gjergi, Ocelli, Dume, Canaj, Demollari, Tahiri, Kepa.

Tirana, 1 May 1991, 10,000

Albania (0) 0

Czechoslovakia (0) 2 *(Kubik 47, Kuka 67)*

Albania: Nallbani; Zmijani, Dema (Kola 73), Daja, Ocelli, Shpuza, Kushta, Memushi, Barbullushi (Dosti 63), Dume (Kole 70), Milori.
Czechoslovakia: Miklosko; Kula, Kadlec, Hasek (Hapal 19), Grussmann, Tittel, Nemec, Kubik, Kuka, Kukleta (Chyleik 84), Moravcik.

Tirana, 26 May 1991, 5000

Albania (0) 1 *(Abazi 56)*

Iceland (0) 0

Albania: Nallbani; Memushi (Josa 17), Ocelli, Lekbello, Shpuza, Daja, Millo, Demollari, Milori, Kushta, Abazi.
Iceland: Sigurdsson; Jonsson Saevar, Bergsson, Gislason, Kristiansson, Kristinsson (Stefansson 62), Orlygsson T, Thordarsson, Gretarson, Sverrison, Gregory (Marteinsson 75).

Reykjavik, 5 June 1991, 5000

Iceland (0) 0

Czechoslovakia (1) 1 *(Hasek 15)*

Iceland: Sigurdsson; Jonsson Saever, Bergsson, Edvaldsson, Gislason, Thordarsson, Gretarson, Orlygsson T, Kristinsson, Gudjohnsen, Sverrison (Stefansson 70).
Czechoslovakia: Miklosko; Grussmann, Kocian, Tittel, Hasek, Hapal, Kubik, Kula, Nemec, Danek (Pecko 89), Skuhravy.

	P	W	D	L	F	A	Pts
France	5	5	0	0	13	3	10
Czechoslovakia	5	4	0	1	8	4	8
Spain	4	2	0	2	14	7	4
Iceland	6	1	0	5	4	7	2
Albania	6	1	0	5	1	19	2

Remaining fixtures: 4.9.91. Czechoslovakia v France; 25.9.91. Iceland v Spain; 12.10.91. Spain v France; 16.10.91. Czechoslovakia v Albania; 13.11.91. Spain v Czechoslovakia, France v Iceland; 18.12.91. Albania v Spain.

Group 2

Geneva, 12 September 1990, 12,000

Switzerland (1) 2 *(Hottiger 19, Bickel 63)*

Bulgaria (0) 0

Switzerland: Walker; Geiger, Herr, Schepull, Hottiger, Koller, Bickel, Hermann, Sutter A (Piffaretti 88), Knup (Chapuisat 64), Turkyilmaz.

Bulgaria: Valov; Dochev, Zhelev, Iliev, Ivanov, Vassev (Bankov 14), Yanchev, Yordanov, Balakov (Todorov 65), Kostadinov, Stoichkov.

Hampden Park, 12 September 1990, 12,081

Scotland (1) 2 *(Robertson 37, McCoist 76)*

Rumania (1) 1 *(Camataru 13)*

Scotland: Goram; McKimmie, Malpas, McAllister (Nevin 73), Irvine, McLeish, Robertson, McStay, McCoist, MacLeod, Connor (Boyd 59).

Rumania: Lung, Petrescu, Klein, Sandoi, Rotariu, Popescu, Lacatus, Mateut (Sabau 79), Camataru (Raducioiu 62), Hagi, Lupescu.

Bucharest, 17 October 1990, 15,350

Rumania (0) 0

Bulgaria (1) 3 *(Sirakov 28, Todorov 48, 76)*

Rumania: Stelea; Petrescu, Klein (Sandoi 46), Andone, Rotariu, Popescu, Lacatus, Sabau, Raducioiu (Balint 46), Hagi, Lupescu.

Bulgaria: Mikhailov; Dochev, Ivanov, Vassev, Iliev, Yankov, Yanchev, Stoichkov, Balakov, Sirakov (Kostadinov 75), Yordanov (Todorov 46).

Hampden Park, 17 October 1990, 20,740

Scotland (1) 2 *(Robertson 34, McAllister 53)*

Switzerland (0) 1 *(Knup 66)*

Scotland: Goram; McKimmie, Nicol, McCall, McPherson, McLeish, Robertson, McAllister (Collins 79), McCoist, MacLeod, Boyd (Durie 68).

Switzerland: Walker; Piffaretti (Sutter B 80), Schepull (Chassot 73), Herr, Egli, Bickel, Knup, Hermann, Turkyilmaz, Sutter A, Chapuisat.

Sofia, 14 November 1990, 40,000

Bulgaria (0) 1 *(Todorov 74)*

Scotland (1) 1 *(McCoist 9)*

Bulgaria: Mikhailov; Dochev, Mladenov, Yankov, Bankov, Yanchev (Todorov 52), Yordanov, Stoichkov, Penev, Sirakov, Balakov (Kostadinov 80).

Scotland: Goram; McKimmie, Malpas, McInally, McPherson, Gillespie, Durie (Nevin 67), McAllister, McCoist, McClair, Boyd.

Serravalle, 14 November 1990, 931

San Marino (0) 0

Switzerland (3) 4 *(Sutter A 7, Chapuisat 27, Knup 43, Chassot 87)*

San Marino: Benedettini; Montironi, Guerra, Gobbi, Muccioli (Toccaceli 46), Bonini (Matteoni 46), Zanotti L, Francini, Ceccoli, Pasolini, Macina.

Switzerland: Walker; Hottiger, Geiger, Herr, Sutter B, Bickel (Piffaretti 59), Chapuisat, Hermann, Sutter A, Turkyilmaz (Chassot 46), Knup.

Bucharest, 5 December 1990, 6380

Rumania (3) 6 *(Sabau 2, Mateut 18, Raducioiu 43, Lupescu 56, Badea 77, Petrescu 85)*

San Marino (0) 0

Rumania: Prunea; Petrescu, Iovan, Popescu, Rednic, Sabau, Mateut, Lupescu (Stanici 65), Dumitrescu (Badea 46), Lacatus, Raducioiu.
San Marino: Benedettini; Montironi, Conti, Guerra, Zanotti L, Toccaceli, Matteoni, Ceccoli, Francini, Passolini (Zanotti P 72), Macina (Bacciochi 46).

Hampden Park, 27 March 1991, 33,119

Scotland (0) 1 *(Collins 84)*

Bulgaria (0) 1 *(Kostadinov 89)*

Scotland: Goram; McPherson, Malpas, McInally, Gough, McLeish, Strachan (Collins 80), McClair, McCoist, McStay, Durie (Robertson 80).
Bulgaria: Mikhailov; Dochev, Ivanov, Kiryakov, Iliev, Yankov, Kostadinov, Yordanov, Penev, Sirakov (Alexandrov 86), Balakov (Tanev 86).

Serravalle, 27 March 1991, 745

San Marino (1) 1 *(Pasolini 30 (pen))*

Rumania (2) 3 *(Hagi 17 (pen), Raducioiu 45, Matteoni (og) 86)*

San Marino: Benedettini; Canti, Guerra, Gobbi (Toccaceli 74), Muccioli, Matteoni, Francini, Pasolini (Mularoni 89), Ceccoli, Mazza M, Mazza P.
Rumania: Prunea; Petrescu, Popescu (Timofte D 46), Lupescu, Klein, Sandoi, Sabau, Mateut (Timofte J 65), Hagi, Lacatus, Raducioiu.

Neuchatel, 3 April 1991, 15,700

Switzerland (0) 0

Rumania (0) 0

Switzerland: Huber; Geiger, Hottiger, Ohrel, Herr, Koller, Bonvin (Bickel 33), Hermann, Aeby, Turkyilmaz (Sutter B 75), Knup.
Rumania: Prunea; Petrescu, Klein, Sandoi, Lupescu, Popescu, Sabau, Hagi (Mateut 85), Lacatus, Raducioiu (Timofte J 89), Timofte D.

Sofia, 1 May 1991, 40,000

Bulgaria (2) 2 *(Kostadinov 11, Sirakov 25)*

Switzerland (0) 3 *(Knup 58, 85, Turkyilmaz 90)*

Bulgaria: Mikhailov; Dochev (Todorov 75), Kiriakov, Yankov, Iliev, Ivanov, Yordanov, Penev, Sirakov (Tanev 65), Balakov, Kostadinov.
Switzerland: Huber; Egli, Herr, Hottiger, Ohrel, Bonvin, Hermann, Knup (Schepull 87), Koller (Chapuisat 75), Sutter B, Turkyilmaz.

Serravalle, 1 May 1991, 3512

San Marino (0) 0

Scotland (0) 2 *(Strachan 63 (pen), Durie 66)*

San Marino: Benedettini; Canti, Muccioli, Zanotti (Toccaceli 60), Gobbi, Guerra, Ceccoli, Mazza M, Mazza P, Francini, Pasolini (Matteoni 79).
Scotland: Goram, McKimmie, Nicol (Robertson 74), McCall, McPherson, Malpas, Gallacher, Strachan, McClair (Nevin 57), McAllister, Durie.

Serrevalle, 22 May 1991, 612

San Marino (0) 0

Bulgaria (2) 3 *(Ivanov Z 12, Sirakov 19, Penev 59)*

San Marino: Benedettini; Canti, Montironi, Muccioli, Gobbi, Guerra, Ceccoli (Matteoni 82), Mazza M, Mazza P, Francini, Pasolini (Bacciocchi 64).

Bulgaria: Mikhailov; Dimitrov, Ivanov I, Kiriakov, Anghelov, Ivanov Z (Todorov 76), Kostadinov E, Gheorghiev, Penev, Sirakov, Yotov (Metkov 56).

St Gallen, 5 June 1991, 12,000

Switzerland (3) 7 *(Knup 2, 86, Hottiger 12, Sutter B 28, Hermann 54, Ohrel 77, Turkyilmaz 89)*

San Marino (0) 0

Switzerland: Huber; Egli (Schepull 74), Herr, Hottiger (Ohrel 74), Hermann, Koller, Sutter A, Sutter B, Turkyilmaz, Knup, Chapuisat.

San Marino: Benedettini; Muccioli, Guerra, Gobbi, Canti, Matteoni (Valentini 46), Mazza M, Francini, Zanotti, Pasolini, Bacciocchi (Malaroni 65)

	P	*W*	*D*	*L*	*F*	*A*	*Pts*
Switzerland	6	4	1	1	17	4	9
Scotland	5	3	2	0	8	4	8
Bulgaria	6	2	2	2	10	7	6
Rumania	5	2	1	2	10	6	5
San Marino	6	0	0	6	1	25	0

Remaining Fixtures: 11.9.91. Switzerland v Scotland; 16.10.91. Bulgaria v San Marino, Rumania v Scotland; 13.11.91. Scotland v San Marino, Rumania v Switzerland; 20.11.91. Bulgaria v Rumania.

Group 3

Moscow, 12 September 1990, 23,000

USSR (1) 2 *(Kontchelskis 22, Kuznetsov 60)*

Norway (0) 0

USSR: Uvarov; Chernishev, Gorlukovich, Kuznetsov, Tishenko (Kulkov 79), Shalimov, Mikhailichenko, Kontchelskis, Getsko (Kolivanov 70), Protasov, Dobrovolski.

Norway: Thorstvedt; Lydersen, Pedersen T, Bratseth, Halle, Berg (Pedersen E 61), Ahlsen, Gulbrandsen, Jakobsen, Andersen A, Fjortoft (Dahlum 66).

Bergen, 10 October 1990, 6300

Norway (0) 0

Hungary (0) 0

Norway: Thorstvedt; Halle, Pedersen T, Bratseth, Lydersen, Pedersen E, Ahlsen, Brandhaug, Jakobsen, (Andersen A 72), Sorloth, Fjortoft (Dahlum 76).

Hungary: Petry; Monos, Pinter, Szalma, Kovacs E, Limperger, Kiprich (Fodor 79), Kozma, Bognar, Lorincz, Kovacs K (Urbanyi 89).

Budapest, 17 October 1990, 24,600

Hungary (1) 1 *(Disztl L 16)*

Italy (0) 1 *(Baggio 54)*

Hungary: Petry; Monos, Disztl L, Garaba (Fodor 60), Szalma, Bognar, Limperger, Kiprich, Kozma (Urbanyi 87), Lorincz, Kovacs K.

Italy: Zenga; Bergomi, De Agostini, Baresi, Ferri, Marocchi, Donadoni, De Napoli, Schillaci (Serena 80), Giannini (Berti 87), Baggio.

Budapest, 31 October 1990, 2300

Hungary (3) 4 *(Lorincz 1, 19, Kiprich 20 (pen), 67 (pen))*

Cyprus (1) 2 *(Xiourouppas 13, Tsolakis 89)*

Hungary: Petry; Disztl L, Monos, Garaba, Limperger, Szalma, Kozma (Discher 56), Bognar, Lorincz, Kiprich (Rugovics 75), Kovacs K.

Cyprus: Onisforu; Kalotheou, Miamiliotis, Christodolou, Socratous, Yiangudakis, Andreou (Tsolakis 59), Savva, Kastanas, Constantinou (Orthanides 73), Xiourouppas.

Rome, 3 November 1990, 52,208

Italy (0) 0

USSR (0) 0

Italy: Zenga; Ferrara, Baresi, Ferri, Maldini, De Napoli, Crippa, De Agostini, Mancini, Schillaci (Serena 70), Baggio.
USSR: Uvarov; Chernishev, Kulkov, Tsvelba, Shalimov, Aleinikov, Mikhailichenko, Kontchelskis, Getsko (Protasov 67), Mostovoi (Tatarchuk 85), Dobrovolski.

Nicosia, 14 November 1990, 2123

Cyprus (0) 0

Norway (1) 3 *(Sorloth 39, Bohinen 50, Brandhaug 64)*

Cyprus: Charitou; Kalotheou (Kantilos 49), Miamiliotis, Kastanas, Socratous, Yiangudakis, Christodolou, Savva, Tsolakis (Constantinou 74), Nicolau, Xiourouppas.
Norway: Thorstvedt; Lydersen, Pedersen T, Bratseth, Lohen (Pedersen E 64), Halle, Brandhaug, Leonhardsen, Bohinen, Sorloth, Dahlum (Fjortoft 80).

Nicosia, 22 December 1990, 9185

Cyprus (0) 0

Italy (3) 4 *(Vierchowod 15, Serena 22, 50, Lombardo 44)*

Cyprus: Onisforu; Kalotheou, Miamiliotis, Christodolou, Socratous, Yiangudakis, Pittas, Savva (Constantinou 56), Tsolakis, Nicolau, Papavasiliu (Xiourouppas 64).
Italy: Zenga; Bergomi, Ferrara, Eranio, Vierchowod, Crippa, Lombardo, Berti, Schillaci, Morocchi, Serena.

Limassol, 3 April 1991, 3000

Cyprus (0) 0

Hungary (2) 2 *(Kiprich 40, Szalma 13).*

Cyprus: Marangos; Constantinou G, Pittas (Kasianos 75), Ioannou, Constantinou C, Yiangudakis, Christofi, Savva (Sotiriu 83), Savvidis, Nicolau, Tsolakis.
Hungary: Petry; Monos, Disztl L, Szalma, Nagy, Limperger, Kiprich, Bognar, Fischer (Maroszan 72), Lorincz, Kovacs K.

Budapest, 17 April 1991, 40,000

Hungary (0) 0

USSR (1) 1 *(Mikhailichenko 30)*

Hungary: Petry; Disztl L, Garaba, Limperger, Monos, Kozma (Detari 63), Bognar (Vincze 71), Lorincz, Szalma, Kiprich, Kovacs K.
USSR: Uvarov; Chernishev, Kulkov, Tsvelba, Galiamin, Shalimov, Mikhailichenko, Kontchelskis, Youran (Kuznetsov D 86), Kolivanov, Aleinikov.

Salerno, 1 May 1991, 45,000

Italy (2) 3 *(Donadoni 4, 16, Vialli 56)*

Hungary (0) 1 *(Bognar 66)*

Italy: Zenga; Ferrara (Vierchowoed 65), Ferri, Baresi, Maldini, Crippa, De Napoli, Giannini, Donadoni (Eranio 36), Vialli, Mancini.
Hungary: Petry; Monos, Disztl L, Palaczky (Kozma 33), Limperger, Garaba, Kiprich (Gregor 46), Lorincz, Bognar, Detari, Kovacs K.

Oslo, 1 May 1991, 7833

Norway (0) 3 *(Lydersen 49 (pen), Dahlum 65, Sorloth 90)*

Cyprus (0) 0

Norway: Thorstvedt; Pedersen T, Bratseth (Ingebritsen 46), Lydersen, Halle (Pedersen E), Ahlsen, Brandhaug, Leonhardsen, Bjornbyre, Sorloth, Dahlum.
Cyprus: Charitou; Nicolau (Sotiriu 89), Constantinou G, Ioannou, Costa, Kalotheu (Constantinou C 84), Savva, Yiangudakis, Pittas, Savvidis, Xiourouppas.

Moscow, 29 May 1991, 20,000
USSR (1) 4 *(Mostovoi 20, Mikhailichenko 51, Korneyev 83, Aleinikov 89)*
Cyprus (0) 0
USSR: Uvarov; Chernishev, Kulkov, Mostovoi (Kuznetsov D 74), Galamin, Shalimov, Mikhailichenko, Kontchelskis, Aleinikov, Kolivanov, Youran (Korneyev 46).
Cyprus: Charitou; Kalotheou, Pittas, Ioannou, Nicolau, Yiangudakis, Costa, Christofi, Savvidis, Christodolou (Constantinou 88), Xiourouppas (Savva 89).

Oslo, 5 June 1991, 27,500
Norway (2) 2 *(Dahlum 4, Bohinen 24)*
Italy (0) 1 *(Schillaci 79)*
Norway: Thorstvedt; Pedersen T, Ahlsen, Bratseth, Lydersen, Dahlum (Pedersen E 46), Bohinen, Lokken, Ingebrigtsen, Jakobsen, Sorloth.
Italy: Zenga; Baresi, Ferrara, Ferri (Bergomi 89), Maldini, Lombardo, Eranio, De Napoli (Schillaci 53), Crippa, Vialli, Mancini.

	P	*W*	*D*	*L*	*F*	*A*	*Pts*
USSR	4	3	1	0	7	0	7
Norway	5	3	1	1	8	3	7
Italy	5	2	2	1	9	4	6
Hungary	6	2	2	2	8	7	6
Cyprus	6	0	0	6	2	20	0

Remaining Fixtures: 28.8.91. Norway v USSR; 25.9.91. USSR v Hungary; 12.10.91. USSR v Italy; 30.10.91. Hungary v Norway; 13.11.91. Italy v Norway, Cyprus v USSR; 21.12.91. Italy v Cyprus.

Group 4
Windsor Park, 12 September 1990, 9008
Northern Ireland (0) 0
Yugoslavia (1) 2 *(Pancev 36, Prosinecki 86)*
Northern Ireland: Kee; Donaghy, Worthington, Taggart, McDonald, Rogan, Dennison (Clarke 66), Wilson D, Dowie, Wilson K, Black.
Yugoslavia: Ivkovic; Spasic, Jozic, Vulic, Hadzibegic, Najdoski, Prosinecki, Savicevic, Pancev (Petrovic 87) Stojkovic, Binic (Stosic 87).

Landskrona, Sweden, 12 September 1990, 1544
Faeroes (0) 1 *(Nielsen 61)*
Austria (0) 0
Faeroes: Knudsen; Jakobsen, Hansen TE, Danielsen, Hansen J, Mordore A, Nielsen, Dam, Hansen A, Reynheim, Morkore K.
Austria: Konsel; Russ, Pecl, Hartmann, Streiter, Peischl, Rodax, Linzmaier, Polster, Herzog (Pacult 63), Reisinger (Wilfurth 63).

Copenhagen, 10 October 1990, 38,500
Denmark (2) 4 *Laudrup M 8, 48, Elstrup 37, Povlsen 89)*
Faeroes (1) 1 *(Morkore A 21)*
Denmark: Schmeichel; Sivebaek, Nielsen K, Olsen L, Heintze, Bartram, Vilfort, Elstrup (Rasmussen E 73), Povlsen, Laudrup M, Laudrup B.
Faeroes: Knudsen; Jakobsen, Hansen TE, Danielsen, Hansen J, Morkore A (Jarnskor 88), Nielsen T, Dam, Hansen A, Reynheim, Morkore K (Mohr 76).

Windsor Park, 17 October 1990, 9079

Northern Ireland (0) 1 *(Clarke 58)*

Denmark (1) 1 *(Bartram 11)*

Northern Ireland: Kee; Donaghy, Worthington, Taggart, McDonald, Rogan, Wilson D, O'Neill C (McBride), Dowie, Clarke, Black.
Denmark: Schmeichel; Sivebaek, Nielsen K, Olsen L, Heintze, Bartram, Larsen, Vilfort, Povlsen, Laudrup M (Helt 80), Laudrup B (Elstrup 70).

Belgrade, 31 October 1990, 11,422

Yugoslavia (2) 4 *(Pancev 32, 52, 85, Katanec 43)*

Austria (1) 1 *(Ogris A 15)*

Yugoslavia: Ivkovic; Vulic, Spasic, Katanec (Jarni 86), Hadzibegic, Josic, Prosinecki, Susic (Boban 63), Bazdarevic, Pancev, Vujovic.
Austria: Konsel; Artner, Aigner, Pecl, Streiter, Hortnagl, Schottel, Herzog Linzmaier 46), Reisinger, Ogris A (Pacult 52), Polster.

Copenhagen, 14 November 1990, 40,000

Denmark (0) 0

Yugoslavia (0) 2 *(Bazdarevic 77, Jarni 84)*

Denmark: Schmeichel; Sivebaek, Nielsen K, Olsen L, Heintze, Vilfort, Molby (Elstrup 72), Laudrup M, Bartram, Laudrup B, Povlsen (Jensen 46).
Yugoslavia: Ivkovic; Vulic, Spasic, Hadzibegic, Jarni, Katanec, Jozic, Susic, Bazdarevic, Pancev (Boban 12), Vujovic (Najdoski 89).

Vienna, 14 November 1990, 7062

Austria (0) 0

Northern Ireland (0) 0

Austria: Konsel; Schottel, Pecl, Polger, Artner, Willfurth, Reischl, Linzmaier, Hortnagl, Ogris A, Polster (Pacult 67).
Northern Ireland: Kee; Donaghy, Worthington, Taggart, McDonald, Rogan, Dennison, Wilson D, Clarke (Dowie 62), Wilson K, Black (Morrow 82).

Belgrade, 27 March 1991, 10,000

Yugoslavia (1) 4 *(Binic 35, Pancev 46, 60, 61)*

Northern Ireland (1) 1 *(Hill 45)*

Yugoslavia: Ivkovic; Vulic (Najdoski 85), Jozic, Jarni, Bazdarevic, Spasic, Hadzibegic, Prosinecki, Savicevic, Pancev, Binic.
Northern Ireland: Kee; Fleming, Rogan, Donaghy, Morrow, Hill, Dennison (Quinn 70), Magilton, Dowie, Wilson K (Clarke 60), Black.

Belgrade, 1 May 1991, 26,000

Yugoslavia (0) 1 *(Pancev 50)*

Denmark (1) 2 *(Christensen 31, 62)*

Yugoslavia: Ivkovic; Vulic, Jarni (Najdoski 84), Spasic, Hadzibegic, Jozic, Prosinecki, Savicevic, Pancev, Bazdarevic, Binic.
Denmark: Schmeichel; Sivebaek (Larsen 54), Nielsen K, Olsen L, Kristensen, Bartram, Jensen (Goldbaek 82), Christofte, Povlsen, Vilfort, Christensen.

Windsor Park, 1 May 1991, 10,000

Northern Ireland (1) 1 *(Clarke 44)*

Faeroes (0) 1 *(Reynheim 65)*

Northern Ireland: Kee; Donaghy, Worthington, Taggart, McDonald, Magilton, Wilson D (Dennison 83), Clarke, Dowie (Williams 83), Wilson K, Black.
Faeroes: Knudson; Jakobsen, Hansen TE, Danielsen, Muller, Morkore A, Nielsen, Dam, Hansen A, Reynheim (Thomassen 74), Morkore K (Rasmussen 85).

Belgrade, 16 May 1991, 8000

Yugoslavia (2) 7 *(Najdoski 20, Prosinecki 24, Pancev 50, 74, Vulic 66, Boban 70, Suker 86)*

Faeroes (0) 0

Yugoslavia: Ivkovic (Lazic 80); Stanojkovic, Jarni (Suker 67), Vulic, Najdoski, Spasic, Prosinecki, Boban, Pancev, Savicevic, Mihajlovic.
Faeroes: Knudsen; Jakobsen, Hansen TE, Danielsen, Jarnskor, Morkore A, Nielsen, Dam, Hansen A, Reynheim, Morkore K (Muller 49).

Vienna, 22 May 1991, 13,000

Austria (1) 3 *(Pfeifenberger 13, Streiter 48, Wetl 63)*

Faeroes (0) 0

Austria: Konsel (Wohlfarht 86); Baur, Russ, Pfeifenberger (Hortnagl 24), Hartman, Stoger, Schottel, Herzog, Streuter, Wetl, Ogris A.
Faeroes: Knudsen; Jakobsen, Morkore A, Danielsen, Hansen TE, Simonsen, Nielsen, Hansen A, Dam (Thomassen 71), Reynheim, Rasmussen (Mohr 85).

Copenhagen, 5 June 1991, 12,521

Denmark (1) 2 *(Christensen 2, 77)*

Austria (0) 1 *(Ogris E 83)*

Denmark: Schmeichel; Hansen, Nielsen K, Olsen L, Bruun, Vilfort, Larsen, Nielsen BS, Nielsen C (Goldbaek 46), Povlsen (Rasmussen 78), Christensen.
Austria: Konrad; Russ (Prosenik 72), Baur, Hartmann, Pfeifenberger, Streiter, Ogris E, Schottel (Hortnagl 66), Herzog, Stoger, Westerhaler.

	P	*W*	*D*	*L*	*F*	*A*	*Pts*
Yugoslavia	6	5	0	1	20	4	10
Denmark	5	3	1	1	9	6	7
Austria	5	1	1	3	5	7	3
Northern Ireland	5	0	3	2	3	8	3
Faroes	5	1	1	3	3	15	3

Remaining fixtures: 11.9.91. Faeroes v Northern Ireland; 25.9.91. Faeroes v Denmark; 9.10.91. Austria v Denmark; 16.10.91. Faeroes v Yugoslavia, Northern Ireland v Austria; 13.11.91. Denmark v Northern Ireland, Austria v Yugoslavia.

Group 5

Ninian Park, 17 October 1990, 12,000

Wales (1) 3 *(Rush 29, Saunders 86, Hughes 88)*

Belgium (1) 1 *(Versavel 24)*

Wales: Southall; Ratcliffe, Blackmore, Young, Aizlewood, Bodin, Horne, Nicholas, Hughes, Rush, Saunders.

Belgium: Preud'homme; Gerets, Grun, Demol, De Wolf, Versavel, Van der Elst, Scifo, Emmers, Ceulemans, Nilis (Wilmots 75).

Luxembourg, 31 October 1990, 9512

Luxembourg (0) 2 *(Girres 57, Langers 65)*

West Germany (2) 3 *(Klinsmann 16, Bein 30, Voller 49)*

Luxembourg: Van Rijswick; Malgret, Petry, Bossi, Birsens, Groff, Hellers, Girres, Salbene (Jeitz 85), Weis, Langers.
West Germany: Illgner; Binz, Berthold, Kohler, Strunz, Hassler, Matthaus, Bein (Reinhardt 73), Brehme, Klinsmann, Voller.

Luxembourg, 14 November 1990, 6800
Luxembourg (0) 0
Wales (1) 1 *(Rush 15)*
Luxembourg: Van Rijswick; Malget, Bossi, Birsens, Petry, Morocutti (Krings 60), Hellers, Girres, Salbene, Weis, Langers.
Wales: Southall; Blackmore, Bodin, Aizlewood, Young, Hughes, Ratcliffe, Horne, Nicholas, Rush (Speed 83), Saunders (Allen 88).

Brussels, 27 February 1991, 24,505
Belgium (3) 3 *(Vandenbergh 7, Ceulemans 17, Scifo 36)*
Luxembourg (0) 0
Belgium: Preud'homme; Grun, Albert, Emmers, Versavel, Dauwen, Scifo, Ceulemans, Degryse, Vandenbergh, Wilmots.
Luxembourg: Koch; Malget (Jeitz 46), Bossi, Birsens, Patry, Groff (Scuto 75), Hellers, Girres, Salbenc, Weis, Krings.

Brussels, 27 March 1991, 25,000
Belgium (0) 1 *(Degryse 47)*
Wales (0) 1 *(Saunders 58)*
Belgium: Preud'homme; Gerets, Albert, Grun, Clijsters, Versavel, Van der Elst, Scifo, Degryse, Vandenbergh, Wilmots.
Wales: Southall; Phillips, Ratcliffe, Young, Aizlewood, Bodin, Horne, Nicholas, Hughes, Rush, Saunders.

Hanover, 1 May 1991, 56,000
West Germany (1) 1 *(Matthaus 5)*
Belgium (0) 0
West Germany: Illgner; Berthold, Reuter, Beiersdorfer, Brehme, Hassler, Sammer, Matthaus, Doll, Klinsmann (Helmer 77), Voller (Riedle 88).
Belgium: Preud'homme; Emmers, Crasson, Grun, Albert, Van der Elst, Scifo, Vervoort, Versavel, Degryse, Wilmots (Nilis 77).

Cardiff (Arms Park), 5 June 1991, 38,000
Wales (0) 1 *(Rush 69)*
West Germany (0) 0
Wales: Southall; Phillips, Melville, Bodin, Aizlewood, Ratcliffe, Nicholas, Saunders (Speed 89), Rush, Hughes, Horne.
West Germany: Illgner; Reuter, Brehme, Kohler, Berthold, Buchwald, Helmer, Sammer (Effenberg 76), Matthaus (Doll 46), Klinsmann, Voller.

	P	*W*	*D*	*L*	*F*	*A*	*Pts*
Wales	4	3	1	0	6	2	7
West Germany	3	2	0	1	4	3	4
Belgium	4	1	1	2	5	5	3
Luxembourg	3	0	0	3	2	7	0

Remaining fixtures: 11.9.91. Luxembourg v Belgium; 16.10.91. West Germany v Wales; 13.11.91. Wales v Luxembourg; 20.11.91. Belgium v West Germany; 17.12.91. West Germany v Luxembourg.

Grroup 6
Helsinki, 12 September 1990, 10,242
Finland (0) 0
Portugal (0) 0
Finland: Huttunen; Rinne, Holmgren, Europaeus, Heikkinen, Petaja, Tarkkio (Paavola 73), Litmanen, Jarvinen (Myyry 84), Hjelm, Paatelainen.

Portugal: Silvino; Joao Pinto, Veloso, Ferreira, Venancio, Fonseca (Pacheco 63), Paneira, Andre, Jaime Pacheco, Rui Barros, Rui Aguas (Cadete 46).

Porto, 17 October 1990, 17,198
Portugal (0) 1 *(Rui Aguas 54)*
Holland (0) 0
Portugal: Silvino; Joao Pinto, Veloso, Venancio, Leal, Paneira, Oceano, Semedo (Ferreira 89), Nelo (Carlos Xavier 87), Rui Aguas, Cadete.
Holland: Van Breukelen; De Boer (Gillhaus 75), Blind, Van Tiggelen (Van't Schip 58), Valckx, Rutjes, Vanenburg, Witschge, Bergkamp, Van Basten, Gullit.

Athens, 31 October 1990, 7768
Greece (2) 4 *(Tsiantakis 37, Karapialis 40, Saravakos 59, Borbokis 88)*
Malta (0) 0
Greece: Papadopoulos T; Apostolakis, Papadopoulos G, Manolas, Kalitzakis, Tsiantakis, Tsalouhidis, Karapialis, Kofidis, Saravakos, Dimitriadis (Borbokis 31).
Malta: Cini; Carabott, Vella S, Galea, Scerri, Buttigieg, Vella R, Suda (De Giorgio 46), Laferla, Zerafa, Busuttil.

Rotterdam, 21 November 1990, 25,430
Holland (2) 2 *(Bergkamp 7, Van Basten 18)*
Greece (0) 0
Holland: Van Breukelen; De Jong, Blind, Rutjes, Vanenburg, Wouters, Bergkamp (Winter 80), Witschge, Van't Schip, Van Basten, Roy.
Greece: Papadopoulos T; Apostolakis, Papadopoulos G, Manolas, Kalitzakis, Tsalouhidis, Kofidis (Karageorgiou 53), Karapialis, Tsiantakis, Saravakos, Bormpokis.

Ta'Qali, 25 November 1990, 7200
Malta (0) 1 *(Suda 74)*
Finland (0) 1 *(Holmgren 87)*
Malta: Cluett; Buttigieg, Vella S, Galea, Scerri, Vella R, Laferla, Degiorgio, Carabott, Busuttil, Zarb (Suda 71).
Finland: Huttunen; Europaeus, Rinne (Petaja 46), Heikkinen, Holmgren, Myyry, Litmanen, Hjelm, Tauriainen, Tarkkio (Tegelberg 79), Paatelainen.

Ta'Qali, 19 December 1990, 10,254
Malta (0) 0
Holland (3) 8 *(Van Basten 9, 20, 23, 64, 80 (pen), Winter 53, Bergkamp 60, 66)*
Malta: Cluett; Camilleri E (Suda 46), Camilleri J, Galea, Laferla, Vella S, Carabott, Degiorgio, Scerri, Busuttil, Vella R.
Holland: Van Breukelen; Blind, De Jong, De Boer, Wouters, Koeman E (Winter 46), Bergkamp (Van den Brom 71), Van't Schip, Gullit, Van Basten, Roy.

Athens, 23 January 1991, 20,000
Greece (1) 3 *(Borbokis 7, Manolas 68, Tsalouhidis 85)*
Portugal (1) 2 *(Rui Aguas 18, Futre 62)*
Greece: Sarganis; Apostolakis, Papadopoulos G, Manolas, Kalitzakis, Tsalouhidis Kofidis (Athanasiadis 69), Tursunides, Tsiantakis, Borbokis (Dimitriadis 65), Saravakos.
Portugal: Vitor Baia; Joao Pinto, Veloso, Leal, Venancio, Paneira, Oceano, Rui Barros (Cadete 71), Futre, Rui Aguas, Sousa.

Ta'Qali, 9 February 1991, 5000
Malta (0) 0
Portugal (1) 1 *(Futre 27)*
Malta: Cluett; Vella S, Azzopardi, Galea, Laferla, Buttigieg, Busuttil, Vella R, Suda, Degiorgio, Zerafa.
Portugal: Vitor Baia; Joao Pinto, Leal, Venancio, Veloso, Oceano, Paneira, Rui Barros (Cadete 67), Rui Aguas, Futre (Sousa 63), Semedo.

Porto, 20 February 1991, 5303
Portugal (3) 5 *(Rui Aguas 5, Leal 33, Paneira 41 (pen), Futre 48, Cadete 81)*
Malta (0) 0
Portugal: Vitor Baia; Joao Pinto (Cadete 46), Leal, Venancio (Madeira 67), Veloso, Oceano, Peneira, Sousa, Rui Aguas, Futre, Semedo.
Malta: Cluett; Vella S, Azzopardi, Camilleri J (Scerri 38), Laferla, Buttigieg, Busuttil, Vella R, Suda (Carabott 51), Degiorgio, Zerafa.

Rotterdam, 13 March 1991, 40,000
Holland (1) 1 *(Van Basten 31 (pen))*
Malta (0) 0
Holland: Van Breukelen; Blind, Vink, De Boer (Kieft 46), Van't Schip, Wouters, Witschge, Gullit, Bergkamp, Van Basten, Roy (Vanenburg 69).
Malta: Cini; Laferla, Camilleri E, Vella S, Brincat (Suda 86), Camilleri J, Azzopardi (Saliba 89), Scerri, Vella R, Degiorgio, Zerafa.

Rotterdam, 17 April 1991, 25,000
Holland (1) 2 *(Van Basten 9, Gullit 75)*
Finland (0) 0
Holland: Van Breukelen; Blind, Vink, De Jong, Gullit, Wouters, Bergkamp (Kieft 72), Witschge, Van't Schip, Van Basten (Rutjes 76), Huistra.
Finland: Huttunen; Kanerva, Heikkinen, Europaeus, Holmgren, Ukkonen, Petaja, Litmanen (Tegelberg 46), Myyry, Tauriainen (Nyssonen 83), Paatelainen.

Helsinki, 16 May 1991, 5150
Finland (0) 2 *(Jarvinen 51, Litmanen 88)*
Malta (0) 0
Finland: Huttunen; Petaja, Holmgren, Heikkinen, Kanerva, Myyry, Litmanen, Ukkonen, Tarkkio (Tauriainen 87), Paatelainen (Paavola 63), Jarvinen.
Malta: Cini, Buttigieg, Brincat, Vella S, Camilleri J (Zerafa 70), Laferla, Busuttil, Vella R, Degiorgio, Scerri, Suda.

Helsinki, 5 June 1991, 21,207
Finland (0) 1 *(Holmgren 78)*
Holland (0) 1 *(De Boer 60)*
Finland: Huttunen; Petaja, Heikkinen, Ukkonen (Hjelm 81), Holmgren, Paavola, Myyry, Litmanen, Jarvinen, Tarkkio, Paatelainen (Tegelberg 66).
Holland: Hiele; Rutjes, Blind, Wouters, De Boer, Koeman R, Winter, Witschge, Van't Schip, Van Basten, Huistra (Kieft 75).

	P	*W*	*D*	*L*	*F*	*A*	*Pts*
Holland	6	4	1	1	14	2	9
Portugal	5	3	1	1	9	3	7
Finland	5	1	3	1	4	4	5
Greece	3	2	0	1	7	4	4
Malta	7	0	1	6	1	22	1

Remaining Fixtures: 11.9.91. Portugal v Finland; 9.10.91. Finland v Greece; 16.10.91. Holland v Portugal; 30.10.91. Greece v Finland; 20.11.91. Portugal v Greece; 4.12.91. Greece v Holland; 22.12.91. Malta v Greece.

Group 7

Wembley 17 October 1990, 77,040

England (1) 2 *(Lineker 39 (pen), Beardsley 89)*

Poland (0) 0

England: Woods; Dixon, Pearce, Parker, Walker, Wright M, Platt, Gascoigne, Bull (Waddle 56), Lineker (Beardsley 56), Barnes.
Poland: Wandzik; Czachowski, Wdowczyk, Szewczyk, Kaczmarek, Nawrocki, Taraiewicz, Warzycha R, Furtok (Warzycha K 75), Ziober, Kosecki (Kubicki 85).

Dublin, 17 October 1990, 46,000

Republic of Ireland (2) 5 *(Aldridge 15, 58, 73 (pen), O'Leary 40, Quinn 66)*

Turkey (0) 0

Republic of Ireland: Bonner; Irwin, Staunton, McCarthy, O'Leary, Hughton, Townsend (Moran 73), Houghton, Quinn (Cascarino 66), Aldridge, Sheridan.
Turkey: Engin; Riza, Tugay, Kemal, Gokhan, Erkan (Tanju 46), Bulent, Oguz, Mehmet, Hami, Sercan (Metin 46).

Dublin, 14 November 1990, 45,000

Republic of Ireland (0) 1 *(Cascarino 79)*

England (0) 1 *(Platt 67)*

Republic of Ireland: Bonner; Morris, Staunton, McCarthy, O'Leary, Whelan (McLoughlin 74), McGrath, Houghton, Quinn (Cascarino 62), Aldridge, Townsend.
England: Woods; Dixon, Pearce, Adams, Walker, Wright M, Platt, Cowans, Beardsley, Lineker, McMahon.

Istanbul, 14 November 1990, 4868

Turkey (0) 0

Poland (1) 1 *(Dziekanowski 37)*

Turkey: Engin; Riza, Uiken (Mehmet 67), Bulent, Gokhan, Yusuf, Muhmmed (Scercan 67), Unal, Oguz, Tanju, Ḥami.
Poland: Wandzik; Kubicki, Kaczmarek, Wdowczyk, Warzycha R, Nawrocki, Tarasiewicz, Prusik, Warzycha K, Dziekanowski (Ziober 74), Kosecki.

Wembley, 27 March 1991, 77,753

England (1) 1 *(Dixon 9)*

Republic of Ireland (1) 1 *(Quinn 27)*

England: Seaman; Dixon, Pearce, Adams (Sharpe 46), Walker, Wright M, Robson, Platt, Beardsley, Lineker (Wright I 75), Barnes.
Republic of Ireland: Bonner; Irwin, Staunton, O'Leary, Moran, Townsend, McGrath, Houghton, Quinn, Aldridge (Cascarino 70), Sheedy.

Warsaw, 17 April 1991, 1000

Poland (0) 3 *(Tarasiewicz 75, Urban 81, Kosecki 88)*

Turkey (0) 0

Poland: Wandzik; Kubicki, Kaczmarek (Czachowski 62), Wdowczyk, Jakolcewicz, Warzycha K, Warzycha R, Tarasiewicz, Urban, Kosecki, Ziober (Soczynski 70).
Turkey: Engin; Riza, Tayfun, Gokhan, Kemal, Bulent, Feyyaz, Ucar (Faruk 80), Muhammed, Mehmet, Tanju, Osman (Abdullah 70).

Dublin, 1 May 1991, 48,000

Republic of Ireland (0) 0

Poland (0) 0

Republic of Ireland: Bonner; Irwin, Staunton, O'Leary, Moran, Townsend, McGrath, Houghton, Quinn (Slaven 70), Aldridge (Cascarino 70), Sheedy.
Poland: Wandzik; Kubicki, Jakolcewicz, Wdowczyk, Soczynski, Warzycha R, Tarasiewicz, Czachowski, Furtok (Kosecki 89), Urban (Warzycha K 88), Szewczyk.

Izmir, 1 May 1991, 20,000
Turkey (0) 0
England (1) 1 *(Wise 32)*

Turkey: Hayrettin, Riza, Ogun, Gokhan, Recap, Muhammed, Unal, Ridvan, Mehmet, Tanju, Ali (Feyyaz 72).
England: Seaman; Dixon, Pearce, Wise, Walker, Pallister, Platt, Thomas G, (Hodge 46), Smith, Lineker, Barnes.

	P	*W*	*D*	*L*	*F*	*A*	*Pts*
England	4	2	2	0	5	2	6
Republic of Ireland	4	1	3	0	7	2	5
Poland	4	2	1	1	4	2	5
Turkey	4	0	0	4	0	10	0

Remaining Fixtures: 16.10.91. Poland v Republic of Ireland, England v Turkey; 13.11.91. Turkey v Republic of Ireland, Poland v England.

SOUTH AMERICAN CHAMPIONSHIP WINNERS

(Copa America)

1916 Uruguay
1917 Uruguay
1919 Brazil
1920 Uruguay
1921 Argentina
1922 Brazil
1923 Uruguay
1924 Uruguay
1925 Argentina
1926 Uruguay
1927 Argentina
1929 Argentina
1935 Uruguay
1937 Argentina
1939 Peru
1941 Argentina
1942 Uruguay
1945 Argentina
1946 Argentina
1947 Argentina
1949 Brazil
1953 Paraguay
1955 Argentina
1956 Uruguay
1957 Argentina
1959 Argentina
1959 Uruguay
1963 Bolivia
1967 Uruguay
1975 Peru
1979 Paraguay
1983 Uruguay
1987 Uruguay
1989 Brazil
1991 Argentina

SOUTH AMERICAN CUP WINNERS

(Copa Libertadores)

1960 Penarol (Uruguay)
1961 Penarol
1962 Santos (Brazil)
1963 Santos
1964 Independiente (Argentina)
1965 Independiente
1966 Penarol
1967 Racing Club (Argentina)
1968 Estudiantes (Argentina)
1969 Estudiantes
1970 Estudiantes
1971 Nacional (Uruguay)
1972 Independiente
1973 Independiente
1974 Independiente
1975 Independiente
1976 Cruzeiro (Brazil)
1977 Boca Juniors (Argentina)
1978 Boca Juniors
1979 Olimpia (Paraguay)
1980 Nacional
1981 Flamengo (Brazil)
1982 Penarol
1983 Gremio Porto Alegre (Brazil)
1984 Independiente
1985 Argentinos Juniors (Argentina)
1986 River Plate (Argentina)
1987 Penarol
1988 Nacional (Uruguay)
1989 Nacional (Colombia)
1990 Olimpia
1991 Colo Colo (Chile)

THE WORLD CUP FINALS

Uruguay 1930

URUGUAY 4, ARGENTINA 2 (1–2) *Montevideo*

Uruguay: Ballesteros; Nasazzi (capt), Mascheroni, Andrade, Fernandez, Gestido, Dorado, Scarone, Castro, Cea, Iriarte. **Scorers:** Dorado, Cea, Iriarte, Castro.

Argentina: Botasso; Della, Torre, Paternoster, Evaristo, J., Monti, Suarez, Peucelle, Varallo, Stabile, Ferreira, (capt), Evaristo, M. **Scorers:** Peucelle, Stabile.

Leading scorer: Stabile (Argentina) 8.

Italy 1934

ITALY 2, CZECHOSLOVAKIA 1 (0–0) (1–1)* *Rome*

Italy: Combi (capt); Monseglio, Allemandi, Ferraris IV, Monti, Bertolini, Guaita, Meazza, Schiavio, Ferrari, Orsi. **Scorers:** Orsi, Schiavio.

Czechoslovakia; Planicka (capt); Zenisek, Ctyroky, Kostalek, Cambal, Krcil, Junek, Svoboda, Sobotka, Nejedly, Puc. **Scorer:** Puc.

Leading scorers: Schiavio (Italy), Nejedly (Czechoslovakia), Conen (Germany) each 4

France 1938

ITALY 4, HUNGARY 2 (3–1) *Paris*

Italy: Olivieri; Foni, Rava, Serantoni, Andreolo, Locatelli, Biavati, Meazza (capt), Piola, Ferrari, Colaussi. **Scorers:** Colaussi 2, Piola 2.

Hungary: Szabo; Polgar, Biro, Szalay, Szucs, Lazar, Vincze, Sarosi (capt), Szengeller, Titkos. **Scorers:** Titkos, Sarosi.

Leading scorer: Leonidas (Brazil) 8.

Brazil 1950

Final pool *(replaced knock-out system)*

Uruguay 2, Spain 2
Brazil 7, Sweden 1
Uruguay 3, Sweden 2
Brazil 6, Spain 1
Sweden 3, Spain 1
Uruguay 2, Brazil 1

Final positions	*P*	*W*	*D*	*L*	*F*	*A*	*Pts*
Uruguay	3	2	1	0	7	5	5
Brazil	3	2	0	1	14	4	4
Sweden	3	1	0	2	6	11	2
Spain	3	0	1	2	4	11	1

Leading scorers: Ademir (Brazil) 7, Schiaffino (Uruguay), Basora (Spain) 5.

Switzerland 1954

WEST GERMANY 3, HUNGARY 2 (2–2) *Berne*

West Germany: Turek; Posipal, Kohlmeyer, Eckel, Liebrich, Mai, Rahn, Morlock, Walter, O., Walter, F. (capt), Schaefer. **Scorers:** Morlock, Rahn 2.

Hungary: Grosics; Buzansky, Lantos, Bozsik, Lorant, Zakarias, Czibor, Kocsis, Hidegkuti, Puskas (capt), Toth, J. **Scorers:** Puskas, Czibor.

Leading scorer: Kocsis (Hungary) 11.

Sweden 1958
BRAZIL 5, SWEDEN 2 (2–1) *Stockholm*
Brazil: Gilmar; Santos, D., Santos, N., Zito, Bellini, Orlando, Garrincha, Didi, Vavà, Pelé, Zagalo. **Scorers:** Vavà 2, Pelé 2, Zagalo.
Sweden: Svensson; Bergmark, Axbom, Boerjesson, Gustavsson, Parling, Hamrin, Gren, Simonsson, Liedholm, Skoglund. **Scorers:** Liedholm, Simonsson.
Leading scorer: Fontaine (France) 13 (present record total).

Chile 1962
BRAZIL 3, CZECHOSLOVAKIA 1 (1–1) *Santiago*
Brazil: Gilmar; Santos, D., Mauro, Zozimo, Santos, N., Zito, Didi, Garrincha, Vavà, Amorildo, Zagalo. **Scorers:** Amarildo, Zito, Vavà.
Czechoslovakia: Schroiff; Tichy, Novak, Pluskal, Popluhar, Masopust, Pospichal, Scherer, Kvasniak, Kadraba, Jelinek. **Scorer:** Masopust.
Leading scorer: Jerkovic (Yugoslavia) 5.

England 1966
ENGLAND 4, WEST GERMANY 2 (1–1) (2–2)* *Wembley*
England: Banks; Cohen, Wilson, Stiles, Charlton, J., Moore, Ball, Hurst, Hunt, Charlton, R., Peters. **Scorers:** Hurst 3, Peters.
West Germany: Tilkowski; Hottges, Schulz, Weber, Schnellinger, Haller, Beckenbauer, Overath, Seeler, Held, Emmerich. **Scorers** Haller, Weber.
Leading scorer: Eusebio (Portugal) 9.

Mexico 1970
BRAZIL 4, ITALY 1 (1–1) *Mexico City*
Brazil: Felix; Carlos Alberto, Piazza, Everaldo, Gerson, Clodoaldo, Jairzinho, Pelé, Tostão, Rivelino. **Scorers:** Pelé, Gerson, Jairzinho, Carlos Alberto.
Italy: Albertosi; Burgnich, Cera, Rosato, Fachetti, Bertini (Juliano), Riva, Domenghini, Mazzola, De Sista, Boninsegna (Riveta). **Scorer:** Boninsegna.
Leading scorer: Müller (West Germany) 10.

West Germany 1974
WEST GERMANY 2, HOLLAND 1 (2–1) *Munich*
West Germany: Maier; Vogts, Schwarzenbeck, Beckenbauer, Breitner, Bonhof, Hoeness, Overath, Grabowski, Müller, Holzenbein. **Scorers:** Breitner (pen), Müller.
Holland: Jongbloed; Suurbier, Rijsbergen (De Jong), Haan, Krol, Jansen, Van Hanegem, Neeskens, Rep (Nanninga), Cruyff, Rensenbrink (Van der Kerhof, R.). **Scorer:** Nanninga (pen).
Leading scorer: Lato (Poland) 7.

Argentina 1978
ARGENTINA 3, HOLLAND 1 (1–1)* *Buenos Aires*
Argentina: Fillol; Olguin, Passarella, Galvan, Tarantini, Ardiles (Larrosa), Gallego, Ortiz (Houseman), Bertoni, Luque, Kempes. **Scorers:** Kempes 2, Bertoni.
Holland: Jongbloed; Poortvliet, Brandts, Krol, Jansen (Suurbier), Neeskens, Van der Kerkhof, W., Van der Kerkhof, R., Haan, Rep (Nanninga), Rensenbrink. **Scorer:** Nanninga.
Leading scorer: Kempes (Argentina) 6.

Spain 1982
ITALY 3, WEST GERMANY 1 (0–0) *Madrid*
Italy: Zoff; Bergomi, Cabrini, Collovati, Scirea, Gentile, Oriali, Tardelli, Conti, Graziani (Altobelli), Rossi (Causio). **Scorers:** Rossi, Tardelli, Altobelli.
West Germany: Schumacher; Kaltz, Forster, K-H., Stielike, Forster, B. Breitner, Dremmler (Hrubesch), Littbarski, Briegel, Fischer, Rummenigge (Müller). **Scorer:** Breitner.
Leading scorer: Rossi (Italy) 6.

Mexico 1986
ARGENTINA 3, WEST GERMANY 2 (1–0) *Mexico City*
Argentina: Pumpido; Cuciuffo, Olarticoechea, Ruggeri, Brown, Giusti, Burruchaga (Trobbiani), Batista, Valdano, Maradona, Enrique. **Scorers:** Brown, Valdano, Burruchaga.
West Germany: Schumacher; Berthold, Briegel, Jakobs, Forster, Eder, Brehme, Matthaus, Allofs (Voller), Magath (Hoeness), Rummenigge. **Scorers:** Rummenigge, Voller.
Leading scorer: Lineker (England) 6.

Italy 1990
WEST GERMANY 1, ARGENTINA 0 (0–0) *Rome*
West Germany: Illgner; Berthold (Reuter 73), Kohler, Augenthaler, Buchwald, Brehme, Littbarski, Hassler, Matthaus, Voller, Klinsmann. **Scorer:** Brehme (pen).
Argentina: Goycochea; Lorenzo, Serrizuela, Sensini, Ruggeri (Monzon 46), Simon, Basualdo, Burruchaga (Calderon 53), Maradona, Troglio, Dezotti.
Referee: Codesal (Mexico). Monzon and Dezotti sent off.
Leading scorer: Schillaci (Italy) 6.

**After extra time*

EUROPEAN SUPER CUP

Played annually between the winners of the European Champions' Cup and the European Cup-Winners' Cup.

Previous Matches

1972 Ajax beat Rangers 3-1, 3-2
1973 Ajax beat AC Milan 0-1, 6-0
1974 Not contested
1975 Dynamo Kiev beat Bayern Munich 1-0, 2-0
1976 Anderlecht beat Bayern Munich 4-1, 1-2
1977 Liverpool beat Hamburg 1-1, 6-0
1978 Anderlecht beat Liverpool 3-1, 1-2
1979 Nottingham F beat Barcelona 1-0, 1-1
1980 Valencia beat Nottingham F 1-0, 1-2
1981 Not contested
1982 Aston Villa beat Barcelona 0-1, 3-0
1983 Aberdeen beat Hamburg 0-0, 2-0
1984 Juventus beat Liverpool 2-0
1985 Juventus v Everton not contested due to UEFA ban on English clubs
1986 Steaua Bucharest beat Dynamo Kiev 1-0
1987 FC Porto beat Ajax 1-0, 1-0
1988 KV Mechelen beat PSV Eindhoven 3-0, 0-1
1989 AC Milan beat Barcelona 1-1, 1-0

1990

First Leg, 10 October 1990, Genoa

Sampdoria (1) 1 *(Mikhailichenko 31)*

AC Milan (1) 1 *(Evani 39)* 25,000

Sampdoria: Pagliuca; Mannini, Invernizzi, Pari, Lanna, Pellegrini, Mikhailichenko, Lombardo, Branca, Mancini, Dossena.
AC Milan: Pazzagli; Tassotti, Costacurta, Gaudenzi, Galli F, Baresi, Donadoni (Rijkaard 59), Ancelotti, Massaro, Gullit, Evani (Stroppa 70).
Referee: Dos Santos (Portugal).

Second Leg, 29 November 1990, Bologna

AC Milan (1) 2 *(Gullit 44, Rijkaard 76)*

Sampdoria (0) 0 25,000

AC Milan: Pazzagli; Tassotti, Baresi, Costacurta (Galli F 78), Maldini, Carbone, Ancelotti, Rijkaard, Evani, Gullit (Donadoni 73), Agostini.
Sampdoria: Pagliuca; Lanna, Pellegrini, Vierchowod, Bonetti, Pari, Mikhailichenko (Dossena 67), Katanec (Branca 83), Lombardo, Vialli, Mancini.
Referee: Petrovic (Yugoslavia)

WORLD CLUB CHAMPIONSHIP

Played annually up to 1974 and intermittently since then between the winners of the European Cup and the winners of the South American Champions Cup – known as the Copa Libertadores. In 1980 the winners were decided by one match arranged in Tokyo in February 1981 and the venue has been the same since.

1960 Real Madrid beat Penarol 0-0, 5-1
1961 Penarol beat Benfica 0-1, 5-0, 2-1
1962 Santos beat Benfica 3-2, 5-2
1963 Santos beat AC Milan 2-4, 4-2, 1-0
1964 Inter-Milan beat Independiente 0-1, 2-0, 1-0
1965 Inter-Milan beat Independiente 3-0, 0-0
1966 Penarol beat Real Madrid 2-0, 2-0
1967 Racing Club beat Celtic 0-1, 2-1, 1-0
1968 Estudiantes beat Manchester United 1-0, 1-1
1969 AC Milan beat Estudiantes 3-0, 1-2
1970 Feyenoord beat Estudiantes 2-2, 1-0
1971 Nacional beat Panathinaikos* 1-1, 2-1
1972 Ajax beat Independiente 1-1, 3-0
1973 Independiente beat Juventus* 1-0
1974 Atlético Madrid* beat Independiente 0-1, 2-0
1975 Independiente and Bayem Munich could not agree dates; no matches.
1976 Bayern Munich beat Cruzeiro 2-0, 0-0
1977 Boca Juniors beat Borussia Moenchengladbach* 2-2, 3-0
1978 Not played
1979 Olimpia beat Malmö* 1-0, 2-1
1980 Nacional beat Nottingham Forest 1-0
1981 Flamengo beat Liverpool 3-0
1982 Penarol beat Aston Villa 2-0
1983 Gremio Porto Alegre beat SV Hamburg 2-1
1984 Independiente beat Liverpool 1-0
1985 Juventus beat Argentinos Juniors 4-2 on penalties after a 2-2 draw
1986 River Plate beat Steaua Bucharest 1-0
1987 FC Porto beat Penarol 2-1 after extra time
1988 Nacional (Uru) beat PSV Eindhoven 7-6 on penalties after 1-1 draw
1989 AC Milan beat Atletico Nacional (Col) 1-0 after extra time

*European Cup runners-up; winners declined to take part.

1990

9 December in Tokyo

AC Milan (1) 3 *(Rijkaard 43, 65, Stroppa 62)*

Olimpia (0) 0 62,228

AC Milan: Pazzagli; Tassotti, Baresi, Costacurta, Maldini (Galli 22), Carbone, Donadoni (Guerreiri 82), Rijkaard, Van Basten, Gullit, Stroppa.
Olimpia: Almeida; Fernandez, Caceres, Guasch, Ramirez (Chamac 48), Suarez, Hoyn (Cubilla 68), Balbuena, Monzon, Amarilla, Samaniego.
Referee: Wright (Brazil).

OTHER BRITISH AND IRISH INTERNATIONAL MATCHES 1990–91

Copenhagen, 11 September 1990, 8700

Denmark (0) 1 *(Laudrup B 64)*

Wales (0) 0

Denmark: Schmeichel; Sivebaek, Nielsen K, Olsen L, Andersen, Larsen, Bartram (Olsen J 73), Vilfort, Povlsen, Christensen (Molby 46), Laudrup B.
Wales: Southall; Phillips, Bodin, Aizlewood, Young, Ratcliffe, Saunders, Horne, Rush, Hughes, Speed (Nicholas 69).

Wembley, 12 September 1990, 51,459

England (1) 1 *(Lineker 44)*

Hungary (0) 0

England: Woods; Dixon, Pearce (Dorigo 46), Parker, Walker, Wright M, Platt, Gascoigne, Bull (Waddle 73), Lineker, Barnes.
Hungary: Petry; Monos (Simon 68), Disztl, Keller, Limperger, Garaba (Aczel 71), Kozma, Bucs (Balog 80), Gregor, Berczy, Kovacs K.

Dublin, 12 September 1990, 19,450

Republic of Ireland (0) 1 *(Kelly D 74)*
Morocco (0) 0

Republic of Ireland: Bonner; Irwin, McCarthy, O'Leary, Staunton, Houghton, Whelan, Townsend (Sheridan 65), Kelly M (McLoughlin 69), Quinn (Cascarino 58), Kelly D.
Morocco: Brazi; Benabicha, Naybat, Mouhcine, Jbilou (Tahar 76), Raghib, El Ghrissi, Majid, Daoudi, Khairi, Nader.

Wembley, 6 February 1991, 61,075

England (1) 2 (*Lineker 20 (pen), 61*)

Cameroon (0) 0

England: Seaman; Dixon, Pearce, Steven, Walker, Wright M, Robson (Pallister 70), Gascoigne (Hodge 67), Wright I, Lineker, Barnes.
Cameroon: Bell; Ebwelle, Onana, Kunde, Tataw, M'Fede, Mbouh-Mbouh, Pagal, Kana-Biyik (Łibiih 42), Omam-Biyik, Ekeke (Tapoko 78).

Hampden Park, 6 February 1991, 20,763

Scotland (0) 0

USSR (0) 1 (*Kuznetsov 89*)

Scotland: Goram; Malpas, Nicol, McCall (McAllister 69), Gough, McLeish (McPherson 46), Strachan, Fleck (Durie 75), McCoist, McStay, Boyd (MacLeod 46).
USSR: Uvarov; Chernishev, Kulkov, Tsvelba, Gorlukovich, Shalimov, Aleinikov, Kontchelskis, Youran (Kolyvanov 62), Mostovoi (Kuznetsov 69), Dobrovolski.

Racecourse Ground, 6 February 1991, 9168

Wales (0) 0
Republic of Ireland (1) 3 *(Quinn 24, 67, Byrne 87)*

Wales: Southall; Hall, Bodin, Aizlewood, Young (Speed 46), Ratcliffe, Horne, Nicholas, Rush (Allen 51), Saunders, Pascoe.

Republic of Ireland: Bonner; Irwin, Staunton, McGrath, Moran, McLoughlin, Townsend, Byrne, Quinn, Slaven (Kelly D 68), Sheedy.

Ninian Park, 1 May 1991, 3656

Wales (1) 1 *(Bodin 35 (pen))*

Iceland (0) 0

Wales: Southall; Phillips, Bodin, Aizlewood, Melville, Ratcliffe, Goss, Horne, Saunders, Hughes (Pascoe 69), Speed.
Iceland: Sigurdsson; Gislasson, Edvaldsson, Kristinsson, Gretarsson, Jonsson, Bergsson, Orlygsson (Stefansson 79), Gudjohnsen, Thordarsson, Gregory (Kristgannsson 73).

Wembley, 21 May 1991, 23,789

England (2) 3 *(Smith 16, Platt 4 (pen), 89)*

USSR (1) 1 *(Wright (og))*

England: Woods; Stevens, Dorigo, Wise (Batty 70), Parker, Wright M, Platt, Thomas, Smith, Wright I (Beardsley 70), Barnes.
USSR: Uvarov; Chernishey, Kulkov, Tsvelba, Galiamin, Shalimov, Mikhailichenko, Kontchelskis, Kolianov, Tatarchuk (Mostovoi 50), Kuznetsov D.

Dublin, 22 May 1991, 32,230

Republic of Ireland (0) 1 *(Kelly D 82)*

Chile (0) 1 *(Estay 64)*

Republic of Ireland: Peyton; Hughton, Staunton, O'Leary (McGrath 6), Moran, Townsend, Keane, Houghton (McLoughlin 64), Sheridan, Kelly D, Sheedy (Cascarino 71).
Chile: Toledo; Romero, Fuentes, Guevara (Miranda 15), Barca, Parraguez, Rubio, Gomez, Vera (Contreras 64), Estay, Guarda (Gonzales 79).

Wembley, 25 May 1991, 44,497

England (1) 2 *(Lineker 15, Platt 50)*

Argentina (0) (2) *(Garcia 66, Franco 70)*

England: Seaman; Dixon, Pearce, Batty, Walker, Wright M, Platt, Thomas, Smith, Lineker, Barnes (Clough 63).
Argentina: Goycochea; Vazquez, Enrique, Basualdo, Gamboa, Ruggeri, Garcia, Franco, Simeone, Martellotto (Mohammed 60), Boldrini.

Radom, 29 May 1991 11,000

Poland (0) 0

Wales (0) 0

Poland: Bako (Wandzik 46); Kubicki, Jakolcewicz, Wdowczyk, Soczynski, Nawrocki, Tarasiewicz, Warzycha K, Furtok, Kosecki, Ziober.
Wales: Southall; Phillips, Bodin, Aizlewood, Melville, Ratcliffe, Nicholas (Goss) Saunders, Rush, Hughes, Horne.

Boston, 1 June 1991, 51,273

USA (0) 1 *(Wynalda 68)*

Republic of Ireland (0) 1 *(Cascarino 56)*

USA: Meola; Balboa, Trittschuh, Michalik, Quinn (Snyder 85), Henderson, Agoos, Savage, Murray, Vermes (Perez 54), Wynalda.
Republic of Ireland: Bonner; Irwin, Staunton, McCarthy, Moran, Townsend, McGrath, Houghton (Sheridan 72), Cascarino, Kelly D, Sheedy.

Sydney, 1 June 1991, 35,472

Australia (0) 0

England (1) 1 *(Gray 40 (og))*

Australia: Zabica; Gray, Durakovic, Zelic, Tobin, Vidmar T, Wade, Petersen, Arnold, Tapai (Brown 76), Vidmar A.
England: Woods; Parker, Pearce, Batty, Walker, Wright M, Platt, Thomas, Clough, Lineker (Wise 81), Hirst (Salako 46).

Auckland, 3 June 1991, 17,500

New Zealand (0) 0

England (0) 1 *(Lineker 90)*

New Zealand: Gosling; Ridenton, Gray, Dunford, Evans, Ironside, McGarry, Halligan, Edge D, De Jong, Ferris.
England: Woods; Parker, Pearce, Batty (Deane 46), Walker, Barrett, Platt, Thomas, Wise, Lineker, Walters (Salako 70).

Wellington, 8 June 1991, 25,000

New Zealand (0) 0

England (1) 2 *(Pearce 12, Hirst 50)*

New Zealand: Schofield; Ridenton, Gray, Dunford, Evans, Ironside, McGarry, Halligan, Edge D (Edge T 62), De Jong, Ferris.
England: Woods; Charles, Pearce, Wise, Walker, Wright M, Platt, Thomas, Deane (Hirst 46), Wright I, Salako.

Kuala Lumpur, 12 June 1991, 45,000

Malaysia (0) 2 *(Matian 52, 76)*

England (3) 4 *(Lineker 1, 23, 30, 70)*

Malaysia: Hassan (Khairul 66); Serbegeth, Lee, Zaid (Azizol 46), Jayakanthan, Chow, Ahmad, Nasir, Matian, Sainal, Dollah.
England: Woods; Charles, Pearce, Batty, Walker, Wright M, Platt, Thomas, Clough, Lineker, Salako.

POST-WAR INTERNATIONAL APPEARANCES
As at 30 June, 1991

ENGLAND

A'Court, A. (5) (Liverpool) 1957/8, 1958/9.
Adams, T.A. (19) (Arsenal) 1986/7, 1987/8, 1988/9, 1990/91.
Allen, C. (5) (QPR) 1983/4, 1986/7 (Tottenham Hotspur) 1987/8.
Allen, R. (5) (West Bromwich Albion) 1951/2, 1953/4, 1954/5.
Allen, T. (3) (Stoke City) 1959/60.
Anderson, S. (2) (Sunderland) 1961/2.
Anderson, V. (30) (Nottingham Forest) 1978/9, 1979/80, 1980/1, 1981/2, 1983/84, (Arsenal) 1984/5, 1985/6, 1986/7, (Manchester United).
Angus, J. (1) (Burnley) 1960/1.
Armfield, J. (43) (Blackpool) 1958/9, 1959/60, 1960/1, 1961/2, 1962/3, 1963/4, 1965/6.
Armstrong, D. (3) (Middlesbrough) 1979/80, (Southampton) 1982/3, 1983/4.
Armstrong, K. (1) (Chelsea) 1954/5.
Astall, G. (2) (Birmingham) 1955/6.
Astle, J. (5) (West Bromwich Albion) 1968/9, 1969/70.
Aston, J. (17) (Manchester United) 1948/9, 1949/50, 1950/1.
Atyeo, J. (6) (Bristol City) 1955/6, 1956/7.

Bailey, G.R. (2) (Manchester United) 1984/5.
Bailey, M. (2) (Charlton) 1963/4, 1964/5.
Baily, E. (9) (Tottenham Hotspur) 1949/50, 1950/1, 1951/2, 1952/3.
Baker, J. (8) (Hibernian) 1959/60, 1965/6, (Arsenal).
Ball, A. (72) (Blackpool) 1964/5, 1965/6, 1966/7, (Everton) 1967/8, 1968/9, 1969/70, 1970/1, 1971/2 (Arsenal) 1972/3, 1973/4, 1974/5.
Banks, G. (73) (Leicester) 1962/3, 1963/4, 1964/5, 1965/6, 1966/7, 1967/8, (Stoke) 1968/9, 1969/70, 1970/1, 1971/2.
Banks, T. (6) (Bolton Wanderers) 1957/8, 1958/9.
Barham, M. (2) (Norwich City) 1982/3.
Barlow, R. (1) (West Bromwich Albion) 1954/5.
Barnes, J. (65) (Watford) 1982/3, 1983/4, 1984/5, 1985/6, 1986/7, (Liverpool) 1987/8, 1988/9, 1989/90, 1990/91.
Barnes, P. (22) (Manchester City) 1977/8, 1978/9, 1979/80 (West Bromwich Albion) 1980/1, 1981/2 (Leeds United).
Barrass, M. (3) (Bolton Wanderers) 1951/2, 1952/3.
Barrett, E.D. (1) (Oldham Athletic) 1990/91.
Batty, D. (5) (Leeds United) 1990/91.

Baynham, R. (3) (Luton Town) 1955/6.
Beardsley P.A. (49) (Newcastle United) 1985/6, 1986/7 (Liverpool) 1987/8, 1988/9, 1989/90, 1990/91.
Beasant, D.J. (2) (Chelsea), 1989/90.
Beattie, T.K. (9) (Ipswich Town) 1974/5, 1975/6, 1976/7, 1977/8.
Bell, C. (48) (Manchester City) 1967/8, 1968/9, 1969/70, 1971/2, 1972/3, 1973/4, 1974/5, 1975/6.
Bentley, R. (12) (Chelsea) 1948/9, 1949/50, 1952/3, 1954/5.
Berry, J. (4) (Manchester United) 1952/3, 1955/6.
Birtles, G. (3) (Nottingham Forest) 1979/80, 1980/1 (Manchester United).
Blissett, L. (14) (Watford) 1982/3, 1983/4 (AC Milan).
Blockley, J. (1) (Arsenal) 1972/3.
Blunstone, F. (5) (Chelsea) 1954/5, 1956/7.
Bonetti, P. (7) (Chelsea) 1965/6, 1966/7, 1967/8, 1969/70.
Bowles, S. (5) (QPR) 1973/4, 1976/7.
Boyer, P. (1) (Norwich City) 1975/6.
Brabrook, P. (3) (Chelsea) 1957/8, 1959/60.
Bracewell, P.W. (3) (Everton) 1984/5, 1985/6.
Bradford, G. (1) (Bristol Rovers) 1955/6.
Bradley, W. (3) (Manchester United) 1958/9.
Bridges, B. (4) (Chelsea) 1964/5, 1965/6.
Broadbent, P. (7) (Wolverhampton Wanderers) 1957/8, 1958/9, 1959/60.
Broadis, I. (14) (Manchester City) 1951/2, 1952/3 (Newcastle United) 1953/4.
Brooking, T. (47) (West Ham United) 1973/4, 1974/5, 1975/6, 1976/7, 1977/8, 1978/9, 1979/80, 1980/1, 1981/2.
Brooks, J. (3) (Tottenham Hotspur) 1956/7.
Brown, A. (1) (West Bromwich Albion) 1970/1.
Brown, K. (1) (West United) 1959/60.
Bull, S.G. (13) (Wolverhampton Wanderers) 1988/9, 1989/90, 1990/91.
Butcher, T. (77) (Ipswich Town) 1979/80, 1980/1, 1981/2, 1982/3, 1983/4, 1984/5, 1985/6, 1986/7 (Rangers) 1987/8, 1988/9, 1989/90.
Byrne, G. (2) (Liverpool) 1962/3, 1965/6.
Byrne, J. (11) (Crystal Palace) 1961/2, 1962/3, (West Ham United) 1963/4, 1964/5.
Byrne, R. (33) (Manchester United) 1953/4, 1954/5, 1955/6, 1956/7, 1957/8.

Callaghan, I. (4) (Liverpool) 1965/6, 1977/8.
Carter, H. (7) (Derby County) 1946/7.
Chamberlain, M. (8) (Stoke City) 1982/3, 1983/4, 1984/5.
Channon, M. (46) (Southampton) 1972/3, 1973/4, 1974/5, 1975/6, 1976/7, (Manchester City) 1977/8.

Charles, G.A. (2) (Nottingham Forest) 1990/91.
Charlton, J. (35) (Leeds United) 1964/5, 1965/6, 1966/7, 1967/8, 1968/9, 1969/70.
Charlton, R. (106) (Manchester United) 1957/8, 1958/9, 1959/60, 1960/1, 1961/2, 1962/3, 1963/4, 1964/5, 1965/6, 1966/7, 1967/8, 1968/9, 1969/70.
Charnley, R. (1) (Blackpool) 1961/2.
Cherry, T. (27) (Leeds United) 1975/6, 1976/7, 1977/8, 1978/9, 1979/80.
Chilton, A. (2) (Manchester United) 1950/1, 1951/2.
Chivers, M. (24) (Tottenham Hotspur) 1970/1, 1971/2, 1972/3, 1973/4.
Clamp, E. (4) (Wolverhampton Wanderers) 1957/8.
Clapton, D. (1) (Arsenal) 1958/9.
Clarke, A. (19) (Leeds United) 1969/70, 1970/1, 1972/3, 1973/4, 1974/5, 1975/6.
Clarke, H. (1) (Tottenham Hotspur) 1953/4.
Clayton, R. (35) (Blackburn Rovers) 1955/6, 1956/7, 1957/8, 1958/9, 1959/60.
Clemence, R (61) (Liverpool) 1972/3, 1973/4, 1974/5, 1975/6, 1976/7, 1977/8, 1978/9, 1979/80, 1980/1, 1981/2, (Tottenham Hotspur) 1982/3, 1983/4.
Clement, D. (5) (QPR) 1975/6, 1976/7.
Clough, B. (2) (Middlesbrough) 1959/60.
Clough, N.H. (4) (Nottingham Forest) 1988/9, 1990/91.
Coates, R. (4) (Burnley) 1969/70, 1970/1, (Tottenham Hotspur).
Cockburn, H. (13) (Manchester United) 1946/7, 1947/8, 1948/9, 1950/1, 1951/2.
Cohen, G. (37) (Fulham) 1963/4, 1964/5, 1965/6, 1966/7, 1967/8.
Compton, L. (2) (Arsenal) 1950/1.
Connelly J. (20) (Burnley) 1959/60, 1961/2, 1962/3, 1964/5 (Manchester United) 1965/6.
Cooper, T. (20) (Leeds United) 1968/9, 1969/70, 1970/1, 1971/2, 1974/5.
Coppell, S. (42) (Manchester United) 1977/8, 1978/9, 1979/80, 1980/1, 1981/2, 1982/3.
Corrigan J. (9) (Manchester City) 1975/6, 1977/8, 1978/9, 1979/80, 1980/1, 1981/2.
Cottee, A.R. (7) (West Ham United) 1986/7, 1987/8, (Everton) 1988/9.
Cowans, G. (10) (Aston Villa) 1982/3, 1985/6 (Bari) 1990/1 (Aston Villa).
Crawford, R. (2) (Ipswich Town) 1961/2.
Crowe, C. (1) (Wolverhampton Wanderers) 1962/3.
Cunningham, L. (6) (West Bromwich Albion) 1978/9 (Real Madrid) 1979/80, 1980/1.
Currie, A. (17) (Sheffield United) 1971/2, 1972/3, 1973/4, 1975/6 (Leeds United) 1977/8, 1978/9.

Davenport, P. (1) (Nottingham Forest) 1984/5.
Deane, B.C. (2) (Sheffield United) 1990/91.
Deeley, N. (2) (Wolverhampton Wanderers) 1958/9.
Devonshire, A. (8) (West Ham United) 1979/80, 1981/2, 1982/3, 1983/4.
Dickinson, J. (48) (Portsmouth) 1948/9, 1949/50, 1950/1, 1951/2, 1952/3, 1953/4, 1954/5, 1955/6, 1956/7.
Ditchburn, E. (6) (Tottenham Hotspur) 1948/9, 1952/3, 1956/7.
Dixon, K.M. (8) (Chelsea) 1984/5, 1985/6, 1986/7.
Dixon, L.M. (8) (Arsenal) 1989/90, 1990/91.
Dobson, M. (5) (Burnley) 1973/4, 1974/5 (Everton).
Dorigo, A.R. (6) (Chelsea) 1989/90, 1990/91.
Douglas, B. (36) (Blackburn Rovers) 1957/8, 1958/9, 1959/60, 1960/1, 1961/2, 1962/3.
Doyle, M. (5) (Manchester City) 1975/6, 1976/7.
Duxbury, M. (10) (Manchester United) 1983/4, 1984/5.

Eastham, G. (19) (Arsenal) 1962/3, 1963/4, 1964/5, 1965/6.
Eckersley, W. (17) (Blackburn Rovers) 1949/50, 1950/1, 1951/2, 1952/3, 1953/4.
Edwards, D. (18) (Manchester United) 1954/5, 1955/6, 1956/7, 1957/8.
Ellerington, W. (2) (Southampton) 1948/9.
Elliott, W. H. (5) (Burnley) 1951/2, 1952/3.

Fantham, J. (1) (Sheffield Wednesday) 1961/2.
Fashanu, J. (2) (Wimbledon) 1988/9.
Fenwick, T. (20) (QPR) 1983/4, 1984/5, 1985/6 (Tottenham Hotspur) 1987/8.
Finney, T. (76) (Preston) 1946/7, 1947/8, 1948/9, 1949/50, 1950/1, 1951/2, 1952/3, 1953/4, 1954/5, 1955/6, 1956/7, 1957/8, 1958/9.
Flowers R. (49) (Wolverhampton Wanderers) 1954/5, 1958/9, 1959/60, 1960/1, 1961/2, 1962/3, 1963/4, 1964/5, 1965/6.
Foster, S. (3) (Brighton) 1981/2.
Foulkes, W. (1) (Manchester United) 1954/5.
Francis, G. (12) (QPR) 1974/5, 1975/6.
Francis, T. (52) (Birmingham City) 1976/7, 1977/8 (Nottingham Forest) 1978/9, 1979/80, 1980/1, 1981/2 (Manchester City) 1982/3, (Sampdoria) 1983/4, 1984/5, 1985/6.
Franklin, N. (27) (Stoke City) 1946/7, 1947/8, 1948/9, 1949/50.
Froggatt, J. (13) (Portsmouth) 1949/50, 1950/1, 1951/2, 1952/3.
Froggatt, R. (4) (Sheffield Wednesday) 1952/3.

Garrett, T. (3) (Blackpool) 1951/2, 1953/4.
Gascoigne, P.J. (20) (Tottenham Hotspur) 1988/9, 1989/90, 1990/91.
Gates, E. (2) (Ipswich Town) 1980/1.

George, F. C. (1) (Derby County) 1976/7.
Gidman, J. (1) (Aston Villa) 1976/7.
Gillard, I. (3) (QPR) 1974/5, 1975/6.
Goddard, P. (1) (West Ham United) 1981/2.
Grainger, C. (7) (Sheffield United) 1955/6, 1956/7 (Sunderland).
Greaves, J. (57) (Chelsea) 1958/9, 1959/60, 1960/1, 1961/2 (Tottenham Hotspur) 1962/3, 1963/4, 1964/5, 1965/6, 1966/7.
Greenhoff, B. (18) (Manchester United) 1975/6, 1976/7, 1977/8, 1979/80.
Gregory, J. (6) (QPR) 1982/3, 1983/4.

Hagan, J. (1) (Sheffield United) 1948/9.
Haines, J. (1) (West Bromwich Albion) 1948/9.
Hall, J. (17) (Birmingham City) 1955/6, 1956/7.
Hancocks, J. (3) (Wolverhampton Wanderers) 1948/9, 1949/50, 1950/1.
Hardwick, G. (13) (Middlesbrough) 1946/7, 1947/8.
Harford, M.G. (2) (Luton Town) 1987/8, 1988/9.
Harris, G. (1) (Burnley) 1965/6.
Harris, P. (2) (Portsmouth) 1949/50, 1953/4.
Harvey, C. (1) (Everton) 1970/1.
Hassall, H. (5) (Huddersfield Town) 1950/1, 1951/2 (Bolton Wanderers) 1953/4.
Hateley, M. (31) (Portsmouth) 1983/4, 1984/5, (AC Milan) 1985/6, 1986/7, (Monaco) 1987/8.
Haynes, J. (56) (Fulham) 1954/5, 1955/6, 1956/7, 1957/8, 1958/9, 1959/60, 1960/1, 1961/2.
Hector, K. (2) (Derby County) 1973/4.
Hellawell, M. (2) (Birmingham City) 1962/3.
Henry, R. (1) (Tottenham Hotspur) 1962/3.
Hill, F. (2) (Bolton Wanderers) 1962/3.
Hill, G. (6) (Manchester United) 1975/6, 1976/7, 1977/8.
Hill, R. (3) (Luton Town) 1982/3, 1985/6.
Hinton A. (3) (Wolverhampton W.) 1962/3, 1964/5 (Nottingham Forest).
Hirst, D.E. (2) (Sheffield Wednesday) 1990/91.
Hitchens, G. (7) (Aston Villa) 1960/1, (Inter Milan) 1961/2.
Hoddle, G. (53) (Tottenham Hotspur) 1979/80, 1980/1, 1981/2, 1982/3, 1983/4, 1984/5, 1985/6, 1986/7 (Monaco) 1987/8.
Hodge, S.B. (24) (Aston Villa) 1985/6, 1986/7, (Tottenham Hotspur), (Nottingham Forest) 1988/9, 1989/90, 1990/91.
Hodgkinson, A. (5) (Sheffield United) 1956/7, 1960/1.
Holden, D. (5) (Bolton Wanderers) 1958/9.
Holliday, E. (3) (Middlesbrough) 1959/60.
Hollins, J. (1) (Chelsea) 1966/7.

Hopkinson, E. (14) (Bolton Wanderers) 1957/8, 1958/9, 1959/60.
Howe, D. (23) (West Bromwich Albion) 1957/8, 1958/9, 1959/60.
Howe, J. (3) (Derby County) 1947/8, 1948/9.
Hudson, A. (2) (Stoke City) 1974/5.
Hughes, E. (62) (Liverpool) 1969/70, 1970/1, 1971/2, 1972/3, 1973/4, 1974/5, 1976/7, 1977/8, 1978/9 (Wolverhampton Wanderers) 1979/80.
Hughes, L. (3) (Liverpool) 1949/50.
Hunt, R. (34) (Liverpool) 1961/2, 1962/3, 1963/4, 1964/5, 1965/6, 1966/7, 1967/8, 1968/9.
Hunt, S. (2) (West Bromwich Albion) 1983/4.
Hunter, N. (28) (Leeds United) 1965/6, 1966/7, 1967/8, 1968/9, 1969/70, 1970/1, 1971/2, 1972/3, 1973/4, 1974/5.
Hurst, G. (49) (West Ham United) 1965/6, 1966/7, 1967/8, 1968/9, 1969/70, 1970/1, 1971/2.

Jezzard, B. (2) (Fulham) 1953/4, 1955/6.
Johnston, D. (8) (Ipswich Town) 1974/5, 1975/6, (Liverpool) 1979/80.
Johnston, H. (10) (Blackpool) 1946/7, 1950/1, 1952/3, 1953/4.
Jones, M. (3) (Sheffield United) 1964/5 (Leeds United) 1969/70.
Jones, W.H. (2) (Liverpool) 1949/50.

Kay, A. (1) (Everton) 1962/3.
Keegan, K. (63) (Liverpool) 1972/3, 1973/4, 1974/5, 1975/6, 1976/7 (SV Hamburg) 1977/8, 1978/9, 1979/80 (Southampton) 1980/1, 1981/2.
Kennedy, A. (2) (Liverpool) 1983/4.
Kennedy, R. (17) (Liverpool) 1975/6, 1977/8, 1979/80.
Kevan, D. (14) (West Bromwich Albion) 1956/7, 1957/8, 1958/9, 1960/1.
Kidd, B. (2) (Manchester United) 1969/70.
Knowles, C. (4) (Tottenham Hotspur) 1967/8.

Labone, B. (26) (Everton) 1962/3, 1966/7, 1967/8, 1968/9, 1969/70.
Lampard, F. (2) (West Ham United) 1972/3, 1979/80.
Langley, J. (3) (Fulham) 1957/8.
Langton, R. (11) (Blackburn Rovers) 1946/7, 1947/8, 1948/9, (Preston North End) 1949/50, (Bolton Wanderers) 1950/1.
Latchford, R. (12) (Everton) 1977/8, 1978/9.
Lawler, C. (4) (Liverpool) 1970/1, 1971/2.
Lawton, T. (15) (Chelsea) 1946/7, 1947/8, (Notts County) 1948/9.
Lee, F. (27) (Manchester City) 1968/9, 1969/70, 1970/1, 1971/2.
Lee, J. (1) (Derby County) 1950/1.
Lee, S. (14) (Liverpool) 1982/3, 1983/4.
Lindsay, A. (4) (Liverpool) 1973/4.
Lineker, G. (68) (Leicester City) 1983/4, 1984/5 (Everton) 1985/6, 1986/7, (Barcelona) 1987/8, 1988/9 (Tottenham H) 1989/90, 1990/91.

Little, B. (1) (Aston Villa) 1974/5.
Lloyd, L. (4) (Liverpool) 1970/1, 1971/2, (Nottingham Forest) 1979/80.
Lofthouse, N. (33) (Bolton Wanderers) 1950/1, 1951/2, 1952/3, 1953/4, 1954/5, 1955/6, 1958/9.
Lowe, E. (3) (Aston Villa) 1946/7.

Mabbutt, G. (13) (Tottenham Hotspur) 1982/3, 1983/4, 1986/7, 1987/8.
Macdonald, M. (14) (Newcastle United) 1971/2, 1972/3, 1973/4, 1974/5, (Arsenal) 1975/6.
Madeley, P. (24) (Leeds United) 1970/1, 1971/2, 1972/3, 1973/4, 1974/5, 1975/6, 1976/7.
Mannion, W. (26) (Middlesbrough) 1946/7, 1947/8, 1948/9, 1949/50, 1950/1, 1951/2.
Mariner, P. (35) (Ipswich Town) 1976/7, 1977/8, 1979/80, 1980/1, 1981/2, 1982/3, 1983/4, 1984/5 (Arsenal)
Marsh, R. (9) (QPR) 1971/2 (Manchester City) 1972/3.
Martin, A. (17) (West Ham United) 1980/1, 1981/2, 1982/3, 1983/4, 1984/5, 1985/6, 1986/7.
Marwood, B. (1) (Arsenal) 1988/9.
Matthews, R. (5) (Coventry City) 1955/6, 1956/7.
Matthews, S. (37) (Stoke City) 1946/7, (Blackpool) 1947/8, 1948/9, 1949/50, 1950/1, 1953/4, 1954/5, 1955/6, 1956/7.
McDermott, T. (25) (Liverpool) 1977/8, 1978/9, 1979/80, 1980/1, 1981/2.
McDonald, C. (8) (Burnley) 1957/8, 1958/9.
McFarland, R. (28) (Derby County) 1970/1, 1971/2, 1972/3, 1973/4, 1975/6, 1976/7.
McGarry, W. (4) (Huddersfield Town) 1953/4, 1955/6.
McGuinness, W. (2) (Manchester United) 1958/9.
McMahon, S. (17) (Liverpool) 1987/8, 1988/9, 1989/90, 1990/91.
McNab, R. (4) (Arsenal) 1968/9.
McNeil, M. (9) (Middlesbrough) 1960/1, 1961/2.
Meadows, J. (1) (Manchester City) 1954/5.
Medley, L. (Tottenham Hotspur) 1950/1, 1951/2.
Melia, J. (2) (Liverpool) 1962/3.
Merrick, G. (23) (Birmingham City) 1951/2, 1952/3, 1953/4.
Metcalfe, V. (2) (Huddersfield Town) 1950/1.
Milburn, J. (13) (Newcastle United) 1948/9, 1949/50, 1950/1, 1951/2, 1955/6.
Miller, B. (1) (Burnley) 1960/1.
Mills, M. (42) (Ipswich Town) 1972/3, 1975/6, 1976/7, 1977/8, 1978/9, 1979/80, 1980/1, 1981/2.
Milne, G. (14) (Liverpool) 1962/3, 1963/4, 1964/5.
Milton, C.A. (1) (Arsenal) 1951/2.

Moore, R. (108) (West Ham United) 1961/2, 1962/3, 1963/4, 1964/5, 1965/6, 1966/7, 1967/8, 1968/9, 1969/70, 1970/1, 1971/2, 1972/3, 1973/4.
Morley, A. (6) (Aston Villa) 1981/2, 1982/3.
Morris, J. (3) (Derby County) 1948/9, 1949/50.
Mortensen, S. (25) (Blackpool) 1946/7, 1947/8, 1948/9, 1949/50, 1950/1, 1953/4.
Mozley, B. (3) (Derby County) 1949/50.
Mullen, J. (12) (Wolverhampton Wanderers) 1946/7, 1948/9, 1949/50, 1953/4.
Mullery, A. (35) (Tottenham Hotspur) 1964/5, 1966/7, 1967/8, 1968/9, 1969/70, 1970/1, 1971/2.

Neal, P. (50) (Liverpool) 1975/6, 1976/7, 1977/8, 1978/9, 1979/80, 1980/1, 1981/2, 1982/3, 1983/4.
Newton, K. (27) (Blackburn Rovers) 1965/6, 1966/7, 1967/8, 1968/9, 1969/70, (Everton).
Nicholls, J. (2) (West Bromwich Albion) 1953/4.
Nicholson W. (1) (Tottenham Hotspur) 1950/1.
Nish, D. (5) (Derby County) 1972/3, 1973/4.
Norman, M. (23) (Tottenham Hotspur) 1961/2, 1962/3, 1963/4, 1964/5.

O'Grady, M. (2) (Huddersfield Town) 1962/3, 1968/9 (Leeds United).
Osgood, P. (4) (Chelsea) 1969/70, 1973/4.
Osman, R. (11) (Ipswich Town) 1979/80, 1980/1, 1981/2, 1982/3, 1983/4.
Owen, S. (3) (Luton Town) 1953/4.

Paine, T. (19) (Southampton) 1962/3, 1963/4, 1964/5, 1965/6.
Pallister, G. (4) (Middlesbrough) 1987/8, 1990/91 (Manchester United).
Parker, P.A. (16) (QPR) 1988/9, 1989/90, 1990/91.
Parkes, P. (1) (QPR) 1973/4.
Parry, R. (2) (Bolton Wanderers) 1959/60.
Peacock, A. (6) (Middlesbrough) 1961/2, 1962/3, 1965/6 (Leeds United).
Pearce, S. (41) (Nottingham Forest) 1986/7, 1987/8, 1988/9, 1989/90, 1990/91.
Pearson, Stan (8) (Manchester United) 1947/8, 1948/9, 1949/50, 1950/1, 1951/2.
Pearson, Stuart (15) (Manchester United) 1975/6, 1976/7, 1977/8.
Pegg, D. (1) (Manchester United) 1956/7.
Pejic, M. (4) (Stoke City) 1973/4.
Perry, W. (3) (Blackpool) 1955/6.
Perryman, S. (1) (Tottenham Hotspur) 1981/2.

Peters, M. (67) (West Ham United) 1965/6, 1966/7, 1967/8, 1968/9, 1969/70, (Tottenham Hotspur) 1970/1, 1971/2, 1972/3, 1973/4.
Phelan, M.C. (1) (Manchester U) 1989/90.
Phillips, L. (3) (Portsmouth) 1951/2, 1954/5.
Pickering, F. (3) (Everton) 1963/4, 1964/5.
Pickering, N. (1) (Sunderland) 1982/3.
Pilkington, B. (1) (Burnley) 1954/5.
Platt, D. (22) (Aston Villa) 1989/90, 1990/91.
Pointer, R. (3) (Burnley) 1961/2.
Pye, J. (1) (Wolverhampton Wanderers) 1949/50.

Quixall, A. (5) (Sheffield Wednesday) 1953/4, 1954/5.

Radford, J. (2) (Arsenal) 1968/9, 1971/2.
Ramsey, A. (32) (Southampton) 1948/9, 1949/50, (Tottenham Hotspur) 1950/1, 1951/2, 1952/3, 1953/4.
Reaney, P. (3) (Leeds United) 1968/9, 1969/70, 1970/1.
Reeves, K. (2) (Norwich City) 1979/80.
Regis, C. (5) (West Bromwich Albion) 1981/2, 1982/3, (Coventry).
Reid, P. (13) (Everton) 1984/5, 1985/6, 1986/7.
Revie, D. (6) (Manchester City) 1954/5, 1955/6, 1956/7.
Richards, J. (1) (Wolverhampton Wanderers) 1972/3.
Rickaby, S. (1) (West Bromwich Albion) 1953/4.
Rimmer, J. (1) (Arsenal) 1975/6.
Rix, G. (17) (Arsenal) 1980/1, 1981/2, 1982/3, 1983/4.
Robb, G. (1) (Tottenham Hotspur) 1953/4.
Roberts, G. (6) (Tottenham Hotspur) 1982/3, 1983/4.
Robson, B. (89) (West Bromwich Albion) 1979/80, 1980/1, 1981/2, (Manchester United) 1982/3, 1983/4, 1984/5, 1985/6, 1986/7, 1987/8, 1988/9, 1989/90, 1990/91.
Robson, R. (20) (West Bromwich Albion) 1957/8, 1959/60, 1960/1, 1961/2.
Rocastle, D. (11) (Arsenal) 1988/9, 1989/90.
Rowley, J. (6) (Manchester United) 1948/9, 1949/50, 1951/2.
Royle, J. (6) (Everton) 1970/1, 1972/3, (Manchester City) 1975/6, 1976/7.

Sadler, D. (4) (Manchester United) 1967/8, 1969/70, 1970/1.
Salako, J.A. (4) (Crystal Palace) 1990/91.
Sansom, K. (86) (Crystal Palace) 1978/9, 1979/80, 1980/1, (Arsenal) 1981/2, 1982/3, 1983/4, 1984/5, 1985/6, 1986/7, 1987/8.
Scott, L. (17) (Arsenal) 1946/7, 1947/8, 1948/9.
Seaman, D.A. (7) (QPR) 1988/9, 1989/90, 1990/91 (Arsenal).
Sewell, J. (6) (Sheffield Wednesday) 1951/2, 1952/3, 1953/4.
Shackleton, L. (5) (Sunderland) 1948/9, 1949/50, 1954/5.

Sharpe, L.S. (1) (Manchester United) 1990/91.
Shaw, G. (5) (Sheffield United) 1958/9, 1962/3.
Shellito, K. (1) (Chelsea) 1962/3.
Shilton, P. (125) (Leicester City) 1970/1, 1971/2, 1972/3, 1973/4, 1974/5, (Stoke City) 1976/7, (Nottingham Forest) 1977/8, 1978/9, 1979/80, 1980/1, 1981/2, (Southampton) 1982/3, 1983/4, 1984/5, 1985/6, 1986/7, (Derby County) 1987/8, 1988/9, 1989/90.
Shimwell, E. (1) (Blackpool) 1948/9.
Sillett, P. (3) (Chelsea) 1954/5.
Slater, W. (12) (Wolverhampton Wanderers) 1954/5, 1957/8, 1958/9, 1959/60.
Smith, A.M. (7) (Arsenal) 1988/9, 1990/91.
Smith, L. (6) (Arsenal) 1950/1, 1951/2, 1952/3.
Smith R. (15) (Tottenham Hotspur) 1960/1, 1961/2, 1962/3, 1963/4.
Smith, Tom (1) (Liverpool) 1970/1.
Smith, Trevor (2) (Birmingham City) 1959/60.
Spink, N. (1) (Aston Villa) 1982/3.
Springett, R. (33) (Sheffield Wednesday) 1959/60, 1960/1, 1961/2, 1962/3, 1965/6.
Staniforth, R. (8) (Huddersfield Town) 1953/4, 1954/5.
Statham, D. (3) (West Bromwich Albion) 1982/3.
Stein, B. (1) (Luton Town) 1983/4.
Stepney, A. (1) (Manchester United) 1967/8.
Sterland, M. (1) (Sheffield Wednesday) 1988/9.
Steven, T.M. (30) (Everton) 1984/5, 1985/6, 1986/7, 1987/8, 1988/9 (Glasgow Rangers) 1989/90, 1990/91.
Stevens, G.A. (7) (Tottenham Hotspur) 1984/5, 1985/6.
Stevens, M.G. (42) (Everton) 1984/5, 1985/6, 1986/7, 1987/8 (Rangers) 1988/9, 1989/90, 1990/91.
Stiles, N. (28) (Manchester United) 1964/5, 1965/6, 1966/7, 1967/8, 1968/9, 1969/70.
Storey-Moore, I. (1) (Nottingham Forest) 1969/70.
Storey, P. (19) (Arsenal) 1970/1, 1971/2, 1972/3.
Streten, B. (1) (Luton Town) 1949/50.
Summerbee, M. (8) (Manchester City) 1967/8, 1971/2, 1972/3.
Sunderland, A. (1) (Arsenal) 1979/80.
Swan, P. (19) (Sheffield Wednesday) 1959/60, 1960/1, 1961/2.
Swift, F. (19) (Manchester City) 1946/7, 1947/8, 1948/9.

Talbot, B. (6) (Ipswich Town) 1976/7, 1979/80.
Tambling, R. (3) (Chelsea) 1962/3, 1965/6.
Taylor, E. (1) (Blackpool) 1953/4.
Taylor, J. (2) (Fulham) 1950/1.
Taylor, P.H. (3) (Liverpool) 1947/8.
Taylor, P.J. (4) (Crystal Palace) 1975/6.

Taylor, T. (19) (Manchester United) 1952/3, 1953/4, 1955/6, 1956/7, 1958/9.
Temple, D. (1) (Everton) 1964/5.
Thomas, Danny (2) (Coventry City) 1982/3.
Thomas, Dave (8) (QPR) 1974/5, 1975/6.
Thomas, G.R. (7) (Crystal Palace) 1990/91.
Thomas, M.L. (2) (Arsenal) 1988/9, 1989/90.
Thompson, P. (16) (Liverpool) 1963/4, 1964/5, 1965/6, 1967/8, 1969/70.
Thompson, P.B. (42) (Liverpool) 1975/6, 1976/7, 1978/9, 1979/80, 1980/1, 1981/2, 1982/3.
Thompson, T. (2) (Aston Villa) 1951/2, (Preston) 1956/7.
Thomson, R. (8) (Wolverhampton Wanderers) 1963/4, 1964/5.
Todd, C. (27) (Derby County) 1971/2, 1973/4, 1974/5, 1975/6, 1976/7.
Towers, T. (3) (Sunderland) 1975/6.
Tueart, D. (6) (Manchester City) 1974/5, 1976/7.

Ufton, D. (1) (Charlton Athletic) 1953/4.

Venables, T. (2) (Chelsea) 1964/5.
Viljoen, C. (2) (Ipswich Town) 1974/5.
Viollet, D. (2) (Manchester United) 1959/60, 1961/2.

Waddle, C.R. (61) (Newcastle United) 1984/5, (Tottenham Hotspur) 1985/6, 1986/7, 1987/8, 1988/9, (Marseille) 1989/90, 1990/91.
Waiters, A. (5) (Blackpool) 1963/4, 1964/5.
Walker, D.S. (36) (Nottingham Forest) 1988/9, 1989/90, 1990/91.
Wallace, D.L. (1) (Southampton) 1985/6.
Walsh, P. (5) (Luton Town) 1982/3, 1983/4.
Walters, K.M. (1) (Rangers) 1990/91.
Ward, P. (1) (Brighton) 1979/80.
Ward, T. (2) (Derby County) 1947/8, 1948/9.
Watson, D. (12) (Norwich City) 1983/4, 1984/5, 1985/6, 1986/7 (Everton) 1987/8.
Watson D.V. (65) (Sunderland) 1973/4, 1974/5, 1975/6 (Manchester City) 1976/7, 1977/8, (Southampton) 1978/9 (Werder Bremen) 1979/80, (Southampton) 1980/1, 1981/2, (Stoke City).
Watson, W. (4) (Sunderland) 1949/50, 1950/1.
Webb, N. (20) (Nottingham Forest) 1987/8, 1988/9 (Manchester United) 1989/90.
Weller, K. (4) (Leicester City) 1973/4.
West, G. (3) (Everton) 1968/9.
Wheeler, J. (1) (Bolton Wanderers) 1954/5.
Whitworth, S. (7) (Leicester City) 1974/5, 1975/6.
Whymark, T. (1) (Ipswich Town) 1977/8.
Wignall, F. (2) (Nottingham Forest) 1964/5.

Wilkins, R. (84) (Chelsea) 1975/6, 1976/7, 1977/8, 1978/9, (Manchester United) 1979/80, 1980/1, 1981/2, 1982/3, 1983/4, 1984/5, (AC Milan) 1985/6, 1986/7.
Williams, B. (24) (Wolverhampton Wanderers) 1948/9, 1949/50, 1950/1, 1951/2, 1954/5, 1955/6.
Williams, S. (6) (Southampton) 1982/3, 1983/4, 1984/5.
Willis, A. (1) (Tottenham Hotspur) 1951/2.
Wilshaw, D. (12) (Wolverhampton Wanderers) 1953/4, 1954/5, 1955/6, 1956/7.
Wilson, R. (63) (Huddersfield Town) 1959/60, 1961/2, 1962/3, 1963/4, 1964/5, (Everton) 1965/6, 1966/7, 1967/8.
Winterburn, N. (1) (Arsenal) 1989/90.
Wise, D.F. (5) (Chelsea) 1990/91.
Withe, P. (11) (Aston Villa) 1980/1, 1981/2, 1982/3, 1983/4, 1984/5.
Wood, R. (3) (Manchester United) 1954/5, 1955/6.
Woodcock, A. (42) (Nottingham Forest) 1977/8, 1978/9, 1979/80 (FC Cologne) 1980/1, 1981/2, (Arsenal) 1982/3, 1983/4, 1984/5, 1985/6.
Woods, C.C.E. (24) (Norwich City) 1984/5, 1985/6, 1986/7, (Rangers) 1987/8, 1988/9, 1989/90, 1990/91.
Worthington, F. (8) (Leicester City) 1973/4, 1974/5.
Wright, I.E. (4) (Crystal Palace) 1990/91.
Wright M. (40) (Southampton) 1983/4, 1984/5, 1985/6, 1986/7, (Derby County) 1987/8, 1988/9, 1989/90, 1990/91.
Wright, T. (11) (Everton) 1967/8, 1968/9, 1969/70.
Wright, W. (105) (Wolverhampton Wanderers) 1946/7, 1947/8, 1948/9, 1949/50, 1950/1, 1951/2, 1952/3, 1953/4, 1954/5, 1955/6, 1956/7, 1957/8, 1958/9.

Young, G. (1) (Sheffield Wednesday) 1964/5.

NORTHERN IRELAND

Aherne, T. (4) (Belfast Celtic) 1946/7, 1947/8, 1948/9, 1949/50 (Luton Town).
Anderson, T. (22) (Manchester United) 1972/3, 1973/4, 1974/5, (Swindon Town) 1975/6, 1976/7, 1977/8, (Peterborough United) 1978/9.
Armstrong, G. (63) (Tottenham Hotspur) 1976/7, 1977/8, 1978/9, 1979/80, 1980/1, (Watford) 1981/2, 1982/3, (Real Mallorca) 1983/4, 1984/5, (West Bromwich Albion) 1985/6 (Chesterfield).

Barr, H. (3) (Linfield) 1961/2, 1962/3, (Coventry City).
Best, G. (37) (Manchester United) 1963/4, 1964/5, 1965/6, 1966/7, 1967/8, 1968/9, 1969/70, 1970/1, 1971/2, 1972/3, 1973/4 (Fulham) 1976/7, 1977/8.

Bingham, W. (56) (Sunderland) 1950/1, 1951/2, 1952/3, 1953/4, 1954/5, 1955/6, 1956/7, 1957/8, 1958/9 (Luton Town) 1959/60, 1960/1 (Everton) 1961/2, 1962/3, 1963/4 (Port Vale).
Black, K. (16) (Luton Town) 1987/8, 1988/9, 1989/90, 1990/91.
Blair, R. (5) (Oldham Athletic) 1974/5, 1975/6.
Blanchflower, D. (54) (Barnsley) 1949/50, 1950/1 (Aston Villa) 1951/2, 1952/3, 1953/4, 1954/5, (Tottenham Hotspur) 1955/6, 1956/7, 1957/8, 1958/9, 1959/60, 1960/1, 1961/2, 1962/3.
Blanchflower J. (12) (Manchester United) 1953/4, 1954/5, 1955/6, 1956/7, 1957/8.
Bowler, G. (3) (Hull City) 1949/50.
Braithwaite, R. (10) (Linfield) 1961/2, 1962/3 (Middlesbrough) 1963/4, 1964/5.
Brennan, R. (5) (Luton Town) 1948/9, 1949/50 (Birmingham City) (Fulham), 1950/1.
Briggs, R. (2) (Manchester United) 1961/2, 1964/5 (Swansea)
Brotherston, N. (27) (Blackburn Rovers) 1979/80, 1980/1, 1981/2, 1982/3, 1983/4, 1984/5.
Bruce, W. (2) (Glentoran) 1960/1, 1966/7.

Campbell, A. (2) (Crusaders) 1962/3, 1964/5.
Campbell, D.A. (10) (Nottingham Forest) 1985/6, 1986/7, 1987/8 (Charlton Athletic).
Campbell, J. (2) (Fulham) 1950/1.
Campbell, R.M. (2) (Bradford City) 1981/2.
Campbell, W. (6) (Dundee) 1967/8, 1968/9, 1969/70.
Carey, J. (7) (Manchester United) 1946/7, 1947/8, 1948/9.
Casey, T. (12) (Newcastle United) 1954/5, 1955/6, 1956/7, 1957/8, 1958/9, (Portsmouth).
Caskey, A. (7) (Derby County) 1978/9, 1979/80, 1981/2 (Tulsa Roughnecks).
Cassidy, T. (24) (Newcastle United) 1970/1, 1971/2, 1973/4, 1974/5, 1975/6, 1976/7, 1979/80 (Burnley) 1980/1, 1981/2.
Caughey, M. (2) (Linfield) 1985/6.
Clarke, C.J. (30) (Bournemouth) 1985/6, 1986/7 (Southampton) 1987/8, 1988/9, 1989/90, 1990/91 (Portsmouth).
Cleary, J. (5) (Glentoran) 1981/2, 1982/3, 1983/4, 1984/5.
Clements, D. (48) (Coventry City) 1964/5, 1965/6, 1966/7, 1967/8, 1968/9, 1969/70, 1970/1, 1971/2 (Sheffield Wednesday) 1972/3 (Everton) 1973/4, 1974/5, 1975/6 (New York Cosmos).
Cochrane, D. (10) (Leeds United) 1946/7, 1947/8, 1948/9, 1949/50.
Cochrane, T. (26) (Coleraine) 1975/6, (Burnley) 1977/8, 1978/9, (Middlesbrough) 1979/80, 1980/1, 1981/2, (Gillingham) 1983/4.
Cowan, J. (1) (Newcastle United) 1969/70.
Coyle, F. (4) (Coleraine) 1955/6, 1956/7, 1957/8 (Nottingham Forest).

Coyle, L. (1) (Derry C) 1988/9.
Coyle, R. (5) (Sheffield Wednesday) 1972/3, 1973/4.
Craig, D. (25) (Newcastle United) 1966/7, 1967/8, 1968/9, 1969/70, 1970/1, 1971/2, 1972/3, 1973/4, 1974/5.
Crossan, E. (3) (Blackburn Rovers) 1949/50, 1950/1, 1954/5.
Crossan, J. (23) (Rotterdam Sparta) 1959/60, 1962/3 (Sunderland) 1963/4, 1964/5, (Manchester City) 1965/6, 1966/7, 1967/8 (Middlesbrough).
Cunningham, W. (30) (St Mirren) 1950/1, 1952/3, 1953/4, 1954/5, 1955/6, 1956/7, (Leicester City) 1957/8, 1958/9, 1959/60, 1960/1 (Dunfermline Athletic) 1961/2.
Cush, W. (26) (Glentoran) 1950/1, 1953/4, 1956/7, 1957/8 (Leeds United) 1958/9, 1959/60, 1960/1 (Portadown) 1961/2.

D'Arcy, S. (5) (Chelsea) 1951/2, 1952/3 (Brentford).
Dennison, R. (12) (Wolverhampton Wanderers) 1987/8, 1988/9, 1989/90, 1990/91.
Devine, J. (1) (Glentoran) 1989/90.
Dickson, D. (4) (Coleraine) 1969/70, 1972/3.
Dickson, T. (1) (Linfield) 1956/7.
Dickson, W. (12) (Chelsea) 1950/1, 1951/2, 1952/3 (Arsenal) 1953/4, 1954/5.
Doherty, L. (2) (Linfield) 1984/5, 1987/8.
Doherty P. (6) (Derby County) 1946/7, (Huddersfield Town) 1947/8, 1948/9, (Doncaster Rovers) 1950/1.
Donaghy, M. (70) (Luton Town) 1979/80, 1980/1, 1981/2, 1982/3, 1983/4, 1984/5, 1985/6, 1986/7, 1987/8, (Manchester United) 1988/9, 1989/90, 1990/91.
Dougan D. (43) (Portsmouth) 1957/8, 1959/60, (Blackburn Rovers) 1960/1, 1962/3 (Aston Villa) 1965/6 (Leicester City), 1966/7 (Wolverhampton Wanderers) 1967/8, 1968/9, 1969/70, 1970/1, 1971/2, 1972/3.
Douglas, J.P. (1) (Belfast Celtic) 1946/7.
Dowd, H. (3) (Glentoran) 1972/3, 1974/5 (Sheffield Wednesday).
Dowie, I. (7) (Luton Town) 1989/90, 1990/91.
Dunlop, G. (4) (Linfield) 1984/5, 1986/7.

Eglington T. (6) (Everton) 1946/7, 1947/8, 1948/9.
Elder, A. (40) (Burnley) 1959/60, 1960/1, 1961/2, 1962/3, 1963/4, 1964/5, 1965/6, 1966/7, (Stoke City) 1967/8, 1968/9, 1969/70.

Farrell, P. (7) (Everton) 1946/7, 1947/8, 1948/9.
Feeney, J. (2) (Linfield) 1946/7 (Swansea City) 1949/50.
Feeney, W. (1) (Glentoran) 1975/6.
Ferguson, W. (2) (Linfield) 1965/6, 1966/7.

Ferris, R. (3) (Birmingham City) 1949/50, 1950/1, 1951/2.
Finney, T. (14) (Sunderland) 1974/5, 1975/6 (Cambridge United) 1979/80.
Fleming, J.G. (12) (Nottingham Forest) 1986/7, 1987/8, 1988/9 (Manchester City) 1989/90, 1990/91 (Barnsley).
Forde, T. (4) (Ards) 1958/9, 1960/1.

Gallogly, C. (2) (Huddersfield Town) 1950/1.
Garton, R. (1) (Oxford United) 1968/9.
Gorman, W. (4) (Brentford) 1946/7, 1947/8.
Graham, W. (14) (Doncaster Rovers) 1950/1, 1951/2, 1952/3, 1953/4, 1954/5, 1955/6, 1958/9.
Gregg, H. (25) (Doncaster Rovers) 1953/4, 1956/7, 1957/8, (Manchester United) 1958/9, 1959/60, 1960/1, 1961/2, 1963/4.

Hamilton, B. (50) (Linfield) 1968/9, 1970/1, 1971/2 (Ipswich Town) 1972/3, 1973/4, 1974/5, 1975/6 (Everton) 1976/7, 1977/8, (Millwall) 1978/9, (Swindon Town).
Hamilton, W. (41) (QPR) 1977/8, 1979/80 (Burnley) 1980/1, 1981/2, 1982/3, 1983/4, 1984/5, (Oxford United) 1985/6.
Harkin, T. (5) (Southport) 1967/8, 1968/9 (Shrewsbury Town) 1969/70, 1970/1.
Harvey, M. (34) (Sunderland) 1960/1, 1961/2, 1962/3, 1963/4, 1964/5, 1965/6, 1966/7, 1967/8, 1968/9, 1969/70, 1970/1.
Hatton, S. (2) (Linfield) 1962/3.
Healy, F. (4) (Coleraine) 1981/2 (Glentoran) 1982/3.
Hegan, D. (7) (West Bromwich Albion) 1969/70, 1971/2 (Wolverhampton Wanderers) 1972/3.
Hill, C.F. (4) (Sheffield U), 1989/90, 1990/91.
Hill, J. (7) (Norwich City) 1958/9, 1959/60, 1960/1, (Everton) 1961/2, 1963/4.
Hinton, E. (7) (Fulham) 1946/7, 1947/8 (Millwall) 1950/1.
Hughes, P. (3) (Bury) 1986/7.
Hughes, W. (1) (Bolton Wanderers) 1950/1.
Humphries, W. (14) (Ards) 1961/2 (Coventry City) 1962/3, 1963/4, 1964/5 (Swansea Town).
Hunter, A. (53) (Blackburn Rovers) 1969/70, 1970/1, 1971/2 (Ipswich Town) 1972/3, 1973/4, 1974/5, 1975/6, 1976/7, 1977/8, 1978/9, 1979/80.

Irvine, R. (8) (Linfield) 1961/2, 1962/3 (Stoke City) 1964/5.
Irvine W. (23) (Burnley) 1962/3, 1964/5, 1965/6, 1966/7, 1967/8, 1968/9 (Preston North End) (Brighton & Hove Albion) 1971/2.

Jackson, T. (35) (Everton) 1968/9, 1969/70, 1970/1 (Nottingham Forest) 1971/2, 1972/3, 1973/4, 1974/5 (Manchester United) 1975/6, 1976/7.
Jamison, A. (1) (Glentoran) 1975/6.
Jennings, P. (119) (Watford) 1963/4, 1964/5, (Tottenham Hotspur) 1965/6, 1966/7, 1967/8, 1968/9, 1969/70, 1970/1, 1971/2, 1972/3, 1973/4, 1974/5, 1975/6, 1976/7, (Arsenal) 1977/8, 1978/9, 1979/80, 1980/1, 1981/2, 1982/3, 1983/4, 1984/5, (Tottenham Hotspur) 1985/6.
Johnston, W. (1) (Glentoran) 1961/2, (Oldham Athletic) 1965/6.
Jones, J. (3) (Glenavon) 1955/6, 1956/7.

Keane, T. (1) (Swansea Town) 1948/9.
Kee, P.V. (7) (Oxford U), 1989/90, 1990/91.
Keith, R. (23) (Newcastle United) 1957/8, 1958/9, 1959/60, 1960/1, 1961/2.
Kelly, H. (4) (Fulham) 1949/50 (Southampton) 1950/1.
Kelly, P. (1) (Barnsley) 1949/50.

Lawther, I. (4) (Sunderland) 1959/60, 1960/1, 1961/2 (Blackburn Rovers).
Lockhart, N. (8) (Linfield) 1946/7, 1949/50, (Coventry City) 1950/1, 1951/2, 1953/4, (Aston Villa) 1954/5, 1955/6.
Lutton, B. (6) (Wolverhampton Wanderers) 1969/70, 1972/3 (West Ham United) 1973/4.

Magill, E. (26) (Arsenal) 1961/2, 1962/3, 1963/4, 1964/5, 1965/6 (Brighton & Hove Albion).
Magilton, J. (3) (Oxford United) 1990/91.
Martin, C. (6) (Glentoran) 1946/7, 1947/8 (Leeds United) 1948/9 (Aston Villa) 1949/50.
McAdams, W. (15) (Manchester City) 1953/4, 1954/5, 1956/7, 1957/8, 1960/1 (Bolton Wanderers) 1961/2 (Leeds United).
McAlinden, J. (2) (Portsmouth) 1946/7, 1948/9, (Southend United).
McBride, S. (2) (Glenavon) 1990/91.
McCabe, J. (6) (Leeds United) 1948/9, 1949/50, 1950/1, 1952/3, 1953/4.
McCavana, T. (3) (Coleraine) 1954/5, 1955/6.
McCleary, J.W. (1) (Cliftonville) 1954/5.
McClelland, J. (6) (Arsenal) 1960/1, 1965/6 (Fulham).
McClelland, J. (53) (Mansfield Town) 1979/80, 1980/1, 1981/2 (Rangers) 1982/3, 1983/4, 1984/5 (Watford) 1985/6, 1986/7, 1987/8, 1988/9 (Leeds U) 1989/90.
McCourt, F. (6) (Manchester City) 1951/2, 1952/3.
McCoy, R. (1) (Coleraine) 1986/7.

McCreery, D. (67) (Manchester United) 1975/6, 1976/7, 1977/8, 1978/9, 1979/80 (QPR) 1980/1 (Tulsa Roughnecks) 1981/2, 1982/3 (Newcastle United), 1983/4, 1984/5, 1985/6, 1986/7, 1987/8, 1988/9 (Hearts) 1989/90.
McCrory, S. (1) (Southend United) 1957/8.
McCullough, W. (10) (Arsenal) 1960/1, 1962/3, 1963/4, 1964/5, 1966/7, (Millwall).
McCurdy, C. (1) (Linfield) 1979/80.
McDonald, A. (29) (QPR) 1985/6, 1986/7, 1987/8, 1988/9, 1990/91.
McElhinney, G. (6) (Bolton Wanderers) 1983/4, 1984/5.
McFaul, I. (6) (Linfield) 1966/7, 1969/70 (Newcastle United) 1970/1, 1971/2, 1972/3, 1973/4.
McGarry, J.K. (3) (Cliftonville) 1950/1.
McGaughey, M. (1) (Linfield) 1984/5.
McGrath, R. (21) (Tottenham Hotspur) 1973/4, 1974/5, 1975/6 (Manchester United) 1976/7, 1977/8, 1978/9.
McIlroy, J. (55) (Burnley) 1951/2, 1952/3, 1953/4, 1954/5, 1955/6, 1956/7, 1957/8, 1958/9, 1959/60, 1960/1, 1961/2, 1962/3, 1965/6 (Stoke City).
McIlroy, S.B. (88) (Manchester United) 1971/2, 1973/4, 1974/5, 1975/6, 1976/7, 1977/8, 1978/9, 1979/80, 1980/1, 1981/2, (Stoke City) 1982/3, 1983/4, 1984/5 (Manchester City) 1985/6, 1986/7.
McKeag, W. (2) (Glentoran) 1967/8.
McKenna, J. (7) (Huddersfield Town) 1949/50, 1950/1, 1951/2.
McKenzie, R. (1) (Airdrieonians) 1966/7.
McKinney, W. (1) (Falkirk) 1965/6.
McKnight, A. (10) (Celtic) 1987/8, (West Ham United) 1988/9.
McLaughlin, J. (12) (Shrewsbury Town) 1961/2, 1962/3 (Swansea City), 1963/4, 1964/5, 1965/6.
McMichael, A. (39) (Newcastle United) 1949/50, 1950/1, 1951/2, 1952/3, 1953/4, 1954/5, 1955/6, 1956/7, 1957/8, 1958/9, 1959/60.
McMillan, S. (2) (Manchester United) 1962/3.
McMordie, E. (21) (Middlesbrough) 1968/9, 1969/70, 1970/1, 1971/2, 1972/3.
McMorran, E. (15) (Belfast Celtic) 1946/7 (Barnsley) 1950/1, 1951/2, 1952/3, (Doncaster Rovers) 1953/4, 1955/6, 1956/7.
McNally, B.A. (5) (Shrewsbury Town) 1985/6, 1986/7, 1987/8.
McParland, P. (34) (Aston Villa) 1953/4, 1954/5, 1955/6, 1956/7, 1957/8, 1958/9, 1959/60, 1960/1, 1961/2 (Wolverhampton Wanderers).
Montgomery, F.J. (1) (Coleraine) 1954/5.
Moore, C. (1) (Glentoran) 1948/9.
Moreland, V. (6) (Derby County) 1978/9, 1979/80.
Morgan, S. (18) (Port Vale) 1971/2, 1972/3, 1973/4 (Aston Villa) 1974/5, 1975/6 (Brighton & Hove Albion) (Sparta Rotterdam) 1978/9.
Morrow, S.J. (4) (Arsenal) 1989/90, 1990/91.

Mullan, G. (4) (Glentoran) 1982/3.

Napier, R. (1) (Bolton Wanderers) 1965/6.
Neill, T. (59) (Arsenal) 1960/1, 1961/2, 1962/3, 1963/4, 1964/5, 1965/6, 1966/7, 1967/8, 1968/9, 1969/70 (Hull City) 1970/1, 1971/2, 1972/3.
Nelson, S. (51) (Arsenal) 1969/70, 1970/1, 1971/2, 1972/3, 1973/4, 1974/5, 1975/6, 1976/7, 1977/8, 1978/9, 1979/80, 1980/1, 1981/2 (Brighton).
Nicholl, C. (51) (Aston Villa) 1974/5, 1975/6, 1976/7 (Southampton) 1977/8, 1978/9, 1979/80, 1980/1, 1981/2, 1982/3 (Grimsby T.) 1983/4.
Nicholl, J.M. (73) (Manchester United) 1975/6, 1976/7, 1977/8, 1978/9, 1979/80, 1980/1, 1981/2 (Toronto Blizzard) 1982/3 (Sunderland) (Toronto Blizzard) (Rangers) 1983/4 (Toronto Blizzard) 1984/5 (West Bromwich Albion), 1985/6.
Nicholson, J. (41) (Manchester United) 1960/1, 1961/2, 1962/3, 1964/5, (Huddersfield Town) 1965/6, 1966/7, 1967/8, 1968/9, 1969/70, 1970/1, 1971/2.

O'Doherty, A. (2) (Coleraine) 1969/70.
O'Driscoll, J. (3) (Swansea City) 1948/9.
O'Kane, L. (20) (Nottingham Forest) 1969/70, 1970/1, 1971/2, 1972/3, 1973/4, 1974/5.
O'Neill, C. (3) (Motherwell) 1988/9, 1989/90, 1990/91.
O'Neill, H.M. (64) (Distillery) 1971/2 (Nottingham Forest) 1972/3, 1973/4, 1974/5, 1975/6, 1976/7, 1977/8, 1978/9, 1979/80, 1980/1 (Norwich City) 1981/2 (Manchester City) (Norwich City) 1982/3 (Notts County) 1983/4, 1984/5.
O'Neill, J. (1) (Sunderland) 1961/2.
O'Neill, J. (39) (Leicester City) 1979/80, 1980/1, 1981/2, 1982/3, 1983/4, 1984/5, 1985/6.
O'Neill, M.A. (13) (Newcastle United) 1987/8, 1988/9 (Dundee United) 1989/90, 1990/91.

Parke, J. (13) (Linfield) 1963/4 (Hibernian), 1964/5 (Sunderland) 1965/6, 1966/7, 1967/8.
Peacock, R. (31) (Glasgow Celtic) 1951/2, 1952/3, 1953/4, 1954/5, 1955/6, 1956/7, 1957/8, 1958/9, 1959/60, 1960/1 (Coleraine) 1961/2.
Penney, S. (17) (Brighton & Hove Albion) 1984/5, 1985/6, 1986/7, 1987/8, 1988/9.
Platt, J.A. (23) (Middlesbrough) 1975/6, 1977/8, 1979/80, 1980/1, 1981/2, 1982/3, (Ballymena United) 1983/4 (Coleraine) 1985/6.

Quinn, J.M. (28) (Blackburn Rovers) 1984/5, 1985/6, 1986/7, 1987/8 (Leicester) 1988/9 (Bradford City) 1989/90 (West Ham United), 1990/91.

Rafferty, P. (1) (Linfield) 1979/80.
Ramsey, P. (14) (Leicester City) 1983/4, 1984/5, 1985/6, 1986/7, 1987/8, 1988/9.
Rice, P. (49) (Arsenal) 1968/9, 1969/70, 1970/1, 1971/2, 1972/3, 1973/4, 1974/5, 1975/6, 1976/7, 1977/8, 1978/9, 1979/80.
Rogan, A. (16) (Celtic) 1987/8, 1988/9, 1989/90, 1990/91.
Ross, E. (1) (Newcastle United) 1968/9.
Russell, A. (1) (Linfield) 1946/7.
Ryan, R. (1) (West Bromwich Albion) 1949/50.

Sanchez, L.P. (3) (Wimbledon) 1986/7, 1988/9.
Scott, J. (2) (Grimsby Town) 1957/8.
Scott, P. (10) (Everton) 1974/5, 1975/6, (York City) 1977/8, (Aldershot) 1978/9.
Sharkey, P. (1) (Ipswich Town) 1975/6.
Shields, J. (1) (Southampton) 1956/7.
Simpson, W. (12) (Glasgow Rangers) 1950/1, 1953/4, 1954/5, 1956/7, 1957/8, 1958/9.
Sloan, D. (2) (Oxford) 1968/9, 1970/1.
Sloan, T. (3) (Manchester United) 1978/9.
Sloan, W. (1) (Arsenal) 1946/7.
Smyth, S. (9) (Wolverhampton Wanderers) 1947/8, 1948/9, 1949/50 (Stoke City) 1951/2.
Smyth, W. (4) (Distillery) 1948/9, 1953/4.
Spence, D. (29) (Bury) 1974/5, 1975/6, (Blackpool) 1976/7, 1978/9, 1979/80, (Southend United) 1980/1, 1981/2.
Stevenson, A. (3) (Everton) 1946/7, 1947/8.
Stewart, A. (7) (Glentoran) 1966/7, 1967/8 (Derby) 1968/9.
Stewart, D. (1) (Hull City) 1977/8.
Stewart, I. (31) (QPR) 1981/2, 1982/3, 1983/4, 1984/5, (Newcastle United) 1985/6, 1986/7.
Stewart, T. (1) (Linfield) 1960/1.

Taggart, G.P. (7) (Barnsley) 1989/90, 1990/91.
Todd, S. (11) (Burnley) 1965/6, 1966/7, 1967/8, 1968/9, 1969/70 (Sheffield Wednesday) 1970/1.
Trainor, D. (1) (Crusaders) 1966/7.
Tully, C. (10) (Glasgow Celtic) 1948/9, 1949/50, 1951/2, 1952/3, 1953/4, 1955/6, 1958/9.

Uprichard, N. (18) (Swindon Town) 1951/2, 1952/3 (Portsmouth) 1954/5, 1955/6, 1957/8, 1958/9.

Vernon, J. (17) (Belfast Celtic) 1946/7 (West Bromwich Albion) 1947/8, 1948/9, 1949/50, 1950/1, 1951/2.

Walker, J. (1) (Doncaster R) 1954/5.
Walsh, D. (9) (West Bromwich Albion) 1946/7, 1947/8, 1948/9, 1949/50.
Walsh, W. (5) (Manchester City) 1947/8, 1948/9.
Watson, P. (1) (Distillery) 1970/1.
Welsh, S. (4) (Carlisle United) 1965/6, 1966/7.
Whiteside, N. (38) (Manchester United) 1981/2, 1982/3, 1983/4, 1984/5, 1985/6, 1986/7, 1987/8, (Everton) 1989/90.
Williams, P. (1) (WBA) 1990/91.
Wilson, D.J. (22) (Brighton & Hove Albion) 1986/7 (Luton) 1987/8, 1988/9, 1989/90, 1990/91.
Wilson, K.J. (21) (Ipswich Town) 1986/7 (Chelsea) 1987/8, 1988/9, 1989/90, 1990/91 (Sheffield Wednesday).
Wilson, S. (12) (Glenavon) 1961/2, 1963/4, (Falkirk) 1964/5 (Dundee) 1965/6, 1966/7, 1967/8.
Worthington, N. (32) (Sheffield Wednesday) 1983/4, 1984/5, 1985/6, 1986/7, 1987/8, 1988/9, 1989/90, 1990/91.
Wright, T.J. (4) (Newcastle) 1988/9, 1989/90.

SCOTLAND

Aird, J. (4) (Burnley) 1953/4.
Aitken, G.G. (8) (East Fife) 1948/9, 1949/50, 1952/3 (Sunderland) 1953/4.
Aitken, R. (56) (Celtic) 1979/80, 1982/3, 1983/4, 1984/5, 1985/6, 1986/7, 1987/8, (Newcastle) 1989/90.
Albiston, A. (14) (Manchester United) 1981/2, 1983/4, 1984/5, 1985/6.
Allan, T. (2) (Dundee) 1973/4.
Anderson, J. (1) (Leicester City) 1953/4.
Archibald, S. (27) (Aberdeen) 1979/80 (Tottenham Hotspur) 1980/1, 1981/2, 1982/3, 1983/4, 1984/5, (Barcelona) 1985/6.
Auld, B. (3) (Celtic) 1958/9, 1959/60.

Baird, H. (1) (Airdrieonians) 1955/6.
Baird, S. (7) (Rangers) 1956/7, 1957/8.
Bannon, E. (11) (Dundee United) 1979/80, 1982/3, 1983/4, 1985/6.
Bauld, W. (3) (Heart of Midlothian) 1949/50.
Baxter, J. (34) (Rangers) 1960/1, 1961/2, 1962/3, 1963/4, 1964/5 (Sunderland) 1965/6, 1966/7, 1967/8.
Bell, W. (2) (Leeds United) 1965/6.
Bett, J. (25) (Rangers) 1981/2, 1982/3 (Lokeren) 1983/4, 1984/5 (Aberdeen) 1985/6, 1986/7, 1987/8, 1988/9, 1989/90.
Black, E. (2) (Metz) 1987/8.
Black, I. (1) (Southampton) 1947/8.
Blacklaw, A. (3) (Burnley) 1962/3, 1965/6.

Blackley, J. (7) (Hibernian) 1973/4, 1975/6, 1976/7.
Blair, J. (1) (Blackpool) 1946/7.
Blyth, J. (2) (Coventry City) 1977/8.
Bone, J. (2) (Norwich City) 1971/2, 1972/3.
Boyd, T. (4) (Motherwell) 1990/91.
Brand, R. (8) (Rangers) 1960/1, 1961/2.
Brazil, A. (13) (Ipswich Town) 1979/80, 1981/2, 1982/3 (Tottenham Hotspur).
Bremner, D. (1) (Hibernian) 1975/6.
Bremner, W. (54) (Leeds United) 1964/5, 1965/6, 1966/7, 1967/8, 1968/9, 1969/70, 1970/1, 1971/2, 1972/3, 1973/4, 1974/5, 1975/6.
Brennan, F. (7) (Newcastle United) 1946/7, 1952/3, 1963/4.
Brogan, J. (4) (Celtic) 1970/1.
Brown, A. (14) (East Fife) 1949/50 (Blackpool) 1951/2, 1952/3, 1953/4.
Brown, H. (3) (Partick Thistle) 1946/7.
Brown, J. (1) (Sheffield United) 1974/5.
Brown, R. (3) (Rangers) 1946/7, 1948/9, 1951/2.
Brown, W. (28) (Dundee) 1957/8, 1958/9, 1959/60 (Tottenham Hotspur) 1961/2, 1962/3, 1963/4, 1964/5, 1965/6.
Brownlie, J. (7) (Hibernian) 1970/1, 1971/2, 1972/3, 1975/6.
Buchan, M. (34) (Aberdeen) 1971/2 (Manchester United), 1972/3, 1973/4, 1974/5, 1975/6, 1976/7, 1977/8, 1978/9.
Buckley, P. (3) (Aberdeen) 1953/4, 1954/5.
Burley, G. (11) (Ipswich Town) 1978/9, 1979/80, 1981/2.
Burns, F. (1) (Manchester United) 1969/70.
Burns, K. (20) (Birmingham City) 1973/4, 1974/5, 1976/7 (Nottingham Forest) 1977/8, 1978/9, 1979/80, 1980/1.
Burns, T. (8) (Celtic) 1980/1, 1981/2, 1982/3, 1987/8.

Caldow, E. (40) (Rangers) 1956/7, 1957/8, 1958/9, 1959/60, 1960/1, 1961/2, 1962/3.
Callaghan, W. (2) (Dunfermline) 1969/70.
Campbell, R. (5) (Falkirk) 1946/7 (Chelsea) 1949/50.
Campbell, W. (5) (Morton) 1946/7, 1947/8.
Carr, W. (6) (Coventry City) 1969/70, 1970/1, 1971/2, 1972/3.
Chalmers, S. (5) (Celtic) 1964/5, 1965/6, 1966/7.
Clark, J. (4) (Celtic) 1965/6, 1966/7.
Clark, R. (17) (Aberdeen) 1967/8, 1969/70, 1970/1, 1971/2, 1972/3.
Clarke, S. (5) (Chelsea) 1987/8.
Collins, J. (6) (Hibernian) 1987/8, 1989/90, 1990/91 (Celtic).
Collins, R. (31) (Celtic) 1950/1, 1954/5, 1955/6, 1956/7, 1957/8, 1958/9, (Everton) 1964/5, (Leeds United).
Colquhoun, E. (9) (Sheffield United) 1971/2, 1972/3.
Colquhoun, J. (1) (Hearts) 1987/8.
Combe, R. (3) (Hibernian) 1947/8.

Conn, A. (1) (Heart of Midlothian) 1955/6.
Conn, A. (2) (Tottenham Hotspur) 1974/5.
Connachan, E. (2) (Dunfermline Athletic) 1961/2.
Connelly, G. (2) (Celtic) 1973/4.
Connolly, J. (1) (Everton) 1972/3.
Connor, R. (4) (Dundee) 1985/6 (Aberdeen) 1987/8, 1988/9, 1990/91.
Cooke, C. (16) (Dundee) 1965/6 (Chelsea) 1967/8, 1968/9, 1969/70, 1970/1, 1974/5.
Cooper, D. (22) (Rangers) 1979/80, 1983/4, 1984/5, 1985/6, 1986/7 (Motherwell) 1989/90.
Cormack, P. (9) (Hibernian) 1965/6, 1969/70 (Nottingham Forest) 1970/1, 1971/2.
Cowan, J. (25) (Morton) 1947/8, 1948/9, 1949/50, 1950/1, 1951/2 (Motherwell).
Cowie, D. (20) (Dundee) 1952/3, 1953/4, 1954/5, 1955/6, 1956/7, 1957/8.
Cox, C. (1) (Hearts) 1947/8.
Cox, S. (25) (Rangers) 1947/8, 1948/9, 1949/50, 1950/1, 1951/2, 1952/3, 1953/4.
Craig, J. (1) (Celtic) 1976/7.
Craig, J.P. (1) (Celtic) 1967/8.
Craig, T. (1) (Newcastle United) 1975/6.
Crerand, P. (16) (Celtic) 1960/1, 1961/2, 1962/3 (Manchester United) 1963/4, 1964/5, 1965/6.
Cropley, A. (2) (Hibernian) 1971/2.
Cruickshank, J. (6) (Heart of Midlothian) 1963/4, 1969/70, 1970/1, 1975/6.
Cullen, M. (1) (Luton Town) 1955/6.
Cumming, J. (9) (Heart of Midlothian) 1954/5, 1959/60.
Cunningham, W. (8) (Preston North End) 1953/4, 1954/5.
Curran, H. (5) (Wolverhampton Wanderers) 1969/70, 1970/1.

Dalglish, K. (102) (Celtic) 1971/2, 1972/3, 1973/4, 1974/5, 1975/6, 1976/7, (Liverpool) 1977/8, 1978/9, 1979/80, 1980/1, 1981/2, 1982/3, 1983/4, 1984/5, 1985/6, 1986/7.
Davidson, J. (8) (Partick Thistle) 1953/4, 1954/5.
Dawson, A. (5) (Rangers) 1979/80, 1982/3.
Deans, D. (2) (Celtic) 1974/5.
Delaney, J. (4) (Manchester United) 1946/7, 1947/8.
Dick, J. (1) (West Ham United) 1958/9.
Dickson, W. (5) (Kilmarnock) 1969/70, 1970/1.
Docherty, T. (25) (Preston North End) 1951/2, 1952/3, 1953/4, 1954/5, 1956/7, 1957/8, 1958/9 (Arsenal).
Dodds, D. (2) (Dundee United) 1983/4.

Donachie, W. (35) (Manchester City) 1971/2, 1972/3, 1973/4, 1975/6, 1976/7, 1977/8, 1978/9.
Dougall, C. (1) (Birmingham City) 1946/7.
Dougan, R. (1) (Heart of Midlothian) 1949/50.
Doyle, J. (1) (Ayr United) 1975/6.
Duncan, A. (6) (Hibernian) 1974/5, 1975/6.
Duncan, D. (3) (East Fife) 1947/8.
Duncanson, J. (1) (Rangers) 1946/7.
Durie, G.S. (12) (Chelsea) 1987/8, 1988/9, 1989/90, 1990/91.
Durrant, I. (5) (Rangers) 1987/8, 1988/9.

Evans, A. (4) (Aston Villa) 1981/2.
Evans, R. (48) (Celtic) 1948/9, 1949/50, 1950/1, 1951/2, 1952/3, 1953/4, 1954/5, 1955/6, 1956/7, 1957/8, 1958/9, 1959/60 (Chelsea).
Ewing, T. (2) (Partick Thistle) 1957/8.

Farm, G. (10) (Blackpool) 1952/3, 1953/4, 1958/9.
Ferguson, D. (2) (Rangers) 1987/8.
Ferguson, I. (3) (Rangers) 1988/9.
Ferguson, R. (7) (Kilmarnock) 1965/6, 1966/7.
Fernie, W. (12) (Celtic) 1953/4, 1954/5, 1956/7, 1957/8.
Flavell, R. (2) (Airdrieonians) 1946/7.
Fleck, R. (4) (Norwich) 1989/90, 1990/91.
Fleming, C. (1) (East Fife) 1953/4.
Forbes, A. (14) (Sheffield United) 1946/7, 1947/8 (Arsenal) 1949/50, 1950/1, 1951/2.
Ford, D. (3) (Heart of Midlothian) 1973/4.
Forrest, J. (1) (Motherwell) 1957/8.
Forrest, J. (5) (Rangers) 1965/6 (Aberdeen) 1970/1.
Forsyth, A. (10) (Partick Thistle) 1971/2, 1972/3 (Manchester United) 1974/5, 1975/6.
Forsyth, C. (4) (Kilmarnock) 1963/4, 1964/5.
Forsyth, T. (22) (Motherwell) 1970/1 (Rangers) 1973/4, 1975/6, 1976/7, 1977/8.
Fraser, D. (2) (West Bromwich Albion) 1967/8, 1968/9.
Fraser, W. (2) (Sunderland) 1954/5.

Gabriel, J. (2) (Everton) 1960/1, 1961/2.
Gallacher, K.W. (5) (Dundee United) 1987/8, 1988/9, 1990/91 (Coventry City).
Gardiner, W. (1) (Motherwell) 1957/8.
Gemmell, T. (2) (St Mirren) 1954/5.
Gemmell, T. (18) (Celtic) 1965/6, 1966/7, 1967/8, 1968/9, 1969/70, 1970/1.

Gemmill, A. (43) (Derby County) 1970/1, 1971/2, 1975/6, 1976/7, 1977/8 (Nottingham Forest) 1978/9 (Birmingham City) 1979/80, 1980/1.
Gibson, D. (7) (Leicester City) 1962/3, 1963/4, 1964/5.
Gillespie, G.T. (13) (Liverpool) 1987/8, 1988/9, 1989/90, 1990/91.
Gilzean, A. (22) (Dundee) 1963/4, 1964/5 (Tottenham Hotspur) 1965/6, 1967/8, 1968/9, 1969/70, 1970/1.
Glavin, R. (1) (Celtic) 1976/7.
Glen, A. (2) (Aberdeen) 1955/6.
Goram, A.L. (15) (Oldham Athletic) 1985/6, 1986/7, (Hibernian) 1988/9, 1989/90, 1990/91.
Gough, C.R. (52) (Dundee United) 1982/3, 1983/4, 1984/5, 1985/6, 1986/7 (Tottenham Hotspur) 1987/8 (Rangers) 1988/9, 1989/90, 1990/91.
Govan, J. (6) (Hibernian) 1947/8, 1948/9.
Graham, A. (10) (Leeds United) 1977/8, 1978/9, 1979/80, 1980/1.
Graham, G. (13) (Arsenal) 1971/2, 1972/3 (Manchester United).
Grant, J. (2) (Hibernian) 1958/9.
Grant, P. (2) (Celtic) 1988/9.
Gray, A. (20) (Aston Villa) 1975/6, 1976/7, 1978/9 (Wolverhampton Wanderers) 1979/80, 1980/1, 1981/2, 1982/3, 1984/5 (Everton).
Gray, E. (12) (Leeds United) 1968/9, 1969/70, 1970/71, 1971/2, 1975/6, 1976/7.
Gray F. (32) (Leeds United) 1975/6, 1978/9, 1979/80 (Nottingham Forest) 1980/1, (Leeds United) 1981/2, 1982/3.
Green, A. (6) (Blackpool) 1970/1 (Newcastle United) 1971/2.
Greig, J. (44) (Rangers) 1963/4, 1964/5, 1965/6, 1966/7, 1967/8, 1968/9, 1969/70, 1970/1, 1975/6.
Gunn, B. (1) (Norwich C) 1989/90.

Haddock, H. (6) (Clyde) 1954/5, 1957/8.
Haffey, F. (2) (Celtic) 1959/60, 1960/1.
Hamilton, A. (24) (Dundee) 1961/2, 1962/3, 1963/4, 1964/5, 1965/6.
Hamilton, G. (5) (Aberdeen) 1946/7, 1950/1, 1953/4.
Hamilton, W. (1) (Hibernian) 1964/5.
Hansen, A. (26) (Liverpool) 1978/9, 1979/80, 1980/1, 1981/2, 1982/3, 1984/5, 1985/6, 1986/7.
Hansen J. (2) (Partick Thistle) 1971/2.
Harper, J. (4) (Aberdeen) 1972/3, 1975/6, 1978/9.
Hartford, A. (50) (West Bromwich Albion) 1971/2, 1975/6 (Manchester City) 1976/7, 1977/8, 1978/9, 1979/80 (Everton) 1980/1, 1981/2 (Manchester City).
Harvey, D. (16) (Leeds United) 1972/3, 1973/4, 1974/5, 1975/6, 1976/7.
Haughney, M. (1) (Celtic) 1953/4.
Hay, D. (27) (Celtic) 1969/70, 1970/1, 1971/2, 1972/3, 1973/4.

Hegarty, P. (8) (Dundee United) 1978/9, 1979/80, 1982/3.
Henderson, J. (7) (Portsmouth) 1952/3, 1953/4, 1955/6, 1958/9 (Arsenal).
Henderson, W. (29) (Rangers) 1962/3, 1963/4, 1964/5, 1965/6, 1966/7, 1967/8, 1968/9, 1969/70.
Herd, D. (5) (Arsenal) 1958/9, 1960/1, 1970/1.
Herd, G. (5) (Clyde) 1957/8, 1959/60, 1960/1.
Herriot, J. (8) (Birmingham City) 1968/9, 1969/70.
Hewie, J. (19) (Charlton Athletic) 1955/6, 1956/7, 1957/8, 1958/9, 1959/60.
Holt, D. (5) (Heart of Midlothian) 1962/3, 1963/4.
Holton, J. (15) (Manchester United) 1972/3, 1973/4, 1974/5.
Hope, R. (2) (West Bromwich Albion) 1967/8, 1968/9.
Houliston, W. (3) (Queen of the South) 1948/9.
Houston, S. (1) (Manchester United) 1975/6.
Howie, H. (1) (Hibernian) 1948/9.
Hughes, J. (8) (Celtic) 1964/5, 1965/6, 1967/8, 1968/9, 1969/70.
Hughes, W. (1) (Sunderland) 1974/5.
Humphries, W. (1) (Motherwell) 1951/2.
Hunter, A. (4) (Kilmarnock) 1971/2, 1972/3, (Celtic) 1973/4.
Hunter, W. (3) (Motherwell) 1959/60, 1960/1
Husband, J. (1) (Partick Thistle) 1946/7.
Hutchison, T. (17) (Coventry City) 1973/4, 1974/5, 1975/6.

Imlach, S. (4) (Nottingham Forest) 1957/8.
Irvine, B. (1) (Aberdeen) 1990/91.

Jackson, C. (8) (Rangers) 1974/5, 1975/6.
Jardine, A. (38) (Rangers) 1970/1, 1971/2, 1972/3, 1973/4, 1974/5, 1976/7, 1977/8, 1978/9, 1979/80.
Jarvie, A. (3) (Airdrieonians) 1970/1.
Johnston, M. (36) (Watford) 1983/4, 1984/5 (Celtic) 1985/6, 1986/7, (Nantes) 1987/8, 1988/9 (Rangers) 1989/90.
Johnston, W. (22) (Rangers) 1965/6, 1967/8, 1968/9, 1969/70, 1970/1 (West Bromwich Albion) 1976/7, 1977/8.
Johnstone, D. (14) (Rangers) 1972/3, 1974/5, 1975/6, 1977/8, 1979/80.
Johnstone, J. (23) (Celtic) 1964/5, 1965/6, 1966/7, 1967/8, 1968/9, 1969/70, 1970/1, 1971/2, 1973/4, 1974/5.
Johnstone, L. (2) (Clyde) 1947/8.
Johnstone, R. (17) (Hibernian) 1950/1, 1951/2, 1952/3, 1953/4, 1954/5, (Manchester City) 1955/6.
Jordan, J. (52) (Leeds United) 1972/3, 1973/4, 1974/5, 1975/6, 1976/7, 1977/8, (Manchester United) 1978/9, 1979/80, 1980/1, 1981/2 (AC Milan).

Kelly, H. (1) (Blackpool) 1951/2.
Kelly, J. (2) (Barnsley) 1948/9.
Kennedy, J. (6) (Celtic) 1963/4, 1964/5.
Kennedy, S. (8) (Aberdeen) 1977/8, 1978/9, 1981/2.
Kennedy, S. (5) (Rangers) 1974/5.
Kerr, A. (2) (Partick Thistle) 1954/5.

Law, D. (55) (Huddersfield Town) 1958/9, 1959/60 (Manchester City) 1960/1, 1961/2 (Torino) 1962/3 (Manchester United) 1963/4, 1964/5, 1965/6, 1966/7, 1967/8, 1968/9, 1971/2, 1973/4 (Manchester City).
Lawrence, T. (3) (Liverpool) 1962/3, 1968/9.
Leggat, G. (18) (Aberdeen) 1955/6, 1956/7, 1957/8, 1958/9 (Fulham) 1959/60.
Leighton, J. (58) (Aberdeen) 1982/3, 1983/4, 1984/5, 1985/6, 1986/7, 1987/8, (Manchester United) 1988/9, 1989/90.
Lennox, R. (10) (Celtic) 1966/7, 1967/8, 1968/9.
Leslie, L. (5) (Airdrieonians) 1960/1.
Levein, C. (6) (Hearts) 1989/90.
Liddell, W. (28) (Liverpool) 1946/7, 1947/8, 1949/50, 1950/1, 1951/2, 1952/3, 1953/4, 1954/5, 1955/6.
Linwood, A. (1) (Clyde) 1949/50.
Little, A. (1) (Rangers) 1952/3.
Logie, J. (1) (Arsenal) 1952/3.
Long, H. (1) (Clyde) 1946/7.
Lorimer, P. (21) (Leeds United) 1969/70, 1970/1, 1971/2, 1972/3, 1973/4, 1974/5, 1975/6.

Macari, L. (24) (Celtic) 1971/2, 1972/3 (Manchester United) 1974/5, 1976/7, 1977/8, 1978/9.
Macaulay, A. (7) (Brentford) 1946/7 (Arsenal) 1947/8.
MacDougall, E. (7) (Norwich City) 1974/5, 1975/6.
Mackay, D. (22) (Heart of Midlothian) 1956/7, 1957/8, 1958/9 (Tottenham Hotspur) 1959/60, 1960/1, 1962/3, 1963/4, 1965/6.
Mackay, G. (4) (Heart of Midlothian) 1987/8.
Malpas, M. (42) (Dundee United) 1983/4, 1984/5, 1985/6, 1986/7, 1987/8, 1988/9, 1989/90, 1990/91.
Martin, F. (6) (Aberdeen) 1953/4, 1954/5.
Martin, N. (3) (Hibernian) 1964/5, 1965/6 (Sunderland).
Martis, J. (1) (Motherwell) 1960/1.
Mason, J. (7) (Third Lanark) 1948/9, 1949/50, 1950/1.
Masson, D. (17) (QPR) 1975/6, 1976/7, 1977/8 (Derby County) 1978/9.
Mathers, D. (1) (Partick Thistle) 1953/4.
McAllister, G. (8) (Leicester C) 1989/90, 1990/91 (Leeds United).
McAvennie, F. (5) (West Ham United) 1985/6 (Celtic) 1987/8.

McBride, J. (2) (Celtic) 1966/7.
McCall, S.M. (11) (Everton) 1989/90, 1990/91.
McCalliog, J. (5) (Sheffield Wednesday) 1966/7, 1967/8, 1968/9, 1970/1 (Wolverhampton Wanderers).
McCann, R. (5) (Motherwell) 1958/9, 1959/60, 1960/1.
McClair, B. (17) (Celtic) 1986/7 (Manchester United) 1987/8, 1988/9, 1989/90, 1990/91.
McCloy, P. (4) (Rangers) 1972/3.
McCoist, A. (31) (Rangers) 1985/6, 1986/7, 1987/8, 1988/9, 1989/90, 1990/91.
McColl, I. (14) (Rangers) 1949/50, 1950/1, 1956/7, 1957/8.
McCreadie, E. (23) (Chelsea) 1964/5, 1965/6, 1966/7, 1967/8, 1968/9.
MacDonald, A. (1) (Rangers) 1975/6.
MacDonald, J. (2) (Sunderland) 1955/6.
McFarlane, W. (1) (Heart of Midlothian) 1946/7.
McGarr, E. (2) (Aberdeen) 1969/70.
McGarvey, F. (7) (Liverpool) 1978/9 (Celtic) 1983/4.
McGhee, M. (4) (Aberdeen) 1982/3, 1983/4.
McGrain, D. (62) (Celtic) 1972/3, 1973/4, 1974/5, 1975/6, 1976/7, 1977/8, 1979/80, 1980/1, 1981/2.
McGrory, J. (3) (Kilmarnock) 1964/5, 1965/6.
McInally, A. (8) (Aston Villa) 1988/9 (Bayern Munich) 1989/90.
McInally, J. (5) (Dundee United) 1986/7, 1987/8, 1990/91.
McKay, D. (14) (Celtic) 1958/9, 1959/60, 1960/1, 1961/2.
McKean, R. (1) (Rangers) 1975/6.
McKenzie, J. (9) (Partick Thistle) 1953/4, 1954/5, 1955/6.
McKimmie, S. (10) (Aberdeen) 1988/9, 1989/90, 1990/91.
McKinnon, R. (28) (Rangers) 1965/6, 1966/7, 1967/8, 1968/9, 1969/70, 1970/1.
McLaren, A. (4) (Preston North End) 1946/7, 1947/8.
McLean, G. (1) (Dundee) 1967/8.
McLean, T. (6) (Kilmarnock) 1968/9, 1969/70, 1970/1.
McLeish, A. (76) (Aberdeen) 1979/80, 1980/1, 1981/2, 1982/3, 1983/4, 1984/5, 1985/6, 1986/7, 1987/8, 1988/9, 1989/90, 1990/91.
McLeod, J. (4) (Hibernian) 1960/1.
MacLeod, M. (20) (Celtic) 1984/5, 1986/7 (Borussia Dortmund) 1987/8, 1988/9, 1989/90, 1990/91 (Hibernian).
McLintock, F. (9) (Leicester City) 1962/3, 1964/5 (Arsenal) 1966/7, 1969/70, 1970/1.
McMillan, I. (6) (Airdrieonians) 1951/2, 1954/5, 1955/6 (Rangers) 1960/1.
McNaught, W. (5) (Raith Rovers) 1950/1, 1951/2, 1954/5.
McNeill, W. (29) (Celtic) 1960/1, 1961/2, 1962/3, 1963/4, 1964/5, 1965/6, 1966/7, 1967/8, 1968/9, 1969/70, 1971/2.
McPhail, J. (5) (Celtic) 1949/50, 1950/1, 1953/4.

McPherson, D. (12) (Hearts) 1988/9, 1989/90, 1990/91.
McQueen, G. (30) (Leeds United) 1973/4, 1974/5, 1975/6, 1976/7, 1977/8, (Manchester United) 1978/9, 1979/80, 1980/1.
McStay, P. (51) (Celtic) 1983/4, 1984/5, 1985/6, 1986/7, 1987/8, 1988/9, 1989/90, 1990/91.
Millar, J. (2) (Rangers) 1962/3.
Miller, W. (6) (Celtic) 1946/7, 1947/8.
Miller, W. (65) (Aberdeen) 1974/5, 1977/8, 1979/80, 1980/1, 1981/2, 1982/3, 1983/4, 1984/5, 1985/6, 1986/7, 1987/8, 1988/9, 1989/90.
Mitchell, R. (2) (Newcastle United) 1950/1.
Mochan, N. (3) (Celtic) 1953/4.
Moir, W. (1) (Bolton Wanderers) 1949/50.
Moncur, R. (16) (Newcastle United) 1967/8, 1969/70, 1970/1, 1971/2.
Morgan, W. (21) (Burnley) 1967/8 (Manchester United) 1971/2, 1972/3, 1973/4.
Morris, H. (1) (East Fife) 1949/50.
Mudie, J. (17) (Blackpool) 1956/7, 1957/8.
Mulhall, G. (3) (Aberdeen) 1959/60, 1962/3 (Sunderland) 1963/4.
Munro, F. (9) (Wolverhampton Wanderers) 1970/1, 1974/5.
Munro, I. (7) (St Mirren) 1978/9, 1979/80.
Murdoch, R. (12) (Celtic) 1965/6, 1966/7, 1967/8, 1968/9, 1969/70.
Murray, J. (5) (Heart of Midlothian) 1957/8.
Murray, S. (1) (Aberdeen) 1971/2.

Narey, D. (35) (Dundee United) 1976/7, 1978/9, 1979/80, 1980/1, 1981/2, 1982/3, 1985/6, 1986/7, 1988/9.
Nevin, P.K.F. (11) (Chelsea) 1985/6, 1986/7, 1987/8 (Everton) 1988/9, 1990/91.
Nicholas, C. (20) (Celtic) 1982/3, (Arsenal) 1983/4, 1984/5, 1985/6, 1986/7, (Aberdeen) 1988/9.
Nicol, S. (26) (Liverpool) 1984/5, 1985/6, 1987/8, 1988/9, 1989/90, 1990/91.

O'Hare, J. (13) (Derby County) 1969/70, 1970/1, 1971/2.
Ormond, W. (6) (Hibernian) 1953/4, 1958/9.
Orr, T. (2) (Morton) 1951/2.

Parker, A. (15) (Falkirk) 1954/5, 1955/6, 1956/7, 1957/8.
Parlane, D. (12) (Rangers) 1972/3, 1974/5, 1975/6, 1976/7.
Paton, A. (2) (Motherwell) 1951/2.
Pearson, T. (2) (Newcastle United) 1946/7.
Penman, A. (1) (Dundee) 1965/6.
Pettigrew, W. (5) (Motherwell) 1975/6, 1976/7.
Plenderleith, J. (1) (Manchester City) 1960/1.

Provan, D. (5) (Rangers) 1963/4, 1965/6.
Provan, D. (10) (Celtic) 1979/80, 1980/1, 1981/2.

Quinn, P. (4) (Motherwell) 1960/1, 1961/2.

Redpath, W. (9) (Motherwell) 1948/9, 1950/1, 1951/2.
Reilly, L. (38) (Hibernian) 1948/9, 1949/50, 1950/1, 1951/2, 1952/3, 1953/4, 1954/5, 1955/6, 1956/7.
Ring, T. (12) (Clydebank) 1952/3, 1954/5, 1956/7, 1957/8.
Rioch, B. (24) (Derby County) 1974/5, 1975/6, 1976/7, (Everton) 1977/8, (Derby County) 1978/9.
Robb, D. (5) (Aberdeen) 1970/1.
Robertson, A. (5) (Clyde) 1954/5, 1957/8.
Robertson, H. (1) (Dundee) 1961/2.
Robertson, J. (1) (Tottenham Hotspur) 1964/5.
Robertson, J. (4) (Heart of Midlothian) 1990/91.
Robertson, J.N. (28) (Nottingham Forest) 1977/8, 1978/9, 1979/80, 1980/1, 1981/2, 1982/3 (Derby County) 1983/4.
Robinson, B. (4) (Dundee) 1973/4, 1974/5.
Rough, A. (53) (Partick Thistle) 1975/6, 1976/7, 1977/8, 1978/9, 1979/80, 1980/1, 1981/2, (Hibernian) 1985/6.
Rougvie, D. (1) (Aberdeen) 1983/4.
Rutherford, E. (1) (Rangers) 1947/8.

St John, I. (21) (Motherwell) 1958/9, 1959/60, 1960/1, 1961/2 (Liverpool) 1962/3, 1963/4, 1964/5.
Schaedler, E. (1) (Hibernian) 1973/4.
Scott, A. (16) (Rangers) 1956/7, 1957/8, 1958/9, 1961/2 (Everton) 1963/4, 1964/5, 1965/6.
Scott, J. (1) (Hibernian) 1965/6.
Scott, J. (2) (Dundee) 1970/1.
Scoular, J. (9) (Portsmouth) 1950/1, 1951/2, 1952/3.
Sharp, G.M. (12) (Everton) 1984/5, 1985/6, 1986/7, 1987/8.
Shaw, D. (8) (Hibernian) 1946/7, 1947/8, 1948/9.
Shaw, J. (4) (Rangers) 1946/7, 1947/8.
Shearer, R. (4) (Rangers) 1960/1.
Simpson, N. (4) (Aberdeen) 1982/3, 1983/4, 1986/7, 1987/8.
Simpson, R. (5) (Celtic) 1966/7, 1967/8, 1968/9.
Sinclair, J. (1) (Leicester City) 1965/6.
Smith, D. (2) (Aberdeen) 1965/6, 1967/8 (Rangers).
Smith, E. (2) (Celtic) 1958/9.
Smith G. (18) (Hibernian) 1946/7, 1947/8, 1951/2, 1954/5, 1955/6, 1956/7.
Smith H.G. (1) (Heart of Midlothian) 1987/8.
Smith J. (4) (Aberdeen) 1967/8, 1973/4 (Newcastle United).

Souness, G. (54) (Middlesbrough) 1974/5 (Liverpool) 1977/8, 1978/9, 1979/80, 1980/1, 1981/2, 1982/3, 1983/4, (Sampdoria) 1984/5, 1985/6.
Speedie, D.R. (10) (Chelsea) 1984/5, 1985/6, (Coventry City) 1988/9.
Stanton, P. (16) (Hibernian) 1965/6, 1968/9, 1969/70, 1970/1, 1971/2, 1972/3, 1973/4.
Steel, W. (30) (Morton) 1946/7, 1947/8 (Derby County) 1948/9, 1949/50, (Dundee) 1950/1, 1951/2, 1952/3.
Stein, C. (21) (Rangers) 1968/9, 1969/70, 1970/1, 1971/2 (Coventry City).
Stephen, J. (2) (Bradford City) 1946/7, 1947/8.
Stewart, D. (1) (Leeds United) 1977/8.
Stewart, J. (2) (Kilmarnock) 1976/7 (Middlesbrough) 1978/9.
Stewart, R. (10) (West Ham United) 1980/1, 1981/2, 1983/4, 1986/7.
Strachan, G. (46) (Aberdeen) 1979/80, 1980/1, 1981/2, 1982/3, 1983/4 (Manchester United) 1984/5, 1985/6, 1986/7, 1987/8, 1988/9 (Leeds U) 1989/90, 1990/91.
Sturrock, P. (20) (Dundee United) 1980/1, 1981/2, 1982/3, 1983/4, 1984/5, 1985/6, 1986/7.

Telfer, W. (1) (St Mirren) 1953/4.
Thomson, W. (7) (St Mirren) 1979/80, 1980/1, 1981/2, 1982/3, 1983/4.
Thornton, W. (7) (Rangers) 1946/7, 1947/8, 1948/9, 1951/2.
Toner, W. (2) (Kilmarnock) 1958/9.
Turnbull, E. (8) (Hibernian) 1947/8, 1950/1, 1957/8.

Ure, I. (11) (Dundee) 1961/2, 1962/3 (Arsenal) 1963/4, 1967/8.

Waddell, W. (17) (Rangers) 1946/7, 1948/9, 1949/50, 1950/1, 1951/2, 1953/4, 1954/5.
Walker, A. (1) (Celtic) 1987/8.
Wallace, I.A. (3) (Coventry City) 1977/8, 1978/9.
Wallace, W.S.B. (7) (Heart of Midlothian) 1964/5, 1965/6, 1966/7 (Celtic) 1967/8, 1968/9.
Wardhaugh, J. (2) (Heart of Midlothian) 1954/5, 1956/7.
Wark, J. (29) (Ipswich Town) 1978/9, 1979/80, 1980/1, 1981/2, 1982/3, 1983/4 (Liverpool) 1984/5.
Watson, J. (2) (Motherwell) 1947/8 (Huddersfield Town) 1953/4.
Watson, R. (1) (Motherwell) 1970/1.
Weir, A. (6) (Motherwell) 1958/9, 1959/60.
Weir, P. (6) (St Mirren) 1979/80, 1982/3, (Aberdeen) 1983/4.
White, J. (22) (Falkirk) 1958/9, 1959/60 (Tottenham Hotspur) 1960/1, 1961/2, 1962/3, 1963/4.
Whyte, D. (3) (Celtic) 1987/8, 1988/9.
Wilson, A. (1) (Portsmouth) 1953/4.
Wilson, D. (22) (Rangers) 1960/1, 1961/2, 1962/3, 1963/4, 1964/5.

Wilson, I.A. (5) (Leicester City) 1986/7, (Everton) 1987/8.
Wilson, P. (1) (Celtic) 1974/5.
Wilson, R. (2) (Arsenal) 1971/2.
Wood, G. (4) (Everton) 1978/9, 1981/2 (Arsenal).
Woodburn, W. (24) (Rangers) 1946/7, 1947/8, 1948/9, 1949/50, 1950/1, 1951/2.
Wright, T. (3) (Sunderland) 1952/3.

Yeats, R. (2) (Liverpool) 1964/5, 1965/6.
Yorston, H. (1) (Aberdeen) 1954/5.
Young, A. (9) (Heart of Midlothian) 1959/60. 1960/1 (Everton) 1965/6.
Young, G. (53) (Rangers) 1946/7, 1947/8, 1948/9, 1949/50, 1950/1, 1951/2, 1952/3, 1953/4, 1954/5, 1955/6, 1956/7.
Younger, T. (24) (Hibernian) 1954/5, 1955/6, 1956/7 (Liverpool) 1957/8.

WALES

Aizlewood, M. (25) (Charlton Athletic) 1985/6, 1986/7 (Leeds United) 1987/8, 1988/9 (Bradford C) 1989/90, 1990/91 (Bristol City).
Allchurch, I. (68) (Swansea City) 1950/1, 1951/2, 1952/3, 1953/4, 1954/5, 1955/6, 1956/7, 1957/8, 1958/9 (Newcastle United) 1959/60, 1960/1, 1961/2, 1962/3 (Cardiff City) 1963/4, 1964/5, 1965/6 (Swansea City).
Allchurch L. (11) (Swansea City) 1954/5, 1955/6, 1957/8, 1958/9, 1961/2, (Sheffield United) 1963/4.
Allen, B. (2) (Coventry City) 1950/1.
Allen, M. (11) (Watford) 1985/6, (Norwich City) 1988/9 (Millwall) 1989/90, 1990/91.

Baker, C. (7) (Cardiff City) 1957/8, 1959/60. 1960/1, 1961/2.
Baker, W. (1) (Cardiff City) 1947/8.
Barnes, W. (22) (Arsenal) 1947/8, 1948/9, 1949/50, 1950/1, 1951/2, 1953/4, 1954/5.
Berry, G. (5) (Wolverhampton Wanderers) 1978/9, 1979/80, 1982/3 (Stoke City).
Blackmore, C.G. (27) (Manchester United) 1984/5, 1985/6, 1986/7, 1987/8, 1988/9, 1989/90, 1990/91.
Bowen, D. (19) (Arsenal) 1954/5, 1956/7, 1957/8, 1958/9.
Bowen, M.R. (11) (Tottenham Hotspur) 1985/6 (Norwich City) 1987/8, 1988/9, 1989/90.
Bodin, P.J. (9) (Swindon T) 1989/90, 1990/91 (Crystal Palace).
Boyle, T. (2) (Crystal Palace) 1980/1.
Burgess, R. (32) (Tottenham Hotspur) 1946/7, 1947/8, 1948/9, 1949/50, 1950/1, 1951/2, 1952/3, 1953/4.

Burton, O. (9) (Norwich City) 1962/3 (Newcastle United) 1963/4, 1968/9, 1971/2.

Cartwright, L. (7) (Coventry City) 1973/4, 1975/6, 1976/7 (Wrexham) 1977/8, 1978/9.
Charles, J. (38) (Leeds United) 1949/50, 1950/1, 1952/3, 1953/4, 1954/5, 1955/6, 1956/7 (Juventus Turin) 1957/8, 1959/60, 1961/2, 1962/3, (Leeds United) (Cardiff City) 1963/4, 1964/5.
Charles, J.M. (19) (Swansea City) 1980/1, 1981/2, 1982/3, 1983/4 (QPR), (Oxford United) 1984/5, 1985/6, 1986/7.
Charles, M. (31) (Swansea City) 1954/5, 1955/6, 1956/7, 1957/8, 1958/9 (Arsenal) 1960/1, 1961/2 (Cardiff City) 1962/3.
Clarke, R. (22) (Manchester City) 1948/9, 1949/50, 1950/1, 1951/2, 1952/3, 1953/4, 1954/5, 1955/6.
Crowe, V. (16) (Aston Villa) 1958/9, 1959/60, 1960/1, 1961/2, 1962/3.
Curtis, A. (35) (Swansea City) 1975/6, 1976/7, 1977/8, 1978/9, 1979/80, 1981/2, 1982/3, 1983/4 (Southampton) 1984/5, 1985/6, 1986/7 (Cardiff City).

Daniel, R. (21) (Arsenal) 1950/1, 1951/2, 1952/3, 1953/4 (Sunderland) 1954/5, 1956/7.
Davies, A. (11) (Manchester United) 1982/3, 1983/4, 1984/5, (Newcastle United) 1985/6 (Swansea City) 1987/8, 1988/9 (Bradford C) 1989/90.
Davies, D. (52) (Everton) 1974/5, 1975/6, 1976/7, 1977/8, (Wrexham) 1978/9, 1979/80, 1980/1 (Swansea City) 1981/2, 1982/3.
Davies, G. (18) (Fulham) 1979/80, 1981/2, 1982/3, 1983/4, 1984/5 (Chelsea), (Manchester City) 1985/6.
Davies, R. Wyn (34) (Bolton Wanderers) 1963/4, 1964/5, 1965/6, 1966/7 (Newcastle United) 1967/8, 1968/9, 1969/70, 1970/1, 1971/2 (Manchester City), (Blackpool) 1972/3 (Manchester United) 1973/4.
Davies, Reg (6) (Newcastle United) 1952/3, 1953/4, 1957/8.
Davies, Ron (29) (Norwich City) 1963/4, 1964/5, 1965/6, 1966/7, (Southampton) 1967/8, 1968/9, 1969/70, 1970/1, 1971/2, 1973/4 (Portsmouth).
Davis, C. (1) (Charlton Athletic) 1971/2.
Davis, G. (4) (Wrexham) 1977/8.
Deacy, N. (11) (PSV Eindhoven) 1976/7. 1977/8 (Beringen) 1978/9.
Derrett, S. (4) (Cardiff City) 1968/9, 1969/70, 1970/1.
Dibble, A. (3) (Luton Town) 1985/6, (Manchester City) 1988/9.
Durban, A. (27) (Derby County) 1965/6, 1966/7, 1967/8, 1968/9, 1969/70, 1970/1, 1971/2.
Dwyer, P. (10) (Cardiff City) 1977/8, 1978/9, 1979/80.

Edwards, I. (4) (Chester) 1977/8, 1978/9, 1979/80.
Edwards, G. (12) (Birmingham City) 1946/7, 1947/8 (Cardiff City) 1948/9, 1949/50.
Edwards, T. (2) (Charlton Athletic) 1956/7.
Emanuel, J. (2) (Bristol City) 1972/3.
England, M. (44) (Blackburn Rovers) 1961/2, 1962/3, 1963/4, 1964/5, 1965/6, 1966/7 (Tottenham Hotspur) 1967/8, 1968/9, 1969/70, 1970/1, 1971/2, 1972/3, 1973/4, 1974/5.
Evans, B. (7) (Swansea City) 1971/2, 1972/3 (Hereford United) 1973/4.
Evans, I. (13) (Crystal Palace) 1975/6, 1976/7, 1977/8.
Evans, R. (1) (Swansea City) 1963/4.

Felgate, D. (1) (Lincoln City) 1983/4.
Flynn, B. (66) (Burnley) 1974/5, 1975/6, 1976/7, 1977/8 (Leeds United) 1978/9, 1979/80, 1980/1, 1981/2, 1982/3 (Burnley) 1983/4.
Ford, T. (38) (Swansea City) 1946/7 (Aston Villa) 1947/8, 1948/9, 1949/50, 1950/1 (Sunderland) 1951/2, 1952/3 (Cardiff City) 1953/4, 1954/5, 1955/6, 1956/7.
Foulkes, W. (11) (Newcastle United) 1951/2, 1952/3, 1953/4.

Giles, D. (12) (Swansea City) 1979/80, 1980/1, 1981/2 (Crystal Palace) 1982/3.
Godfrey, B. (3) (Preston North End) 1963/4, 1964/5.
Goss, J. (2) (Norwich City) 1990/91.
Green, C. (15) (Birmingham City) 1964/5, 1965/6, 1966/7, 1967/8, 1968/9.
Griffiths, A. (17) (Wrexham) 1970/1, 1974/5, 1975/6, 1976/7.
Griffiths, H. (1) (Swansea City) 1952/3.
Griffiths, M. (11) (Leicester City) 1946/7, 1948/9, 1949/50, 1950/1, 1953/4.

Hall, G.D. (8) (Chelsea) 1987/8, 1988/9, 1990/91.
Harrington, A. (11) (Cardiff City) 1955/6, 1956/7, 1957/8, 1960/1, 1961/2.
Harris, C. (24) (Leeds United) 1975/6, 1977/8, 1978/9, 1979/80, 1980/1, 1981/2.
Harris, W. (6) (Middlesbrough) 1953/4, 1956/7, 1957/8.
Hennessey, T. (39) (Birmingham City) 1961/2, 1962/3, 1963/4, 1964/5, 1965/6, (Nottingham Forest) 1966/7, 1967/8, 1968/9, 1969/70 (Derby County) 1971/2, 1972/3.
Hewitt, R. (5) (Cardiff City) 1957/8.
Hill, M. (2) (Ipswich Town) 1971/2.
Hockey, T. (9) (Sheffield United) 1971/2, 1972/3 (Norwich City) 1973/4, (Aston Villa).

Hodges, G. (13) (Wimbledon) 1983/4, 1986/7 (Newcastle United) 1987/8, (Watford) 1989/90.
Holden, A. (1) (Chester City) 1983/4.
Hole, B. (30) (Cardiff City) 1962/3, 1963/4, 1964/5, 1965/6, 1966/7, (Blackburn Rovers) 1967/8, 1968/9 (Aston Villa) 1969/70 (Swansea City) 1970/71.
Hollins, D. (11) (Newcastle United) 1961/2, 1962/3, 1963/4, 1964/5, 1965/6.
Hopkins, J. (16) (Fulham) 1982/3, 1983/4, 1984/5 (Crystal P) 1989/90.
Hopkins M. (34) (Tottenham Hotspur) 1955/6, 1956/7, 1957/8, 1958/9, 1959/60, 1960/1, 1961/2, 1962/3.
Horne, B. (22) (Portsmouth) 1987/8, (Southampton) 1988/9, 1989/90, 1990/91.
Howells, R. (2) (Cardiff City) 1953/4.
Hughes, I. (4) (Luton Town) 1950/1.
Hughes, L.M. (35) (Manchester United) 1983/4, 1984/5, 1985/6, 1986/7 (Barcelona) 1987/8, 1988/9 (Manchester United) 1989/90, 1990/91.
Hughes, W. (3) (Birmingham City) 1946/7.
Hughes, W.A. (5) (Blackburn Rovers) 1948/9.
Humphreys, J. (1) (Everton) 1946/7.

Jackett, K. (31) (Watford) 1982/3, 1983/4, 1984/5, 1985/6, 1986/7, 1987/8.
James, G. (9) (Blackpool) 1965/6, 1966/7, 1967/8, 1970/1.
James, L. (54) (Burnley) 1971/2, 1972/3, 1973/4, 1974/5, 1975/6 (Derby County) 1976/7, 1977/8 (QPR) (Burnley) 1978/9, 1979/80 (Swansea City) 1980/1, 1981/2 (Sunderland) 1982/3.
James, R.M. (47) (Swansea City) 1978/9, 1979/80, 1981/2, 1982/3 (Stoke City) 1983/4, 1984/5 (QPR) 1985/6, 1986/7 (Leicester City) 1987/8 (Swansea City).
Jarvis, A. (3) (Hull City) 1966/7.
Johnson, M. (1) (Swansea City) 1963/4.
Jones, A. (6) (Port Vale) 1986/7, 1987/8 (Charlton Athletic) 1989/90.
Jones, Barrie (15) (Swansea City) 1962/3, 1963/4, 1964/5 (Plymouth Argyle) 1968/9 (Cardiff City).
Jones, Bryn. (4) (Arsenal) 1946/7, 1947/8, 1948/9.
Jones, C. (59) (Swansea City) 1953/4, 1955/6, 1956/7, 1957/8 (Tottenham Hotspur) 1958/9, 1959/60, 1960/1, 1961/2, 1962/3, 1963/4, 1964/5, 1966/7, 1967/8, 1968/9 (Fulham) 1969/70.
Jones D. (8) (Norwich City) 1975/6, 1977/8, 1979/80.
Jones, E. (4) (Swansea City) 1947/8 (Tottenham Hotspur) 1948/9.
Jones, J. (72) (Liverpool) 1975/6, 1976/7, 1977/8 (Wrexham) 1978/9, 1979/80, 1980/1, 1981/2, 1982/3 (Chelsea) 1983/4, 1984/5 (Huddersfield Town) 1985/6.
Jones K. (1) (Aston Villa) 1949/50.

Jones, T.G. (13) (Everton) 1946/7, 1947/8, 1948/9, 1949/50.
Jones W. (1) (Bristol City) 1970/1.

Kelsey, J. (41) (Arsenal) 1953/4, 1954/5, 1955/6, 1956/7, 1957/8, 1958/9, 1959/60, 1960/1, 1961/2.
King, J. (1) (Swansea City) 1954/5.
Kinsey, N. (7) (Norwich City) 1950/1, 1951/2, 1953/4 (Birmingham City) 1955/6.
Knill, A.R. (1) (Swansea City) 1988/9.
Krzywicki, R. (West Bromwich Albion) 1969/70 (Huddersfield Town) 1970/1, 1971/2.

Lambert, R. (5) (Liverpool) 1946/7, 1947/8, 1948/9.
Law, B.J. (1) (QPR), 1989/90.
Lea, C. (2) (Ipswich Town) 1964/5.
Leek, K. (13) (Leicester City) 1960/1, 1961/2 (Newcastle United) (Birmingham City) 1962/3, 1964/5.
Lever, A. (1) (Leicester City) 1952/3.
Lewis, D. (1) (Swansea City) 1982/3.
Lloyd, B. (3) (Wrexham) 1975/6.
Lovell, S. (6) (Crystal Palace) 1981/2 (Millwall) 1984/5, 1985/6.
Lowndes, S. (10) (Newport County) 1982/3 (Millwall) 1984/5, 1985/6, 1986/7, (Barnsley) 1987/8.
Lowrie, G. (4) (Coventry City) 1947/8, 1948/9 (Newcastle United).
Lucas, M. (4) (Leyton Orient) 1961/2, 1962/3.
Lucas, W. (7) (Swansea City) 1948/9, 1949/50, 1950/1.

Maguire, G.T. (5) (Portsmouth) 1989/90.
Mahoney, J. (51) (Stoke City) 1967/8, 1968/9, 1970/1, 1972/3, 1973/4, 1974/5, 1975/6, 1976/7 (Middlesbrough) 1977/8, 1978/9 (Swansea City) 1979/80, 1981/2, 1982/3.
Marustik, C. (6) (Swansea City) 1981/2, 1982/3.
Medwin, T. (30) (Swansea City) 1952/3, 1956/7 (Tottenham Hotspur) 1957/8, 1958/9, 1959/60, 1960/1, 1962/3.
Melville, A.K. (7) (Swansea C), 1989/90, 1990/91 (Oxford United).
Mielczarek, R. (1) (Rotherham United) 1970/1.
Millington, A. (21) (West Bromwich Albion) 1962/3, 1964/5 (Crystal Palace) 1965/6 (Peterborough United) 1966/7, 1967/8, 1968/9, 1969/70 (Swansea City) 1970/1, 1971/2.
Moore, G. (21) (Cardiff City) 1959/60, 1960/1, 1961/2 (Chelsea) 1962/3, (Manchester United) 1963/4 (Northampton Town) 1965/6, 1968/9 (Charlton Athletic) 1969/70, 1970/1.
Morris, W. (5) (Burnley) 1946/7, 1948/9, 1951/2.

Nardiello, D. (2) (Coventry City) 1977/8.
Nicholas, P. (72) (Crystal Palace) 1978/9, 1979/80, 1980/1 (Arsenal) 1981/2, 1982/3, 1983/4 (Crystal Palace) 1984/5, (Luton Town) 1985/6, 1986/7, 1987/8 (Aberdeen), (Chelsea) 1988/9, 1989/90, 1990/91 (Watford).
Niedzwiecki, E.A. (2) (Chelsea) 1984/5, 1987/8.
Norman, A.J. (5) (Hull City) 1985/6, 1987/8.
Nurse, M. (12) (Swansea City) 1959/60, 1960/1, 1962/3 (Middlesbrough) 1963/4.

O'Sullivan, P. (3) (Brighton & Hove Albion) 1972/3, 1975/6, 1978/9.

Page, M. (28) (Birmingham City) 1970/1, 1971/2, 1972/3, 1973/4, 1974/5, 1975/6, 1976/7, 1977/8, 1978/9.
Palmer, D. (3) (Swansea City) 1956/7, 1957/8.
Parry, J. (1) (Swansea City) 1950/1.
Pascoe, C. (9) (Swansea City) 1983/4, (Sunderland) 1988/9, 1989/90 1990/91.
Paul, R. (33) (Swansea City) 1948/9, 1949/50 (Manchester City) 1950/1, 1951/2, 1952/3, 1953/4, 1954/5, 1955/6.
Phillips, D. (32) (Plymouth Argyle) 1983/4 (Manchester City) 1984/5, 1985/6, 1986/7 (Coventry City) 1987/8, 1988/9 (Norwich City) 1989/90, 1990/91.
Phillips, J. (4) (Chelsea) 1972/3, 1973/4, 1974/5, 1977/8.
Phillips, L. (58) (Cardiff City) 1970/1, 1971/2, 1972/3, 1973/4, 1974/5, (Aston Villa) 1975/6, 1976/7, 1977/8, 1978/9 (Swansea City) 1979/80, 1980/1, 1981/2 (Charlton Athletic).
Pontin, K. (2) (Cardiff City) 1979/80.
Powell, A. (8) (Leeds United) 1946/7, 1947/8, 1948/9 (Everton) 1949/50, 1950/1 (Birmingham City).
Powell, D. (11) (Wrexham) 1967/8, 1968/9 (Sheffield United) 1969/70, 1970/1.
Powell, I. (8) (QPR) 1946/7, 1947/8, 1948/9 (Aston Villa) 1949/50, 1950/1.
Price, P. (25) (Luton Town) 1979/80, 1980/1, 1981/2 (Tottenham Hotspur) 1982/3, 1983/4.
Pring, K. (3) (Rotherham United) 1965/6, 1966/7.
Pritchard, H.K. (1) (Bristol City) 1984/5.

Rankmore, F. (1) (Peterborough United) 1965/6.
Ratcliffe, K. (56) (Everton) 1980/1, 1981/2, 1982/3, 1983/4, 1984/5, 1985/6, 1986/7, 1987/8, 1988/9, 1989/90, 1990/91.
Reece, G. (29) (Sheffield United) 1965/6, 1966/7, 1969/70, 1970/1, 1971/2, (Cardiff City) 1972/3, 1973/4, 1974/5.
Reed, W. (2) (Ipswich Town) 1954/5.

Rees, A. (1) (Birmingham City) 1983/4.
Rees, R. (39) (Coventry City) 1964/5, 1965/6, 1966/7, 1967/8 (West Bromwich Albion) 1968/9 (Nottingham Forest) 1969/70, 1970/1, 1971/2.
Rees, W. (4) (Cardiff City) 1948/9 (Tottenham Hotspur) 1949/50.
Richards, S. (1) (Cardiff City) 1946/7.
Roberts D. (17) (Oxford United) 1972/3, 1973/4, 1974/5 (Hull City) 1975/6, 1976/7, 1977/8.
Roberts, I.W. (1) (Watford) 1989/90.
Roberts, J.G. (22) (Arsenal) 1970/1, 1971/2, 1972/3, (Birmingham City) 1973/4, 1974/5, 1975/6.
Roberts, J. H. (1) (Bolton Wanderers) 1948/9.
Roberts, P. (4) (Portsmouth) 1973/4, 1974/5.
Rodrigues, P. (40) (Cardiff City) 1964/5, 1965/6 (Leicester City) 1966/7, 1967/8, 1968/9, 1969/70 (Sheffield Wednesday) 1970/1, 1971/2, 1972/3, 1973/4.
Rouse, V. (1) (Crystal Palace) 1958/9.
Rowley, T. (1) (Tranmere Rovers) 1958/9.
Rush, I. (51) (Liverpool) 1979/80, 1980/1, 1981/2, 1982/3, 1983/4, 1984/5, 1985/6, 1986/7 (Juventus) 1987/8, (Liverpool) 1988/9, 1989/90, 1990/91.

Saunders, D. (27) (Brighton & Hove Albion) 1985/6, 1986/7 (Oxford United) 1987/8, (Derby County) 1988/9, 1989/90, 1990/91.
Sayer, P. (7) (Cardiff City) 1976/7, 1977/8.
Scrine, F. (2) (Swansea City) 1949/50.
Sear, C. (1) (Manchester City) 1962/3.
Sherwood, A. (41) (Cardiff City) 1946/7, 1947/8, 1948/9, 1949/50, 1950/1, 1951/2, 1952/3, 1953/4, 1954/5, 1955/6, 1956/7 (Newport County).
Shortt, W. (12) (Plymouth Argyle) 1946/7, 1949/50, 1951/2, 1952/3.
Showers, D. (2) (Cardiff City) 1974/5.
Sidlow, C. (7) (Liverpool) 1946/7, 1947/8, 1948/9, 1949/50.
Slatter, N. (22) (Bristol Rovers) 1982/3, 1983/4, 1984/5 (Oxford United) 1985/6, 1986/7, 1987/8, 1988/9.
Smallman, D. (7) (Wrexham) 1973/4 (Everton) 1974/5, 1975/6.
Southall, N. (52) (Everton) 1981/2, 1982/3, 1983/4, 1984/5, 1985/6, 1986/7, 1987/8, 1988/9, 1989/90, 1990/91.
Speed, G.A. (6) (Leeds U), 1989/90, 1990/91.
Sprake, G. (37) (Leeds United) 1963/4, 1964/5, 1965/6, 1966/7, 1967/8, 1968/9, 1969/70, 1970/1, 1971/2, 1972/3, 1973/4 (Birmingham City) 1974/5.
Stansfield, F. (1) (Cardiff City) 1948/9.
Stevenson, B. (15) (Leeds United) 1977/8, 1978/9, 1979/80, 1981/2 (Birmingham City).

Stevenson, N. (4) (Swansea City) 1981/2, 1982/3.
Stitfall, R. (2) (Cardiff City) 1952/3, 1956/7.
Sullivan, D. (17) (Cardiff City) 1952/3, 1953/4, 1954/5, 1956/7, 1957/8, 1958/9, 1959/60.

Tapscott, D. (14) (Arsenal) 1953/4, 1954/5, 1955/6, 1956/7, 1958/9 (Cardiff City).
Thomas, D. (2) (Swansea City) 1956/7, 1957/8.
Thomas, M. (51) (Wrexham) 1976/7, 1977/8, 1978/9 (Manchester United) 1979/80, 1980/1, 1981/2 (Everton) (Brighton) 1982/3 (Stoke City) 1983/4, (Chelsea) 1984/5, 1985/6 (West Bromwich Albion).
Thomas, M.R. (1) (Newcastle United) 1986/7.
Thomas, R. (50) (Swindon Town) 1966/7, 1967/8, 1968/9, 1969/70, 1970/1, 1971/2, 1972/3, 1973/4 (Derby County) 1974/5, 1975/6, 1976/7, 1977/8 (Cardiff City).
Thomas, S. (4) (Fulham) 1947/8, 1948/9.
Toshack, J. (40) (Cardiff City) 1968/9, 1969/70 (Liverpool) 1970/1, 1971/2, 1972/3, 1974/5, 1975/6, 1976/7, 1977/8 (Swansea City) 1978/9, 1979/80.

Van den Hauwe, P.W.R. (13) (Everton) 1984/5, 1985/6, 1986/7, 1987/8, 1988/9.
Vaughan, N. (10) (Newport County) 1982/3, 1983/4 (Cardiff City) 1984/5.
Vearncombe, G. (2) (Cardiff City) 1957/8, 1960/1.
Vernon, R. (32) (Blackburn Rovers) 1956/7, 1957/8, 1958/9, 1959/60 (Everton) 1960/1, 1961/2, 1962/3, 1963/4, 1964/5 (Stoke City) 1965/6, 1966/7, 1967/8.
Villars, A. (3) (Cardiff City) 1973/4.

Walley, T. (1) (Watford) 1970/1.
Walsh, I. (18) (Crystal Palace) 1979/80, 1980/1, 1981/2 (Swansea City).
Ward, D. (2) (Bristol Rovers) 1958/9, 1961/2 (Cardiff City).
Webster, C. (4) (Manchester United) 1956/7, 1957/8.
Williams, D.G. (11) 1987/8 (Derby County) 1988/9, 1989/90.
Williams, D.M. (5) (Norwich City) 1985/6, 1986/7.
Williams, G. (1) (Cardiff City) 1950/1.
Williams, G.E. (26) (West Bromwich Albion) 1959/60, 1960/1, 1962/3, 1963/4, 1964/5, 1965/6, 1966/7, 1967/8, 1968/9.
Williams, G.G. (5) (Swansea City) 1960/1, 1961/2.
Williams, H. (4) (Newport County) 1948/9 (Leeds United) 1949/50, 1950/1.
Williams, Herbert (3) (Swansea City) 1964/5, 1970/1.

Williams, S. (43) (West Bromwich Albion) 1953/4, 1954/5, 1955/6, 1957/8, 1958/9, 1959/60, 1960/1, 1961/2, 1962/3 (Southampton) 1963/4, 1964/5, 1965/6.
Witcomb, D. (3) (West Bromwich Albion) 1946/7 (Sheffield Wednesday).
Woosnam, P. (17) (Leyton Orient) 1958/9 (West Ham United) 1959/60, 1960/1, 1961/2, 1962/3 (Aston Villa).

Yorath, T. (59) (Leeds United) 1969/70, 1970/1, 1971/2, 1972/3, 1973/4, 1974/5, 1975/6 (Coventry City) 1976/7, 1977/8, 1978/9 (Tottenham Hotspur) 1979/80, 1980/1.
Young, E. (6) (Wimbledon) 1989/90, 1990/91 (Crystal Palace).

EIRE

Aherne, T. (16) (Belfast Celtic) 1945/6 (Luton Town) 1949/50, 1950/1, 1951/2, 1952/3, 1953/4.
Aldridge, J.W. (39) (Oxford United) 1985/6, 1986/7 (Liverpool) 1987/8, 1988/9 (Real Sociedad) 1989/90, 1990/91.
Ambrose, P. (5) (Shamrock Rovers) 1954/5, 1963/4.
Anderson, J. (16) (Preston North End) 1979/80, 1981/2 (Newcastle United) 1983/4, 1985/6, 1986/7, 1987/8, 1988/9.

Bailham, E. (1) (Shamrock Rovers) 1963/4.
Barber, E. (2) (Shelbourne) 1965/6 (Birmingham City) 1965/6.
Beglin, J. (15) (Liverpool) 1983/4, 1984/5, 1985/6, 1986/7.
Bonner, P. (50) (Celtic) 1980/1, 1981/2, 1983/4, 1984/5, 1985/6, 1986/7, 1987/8, 1988/9, 1989/90, 1990/91.
Braddish, S. (1) (Dundalk) 1977/8.
Brady T.R. (6) (QPR) 1963/4.
Brady, W. L. (72) (Arsenal) 1974/5, 1975/6, 1976/7, 1977/8, 1978/9, 1979/80 (Juventus) 1980/1, 1981/2 (Sampdoria) 1982/3, 1983/4 (Internazionale) 1984/5, 1985/6 (Ascoli) 1986/7 (West Ham United) 1987/8, 1988/9, 1989/90.
Breen, T. (3) (Shamrock Rovers) 1946/7.
Brennan, F. (1) (Drumcondra) 1964/5.
Brennan, S.A. (19) (Manchester United) 1964/5, 1965/6, 1966/7, 1968/9, 1969/70 (Waterford) 1970/1.
Browne, W. (3) (Bohemians) 1963/4.
Buckley, L. (2) (Shamrock Rovers) 1983/4 (Waregem) 1984/5.
Burke, F. (1) (Cork Athletic) 1951/2.
Byrne, A.B. (14) (Southampton) 1969/70, 1970/1, 1972/3, 1973/4.
Byrne, J. (20) (QPR) 1984/5, 1986/7, 1987/8 (Le Havre) 1989/90, 1990/91 (Brighton & Hove Albion).
Byrne, P. (9) (Shamrock Rovers) 1983/4, 1984/5, 1985/6.

Campbell, A. (3) (Santander) 1984/5.
Campbell, N. (11) (St Patrick's Athletic) 1970/1 (Fortuna Cologne) 1971/2, 1972/3, 1974/5, 1975/6.
Cantwell, N. (36) (West Ham United) 1953/4, 1955/6, 1956/7, 1957/8, 1958/9, 1959/60, 1960/1 (Manchester United) 1960/1, 1961/2, 1962/3, 1963/4, 1964/5, 1965/6, 1966/7.
Carey, J.J. (21) (Manchester United) 1945/6, 1946/7, 1947/8, 1948/9, 1949/50, 1950/1, 1952/3.
Carolan, J. (2) (Manchester United) 1959/60.
Carroll, B. (2) (Shelbourne) 1948/9, 1949/50.
Carroll, T.R. (17) (Ipswich Town) 1967/8, 1968/9, 1969/70, 1970/1 (Birmingham City) 1971/2, 1972/3.
Cascarino, A.G. (33) (Gillingham) 1985/6 (Millwall) 1987/8, 1988/9, 1989/90 (Aston Villa), 1990/91.
Chandler, J. (2) (Leeds United) 1979/80.
Clarke, J. (1) (Drogheda United) 1977/8.
Clarke, K. (2) (Drumcondra) 1947/8.
Clarke, M. (1) (Shamrock Rovers) 1949/50.
Clinton, T.J. (3) (Everton) 1950/1, 1953/4.
Coad, P. (11) (Shamrock Rovers) 1946/7, 1947/8, 1948/9, 1950/1, 1951/2.
Coffey, T. (1) (Drumcondra) 1949/50.
Colfer, M.D. (2) (Shelbourne) 1949/50, 1950/1.
Conmy, O.M. (5) (Peterborough United) 1964/5, 1966/7, 1967/8, 1969/70.
Conroy, G.A. (27) (Stoke City) 1969/70, 1970/1, 1972/3, 1973/4, 1974/5, 1975/6, 1976/7.
Conway, J.P. (20) (Fulham) 1966/7, 1967/8, 1968/9, 1969/70, 1970/1, 1973/4, 1974/5, 1975/6 (Manchester City) 1976/7.
Corr, P.J. (4) (Everton) 1948/9.
Courtney, E. (1) (Cork United) 1945/6.
Cummins, G.P. (19) (Luton Town) 1953/4, 1954/5, 1955/6, 1957/8, 1958/9, 1959/60, 1960/1.
Cuneen, T. (1) (Limerick) 1950/1.
Curtis, D.P. (17) (Shelbourne) 1956/7 (Bristol City) 1956/7, 1957/8, (Ipswich Town) 1958/9, 1959/60, 1960/1, 1961/2, 1962/3 (Exeter City) 1963/4.
Cusack, S. (1) (Limerick) 1952/3.

Daly, G.A. (47) (Manchester United) 1972/3, 1973/4, 1974/5, 1976/7 (Derby County) 1977/8, 1978/9, 1979/80 (Coventry City) 1980/1, 1981/2, 1982/3, 1983/4 (Birmingham City) 1984/5, 1985/6 (Shrewsbury Town) 1986/7.
Daly, M. (2) (Wolverhampton Wanderers) 1977/8.
Daly, P. (1) (Shamrock Rovers) 1949/50.

De Mange, K.J.P.P. (2) (Liverpool) 1986/7, (Hull City) 1988/9.
Deacy, E. (4) (Aston Villa) 1981/2.
Dempsey, J.T. (19) (Fulham) 1966/7, 1967/8, 1968/9 (Chelsca) 1968/9, 1969/70, 1970/1, 1971/2.
Dennehy, J. (11) (Cork Hibernian) 1971/2 (Nottingham Forest) 1972/3, 1973/4, 1974/5 (Walsall) 1975/6, 1976/7.
Desmond, P. (4) (Middlesbrough) 1949/50.
Devine, J. (12) (Arsenal) 1979/80, 1980/1, 1981/2, 1982/3 (Norwich City) 1983/4, 1984/5.
Donovan, D.C. (5) (Everton) 1954/5, 1956/7.
Donovan, T. (1) (Aston Villa) 1979/80.
Doyle, C. (1) (Shelbourne) 1958/9.
Duffy, B. (1) (Shamrock Rovers) 1949/50.
Dunne, A.P. (33) (Manchester United) 1961/2, 1962/3, 1963/4, 1964/5, 1965/6, 1966/7, 1968/9, 1969/70, 1970/1 (Bolton Wanderers) 1973/4, 1974/5, 1975/6.
Dunne, J.C. (1) (Fulham) 1970/1.
Dunne, P.A.J. (5) (Manchester United) 1964/5, 1965/6, 1966/7.
Dunne, S. (15) (Luton Town) 1952/3, 1953/4, 1955/6, 1956/7, 1957/8, 1958/9, 1959/60.
Dunne, T. (3) (St Patrick's Athletic) 1955/6, 1956/7.
Dunning, P. (2) (Shelbourne) 1970/1.
Dunphy, E.M. (23) (York City) 1965/6 (Millwall) 1965/6, 1966/7, 1967/8, 1968/9, 1969/70, 1970/1.
Dwyer, N.M. (14) (West Ham United) 1959/60 (Swansea Town) 1960/1, 1961/2, 1963/4, 1964/5.

Eccles, P. (1) (Shamrock Rovers) 1985/6.
Eglington, T.J. (24) (Shamrock Rovers) 1945/6 (Everton) 1946/7, 1947/8, 1948/9, 1950/1, 1951/2, 1952/3, 1953/4, 1954/5, 1955/6.

Fagan, E. (1) (Shamrock Rovers) 1972/3.
Fagan, F. (8) (Manchester City) 1954/5, 1959/60 (Derby County) 1959/60, 1960/1.
Fairclough, M. (2) (Dundalk) 1981/2.
Fallon, S. (8) (Celtic) 1950/1, 1951/2, 1952/3, 1954/5.
Farrell, P.D. (28) (Shamrock Rovers) 1945/6 (Everton) 1946/7, 1947/8, 1948/9, 1949/50, 1950/1, 1951/2, 1952/3, 1953/4, 1954/5, 1955/6, 1956/7.
Finucane, A. (11) (Limerick) 1966/7, 1968/9, 1969/70, 1970/1, 1971/2.
Fitzgerald, F.J. (2) (Waterford) 1954/5, 1955/6.
Fitzgerald, P.J. (5) (Leeds United) 1960/1, 1961/2.
Fitzpatrick, K. (1) (Limerick) 1969/70.
Fitzsimons, A.G. (26) (Middlesbrough) 1949/50, 1951/2, 1952/3, 1953/4, 1954/5, 1955/6, 1956/7, 1957/8, 1958/9 (Lincoln City) 1958/9.

Fogarty, A. (11) (Sunderland) 1959/60, 1960/1, 1961/2, 1962/3, 1963/4, (Hartlepool United) 1963/4.
Foley, T.C. (9) (Northampton Town) 1963/4, 1964/5, 1965/6, 1966/7.
Fullam, J. (Preston North End) 1960/1 (Shamrock Rovers) 1963/4, 1965/6, 1967/8, 1968/9, 1969/70.

Gallagher, C. (2) (Celtic) 1966/7.
Gallagher, M. (1) (Hibernian) 1953/4.
Galvin, A. (29) (Tottenham Hotspur) 1982/3, 1983/4, 1984/5, 1985/6, 1986/7 (Sheffield Wednesday) 1987/8, 1988/9, 1989/90.
Gannon, E. (14) (Notts County) 1948/9 (Sheffield Wednesday) 1948/9, 1949/50, 1950/1, 1951/2, 1953/4, 1954/5 (Shelbourne) 1954/5.
Gannon, M. (1) (Shelbourne) 1971/2.
Gavin, J.T. (7) (Norwich City) 1949/50, 1952/3, 1953/4 (Tottenham Hotspur) 1954/5 (Norwich City) 1956/7.
Gibbons, A. (4) (St Patrick's Athletic) 1951/2, 1953/4, 1955/6.
Gilbert, R. (1) (Shamrock Rovers) 1965/6.
Giles, C. (1) (Doncaster Rovers) 1950/1.
Giles, M.J. (60) (Manchester United) 1959/60, 1960/1, 1961/2, 1962/3 (Leeds United) 1963/4, 1964/5, 1965/6, 1966/7, 1968/9, 1969/70, 1970/1, 1972/3, 1973/4, 1974/5 (West Bromwich Albion) 1975/6, 1976/7 (Shamrock Rovers) 1977/8, 1978/9.
Givens, D.J. (56) (Manchester United) 1968/9, 1969/70 (Luton Town) 1969/70, 1970/1, 1971/2 (QPR) 1972/3, 1973/4, 1974/5, 1975/6, 1976/7, 1977/8 (Birmingham City) 1978/9, 1979/80, 1980/1 (Neuchatel Xamax) 1981/2.
Glynn, D. (2) (Drumcondra) 1951/2, 1954/5.
Godwin, T.F. (13) (Shamrock Rovers) 1948/9, 1949/50 (Leicester City) 1949/50, 1950/1 (Bournemouth) 1955/6, 1956/7, 1957/8.
Gorman, W.C. (2) (Brentford) 1946/7.
Grealish, A. (44) (Orient) 1975/6, 1978/9 (Luton Town) 1979/80, 1980/1, (Brighton & Hove Albion) 1981/2, 1982/3, 1983/4 (West Bromwich Albion) 1984/5, 1985/6.
Gregg, E. (9) (Bohemians) 1977/8, 1978/9, 1979/80.
Grimes, A.A. (17) (Manchester United) 1977/8, 1979/80, 1980/1, 1981/2, 1982/3 (Coventry City) 1983/4 (Luton Town) 1987/8.

Hale, A. (13) (Aston Villa) 1961/2 (Doncaster Rovers) 1962/3, 1963/4, (Waterford) 1966/7, 1967/8, 1968/9, 1969/70, 1970/1, 1971/2.
Hamilton, T. (2) (Shamrock Rovers) 1958/9.
Hand, E.K. (20) (Portsmouth) 1968/9, 1969/70, 1970/1, 1972/3, 1973/4, 1974/5, 1975/6.
Hartnett, J.B. (2) (Middlesbrough) 1948/9, 1953/4.

Haverty, J. (32) (Arsenal) 1955/6, 1956/7, 1957/8, 1958/9, 1959/60, 1960/1, (Blackburn Rovers) 1961/2 (Millwall) 1962/3, 1963/4 (Celtic) 1964/5, (Bristol Rovers) 1964/5 (Shelbourne) 1965/6, 1966/7.
Hayes, A.W.P. (1) (Southampton) 1978/9.
Hayes, W.E. (2) (Huddersfield Town) 1946/7.
Hayes, W.J. (1) (Limerick) 1948/9.
Healey, R. (2) (Cardiff City) 1976/7, 1979/80.
Heighway, S.D. (34) (Liverpool) 1970/1, 1972/3, 1974/5, 1975/6, 1976/7, 1977/8, 1978/9, 1979/80, 1980/1 (Minnesota Kicks) 1981/2.
Henderson, B. (2) (Drumcondra) 1947/8.
Hennessy, J. (5) (Shelbourne) 1955/6, 1965/6 (St Patrick's Athletic) 1968/9.
Herrick, J. (3) (Cork Hibernians) 1971/2 (Shamrock Rovers) 1972/3.
Higgins, J. (1) (Birmingham City) 1950/1.
Holmes, J. (Coventry City) 1970/1, 1972/3, 1973/4, 1974/5, 1975/6, 1976/7 (Tottenham Hotspur) 1977/8, 1978/9, 1980/1 (Vancouver Whitecaps) 1980/1.
Houghton, R.J. (41) (Oxford United) 1985/6, 1986/7, 1987/8 (Liverpool) 1987/8, 1988/9, 1989/90, 1990/91.
Howlett, G. (1) (Brighton & Hove Albion) 1983/4.
Hughton, C. (52) (Tottenham Hotspur) 1979/80, 1980/1, 1981/2, 1982/3, 1983/4, 1984/5, 1985/6, 1986/7, 1987/8, 1988/9, 1989/90, 1990/91 (West Ham United).
Hurley, C.J. (40) (Millwall) 1956/7, 1957/8 (Sunderland) 1958/9, 1959/60, 1960/1, 1961/2, 1962/3, 1963/4, 1964/5, 1965/6, 1966/7, 1967/8 (Bolton Wanderers) 1968/9.

Irwin, D.J. (6) (Manchester United) 1990/91.

Keane, R.M. (1) (Nottingham Forest) 1990/91.
Keane, T.R. (4) (Swansea Town) 1948/9.
Kearin, M. (1) (Shamrock Rovers) 1971/2.
Kearns, F.T. (1) (West Ham United) 1953/4.
Kearns, M. (18) (Oxford United) 1969/70 (Walsall) 1973/4, 1975/6, 1976/7, 1977/8, 1978/9 (Wolverhampton Wanderers) 1979/80.
Kelly, D.T. (10) (Walsall) 1987/8 (West Ham) 1988/9 (Leicester City) 1989/90, 1990/91.
Kelly J.A. (47) (Drumcondra) 1956/7 (Preston North End) 1961/2, 1962/3, 1963/4, 1964/5, 1965/6, 1966/7, 1967/8, 1969/70, 1970/1, 1971/2, 1972/3.
Kelly, J.P.V. (5) (Wolverhampton Wanderers) 1960/1, 1961/2.
Kelly, M.J. (4) (Portsmouth) 1987/8, 1988/9, 1990/91.
Kelly, N. (1) (Nottingham Forest) 1953/4.
Kennedy, M.F. (2) (Portsmouth) 1985/6.
Keogh, J. (1) (Shamrock Rovers) 1965/6.

Keogh, S. (1) (Shamrock Rovers) 1958/9.
Kiernan, F.W. (5) (Shamrock Rovers) 1950/1 (Southampton) 1951/2.
Kinnear, J.P. (26) (Tottenham Hotspur) 1966/7, 1967/8, 1968/9, 1969/70, 1970/1, 1971/2, 1972/3, 1973/4, 1974/5 (Brighton & Hove Albion) 1975/6.

Langan, D. (25) (Derby County) 1977/8, 1979/80 (Birmingham City) 1980/1, 1981/2 (Oxford United) 1984/5, 1985/6, 1986/7, 1987/8.
Lawler, J.F. (8) (Fulham) 1952/3, 1953/4, 1954/5, 1955/6.
Lawlor, J.C. (3) (Drumcondra) 1948/9 (Doncaster Rovers) 1950/1.
Lawlor, M. (5) (Shamrock Rovers) 1970/1, 1972/3.
Lawrenson, M. (38) (Preston North End) 1976/7 (Brighton & Hove Albion) 1977/8, 1978/9, 1979/80, 1980/1 (Liverpool) 1981/2, 1982/3, 1983/4, 1984/5, 1985/6, 1986/7, 1987/8.
Leech, M. (8) (Shamrock Rovers) 1968/9, 1971/2, 1972/3.
Lowry, D. (1) (St Patrick's Athletic) 1961/2.

McAlinden, J. (2) (Portsmouth) 1945/6.
McCann, J. (1) (Shamrock Rovers) 1956/7.
McCarthy, M. (51) (Manchester City) 1983/4, 1984/5, 1985/6, 1986/7 (Celtic) 1987/8, 1988/9 (Lyon) 1989/90, 1990/91 (Millwall).
McConville, T. (6) (Dundalk) 1971/2 (Waterford) 1972/3.
McDonagh, J. (24) (Everton) 1980/1 (Bolton Wanderers) 1981/2, 1982/3, (Notts County) 1983/4, 1984/5, 1985/6.
McDonagh, Joe (3) (Shamrock Rovers) 1983/4, 1984/5.
McEvoy, M.A. (17) (Blackburn Rovers) 1960/1, 1962/3, 1963/4, 1964/5, 1965/6, 1966/7.
McGee, P. (15) (QPR) 1977/8, 1978/9, 1979/80 (Preston North End) 1980/1.
McGowan, D. (3) (West Ham United) 1948/9.
McGowan, J. (1) (Cork United) 1946/7.
McGrath, M. (22) (Blackburn Rovers) 1957/8, 1958/9, 1959/60, 1960/1, 1961/2, 1962/3, 1963/4, 1964/5, 1965/6 (Bradford Park Avenue) 1965/6, 1966/7.
McGrath, P. (47) (Manchester United) 1984/5, 1985/6, 1986/7, 1987/8, 1988/9 (Aston Villa) 1989/90, 1990/91.
Macken, A. (1) (Derby County) 1976/7.
Mackey, G. (3) (Shamrock Rovers) 1956/7.
McLoughlin, A.F. (7) (Swindon T) 1989/90, 1990/91 (Southampton).
McMillan, W. (2) (Belfast Celtic) 1945/6.
McNally, J.B. (3) (Luton Town) 1958/9, 1960/1, 1962/3.
Malone, G. (1) (Shelbourne) 1948/9.
Mancini, T.J. (5) (QPR) 1973/4 (Arsenal) 1974/5.

Martin, C.J. (30) (Glentoran) 1945/6, 1946/7 (Leeds United) 1946/7, 1947/8, (Aston Villa) 1948/9, 1949/50 1950/1, 1951/2, 1953/4, 1954/5, 1955/6.
Martin, M.P. (51) (Bohemians) 1971/2, 1972/3 (Manchester United) 1972/3, 1973/4, 1974/5 (West Bromwich Albion) 1975/6, 1976/7 (Newcastle United) 1978/9, 1979/80, 1981/2, 1982/3.
Meagan, M.K. (17) (Everton) 1960/1, 1961/2, 1962/3, 1963/4 (Huddersfield Town) 1964/5, 1965/6, 1966/7, 1967/8 (Drogheda) 1969/70.
Mooney, J. (2) (Shamrock Rovers) 1964/5.
Moran, K. (60) (Manchester United) 1979/80, 1980/1, 1981/2, 1982/3, 1983/4, 1984/5, 1985/6, 1986/7, 1987/8 (Sporting Gijon) 1988/9 (Blackburn Rovers) 1989/90, 1990/91.
Moroney, T. (12) (West Ham United) 1947/8, 1948/9, 1949/50, 1950/1, 1951/2, 1953/4.
Morris, C.B. (27) (Celtic) 1987/8, 1988/9, 1989/90, 1990/91.
Moulson, G.B. (3) (Lincoln City) 1947/8, 1948/9.
Mucklan, C. (1) (Drogheda) 1977/8
Mulligan, P.M. (50) (Shamrock Rovers) 1968/9, 1969/70 (Chelsea) 1969/70, 1970/1, 1971/2 (Crystal Palace) 1972/3, 1973/4, 1974/5 (West Bromwich Albion) 1975/6, 1976/7, 1977/8, 1978/9 (Shamrock Rovers) 1979/80.
Munroe, L. (1) (Shamrock Rovers) 1953/4.
Murphy, A. (1) (Clyde) 1955/6.
Murphy, B. (1) (Bohemians) 1985/6.
Murphy, J. (1) (Crystal Palace) 1979/80.
Murray, T. (1) (Dundalk) 1949/50.

Newman, W. (1) (Shelbourne) 1968/9.
Nolan, R. (10) (Shamrock Rovers) 1956/7, 1957/8, 1959/60, 1961/2, 1962/3.

O'Brien, F. (4) (Philadelphia Fury) 1979/80.
O'Brien, L. (8) (Shamrock Rovers) 1985/6 (Manchester United) 1986/7, 1987/8, (Newcastle United) 1988/9.
O'Brien R. (4) (Notts County) 1975/6, 1976/7.
O'Byrne, L.B. (1) (Shamrock Rovers) 1948/9.
O'Callaghan, B.R. (6) (Stoke City) 1978/9, 1979/80, 1980/1, 1981/2.
O'Callaghan, K. (20) (Ipswich Town) 1980/1, 1981/2, 1982/3, 1983/4, 1984/5, (Portsmouth) 1985/6, 1986/7.
O'Connell, A. (2) (Dundalk) 1966/7 (Bohemians) 1970/1.
O'Connor, T. (4) (Shamrock Rovers) 1949/50.
O'Connor, T. (7) (Fulham) 1967/8 (Dundalk) 1971/2 (Bohemians) 1972/3.
O'Driscoll, J.F. (3) (Swansea Town) 1948/9.

O'Driscoll, S. (3) (Fulham) 1981/2.
O'Farrell, F. (9) (West Ham United) 1951/2, 1952/3, 1953/4, 1954/5, 1955/6 (Preston North End) 1957/8, 1958/9.
O'Flanagan, K.P. (3) (Arsenal) 1946/7.
O'Flanagan, M. (1) (Bohemians) 1946/7.
O'Hanlon, K.G. (1) (Rotherham United) 1987/8.
O'Keefe, E. (5) (Everton) 1980/1 (Port Vale) 1983/4.
O'Leary, D. (57) (Arsenal) 1976/7, 1977/8, 1978/9, 1979/80, 1980/1, 1981/2, 1982/3, 1983/4, 1984/5, 1985/6, 1988/9, 1989/90, 1990/91.
O'Leary, P. (7) (Shamrock Rovers) 1979/80, 1980/1.
O'Neill, F.S. (20) (Shamrock Rovers) 1961/2, 1964/5, 1965/6, 1966/7, 1968/9, 1971/2.
O'Neill, J. (17) (Everton) 1951/2, 1952/3, 1953/4, 1954/5, 1955/6, 1956/7, 1957/8, 1958/9.
O'Neill, J. (1) (Preston North End) 1960/1.
O'Regan, K. (4) (Brighton & Hove Albion) 1983/4, 1984/5.
O'Reilly, J. (2) (Cork United) 1945/6.

Peyton, G. (29) (Fulham) 1976/7, 1977/8, 1978/9, 1979/80, 1980/1, 1981/2, 1984/5, 1985/6 (Bournemouth) 1987/8, 1988/9, 1989/90, 1990/91.
Peyton, N. (6) (Shamrock Rovers) 1956/7 (Leeds United) 1959/60, 1960/1, 1962/3.

Quinn, N.J. (24) (Arsenal) 1985/6, 1986/7, 1987/8, 1988/9 (Manchester City) 1989/90, 1990/91.

Richardson, D.J. (3) (Shamrock Rovers) 1971/2 (Gillingham) 1972/3, 1979/80.
Ringstead, A. (20) (Sheffield United) 1950/1, 1951/2, 1952/3, 1953/4, 1954/5, 1955/6, 1956/7, 1957/8, 1958/9.
Robinson, M. (23) (Brighton & Hove Albion) 1980/1, 1981/2, 1982/3, (Liverpool) 1983/4, 1984/5 (QPR) 1985/6.
Roche, P.J. (8) (Shelbourne) 1971/2 (Manchester United) 1974/5, 1975/6.
Rogers, E. (19) (Blackburn Rovers) 1967/8, 1968/9, 1969/70, 1970/1, (Charlton Athletic) 1971/2, 1972/3.
Ryan, G. (16) (Derby County) 1977/8 (Brighton & Hove Albion) 1978/9, 1979/80, 1980/1, 1981/2, 1983/4, 1984/5.
Ryan, R.A. (16) (West Bromwich Albion) 1949/50, 1950/1, 1951/2, 1952/3, 1953/4, 1954/5 (Derby County) 1955/6.

Saward, P. (18) (Millwall) 1953/4 (Aston Villa) 1956/7, 1957/8, 1958/9, 1959/60, 1960/1 (Huddersfield Town) 1960/1, 1961/2, 1962/3.
Scannell, T. (1) (Southend United) 1953/4.
Scully, P.J. (1) (Arsenal) 1988/9.

Sheedy, K. (37) (Everton) 1983/4, 1984/5, 1985/6, 1986/7, 1987/8, 1988/9, 1989/90, 1990/91.
Sheridan, J.J. (13) (Leeds United) 1987/8, 1988/9 (Sheffield Wed) 1989/90, 1990/91.
Slaven, B. (6) (Middlesbrough) 1989/90, 1990/91.
Sloan, J.W. (2) (Arsenal) 1945/6.
Smyth, M. (1) (Shamrock Rovers) 1968/9.
Stapleton, F. (70) (Arsenal) 1976/7, 1977/8, 1978/9, 1979/80, 1980/1 (Manchester United) 1981/2, 1982/3, 1983/4, 1984/5, 1985/6, 1986/7 (Ajax) 1987/8 (Derby County) 1987/8 (Le Havre) 1988/9 (Blackburn Rovers) 1989/90.
Staunton, S. (26) (Liverpool) 1988/9, 1989/90, 1990/91.
Stevenson, A.E. (6) (Everton) 1946/7, 1947/8, 1948/9.
Strahan, F. (5) (Shelbourne) 1963/4, 1964/5, 1965/6.
Swan, M.M.G. (1) (Drumcondra) 1959/60.
Synott, N. (3) (Shamrock Rovers) 1977/8, 1978/9.

Thomas, P. (2) (Waterford) 1973/4.
Townsend, A.D. (25) (Norwich City) 1988/9, 1989/90, 1990/91 (Chelsea).
Traynor, T.J. (8) (Southampton) 1953/4, 1961/2, 1962/3, 1963/4.
Treacy, R.C.P. (43) (West Bromwich Albion) 1965/6, 1966/7, 1967/8 (Charlton Athletic) 1967/8, 1968/9, 1969/70, 1970/1 (Swindon Town) 1971/2, 1972/3, 1973/4 (Preston North End) 1973/4, 1974/5, 1975/6 (West Bromwich Albion) 1976/7, 1977/8 (Shamrock Rovers) 1979/80.
Tuohy, L. (8) (Shamrock Rovers) 1955/6, 1958/9 (Newcastle United) 1961/2, 1962/3 (Shamrock Rovers) 1963/4, 1964/5.
Turner, A. (2) (Celtic) 1962/3, 1963/4.

Vernon, J. (2) (Belfast Celtic) 1945/6.

Waddock, G. (20) (QPR) 1979/80, 1980/1, 1981/2, 1982/3, 1983/4, 1984/5, 1985/6 (Millwall) 1989/90.
Walsh, D.J. (20) (West Bromwich Albion) 1945/6, 1946/7, 1947/8, 1948/9, 1949/50, 1950/1 (Aston Villa) 1951/2, 1952/3, 1953/4.
Walsh, J. (1) (Limerick 1981/2.
Walsh, M. (22) (Blackpool) 1975/6, 1976/7 (Everton) 1978/9 (QPR) 1978/9 (Porto) 1980/1, 1981/2, 1982/3, 1983/4, 1984/5.
Walsh, M. (5) (Everton) 1981/2, 1982/3 (Norwich City) 1982/3.
Walsh, W. (9) (Manchester City) 1946/7, 1947/8, 1948/9, 1949/50.
Waters, J. (2) (Grimsby Town) 1976/7, 1979/80.
Whelan, R. (2) (St Patrick's Athletic) 1963/4.
Whelan, R. (41) (Liverpool) 1980/1, 1981/2, 1982/3, 1983/4, 1984/5, 1985/6, 1986/7, 1987/8, 1988/9, 1989/90, 1990/91.
Whelan, W. (4) (Manchester United) 1955/6, 1956/7.
Whittaker, R. (1) (Chelsea) 1958/9.

BRITISH ISLES INTERNATIONAL GOALSCORERS SINCE 1946

ENGLAND

A'Court, A.....1
Adams, T.A.....4
Allen, R.....2
Anderson, V.....2
Astall, G.....1
Atyco, P.J.W.....5

Baily, E.F.....5
Baker, J.H.....3
Ball, A.J.....8
Barnes, J.....10
Barnes, P.S.....4
Beardsley, P.A.....8
Beattie, T.K.....1
Bell, C.....9
Bentley, R.T.F.....9
Blissett, L.....3
Bowles, S.....1
Bradford, G.R.W.....1
Bradley, W.....2
Bridges, B.J.....1
Broadbent, P.F.....2
Broadis, I.A.....8
Brooking, T.D.....5
Brooks, J.....2
Bull, S.G.....4
Butcher, T.....3
Byrne, J.J.....8

Carter, H.S.....7
(inc. 2 scored pre-war)
Chamberlain, M.....1
Channon, M.R.....21
Charlton, J.....6
Charlton, R.....49
Chivers, M.....13
Clarke, A.J.....10
Connelly, J.M.....7
Coppell, S.J.....7
Cowans, G.....2
Crawford, R.....1
Currie, A.W.....3

Dixon, L.M.....1
Dixon, K.M.....4
Douglas, B.....11

Eastham, G.....2
Edwards, D.....5
Elliott, W.H.....3

Finney, T.....30
Flowers, R.....10
Francis, G.C.J.....3
Francis, T.....12
Froggatt, J.....2
Froggatt, R.....2

Gascoigne, P.J.....2
Goddard, P.....1
Grainger, C.....3
Greaves, J.....44

Haines, J.T.W.....2
Hancocks, J.....2
Hassall, H.W.....4
Hateley, M.....9
Haynes, J.N.....18
Hirst, D.E.....1
Hitchens, G.A.....5
Hoddle, G.....8
Hughes, E.W.....1
Hunt, R.....18
Hunter, N.....2
Hurst, G.C.....24

Johnson, D.E.....6

Kay, A.H.....1
Keegan, J.K.....21
Kennedy, R.....3
Kevan, D.T.....8
Kidd, B.....1

Langton, R.....1
Latchford, R.D.....5
Lawler, C.....1
Lawler, T.....22
(inc. 6 scored pre-war)
Lee, F.....10
Lee, J.....1
Lee, S.....2
Lineker, G.....45
Lofthouse, N.....30

Mabbutt, G.....1
McDermott, T.....3
Macdonald, M.....6
Mannion, W.J.....11
Mariner, P.....13
Marsh, R.W.....1

Matthews, S.....11
(inc. 8 scored pre-war)
Medley, L.D.....1
Melia, J.....1
Milburn, J.E.T.....10
Moore, R.F.....2
Morris, J.....3
Mortensen, S.H.....23
Mullen, J.....6
Mullery, A.P.....1

Neal, P.G.....5
Nicholls, J.....1
Nicholson, W.E.....1

O'Grady, M.....3
Own goals.....15

Paine, T.L.....7
Parry, R.A.....1
Peacock, A.....3
Pearce, S.....2
Pearson, J.S.....5
Pearson, S.C.....5
Perry, W.....2
Peters, M.....20
Pickering, F.....5
Platt, D.....7
Pointer, R.....2

Ramsay, A.E.....3
Revie, D.G.....4
Robson, B.....26
Robson, R.....4
Rowley, J.F.....6
Royle, J.....2

Sansom, K.....1
Sewell, J.....3
Shackleton, L.F.....1
Smith, A.M.....1
Smith, R.....13
Steven, T.M.....3
Stiles, N.P.....13
Summerbee, M.G.....1

Tambling, R.V.....1
Taylor, P.J.....2
Taylor, T.....16
Thompson, P.B.....1
Tueart, D.....2

Viollet, D.S 1

Waddle, C.R 6
Wallace, D.L 1
Walsh, P 1
Watson, D.V 4
Webb, N 3
Weller, K 1
Wignall, F 2
Wilkins, R.G 3
Wilshaw, D.J 10
Wise, D.F 1
Withe, P 1
Woodcock, T 16
Worthington, F.S 2
Wright, M 1
Wright, W.A 3

SCOTLAND

Aitken, R 1
Archibald, S 4

Baird, S 2
Bannon, E 1
Bauld, W 2
Baxter, J.C 3
Bett, J 1
Bone, J 1
Brand, R 8
Brazil, A 1
Bremner, W.J 3
Brown, A.D 6
Buckley, P 1
Burns, K 1

Caldow, E 4
Campbell, R 1
Chalmers, S 3
Collins, J 2
Collins, R.V 10
Combe, J.R 1
Conn, A 1
Cooper, D 6
Craig, J 1
Curran, H.P 1

Dalglish, K 30
Davidson, J.A 1
Docherty, T.H 1
Dodds, D 1
Duncan, D.M 1
Durie, G.S 2

Fernie, W 1
Flavell, R 2
Fleming, C 2

Gemmell, T. (*St Mirren*) 1
Gemmell T. (*Celtic*) 1
Gemmill, A 8
Gibson, D.W 3
Gilzean, A.J 10
Gough, C.R 5
Graham, A 2
Graham, G 3
Gray, A 7
Gray, E 3
Gray, F 1
Greig, J 3

Hamilton, G 4
Harper, J.M 2
Hartford, R.A 4
Henderson, J.G 1
Henderson, W 5
Herd, D.G 4
Hewie, J.D 2
Holton, J.A 2
Houliston, W 2
Howie, H 1
Hughes, J 1
Hunter, W 1
Hutchison, T 1

Jackson, C 1
Jardine, A 1
Johnston, L.H 1
Johnston, M 14
Johnstone, D 2
Johnstone, J 4
Johnstone, R 9
Jordan, J 11

Law, D 30
Leggat, G 8
Lennox, R 3
Liddell, W 6
Linwood, A.B 1
Lorimer, P 4

Macari, L 5
McAllister, G 1
MacDougall, E.J 3
MacKay, D.C 4
Mackay, G 1
MacKenzie, J.A 1
MacLeod, M 1
McAvennie, F 1
McCall, S.M 1
McCalliog, J 1
McCoist, A 8
McGhee, M 2
McInally, A 3
McKimmie, S.I 1
McKinnon, R 1
McLaren, A 4
McLean, T 1
McLintock, F 1
McMillan, I.L 2
McNeill, W 3
McPhail, J 3
McQueen, G 5
McStay, P 6
Mason, J 4
Masson, D.S 5
Miller, W 1
Mitchell, R.C 1
Morgan, W 1
Morris, H 3
Mudie, J.K 9
Mulhall, G 1
Murdoch, R 5
Murray, J 1

Narey, D 1
Nicholas, C 5

O'Hare, J 5
Ormond, W.E 1
Orr, T 1
Own goals 7

Parlane, D 1
Pettigrew, W 2
Provan, D 1

Quinn, J 7
Quinn, P 1

Reilly, L 22
Ring, T 2
Rioch, B.D 6
Robertson, A 2
Robertson, J 2
Robertson, J.N 8

St John, I 9
Scott, A.S 5
Sharp, G 1
Smith, G 4
Souness, G.J 3
Steel, W 12
Stein, C 10
Stewart, R 1
Strachan, G 5
Sturrock, P 3

Thornton, W 1

Waddell, W 6
Wallace, I.A 1
Wark, J 7
Weir, A 1
White, J.A 3
Wilson, D 9

Young, A 2

WALES

Allchurch, I.J 23
Allen, M 3

Barnes, W 1
Bodin, P.J 1
Bowen, D.L 1
Bowen, M 1
Boyle, T 1
Burgess, W.A.R 1

Charles, J 1
Charles, M 6
Charles, W.J 15
Clarke, R.J 5
Curtis, A 6

Davies, G 2
Davies, R.T 8
Davies, R.W 7
Deacy, N 4
Durban, A 2
Dwyer, P 2

Edwards, G 2
Edwards, R.I 5
England, H.M 3
Evans, I 1

Flynn, B 6
Ford, T 23
Foulkes, W.I 1

Giles, D 2
Godfrey, B.C 2
Griffiths, A.T 6
Griffiths, M.W 2

Harris, C.S 1
Hewitt, R 1
Hockey, T 1
Hodges, G 2
Horne, B 2
Hughes, L.M 9

James, L 10
James, R 7
Jones, A 1
Jones, B.S 2
Jones, Cliff 15
Jones, D.E 1
Jones, J.P 1

Kryzwicki, R.L 1

Leek, K 5
Lovell, S 1
Lowrie, G 2

Mahoney, J.F 1
Medwin, T.C 6
Moore, G 1

Nicholas, P 2

O'Sullivan, P.A 1
Own goals 5

Palmer, D 1
Paul, R 1
Phillips, D 1
Powell, A 1
Powell, D 1
Price, P 1

Reece, G.I 2
Rees, R.R 3
Roberts, P.S 1
Rush, I 19

Saunders, D 9
Slatter, N 2
Smallman, D.P 1

Tapscott, D.R 4
Thomas, M 4
Toshack, J.B 13

Vernon, T.R 8

Walsh, I 7
Williams, G.E 2
Woosnam, A.P 4

Yorath, T.C 2

NORTHERN IRELAND

Anderson, T 3
Armstrong, G 12
Barr, H.H 1
Best, G 9
Bingham, W.L 10
Blanchflower, D 2
Blanchflower, J 1
Brennan, R.A 1
Brotherston, N 3

Campbell, W.G 1
Casey, T 2
Caskey, W 1
Cassidy, T 1
Clarke, C.J 8
Clements, D 2
Cochrane, T 1
Crossan, E 1
Crossan, J.A 10
Cush, W.W 5

D'Arcy, S.D 1
Doherty, L 1
Doherty, P.D 3
(inc. 1 scored pre-war)
Dougan, A.D 8

Elder, A.R 1

Ferguson, W 1
Ferris, R.O 1
Finney, T 2

Hamilton, B 4
Hamilton, W 5
Harkin, J.T 2
Harvey, M 3
Hill, C.F 1
Humphries, W 1
Hunter, A 1

Irvine, W.J 8

Johnston, W.C 1
Jones, J 1

Lockhart, N 3

Magilton, J 1
McAdams, W.J 7
McClelland, J 1
McCrory, S 1
McCurdy, C 1
McDonald, A 1
McGarry, J.K 1
McGrath, R.C 4
McIlroy, J 10
McIlroy, S.B 5

McLaughlin, J.C..........6
McMordie, A.S............3
McMorran, E.J............4
McParland, P.J...........10
Moreland, V..................1
Morgan, S.....................3

Neill, W.J.T..................2
Nelson, S......................1
Nicholl, C.J...................3
Nicholl, J.M..................2
Nicholson, J.J...............6

O'Kane, W.J.................1
O'Neill, J......................1
O'Neill, M....................1
O'Neill, M.H.................8
Own goals.....................4

Peacock, R...................2
Penney, S.....................2

Quinn, J.M...................6

Simpson, W.J................5
Smyth, S.......................5
Spence, D.W.................3
Stewart, I......................2

Taggart, G.P.................2
Tully, C.P......................3

Walker, J......................1
Walsh, D.J....................5
Welsh, E........................1
Whiteside, N.................9
Wilson, D......................1
Wilson, K.J...................2
Wilson, S.J....................7

EIRE

Aldridge, J....................6
Ambrose, P...................1
Anderson, J...................1

Bermingham, P.............1
Bradshaw, P..................4
Brady, L.......................9
Brown, D......................1
Byrne, J. (*Bray*)............1
Byrne, J. (*QPR*)............3

Cantwell, J..................14
Carey, J........................3
Carroll, T......................1
Cascarino, A.................7

Coad, P........................3
Conroy, T.....................2
Conway, J.....................3
Cummings, G...............5
Curtis, D......................8

Daly, G.......................13
Davis, T.......................4
Dempsey, J..................1
Dennehy, M.................2
Donnelly, J..................3
Donnelly, T..................1
Duffy, B.......................1
Duggan, H...................1
Dunne, J.....................12
Dunne, L......................1

Eglinton, T..................2
Ellis, P.........................1

Fagan, F......................5
Fallon, S......................2
Fallon, W.....................2
Farrell, P.....................3
Fitzgerald, J.................1
Fitzgerald, P................2
Fitzsimons, A...............7
Flood, J.J.....................4
Fogarty, A....................3
Fullam, J......................1
Fullam, R.....................1

Galvin, A.....................1
Gavin, J.......................2
Geoghegan, M.............2
Giles, J........................5
Givens, D...................19
Glynn, D......................1
Grealish, T...................8
Grimes, A.A.................1

Hale, A........................2
Hand, E.......................2
Haverty, J....................3
Holmes, J....................1
Horlacher, A................2
Houghton, R................3
Hughton, C...................1
Hurley, C.....................2

Jordan, D.....................1

Kelly, D.......................6
Kelly, J........................2

Lacey, W......................1

Lawrenson, M..............5
Leech, M....................22

McCann, J....................1
McCarthy, M................1
McEvoy, A...................6
McGee, P.....................4
McGrath, P..................4
Madden, O...................1
Mancini, T...................1
Martin, C.....................6
Martin, M....................4
Mooney, J....................1
Moore, P......................7
Moran, K.....................6
Moroney, T..................1
Mulligan, P..................1

O'Callaghan, K............1
O'Connor, T.................2
O'Farrell, F..................2
O'Flanagan, K.............3
O'Keefe, E...................1
O'Leary, D.A...............1
O'Neill, F....................1
O'Reilly, J....................2
O'Reilly, J....................1
Own goals...................5

Quinn, N......................7

Ringstead, A...............7
Robinson, M................4
Rogers, E.....................5
Ryan, G.......................1
Ryan, R.......................3

Sheedy, K....................6
Sheridan, J..................1
Slaven, B.....................1
Sloan, W.....................1
Squires, J....................1
Stapleton, F...............20
Staunton, S.................1
Strahan, F...................1
Sullivan, J...................1

Townsend, A.D............1
Treacy, R....................5
Tuohy, L.....................4

Waddock, G................3
Walsh, D.....................5
Walsh, M....................3
Waters, J.....................1
White, J.J....................2
Whelan, R...................3

ENGLAND UNDER-21 RESULTS 1976–91

EC UEFA Competition for Under-21 Teams

Year	Date		Venue	Eng	Opp
			v ALBANIA		
				Eng	Alb
EC1989	Mar	7	Shkroda	2	1
EC1989	April	25	Ipswich	2	0
			v BULGARIA	Eng	Bulg
EC1979	June	5	Pernik	3	1
EC1979	Nov	20	Leicester	5	0
1989	June	5	Toulon	2	3
			v CZECHOSLOVAKIA	Eng	Cz
1990	May	28	Toulon	2	1
			v DENMARK	Eng	Den
EC1978	Sept	19	Hvidovre	2	1
EC1979	Sept	11	Watford	1	0
EC1982	Sept	21	Hvidovre	4	1
EC1983	Sept	20	Norwich	4	1
EC1986	Mar	12	Copenhagen	1	0
EC1986	Mar	26	Manchester	1	1
1988	Sept	13	Watford	0	0
			v EAST GERMANY	Eng	EG
EC1980	April	16	Sheffield	1	2
EC1980	April	23	Jena	0	1
			v FINLAND	Eng	Fin
EC1977	May	26	Helsinki	1	0
EC1977	Oct	12	Hull	8	1
EC1984	Oct	16	Southampton	2	0
EC1985	May	21	Mikkeli	1	3
			v FRANCE	Eng	Fra
EC1984	Feb	28	Sheffield	6	1
EC1984	Mar	28	Rouen	1	0
1987	June	11	Toulon	0	2
EC1988	April	13	Besancon	2	4
EC1988	April	27	Highbury	2	2
1988	June	12	Toulon	2	4
1990	May	23	Toulon	7	3
1991	June	3	Toulon	1	0
			v GREECE	Eng	Gre
EC1982	Nov	16	Piraeus	0	1
EC1983	Mar	29	Portsmouth	2	1
1989	Feb	7	Patras	0	1
			v HUNGARY	Eng	Hun
EC1981	June	5	Keszthely	2	1
EC1981	Nov	17	Nottingham	2	0
EC1983	April	26	Newcastle	1	0
EC1983	Oct	11	Nyiregyhaza	2	0
1990	Sept	11	Southampton	3	1
			v ITALY	Eng	Italy
EC1978	Mar	8	Manchester	2	1
EC1978	April	5	Rome	0	0

EC1984	April	18	Manchester	3	1
EC1984	May	2	Florence	0	1
EC1986	April	9	Pisa	0	2
EC1986	April	23	Swindon	1	1
			v ISRAEL	Eng	Isr
1985	Feb	27	Tel Aviv	2	1
			v MEXICO	Eng	Mex
1988	June	5	Toulon	2	1
1991	May	29	Toulon	6	0
			v MOROCCO	Eng	Mor
1987	June	7	Toulon	2	0
1988	June	9	Toulon	1	0
			v NORWAY	Eng	Nor
EC1977	June	1	Bergen	2	1
EC1977	Sept	6	Brighton	6	0
1980	Sept	9	Southampton	3	0
1981	Sept	8	Drammen	0	0
			v POLAND	Eng	Pol
EC1982	Mar	17	Warsaw	2	1
EC1982	April	7	West Ham	2	2
EC1989	June	2	Plymouth	2	1
EC1989	Oct	10	Jastrzebie	3	1
EC1990	Oct	16	Tottenham	0	1
			v PORTUGAL	Eng	Por
1987	June	13	Toulon	0	0
1990	May	21	Toulon	0	1
			v REPUBLIC OF IRELAND	Eng	Rep Ire
1981	Feb	25	Liverpool	1	0
1985	Mar	25	Portsmouth	3	2
1989	June	9	Toulon	0	0
EC1990	Nov	13	Cork	3	0
EC1991	Mar	26	Brentford	3	0
			v ROMANIA	Eng	Rom
EC1980	Oct	14	Ploesti	0	4
EC1981	April	28	Swindon	3	0
EC1985	April	30	Brasov	0	0
EC1985	Sept	10	Ipswich	3	0
			v SENEGAL	Eng	Sen
1989	June	7	Toulon	6	1
1991	May	27	Toulon	2	1
			v SCOTLAND	Eng	Scot
1977	April	27	Sheffield	1	0
EC1980	Feb	12	Coventry	2	1
EC1980	Mar	4	Aberdeen	0	0
EC1982	April	19	Glasgow	1	0
EC1982	April	28	Manchester	1	1

EC1988	Feb	16	Aberdeen	1	0
EC1988	Mar	22	Nottingham	1	0
			v SPAIN	Eng	Spa
EC1984	May	17	Seville	1	0
EC1984	May	24	Sheffield	2	0
1987	Feb	18	Burgos	2	1
			v SWEDEN	Eng	Swe
1979	June	9	Vasteras	2	1
1986	Sept	9	Ostersund	1	1
EC1988	Oct	18	Coventry	1	1
EC1989	Sept	5	Uppsala	0	1
			v SWITZERLAND	Eng	Swit
EC1980	Nov	18	Ipswich	5	0
EC1981	May	31	Neuenburg	0	0
1988	May	28	Lausanne	1	1
			v USA	Eng	USA
1989	June	11	Toulon	0	2
			v TURKEY	Eng	Tur
EC1984	Nov	13	Bursa	0	0
EC1985	Oct	15	Bristol	3	0
EC1987	April	28	Izmir	0	0
EC1987	Oct	13	Sheffield	1	1
EC1991	April	30	Izmir	2	2
			v USSR	Eng	USSR
1987	June	9	Toulon	0	0
1988	June	7	Toulon	1	0
1990	May	25	Toulon	2	1
1991	May	31	Toulon	2	1
			v WALES	Eng	Wales
1976	Dec	15	Wolverhampton	0	0
1979	Feb	6	Swansea	1	0
1990	Dec	5	Tranmere	0	0
			v WEST GERMANY	Eng	WG
EC1982	Sept	21	Sheffield	3	1
EC1982	Oct	12	Bremen	2	3
1987	Sept	8	Ludenscheid	0	2
			v YUGOSLAVIA	Eng	Yugo
EC1978	April	19	Novi Sad	1	2
EC1978	May	2	Manchester	1	1
EC1986	Nov	11	Peterborough	1	1
EC1987	Nov	10	Zemun	5	1

9th UEFA UNDER-16 CHAMPIONSHIP 1991

Group 1: Greece 1, Turkey 1; Turkey 0, Greece 2. Greece qualified.
Group 2: Cyprus 1, Yugoslavia 5; Yugoslavia 1, Cyprus 0. Yugoslavia qualified.
Group 3: Romania 2, Czechoslovakia 0; Czechoslovakia 2, Romania 1. Romania qualified.
Group 4: Malta 1, Spain 1; Spain 5, Malta 0. Spain qualified.
Group 5: Albania 1, Bulgaria 2; Bulgaria 1, Albania 0. Bulgaria qualified.
Group 6: Liechtenstein 1, France 7; France 5, Liechtenstein 0. France qualified.
Group 7: Finland 4, Belgium 1; Belgium 0, Finland 0. Finland qualified.
Group 8: Wales 1, Iceland 0; Iceland 6, Wales 0. Iceland qualified.
Group 9: Sweden 4, Luxembourg 0; Luxembourg 1, Sweden 1. Sweden qualified.
Group 10: West Germany 3, Northern Ireland 0; Northern Ireland 0, West Germany 1. West Germany qualified.
Group 11: Italy 0, Portugal 0; Portugal 0, Italy 0. Portugal qualified.
Group 12: Holland 0, Austria 1; Austria 1, Holland 1. Austria qualified.
Group 13: Poland 4, Scotland 0; Scotland 0, Poland 1. Poland qualified.
Group 14: Norway 1, Denmark 3; Norway 1, Republic of Ireland 1; Denmark 3, Norway 0; Denmark 1, Republic of Ireland 0; Republic of Ireland 2, Denmark 3; Republic of Ireland 1, Norway 0. Denmark qualified.
Group 15: Hungary 1, USSR 1; USSR 2, Hungary 1; USSR 1, Israel 1; Israel 1, Hungary 0; Hungary 0, Israel 1; Israel 0, USSR 1. USSR qualified.

FINAL TOURNAMENT IN SWITZERLAND

GROUP A

Austria (0) 3, West Germany (1) 1	St Gallen, 8 May 1991
Bulgaria (0) 0, Sweden (0) 1	Frauenfeld, 8 May 1991
Bulgaria (0) 1, Austria (0) 2	Wil, 10 May 1991
Sweden (0) 0, West Germany (0) 1	Weinfelden, 10 May 1991
Bulgaria (0) 0, West Germany (2) 5	Kreuzlingen, 12 May 1991
Sweden (0) 1, Austria (0) 0	St Gallen, 12 May 1991

	P	*W*	*D*	*L*	*F*	*A*	*Pts*
West Germany	3	2	0	1	7	3	4
Austria	3	2	0	1	5	3	4
Sweden	3	2	0	1	2	1	4
Bulgaria	3	0	0	3	1	8	0

GROUP B

Greece (1) 1, Poland (0) 0	Lenzburg, 8 May 1991
Portugal (0) 2, Switzerland (0) 0	Muri, 8 May 1991
Portugal (1) 1, Greece (0) 1	Baden, 10 May 1991
Switzerland (0) 1, Poland (0) 1	Zofingen, 10 May 1991
Portugal (1) 1, Poland (0) 0	Wettingen, 12 May 1991
Switzerland (0) 0, Greece (0) 4	Aarau, 12 May 1991

	P	*W*	*D*	*L*	*F*	*A*	*Pts*
Greece	3	2	1	0	6	1	5
Portugal	3	2	1	0	4	1	5
Poland	3	0	1	2	1	3	1
Switzerland	3	0	1	2	1	7	1

GROUP C

France (0) 0, Finland (0) 0	Vevey, 8 May 1991
Romania (0) 1, Denmark (0) 1	Yverdon, 8 May 1991
Finland (1) 2, Denmark (1) 1	Renens, 10 May 1991
France (2) 3, Romania (0) 0	Yverdon, 10 May 1991

Finland (1) 1, Romania (1) 2	Vevey, 12 May 1991
France (1) 4, Denmark (0) 1	Renens, 12 May 1991

	P	*W*	*D*	*L*	*F*	*A*	*Pts*
France	3	2	1	0	7	1	5
Finland	3	1	1	1	3	3	3
Romania	3	1	1	1	3	5	3
Denmark	3	0	1	2	3	7	1

GROUP D

USSR (1) 1, Spain (2) 4	Baar, 8 May 1991
Yugoslavia (1) 1, Iceland (1) 2	Surse, 8 May 1991
Iceland (0) 1, Spain (1) 2	Hochdorf, 10 May 1991
Yugoslavia (0) 1, USSR (0) 3	Kussnacht, 10 May 1991
Iceland (0) 0, USSR (1) 2	Entlebuch, 12 May 1991
Yugoslavia (2) 3, Spain (2) 2	Menzingen, 12 May 1991

	P	*W*	*D*	*L*	*F*	*A*	*Pts*
Spain	3	2	0	1	8	5	4
USSR	3	2	0	1	6	5	4
Yugoslavia	3	1	0	2	5	7	2
Iceland	3	1	0	2	3	5	2

Semi-finals

West Germany (0) 1, France (0) 1 *aet* — Bulle, 15 May 1991
West Germany won on penalties

Greece (0) 0, Spain (0) 1 — Langenthal, 15 May 1991

Third-place match

France (1) 1, Greece (1) 1 *aet* — Berne, 18 May 1991
Greece won on penalties

Final

West Germany (0) 0, Spain (2) 2 — Berne, 18 May 1991

8th UEFA UNDER-18 CHAMPIONSHIP 1990–92

Group 1 *(Israel, Greece, Turkey, Switzerland)*

Greece (1) 1, Switzerland (0) 1	Rhodes, 10 October 1990
Israel (2) 2, Switzerland (0) 0	Herzelia, 16 October 1990
Turkey (1) 1, Israel (1) 1	Istanbul, 18 November 1990

Group 2 *(Cyprus, Romania, Hungary, Bulgaria)*

Hungary (0) 1, Romania (0) 0	Debrecen, 26 September 1990
Hungary (0) 0, Cyprus (0) 1	Budapest, 31 October 1990
Cyprus (1) 3, Bulgaria (1) 1	Lymbia, 14 November 1990
Romania (0) 3, Cyprus (0) 2	Tirgovist, 5 December 1990

Group 3 *(Portugal, France, Denmark, Luxembourg)*

Denmark (2) 7, Luxembourg (0) 0	Slagelse, 31 October 1990
Portugal (0) 0, France (0) 0	Lisbon, 31 October 1990
France (0) 2, Denmark (0) 0	Istres, 13 November 1990
Luxembourg (0) 0, Portugal (3) 5	Dudelange, 1 December 1990
France (0) 0, Portugal (2) 3	Sedan, 5 December 1990

Group 4 *(Italy, Spain, Malta, FR Germany)*

Italy (2) 9, Malta (0) 0	Siderno, 21 November 1990
Spain (0) 0, Italy (1) 2	Murcia, 20 December 1990
Malta (0) 1, Spain (0) 1	Ta'Qali, 13 February 1991

Group 5 *(England, Belgium, Iceland, Wales)*

Iceland (1) 2, England (1) 3	Varmarvol, 12 September 1990
Belgium (1) 1, Iceland (1) 1	Marche-en, 3 October 1990
England (0) 0, Belgium (0) 0	Sunderland, 16 October 1990

Group 6 *(Poland, Republic of Ireland, Scotland, Northern Ireland)*

Northern Ireland (0) 0, Republic of Ireland (1) 2	Lurgan, 9 October 1990
Poland (0) 1, Scotland (0) 0	Warjaw, 10 October 1990
Republic of Ireland (2) 2, Scotland (0) 1	Dublin, 6 November 1990
Poland (1) 3, Northern Ireland (0) 0	Warjaw, 7 November 1990

Group 7 *(Norway, Finland, Holland, Austria)*

Finland (0) 0, Norway (2) 2	Valkeakos, 18 September 1990
Norway (2) 4, Holland (0) 1	Stavanger, 10 October 1990

Group 8 *(Yugoslavia, USSR, Sweden, Czechoslovakia)*

Yugoslavia (2) 3, USSR (1) 2	Bogatic, 20 September 1990
Czechoslovakia (0) 2, Sweden (2) 2	Turnov, 26 September 1990
USSR (2) 3, Czechoslovakia (0) 0	Ternobol, 17 October 1990
Sweden (1) 1, Yugoslavia (0) 1	Kalmar, 18 October 1990

8th UEFA UNDER-21 TOURNAMENT 1990–92

Group 1 *(Czechoslovakia, Spain, France, Albania, Iceland)*

Iceland (0) 0, Albania (0) 0	Kopavoqur, 29 May 1990
Iceland (0) 0, France (0) 1	Reykjavik, 4 September 1990
Czechoslovakia (5) 7, Iceland (0) 0	Michalovc, 25 September 1990
Spain (2) 2, Iceland (0) 0	Puerto Sa, 9 October 1990
France (1) 1, Czechoslovakia (1) 2	Le Mans, 12 October 1990
Czechoslovakia (3) 3, Spain (0) 1	Ceske Bud, 13 November 1990
Albania (0) 0, France (0) 0	Berati, 16 November 1990
Spain (0) 1, Albania (0) 0	Huelva, 18 December 1990
France (0) 0, Spain (0) 1	Tours, 19 February 1991
France (0) 3, Albania (0) 0	29 March 1991
Albania (1) 1, Czechoslovakia (2) 5	30 April 1991
Albania (0) 2, Iceland (0) 1	25 May 1991

Group 2 *(Bulgaria, Scotland, Romania, Switzerland)*

Scotland (1) 2, Romania (0) 0	Edinburgh, 11 September 1990
Switzerland (0) 0, Bulgaria (0) 2	Yverdon, 11 September 1990
Romania (0) 0, Bulgaria (1) 1	Ploiesti, 16 October 1990
Scotland (2) 4, Switzerland (1) 2	Dunfermline, 16 October 1990
Bulgaria (2) 2, Scotland (0) 0	Sofia, 13 November 1990
Scotland (1) 1, Bulgaria (0) 0	26 March 1991
Switzerland (0) 0, Romania (1) 2	2 April 1991
Bulgaria (1) 1, Switzerland (0) 0	30 April 1991

Group 3 *(Norway, Italy, USSR, Hungary)*

USSR (1) 2, Norway (0) 2	Moscow, 11 September 1990
Norway (2) 3, Hungary (0) 1	Kristiansand, 9 October 1990
Italy (0) 1, Hungary (0) 0	Ferrara, 19 October 1990
Hungary (0) 0, USSR (0) 0	18 April 1991
Hungary (0) 0, Italy (0) 1	2 May 1991

Group 4 *(Denmark, Austria, Yugoslavia, San Marino, Liechtenstein)*

Liechtenstein (0) 0, Austria (3) 6	Balzers, 11 September 1990
Austria (6) 10, Liechtenstein (0) 0	Wien-Neud, 16 October 1990
San Marino (0) 0, Denmark (1) 3	San Marin, 17 October 1990
Yugoslavia (0) 1, Austria (0) 0	Maribor, 30 October 1990
Denmark (1) 3, Yugoslavia (0) 0	Aalborg, 13 November 1990
San Marino (0) 0, Austria (2) 2	San Marin, 21 November 1990
Yugoslavia (4) 5, San Marino (0) 0	13 March 1991
Austria (0) 3, San Marino (0) 0	Schwechat, 3 April 1991
Denmark (4) 7, San Marino (0) 0	17 April 1991
Yugoslavia (0) 2, Denmark (1) 6	30 April 1991

Group 5 *(Germany, Luxembourg, Belgium)*

Luxembourg (0) 0, Germany (0) 3	Lux.-Verl, 30 October 1990
Belgium (0) 2, Luxembourg (0) 0	Charleroi, 26 February 1991
Germany (1) 3, Belgium (1) 1	Osnabruck, 30 April 1991

Group 6 *(Portugal, Holland, Finland, Malta)*

Finland (0) 0, Portugal (1) 1	Lahti, 11 September 1990
Portugal (0) 0, Holland (0) 0	Porto, 16 October 1990
Malta (1) 1, Holland (2) 4	Ta'Qali, 18 December 1990
Malta (0) 1, Portugal (1) 3	Ta'Qali, 8 February 1991
Portugal (2) 2, Malta (0) 0	Porto, 19 February 1991
Holland (3) 7, Malta (0) 1	Utrecht, 12 March 1991
Holland (0) 1, Finland (0) 0	16 April 1991

Group 7 *(Poland, England, Republic of Ireland, Turkey)*

England (0) 0, Poland (0) 1	Tottenham, 16 October 1990
Republic of Ireland (1) 3, Turkey (1) 2	Dublin, 16 October 1990
Republic of Ireland (0) 0, England (1) 3	Cork, 13 November 1990
Turkey (0) 0, Poland (0) 1	Istanbul, 13 November 1990
England (1) 3, Republic of Ireland (0) 0	26 March 1991
Poland (1) 2, Turkey (0) 0	16 April 1991
Republic of Ireland (0) 1, Poland (0) 2	Dundalk, 30 April 1991
Turkey (1) 2, England (1) 2	30 April 1991

Group 8 *(Sweden, Israel, Cyprus, Greece)*

Sweden (2) 5, Greece (0) 0	Malmo, 31 October 1990
Cyprus (0) 1, Sweden (0) 1	Paphos, 21 November 1990
Greece (2) 2, Israel (1) 2	Xanthi, 21 November 1990
Israel (1) 4, Cyprus (0) 0	Haifa, 20 March 1991
Cyprus (1) 1, Greece (0) 0	Limassol, 17 April 1991
Sweden (2) 6, Cyprus (0) 0	Halsingborg, 1 May 1991

7th UEFA UNDER-21 TOURNAMENT 1988–90

Final
First leg

Yugoslavia (1) 2, USSR (2) 4	Sarajevo, 5 September 1990

Second leg

USSR (1) 3, Yugoslavia (0) 1	Simferopol, 17 October 1990

GM VAUXHALL CONFERENCE 1990–91

GM VAUXHALL CONFERENCE TABLE 1990–91

		Home			*Goals*		*Away*			*Goals*		
	P	*W*	*D*	*L*	*F*	*A*	*W*	*D*	*L*	*F*	*A*	*Pts*
Barnet	42	13	4	4	50	23	13	5	3	53	29	87
Colchester United	42	16	4	1	41	13	9	6	6	27	22	85
Altrincham	42	12	6	3	48	22	11	7	3	39	24	82
Kettering Town	42	12	6	3	38	19	11	5	5	29	26	80
Wycombe Wanderers	42	15	3	3	46	17	6	8	7	29	29	74
Telford United	42	11	3	7	30	21	9	4	8	32	31	67
Macclesfield Town	42	11	4	6	38	22	6	8	7	25	30	63
Runcorn	42	12	4	5	44	29	4	6	11	25	38	58
Merthyr Tydfil	42	9	5	7	37	24	7	4	10	25	37	57
Barrow	42	10	8	3	34	24	5	4	12	25	41	57
Welling United	42	7	10	4	33	27	6	5	10	22	30	54
Northwich Victoria	42	8	7	6	33	30	5	6	10	32	45	52
Kidderminster Harriers	42	8	5	8	33	30	6	5	10	23	37	52
Yeovil Town	42	9	5	7	38	29	4	6	11	20	29	50
Stafford Rangers	42	7	9	5	30	26	5	5	11	18	25	50
Cheltenham Town	42	8	6	7	29	25	4	6	11	25	47	48
Gateshead	42	10	3	8	32	38	4	3	14	20	54	48
Boston United	42	9	4	8	40	31	3	7	11	15	38	47
Slough Town	42	9	4	8	31	29	4	2	15	20	51	45
Bath City	42	9	4	8	39	27	1	8	12	16	34	42
Sutton United	42	6	6	9	29	33	4	3	14	33	49	39
Fisher Athletic	42	3	9	9	22	30	2	6	13	16	49	30

GM VAUXHALL CONFERENCE LEADING GOALSCORERS 1990–91

GMVC			*FA*	*BL*	*FT*
30	Gary Bull (Barnet	+	2	—	—
24	Mark West (Wycombe Wanderers)	+	6	—	3
22	Ken McKenna (Altrincham	+	3	2	3
19	Mark Carter (Barnet)	+	—	1	1
	Paul Randall (Bath City)	+	—	—	3
18	Colin Cowperthwaite (Barrow)	+	—	2	1
	Terry Robbins (Welling United)	+	2	1	—
17	Mario Walsh (Colchester United)	+	—	—	1
16	Paul Cavell (Boston United)	+	5	1	2
	Nicky Evans (Barnet)	+	5	—	—
15	Charlie Butler (Gateshead)	+	—	1	—
	Peter Howell (Kidderminster Harriers)	+	—	1	4
14	John Askey (Macclesfield Town)	+	—	—	—
	John Brady (Altrincham)	+	1	—	2
	Kim Casey (Cheltenham Town)	+	2	—	1

FA: FA Cup. *BL:* Bob Lord Trophy. *FT:* FA Challenge Trophy.

GM VAUXHALL CONFERENCE RESULTS 1990–91

	Altrincham	Barnet	Barrow	Bath City	Boston United	Cheltenham Town	Colchester United	Fisher Athletic	Gateshead	Kettering Town	Kidderminster Harriers	Macclesfield Town	Merthyr Tydfil	Northwich Victoria	Runcorn	Slough Town	Stafford Rangers	Sutton United	Telford United	Welling United	Wycombe Wanderers	Yeovil Town
Altrincham	—	4-1	1-1	2-0	1-1	3-0	2-2	0-0	4-1	3-2	1-2	5-2	9-2	0-2	1-0	3-0	0-0	4-1	2-1	0-1	1-0	2-2
Barnet	0-0	—	3-1	2-0	5-0	2-1	1-3	8-1	1-1	0-1	2-3	3-1	2-3	1-1	2-0	6-1	2-0	1-0	0-0	3-2	3-2	3-2
Barrow	1-0	4-2	—	1-1	1-1	0-0	2-2	3-1	3-1	0-1	1-3	1-1	0-2	2-2	2-1	2-1	2-0	3-1	2-1	1-1	2-2	1-0
Bath City	2-3	1-4	1-1	—	1-0	2-0	1-2	0-1	3-0	3-3	4-1	0-2	0-0	4-1	6-1	4-0	0-1	2-2	0-1	2-1	1-2	2-1
Boston United	2-6	1-3	0-2	3-0	—	2-1	1-3	4-1	5-1	1-2	3-1	1-1	3-0	4-1	2-2	0-1	0-2	2-2	2-1	0-0	0-1	4-0
Cheltenham Town	1-4	1-4	3-1	0-0	5-0	—	1-2	0-0	1-0	2-2	0-0	2-2	0-1	1-1	1-3	2-0	1-2	3-2	0-1	3-0	1-0	1-0
Colchester United	1-1	0-0	1-0	2-0	3-1	3-1	—	2-1	3-0	3-1	2-0	1-0	3-1	4-0	2-2	2-1	2-0	1-0	2-0	2-1	2-2	0-1
Fisher Athletic	0-0	2-4	1-2	0-3	1-2	1-1	0-0	—	0-2	0-0	1-1	1-2	0-0	5-2	0-1	1-1	1-3	1-1	2-0	1-1	2-3	2-1
Gateshead	0-3	1-3	5-1	2-0	0-1	3-3	1-2	1-0	—	1-2	2-1	1-1	1-0	0-4	3-1	1-0	2-1	0-9	5-1	0-3	2-1	1-1
Kettering Town	1-1	1-3	2-0	1-1	1-1	5-1	1-0	3-2	1-0	—	4-1	2-0	2-0	1-0	3-0	0-0	2-0	5-2	2-5	0-0	0-1	1-1
Kidderminster Harriers	0-1	0-3	3-1	3-2	3-3	2-0	0-0	3-3	2-3	3-0	—	0-0	1-2	3-1	3-1	1-2	2-1	1-0	1-3	1-2	1-2	0-0
Macclesfield Town	0-1	3-2	3-0	3-1	2-0	5-1	1-0	1-1	4-0	1-2	0-0	—	0-1	1-2	2-1	1-2	2-1	4-2	1-2	2-1	0-0	2-1
Merthyr Tydfil	0-2	1-1	0-2	0-0	2-0	3-0	3-0	7-0	3-1	1-3	1-2	0-2	—	3-2	0-0	3-0	1-1	3-0	2-3	1-0	2-4	1-1
Northwich Victoria	1-1	0-2	2-2	2-0	3-1	5-2	2-2	0-0	3-2	0-1	1-1	4-1	0-3	—	1-4	1-0	1-1	1-0	2-4	1-2	1-1	2-0
Runcorn	1-3	3-2	3-1	1-1	2-1	2-2	0-3	5-1	2-0	2-1	5-1	1-2	2-1	2-1	—	3-1	1-0	5-1	0-0	2-3	1-1	0-3
Slough Town	3-3	1-3	3-0	2-0	2-0	0-3	0-2	1-0	1-1	0-3	0-0	0-1	1-2	2-4	2-1	—	2-1	1-2	2-0	3-0	3-3	2-0
Stafford Rangers	2-1	2-2	2-2	2-1	1-2	2-2	0-2	2-0	0-1	0-0	3-1	2-2	2-0	0-0	1-1	3-4	—	1-2	1-1	1-0	2-1	1-1
Sutton United	1-2	0-1	2-1	1-1	0-0	2-3	0-1	3-1	3-3	1-2	1-2	3-1	1-1	2-2	1-3	5-2	0-3	—	0-3	1-1	1-0	1-0
Telford	1-2	1-1	0-1	2-2	1-0	1-2	2-0	3-1	1-2	0-1	1-0	1-2	3-1	1-0	2-0	2-1	0-0	4-2	—	2-1	1-0	1-2
Welling United	2-2	1-4	4-2	2-1	0-0	0-0	1-1	1-1	6-0	0-0	1-0	0-0	2-1	4-5	2-2	2-0	2-1	1-2	1-1	—	1-1	0-3
Wycombe Wanderers	3-0	1-3	2-1	0-0	3-0	0-2	1-0	2-0	4-0	5-1	2-3	0-0	2-1	3-0	1-1	2-1	3-0	4-1	3-2	4-1	—	2-0
Yeovil Town	2-3	1-4	0-3	3-2	1-1	4-0	2-0	0-1	4-1	0-1	2-0	2-1	3-3	1-1	1-0	7-2	0-0	2-1	1-2	0-1	2-2	—

OVENDEN PAPERS FOOTBALL COMBINATION

	P	*W*	*D*	*L*	*F*	*A*	*Pts*
Chelsea	38	24	7	7	93	43	79
Tottenham Hotspur	38	24	6	8	79	37	78
Crystal Palace	38	21	10	7	90	44	73
Wimbledon	38	22	7	9	64	36	73
Southampton	38	20	8	10	68	50	68
Portsmouth	38	19	8	11	67	46	65
Arsenal	38	19	8	11	65	54	65
Norwich City	38	15	12	11	61	52	57
Luton Town	38	15	9	14	66	52	54
QPR	38	14	8	16	60	62	50
Charlton Athletic	38	14	7	17	66	65	49
Oxford Utd	38	14	6	18	57	57	48
Millwall	38	11	11	16	63	69	44
West Ham Utd	38	12	8	18	57	90	44
Swindon Town	38	12	7	19	60	77	43
Ipswich Town	38	11	7	20	40	[illegible]	40
Brighton & Hove Albion	38	11	6	21	48	69	39
Fulham	38	11	6	21	42	75	39
Watford	38	9	9	20	46	84	36
Reading	38	4	6	28	24	88	18

PONTIN'S CENTRAL LEAGUE

Division One

	P	*W*	*D*	*L*	*F*	*A*	*Pts*
Sheffield Wednesday	34	23	6	5	69	36	75
Nottingham Forest	34	21	6	7	92	51	69
Manchester United	34	20	5	9	55	35	65
Liverpool	34	17	5	12	60	39	56
Everton	34	16	5	13	59	51	53
Rotherham United	34	14	9	11	56	51	51
Aston Villa	34	12	11	11	39	48	47
Sunderland	34	13	7	14	63	60	46
Leeds United	34	11	12	11	44	47	45
Blackburn Rovers	34	12	8	14	56	51	44
Coventry City	34	10	13	11	46	48	43
Sheffield United	34	12	6	16	58	72	42
Newcastle United	34	12	5	17	46	52	41
Manchester City	34	11	6	17	47	59	39
Derby County	34	9	10	15	30	42	37
Huddersfield Town	34	8	10	16	36	66	34
Wolverhampton Wanderers	34	8	8	18	42	73	32
Leicester City	34	7	8	19	41	62	29

Division Two

	P	W	D	L	F	A	Pts
West Bromwich Albion	34	23	7	4	77	27	76
Barnsley	34	23	7	4	84	39	76
Bolton Wanderers	34	17	9	8	70	42	60
Bradford City	34	19	3	12	71	52	60
Hull City	34	18	5	11	61	49	59
Notts County	34	16	6	12	56	46	54
Middlesbrough	34	15	8	11	62	50	53
Burnley	34	13	11	10	53	48	50
Port Vale	34	14	5	15	61	72	47
Oldham Athletic	34	12	7	15	81	79	43
Stoke City	34	12	5	17	51	67	41
Scunthorpe United	34	10	10	14	45	60	40
Mansfield Town	34	10	8	16	45	49	38
York City	34	11	5	18	53	78	38
Grimsby Town	34	10	5	19	28	56	35
Blackpool	34	9	6	19	62	84	33
Wigan Athletic	34	9	3	22	56	94	30
Preston North End	34	6	8	20	59	83	26

HIGHLAND LEAGUE

	P	W	D	L	F	A	Pts
Ross County	34	24	4	6	91	37	76
Inverness Caledonian	34	23	4	7	87	40	73
Cove Rangers	34	23	2	9	95	52	71
Forres Mechanics	34	22	3	9	77	49	69
Inverness Thistle	34	20	5	9	55	38	65
Huntly	34	17	10	7	79	52	61
Elgin City	34	17	6	11	84	53	57
Peterhead	34	13	11	10	50	45	50
Brora Rangers	34	13	10	11	66	54	49
Lossiemouth	34	14	5	15	69	61	47
Buckie Thistle	34	12	7	15	47	52	43
Fort William	34	11	10	13	76	85	43
Fraserburgh	34	11	8	15	54	56	41
Keith	34	11	4	19	37	55	37
Deveronvale	34	7	9	18	37	91	30
Clachnacuddin	34	8	2	24	42	92	26
Nairn County	34	4	3	27	36	104	15
Rothes	34	2	5	27	36	102	11

FA CHALLENGE YOUTH CUP 1990–91

First Round Qualifying

Stockton v Billingham Synthonia 2-0
Guisborough Town v Murton 4-1
Rotherham United v Huddersfield Town 2-1
York City v Scarborough 1-0
Accrington Stanley v Blackpool Mechanics 3-1
Bolton Wanderers v Marine 5-1
Bury v Shrewsbury Town 2-0
Rochdale v Chester City 2-2, 2-1*
*(*Replay at Rochdale*)
Lye Town v Willenhall Town 1-2
Leek Town v Telford United 0-3
Alvechurch v Burton Albion 4-0
Moor Green v Kidderminster Harriers 0-3
Cambridge City v Rothwell Town 9-1
Norwich City v Nuneaton Borough 9-0
Bishops Stortford v Witham Town 5-1
Canvey Island v Basildon United 3-4
(*at Basildon United*)
East Thurrock United v St Albans City 0-5
Enfield v Boreham Wood 5-0
Fisher Athletic v Kingsbury Town 1-1, 5-0
Finchley v Clapton 0-1
Slough Town v Wycombe Wanderers 2-6
Bedfont Town v Hillingdon Borough 2-1
Northwood v Maidenhead United 3-5
Uxbridge v Egham Town 0-3
Ringmer v Chatham Town 0-6
Herne Bay v Dover Athletic 0-2
Three Bridges v Worthing 1-3
Shoreham v Horsham YMCA 4-2
Malden Vale v Walton & Hersham 1-10
Feltham v Carshalton Athletic 1-2
Bicester Town v Hungerford Town 1-1. 5-1
(*at Witney Town*)
Basingstoke Town v Aldershot 0-7
Frome Town v Torquay United 0-7
Romsey Town v Exeter City 0-3
Gloucester City v Bristol Rovers 2-4
Trowbridge Town v Worcester City 3-3, 0-3

Second Round Qualifying

Stockton v Guisborough Town 1-5
Rotherham United v York City 1-2
Accrington Stanley v Bolton Wanderers 0-3
Bury v Rochdale 4-1
Willenhall Town v Telford United 1-2
Alvechurch v Kidderminster Harriers 4-3
Cambridge City v Norwich City 3-3, 1-2
Bishops Stortford v Basildon United 1-2
St Albans City v Enfield 0-3
Fisher Athletic v Clapton 0-1
Wycombe Wanderers v Bedfont Town 3-1
Maidenhead United v Egham Town 2-6
Chatham Town v Dover Athletic 0-1
Worthing v Shoreham 2-2, 0-4
Walton & Hersham v Carshalton Athletic 2-2, 0-6
Bicester Town v Aldershot 1-3
(*at Witney Town*)
Torquay United v Exeter City 1-1, 1-2
Bristol Rovers v Worcester City 11-0

First Round Proper

Oldham Athletic v Bolton Wanderers 2-0
Wigan Athletic v Burnley 0-3
Bury v Tranmere Rovers 3-0
York City v Sunderland 3-0
Port Vale v Wolverhampton Wanderers 0-1
Oxford United v Hendon 3-0
Wokingham Town v Egham Town 1-1, 1-3
Epsom & Ewell v Dover Athletic 4-0
Basildon United v Carshalton Athletic 0-0, 2-5
Whyteleafe v Enfield 3-3, 2-1
Clapton v Gillingham 1-4
Bristol City v Exeter City 1-2
Newbury Town v Swansea City 1-9

Second Round Proper

Bradford City v Sheffield United 3-0
Everton v Scunthorpe United 1-0
Hull City v York City 1-1, 2-1
Liverpool v Middlesbrough 3-0
Sheffield Wednesday v Bury 4-1
Newcastle United v Oldham Athletic 2-0
Darlington v Manchester United 0-6
Manchester City v Barnsley 0-1

Doncaster Rovers v Burnley 4-0
Blackburn Rovers v Leeds United 1-1, 1-3
Leyton Orient v Ipswich Town 2-1
West Bromwich Albion v Peterborough United 3-2
Wolverhampton Wanderers v Walsall 0-2
Notts County v Arsenal 0-0, 1-1, 2-1
Leicester City v Coventry City 2-3
Birmingham City v Tottenham Hotspur 1-0
Alvechurch v Crewe Alexandra 0-4
Watford v Luton Town 1-0
Southend United v Stoke City 0-0, 3-2
Derby County v Aston Villa 0-3
Colchester United v Carshalton Athletic 3-2
Whyteleafe v Epsom & Ewell 2-3
Egham Town v Exeter City 0-0, 0-2
Charlton Athletic v Plymouth Argyle 1-2
Portsmouth v Hereford United 2-1
Wimbledon v Oxford United 3-0
Reading v Swansea City 1-1, 1-2
Brentford v Chelsea 2-2, 1-1, 4-7
Swindon Town v Millwall 0-1
Aldershot v West Ham United 1-1, 0-4
Crystal Palace v Queens Park Rangers 3-3, 1-0
Gillingham v Southampton 2-3

Third Round Proper
Bradford City v Barnsley 2-1
Aston Villa v Sheffield Wednesday 2-3
Doncaster Rovers v Leeds United 0-3
Walsall v Liverpool 2-2, 1-4
Manchester United v Everton 1-1, 2-1
Newcastle United v West Bromwich Albion 1-2
Crewe Alexandra v Hull City 0-2
Millwall v Portsmouth 3-1
Leyton Orient v Birmingham City 1-2
Swansea City v Colchester United 1-3
Plymouth Argyle v Epsom & Ewell 2-0
Wimbledon v Coventry City 2-0
Watford v Notts County 0-0, 1-2
Southend United v West Ham United 1-5
Southampton v Exeter City 6-0
Chelsea v Crystal Palace 4-0

Fourth Round Proper
Plymouth Argyle v Millwall 0-1
Liverpool v Manchester United 1-3
Chelsea v Wimbledon 2-2, 0-2
Sheffield Wednesday v West Bromwich Albion 2-1
West Ham United v Birmingham City 2-0
Southampton v Bradford City 4-0
Leeds United v Hull City 1-2
Notts County v Colchester United 2-0

Fifth Round Proper
Sheffield Wednesday v Hull City 1-1, 1-1, 5-1
Southampton v Manchester United 0-2
West Ham United v Notts County 3-1
Millwall v Wimbledon 1-1, 3-2

Semi-final first leg
West Ham United v Millwall 1-2
Sheffield Wednesday v Manchester United 1-1

Second leg
Millwall v West Ham United 2-0
Manchester United v Sheffield Wednesday 0-1

FINAL First Leg
1 May
Sheffield Wednesday (0) 0
Millwall (1) 3 (*Lee, Devine, Walker)* 1666
Sheffield Wednesday: Robinson P; Linighan, Dunn, Simpson, Stewart, Burton, Rowntree, Jones, Robinson N, Chambers, Curzon.
Millwall: Emberson; McArthur, Dolby, Roberts, Foran, Lee, Dickson, Devine, Walker, Manning, Smith.
Referee: I. Borrett

Second Leg
7 May
Millwall (0) 0
Sheffield Wednesday (0) 0 4271
Millwall: Emberson; McArthur, Dolby, Roberts, Foran, Lee, Dickson, Devine, Walker, Manning, Smith.
Sheffield Wednesday: Robinson P; Linighan, Dunn, Simpson, Stewart, Burton, Rowntree, Jones, Robinson N, Chambers, Curzon.
Referee: I. Borrett

OTHER AWARDS 1990–91

FOOTBALLER OF THE YEAR

The Football Writers' Association Award for the Footballer of the Year went to Gordon Strachan of Leeds United and Scotland.

Past Winners

1947–48 Stanley Matthews (Blackpool), 1948–49 Johnny Carey (Manchester U), 1949–50 Joe Mercer (Arsenal), 1950–51 Harry Johnston (Blackpool), 1951–52 Billy Wright (Wolverhampton W), 1952–53 Nat Lofthouse (Bolton W), 1953–54 Tom Finney (Preston NE), 1954–55 Don Revie (Manchester C), 1955–56 Bert Trautmann (Manchester C), 1956–57 Tom Finney (Preston NE), 1957–58 Danny Blanchflower (Tottenham H), 1958–59 Syd Owen (Luton T), 1959–60 Bill Slater (Wolverhampton W), 1960–61 Danny Blanchflower (Tottenham H), 1961–62 Jimmy Adamson (Burnley), 1962–63 Stanley Matthews (Stoke C), 1963–64 Bobby Moore (West Ham U), 1964–65 Bobby Collins (Leeds U), 1965–66 Bobby Charlton (Manchester U), 1966–67 Jackie Charlton (Leeds U), 1967–68 George Best (Manchester U), 1968–69 Dave Mackay (Derby Co) shared with Tony Book (Manchester C), 1969–70 Billy Bremner (Leeds U), 1970–71 Frank McLintock (Arsenal), 1971–72 Gordon Banks (Stoke C), 1972–73 Pat Jennings (Tottenham H), 1973–74 Ian Callaghan (Liverpool), 1974–75 Alan Mullery (Fulham), 1975–76 Kevin Keegan (Liverpool), 1976–77 Emlyn Hughes (Liverpool), 1977–78 Kenny Burns (Nottingham F), 1978–79 Kenny Dalglish (Liverpool), 1979–80 Terry McDermott (Liverpool), 1980–81 Frans Thijssen (Ipswich T), 1981–82 Steve Perryman (Tottenham H), 1982–83 Kenny Dalglish (Liverpool), 1983–84 Ian Rush (Liverpool), 1984–85 Neville Southall (Everton), 1985–86 Gary Lineker (Everton), 1986–87 Clive Allen (Tottenham H), 1987–88 John Barnes (Liverpool), 1988–89 Steve Nicol (Liverpool), 1989–90 John Barnes (Liverpool).

THE PFA AWARDS 1991

Player of the Year: Mark Hughes (Manchester U).

Previous Winners: 1974 Norman Hunter (Leeds U); 1975 Colin Todd (Derby Co); 1976 Pat Jennings (Tottenham H); 1977 Andy Gray (Aston Villa); 1978 Peter Shilton (Nottingham F); 1979 Liam Brady (Arsenal); 1980 Terry McDermott (Liverpool); 1981 John Wark (Ipswich T); 1982 Kevin Keegan (Southampton); 1983 Kenny Dalglish (Liverpool); 1984 Ian Rush (Liverpool); 1985 Peter Reid (Everton); 1986 Gary Lineker (Everton); 1987 Clive Allen (Tottenham H); 1988 John Barnes (Liverpool); 1989 Mark Hughes (Manchester U); 1990 David Platt (Aston Villa).

Young Player of the Year: Lee Sharpe (Manchester U).

Previous Winners: 1974 Kevin Beattie (Ipswich T); 1975 Mervyn Day (West Ham U); 1976 Peter Barnes (Manchester C); 1977 Andy Gray (Aston Villa); 1978 Tony Woodcock (Nottingham F); 1979 Cyrille Regis (WBA); 1980 Glenn Hoddle (Tottenham H); 1981 Gary Shaw (Aston Villa); 1982 Steve Moran (Southampton); 1983 Ian Rush (Liverpool); 1984 Paul Walsh (Luton T); 1985 Mark Hughes (Manchester U); 1986 Tony Cottee (West Ham U); 1987 Tony Adams (Arsenal); 1988 Paul Gascoigne (Tottenham H); 1989 Paul Merson (Arsenal); 1990 Matthew Le Tissier (Southampton).

Merit Award: Tommy Hutchison.

Previous Winners: 1974 Bobby Charlton CBE, Cliff Lloyd OBE; 1975 Denis Law; 1976 George Eastham OBE; 1977 Jack Taylor OBE; 1978 Bill Shankly OBE; 1979 Tom Finney OBE; 1980 Sir Matt Busby CBE; 1981 John Trollope MBE; 1982 Joe Mercer OBE; 1983 Bob Paisley OBE; 1984 Bill Nicholson; 1985 Ron Greenwood; 1986 The 1966 England World Cup team, Sir Alf Ramsey, Harold Shepherdson; 1987 Sir Stanley Matthews; 1988 Billy Bonds MBE; 1989 Nat Lofthouse; 1990 Peter Shilton.

BARCLAYS BANK MANAGER OF THE YEAR 1990–91

George Graham of Barclays League Champions Arsenal, was named Barclays Bank Manager of the Year for the second time in three years by a panel of 30 leading football journalists and commentators. He received the Barclays trophy and a Barclays Higher Rate Deposit Account cheque for £5,000 prior to the Gunners last home match of the seasons. The presentation was made by Sir John Quinton, chairman of Barclays Bank.

It was Graham's twelfth managerial award in eight years – his eighth in the past five years since being appointed at Arsenal: the first four were at Millwall.

It is the fifth time a Scot has won the award in the past six years – Kenny Dalglish, having received the accolade in 1986, 1988 and 1990; and the ninth time a Scot has taken the top manager title in 26 years (Jock Stein in 1966 and 1967, Matt Busby in 1968 and Bill Shankly in 1973).

BARCLAYS BANK DIVISIONAL MANAGERS OF THE SEASON 1990–91

Barclays Bank Managers of the Season 1990–91 – each manager of the winning Barclays League Championship club in Divisions Two, Three and Four – received their awards at the Barclays Bank Managers Awards Luncheon at the Savoy Hotel in London.

Joe Royle (Oldham Athletic) in Division Two, John Beck (Cambridge United) and Brian Little (Darlington) each received a Silver Eagle trophy and a cheque for £1,000 from Mr Alastair Robinson, executive director of Barclays Bank.

Alex Ferguson, European Cup Winners' Cup-winning manager for a second time when Manchester United triumphed in Rotterdam, was named for a Barclays Bank Special Award – a Silver Eagle and a cheque for £1,000; and Ron Atkinson of Sheffield Wednesday, promoted to Division One and League Cup victors, was nominated for a Barclays Bank Special Award (a Silver Eagle plus a cheque for £1,000) by The football League.

BARCLAYS YOUNG EAGLE OF THE YEAR 1991

Lee Sharpe of Manchester United, whose exciting wing play helped take the Old Trafford club to their second major final, was named Barclays Young Eagle of the Year 1991 by a panel, chaired by England team manager Graham Taylor, which includes Jack Charlton, Jimmy Armfield, Ron Greenwood, Bill Nicholson, Stan Cullis, Trevor Cherry and Terry Yorath.

Nineteen-year-old Lee – named PFA Young Player of the Year by his fellow professionals in March – received a Silver Eagle trophy and a Barclays Higher Rate Deposit Account cheque for £5,000.

BRITISH FOOTBALL RECORDS

HIGHEST SCORES

First class match
Arbroath 36 Bon Accord 0 *Scottish Cup 1st Rd, 12.9.1885.*
International match
England 13 Ireland 0 *Belfast, 18.2.1882.*
Football League Tranmere R 13, Oldham Ath 4, *Division 3 (N) 26.12.1935*
FA Cup
Preston NE 26 Hyde U 0 *1st Rd, 15.10.1887*
League Cup
West Ham U 10 Bury 0 *2nd Rd, 2nd leg, 25.10.1983*
Liverpool 10 Fulham 0 *2nd Rd, 1st leg, 23.9.1986*
Scottish League
East Fife 13 Edinburgh C 2 *Division 2, 11.12.1937*

MOST GOALS IN A SEASON

Football League
128 in 42 games, Aston Villa *Division 1, 1930–31*
128 in 42 games, Bradford C *Division 3 (N), 1928–29*
134 in 46 games, Peterborough U *Division 4, 1960–61*
Scottish League
142 in 34 games, Raith R *Division 2, 1937–38*

FEWEST GOALS IN A SEASON

Football League *(minimun 42 games)*
24 in 42 games, Stoke C *Division 1, 1984–85*
24 in 42 games, Watford *Division 2, 1971–72*
27 in 46 games, Stockport Co *Division 3, 1969–70*
Scottish League *(minimum 30 games)*
18 in 39 games, Stirling A *Division 1, 1980–81*

MOST GOALS AGAINST IN A SEASON

Football League
141 in 34 games, Darwen *Division 2, 1898–99*
Scottish League
146 in 38 games, Edinburgh C *Division 2, 1931–32*

FEWEST GOALS AGAINST IN A SEASON

Football League *(Minimum 42 games)*
16 in 42 games, Liverpool *Division 1, 1978–79*
21 in 46 games, Port Vale *Division 3 (N), 1953–54*
Scottish League *(minimum 30 games)*
14 in 38 games, Celtic *Division 1, 1913–14*

MOST POINTS IN A SEASON

Football League *(2 points for a win)*
72 in 42 games, Doncaster R *Division 3 (N), 1946–47*
74 in 46 games, Lincoln C *Division 4, 1975–76*

Football League *(3 points for a win)*
76 in 38 games, Arsenal *Division 1, 1988–89*
76 in 38 games, Liverpool *Division 1, 1988–89*
90 in 40 games, Liverpool *Division 1, 1987–88*
90 in 42 games, Everton *Division 1, 1984–85*
102 in 46 games, Swindon T *Division 4, 1985–86*
Scottish League
72 in 44 games, Celtic *Premier Division, 1987–88*
69 in 38 games, Morton *Division 2, 1966–67*
76 in 42 games, Rangers *Division 1, 1920–21*

FEWEST POINTS IN A SEASON

Football League *(minimum 34 games)*
8 in 34 games, Doncaster R *Division 2, 1904–5*
8 in 34 games, Loughborough T *Division 2, 1899–1900*
11 in 40 games, Rochdale *Division 3 (N), 1931–32*
17 in 42 games, Stoke C *Division 1, 1984–85*
19 in 46 games, Workington *Division 4, 1976–77*
Scottish League *(minimum 30 games)*
6 in 30 games, Stirling A *Division 1, 1954–55*
7 in 34 games, Edinburgh C *Division 2, 1936–37*
11 in 36 games, St Johnstone *Premier Division, 1975–76*

MOST WINS IN A SEASON

Football League
33 in 42 games, Doncaster R *Division 3 (N), 1946–47*
Scottish League
27 in 36 games, Aberdeen *Premier Division, 1984–85*
33 in 38 games, Morton *Division 2, 1966–67*
35 in 42 games, Rangers *Division 1, 1920–21*
Home
Brentford won all 21 games in Division 3(S) in 1929–30
Away
Doncaster R won 18 out of 21 games in Division 3(N) in 1946–47

FEWEST WINS IN A SEASON

Football League *(Minimum 34 games)*
1 in 34 games, Loughborough T *Division 2, 1899–1900*
2 in 46 games, Rochdale *Division 3, 1973–74*
Scottish League *(mimimum 22 games)*
0 in 22 games, Vale of Leven *Division 1, 1891–92*
1 in 38 games, Forfar Ath *Division 2, 1974–75*

MOST DEFEATS IN A SEASON

Football League
33 in 40 games, Rochdale *Division 3(N), 1931–32*
Scottish League
30 in 36 games, Brechin C *Division 2, 1962–63*
31 in 42 games, St Mirren *Division 1, 1920–21*

FEWEST DEFEATS IN A SEASON

Football League *(minimum 20 games)*
0 in 22 games, Preston NE *Division 1, 1888–89*
0 in 28 games, Liverpool *Division 2, 1893–94*
1 in 38 games, Arsenal *Division 1, 1990–91*
2 in 40 games, Liverpool *Division 1, 1987–88*
2 in 42 games, Leeds U *Division 1, 1968–69*
3 in 46 games, Port Vale *Division 3(N), 1953–54*
Scottish League *(minimum 20 games)*
1 in 42 games, Rangers *Division 1, 1920–21*

MOST DRAWS IN A SEASON

Football League
23 in 42 games, Norwich C *Division 1, 1978–79*
23 in 46 games, Exeter C, *Division 4, 1986–87*
Scottish League
19 in 44 games, Hibernian *Premier Division, 1987–88*
21 in 44 games, East Fife *Division 1, 1986–87*

MOST GOALS IN A GAME

Football League
10, Joe Payne, for Luton T v Bristol R *Division 3(S), 13.4.1936*
Scottish League
8, Jimmy McGrory, for Celtic v Dunfermline Ath *Division 1, 14.9.1928*
8, Owen McNally, for Arthurlie v Armadale *Division 2, 1.10.1927*
8, Jim Dyet, for King's Park v Forfar Ath *Division 2, 2.1.1930*
8, John Calder, for Morton v Raith R *Division 2, 18.4.1936*
FA Cup
9, Ted McDougall, for Bournemouth v Margate *1st Rd, 20.11.1971*
Scottish Cup
13, John Petrie, for Arbroath v Bon Accord *1st Rd, 12.9.1885*

MOST LEAGUE GOALS IN A SEASON

Football League
60 in 39 games, W.R. "Dixie" Dean (Everton) *Division 1, 1927–28*
59 in 37 games, George Camsell (Middlesbrough) *Division 2, 1926–27*
Scottish League
66 in 38 games, Jim Smith (Ayr U) *Division 2, 1927–28*
52 in 34 games, William McFadyen (Motherwell) *Division 1, 1931–32*

MOST LEAGUE GOALS IN A CAREER

Football League
434 in 619 games, Arthur Rowley *(WBA, Fulham, Leicester C, Shrewsbury T, 1946–65)*
Scottish League
410 in 408 games, Jimmy McGrory *(Celtic, Clydebank, Celtic, 1922–38)*

MOST CUP WINNERS' MEDALS

FA Cup
5, James Forrest (Blackburn R) *1884, 1885, 1886, 1890, 1891*
5, Hon. A.F. Kinnaird (Wanderers) *1873, 1877, 1878,* (Old Etonians) *1879, 1882*
5, C.H.R. Wollaston (Wanderers) *1872, 1873, 1876, 1877, 1878*

Scottish Cup
7, Jimmy McMenemy, (Celtic) *1904, 1907, 1908, 1911, 1912, 1914,* (Partick T) *1921*
7, Bob McPhail, (Airdrieonians) *1924,* (Rangers) *1928, 1930, 1932, 1934, 1935, 1936*
7, Billy McNeill (Celtic) *1965, 1967, 1969, 1971, 1972, 1974, 1975*

RECORD ATTENDANCES
Football League
83,260 Manchester U v Arsenal, Maine Road, 17.1.1948
Scottish League
118,567, Rangers v Celtic, Ibrox Stadium, 2.1.1939
FA Cup-tie (other than the final)
84,569, Manchester C v Stoke C, 6th Rd at Maine Road, 3.3.1934 (*a British record for any game outside London or Glasgow*)
FA Cup Final
126,047*, Bolton W v West Ham U, Wembley, 28.4.1923 **The figure stated is the official one. Perhaps as many as 70,000 more got in without paying.*
European Cup
135,826, Celtic v Leeds U, semi-final at Hampden Park, 15.4.1970

TRANSFER MILESTONES
First four-figure transaction
Alf Common: Sunderland to Middlesbrough £1,000, February 1905.
First five-figure transaction
David Jack: Bolton W to Arsenal £10,340, October 1928.
First six-figure transaction
Alan Ball: Blackpool to Everton £112,000, August 1966.
First £200,000 transaction
Martin Peters: West Ham U to Tottenham H £200,000, March 1970
First seven-figure transaction
Trevor Francis: Birmingham C to Nottingham F £1,000,000, February 1979.
First £2,000,000 transaction
Paul Gascoigne: Newcastle U to Tottenham H £2,000,000, July 1988.
Highest British Transaction
David Platt: Aston Villa to Bari £5,500,000, July 1991.

MOST GOALS IN AN INTERNATIONAL MATCH
England
5, Malcolm Macdonald (Newcastle U) v Cyprus, Wembley, 16.4.1975
5, Willie Hall (Tottenham H) v Ireland, Old Trafford, 16.11.1938
5, G.O. Smith (Corinthians) v Ireland, Sunderland, 18.2.1899
5*, Steve Bloomer (Derby Co) v Wales, Cardiff, 16.3.1896 *(*one of which was credited to him in only some sources)*
5, Oliver Vaughton (Aston Villa) v Ireland, Belfast 18.2.1882
Scotland
5, Charles Heggie (Rangers) v Ireland, Belfast, 20.3.1886
Ireland
6, Joe Bambrick (Linfield) v Wales, Belfast, 1.2.1930
Wales
4, James Price (Wrexham) v Ireland, Wrexham, 25.2.1882
4, Mel Charles (Cardiff C) v N. Ireland, Cardiff, 11.4.1962
4, Ian Edwards (Chester) v Malta, Wrexham, 25.10.1978

MOST GOALS IN AN INTERNATIONAL CAREER

England
49 in 106 games, Bobby Charlton *(Manchester U)*

Scotland
30 in 55 games, Denis Law *(Huddersfield T, Manchester C, Torino, Manchester U)*
30 in 102 games, Kenny Dalglish *(Celtic, Liverpool)*

Ireland
12 in 25 games, Billy Gillespie *(Sheffield U)*
12 in 63 games, Gerry Armstrong *(Tottenham H, Watford, Real Mallorca, WBA, Chesterfield)*
12 in 11 games, Joe Bambrick *(Linfield, Chelsea)*

Wales
23 in 38 games, Trevor Ford *(Swansea T, Aston Villa, Sunderland, Cardiff C)*
23 in 68 games, Ivor Allchurch *(Swansea T, Newcastle U, Cardiff C)*

Republic of Ireland
20 in 70 games, Frank Stapleton *(Arsenal, Manchester U, Ajax, Derby Co, Le Havre, Blackburn R)*

OLYMPIC FOOTBALL

Previous winners

1896	Athens*	1.	Denmark
		2.	Greece
1900	Paris*	1.	England
		2.	France
1904	St Louis**	1.	Canada
		2.	USA
1908	London	1.	England
		2.	Denmark
		3.	Holland
1912	Stockholm	1.	England
		2.	Denmark
		3.	Holland
1920	Antwerp	1.	Belgium
		2.	Spain
		3.	Holland
1924	Paris	1.	Uruguay
		2.	Switzerland
		3.	Sweden
1928	Amsterdam	1.	Uruguay
		2.	Argentina
		3.	Italy
1932	Los Angeles	no competition	
1936	Berlin	1.	Italy
		2.	Austria
		3.	Norway
1948	London	1.	Sweden
		2.	Yugoslavia
		3.	Denmark
1952	Helsinki	1.	Hungary
		2.	Yugoslavia
		3.	Sweden
1956	Melbourne	1.	USSR
		2.	Yugoslavia
		3.	Bulgaria
1960	Rome	1.	Yugoslavia
		2.	Denmark
		3.	Hungary
1964	Tokyo	1.	Hungary
		2.	Czechoslovakia
		3.	East Germany
1968	Mexico City	1.	Hungary
		2.	Bulgaria
		3.	Japan
1972	Munich	1.	Poland
		2.	Hungary
		3.	East Germany/ USSR joint bronze
1976	Montreal	1.	East Germany
		2.	Poland
		3.	USSR
1980	Moscow	1.	Czechoslovakia
		2.	East Germany
		3.	USSR
1984	Los Angeles	1.	France
		2.	Brazil
		3.	Yugoslavia
1988	Seoul	1.	USSR
		2.	Brazil
		3.	West Germany

*No official tournament
**No official tournament but gold medal later awarded by IOC

GM VAUXHALL CONFERENCE FIXTURES 1991-92

	Altrincham	Barrow	Bath C.	Boston U.	Cheltenham T.	Colchester U.	Farnborough T.	Gateshead	Kettering T.
Altrincham	—	3-9	23-11	9-11	14-12	29-2	18-1	24-9	17-8
Barrow	21-3	—	7-9	2-11	15-2	24-8	21-9	26-12	18-1
Bath C.	15-2	4-4	—	14-12	28-9	14-3	8-10	9-11	18-4
Boston U.	4-4	25-1	7-3	—	7-9	22-4	5-10	19-2	26-12
Cheltenham T.	18-4	31-8	7-12	28-3	—	21-9	11-4	25-1	25-9
Colchester U.	5-10	2-5	31-8	1-2	18-1	—	10-9	7-3	22-2
Farnborough T.	12-10	16-11	25-1	14-3	21-3	9-11	—	18-4	30-11
Gateshead	6-11	1-1	28-12	7-12	8-2	14-12	7-9	—	21-3
Kettering T.	25.4	8-2	2-11	1-1	31-3	25-1	7-3	4-4	—
Kidderminster H.	25-11	4-1	22-2	30-3	20-4	8-2	23-11	24-8	1-2
Macclesfield T.	26-12	14-3	8-2	12-10	26-8	25-4	19-10	28-3	9-11
Merthyr Tydfil	7-3	28-3	26-8	25-4	1-1	4-4	7-12	29-2	18-2
Northwich V.	2-11	24-9	17-8	21-9	1-2	30-11	2-5	4-1	29-2
Redbridge F.	21-9	19-10	26-11	22-2	5-10	26-12	28-3	30-11	24-8
Runcorn	4-1	9-11	21-9	24-8	16-11	28-12	8-2	20-4	7-9
Slough T.	8-2	5-10	21-12	15-2	25-2	26-8	20-4	18-1	14-3
Stafford R.	21-12	20-4	2-5	26-11	7-3	3-12	17-8	19-10	28-12
Telford U.	26-8	14-9	5-10	29-2	4-4	19-10	31-8	21-12	11-4
Welling U.	7-9	30-11	21-3	25-9	24-8	15-2	26-12	5-10	14-12
Witton A.	7-12	14-12	19-10	4-1	25-4	7-9	29-2	7-4	12-10
Wycombe W.	31-8	29-2	20-4	7-3	30-11	28-9	1-2	17-8	28-3
Yeovil T.	2-5	17-8	1-1	18-4	9-11	30-10	21-12	31-8	19-10

Kidderminster H.	Macclesfield T.	Merthyr Tydfil	Northwich V.	Redbridge F.	Runcorn	Slough T.	Stafford R.
1-1	20-4	30-11	22-2	11-4	28-9	19-10	14-9
18-4	26-11	12-10	11-4	21-12	7-12	7-3	26-8
30-11	14-4	1-2	25-4	18-1	29-2	12-10	24-8
31-8	18-1	17-8	8-2	21-3	2-5	4-12	11-
21-12	22-2	26-12	19-10	29-2	2-11	11-9	2
28-3	17-8	16-11	21-3	1-1	12-10	11-4	
15-2	14-12	14-4	24-8	24-9	14-9	22-2	
2-5	1-2	21-9	12-10	15-2	26-8	16-	
21-9	4-1	21-12	7-12	2-5	15-2	2	
—	23-9	21-3	26-8	7-9	11-4		
7-12	—	15-2	28-9	18-4	17-9		
2-11	5-10	—	7-9	8-2	23-1		
14-3	21-12	18-1	—	23-11	5-2		
9-11	31-8	20-4	7-3	—			
19-10	7-3	14-3	24-1	14-12			
17-8	2-5	26-11	4-4	28-9			
4-4	1-1	31-8	9-11	14-			
10-9	23-11	2-5	1-1	1			
29-2	2-11	11-4	16-11				
5-10	21-3	14-9	20-4				
18-1	21-9	9-11	14-1				
25-1	7-9	22-2	28				

…ford U.	Witton A.	Wycombe W.	Yeovil T.
	29-10	14-3	24-8
	1-2	23-11	25-4
	28-3	4-1	26-12
	11-9	19-10	23-11
	17-8	22-1	4-1
	21-12	7-12	14-9
	28-9	4-4	2-11
	23-11	25-4	11-4
	31-8	25-2	16-11
	7-3	26-10	12-10
	30-11	25-1	29-2
	18-4	17-9	28-9
	26-12	15-2	5-10
	4-4	17-3	21-1
	22-2	5-10	4-4
1	2-11	26-12	7-12
1	8-10	7-9	15-2
3	15-2	8-2	14-12
-	21-9	4-9	20-4
12	—	24-8	14-3
4	2-5	—	26-8
2	18-1	7-3	—

BARCLYS LEAGUE FIXTURES 1991–92

DIVISIONE

	Aston Villa	Chelsea	Coventry C	Crystal Palace	Everton	Leeds U	Liverpool	Luton T	Manchester C
Arsenal	1.1	5.10	7.9	11.4	21.12	21.3	20.4	27.8	31.8
Aston Villa	—	20.4	2.5	4.9	1.2	23.11	11.4	5.10	7.12
Chelsea	.9	—	14.3	8.2	28.9	14.9	19.10	31.8	1.1
Coventry C	9	2.11	—	19.10	18.4	18.9	8.2	21.8	17.8
Crystal Pal		26.10	1.2	—	4.4	17.8	14.3	15.12	11.1
Everton	0	2.5	21.9	7.9	—	22.2	28.12	14.3	20.4
Leeds U		11.4	21.4	18.1	30.11	—	21.9	29.2	7.9
Liverpool		1.2	26.10	2.11	31.8	18.4	—	11.1	21.12
Luton T		28.12	20.12	7.3	2.11	7.12	24.8	—	23.11
Manchest		28.3	18.1	24.8	17.9	4.4	21.8	15.2	—
Manches		7.3	7.12	22.2	11.1	31.8	5.10	21.9	11.3
Norwich		11.3	23.11	7.12	21.3	28.9	22.2	26.10	28.8
Notting		22.2	16.11	23.11	17.8	22.12	7.3	1.1	21.3
Notts C		6.12	11.4	28.3	15.2	19.10	7.9	2.5	6.10
Oldham		.8	3.9	21.9	14.12	8.2	18.1	11.4	2.5
QPR		.9	24.8	2.5	26.10	11.3	26.12	20.4	7.3
Sheffiel		9	26.12	28.12	14.9	25.4	28.3	30.11	8.2
Sheffiel		2	7.3	5.10	28.8	11.1	2.5	1.2	11.4
Southa		1	22.2	11.3	1.1	28.8	7.12	21.3	2.11
Totten			28.3	26.11	25.4	7.3	18.12	16.11	19.10
West			5.10	20.4	29.2	1.1	16.11	17.8	21.9
Wimb			28.12	26.12	10.3	2.11	23.11	7 .9	22.2

Manchester U	Norwich C	Nottingham F	Notts Co	Oldham Ath	QPR	Sheffield U	Sheffield W	Southampton	Tottenham H	West Ham U	Wimbledon
1.2	14.12	29.2	26.10	10.3	17.8	21.9	15.2	2.5	30.11	2.11	1.1
21.8	28.3	21.9	16.11	22.2	14.3	7.3	18.1	28.12	7.9	26.12	26.10
14.12	16.11	30.11	28.8	21.12	18.4	21.3	29.2	13.2	11.1	4.4	17.8
29.2	15.2	11.3	14.9	21.3	11.1	28.8	14.12	30.11	1.1	25.4	31.8
30.11	29.2	15.2	1.1	18.4	28.9	31.8	25.4	16.11	22.12	17.9	27.8
24.8	3.9	18.1	23.11	7.3	8.2	11.4	26.12	28.3	5.10	7.12	16.11
28.12	2.5	18.8	1.2	26.10	16.11	5.10	24.8	26.12	14.12	28.3	14.3
25.4	30.11	14.12	4.4	17.8	27.8	1.1	28.9	29.2	21.3	10.3	15.2
18.4	8.2	28.3	28.9	14.9	18.9	22.2	19.10	4.9	11.3	18.1	4.4
16.11	26.12	4.9	25.4	28.9	14.12	26.10	14.9	14.3	1.2	18.4	30.11
—	7.9	20.4	17.8	28.8	1.1	2.11	8.2	11.4	2.5	23.11	21.3
4.4	—	2.11	18.4	11.1	21.12	17.8	18.9	1.2	31.8	14.9	25.4
29.1	14.3	—	11.1	31.8	25.4	1.2	4.4	26.10	28.8	28.9	14.9
18.1	21.9	24.8	—	2.11	30.11	20.4	3.9	18.8	29.2	28.12	14.12
26.12	24.8	28.12	14.3	—	15.2	7.9	28.3	5.10	20.4	19.10	29.2
28.3	21.8	5.10	22.2	23.11	—	7.12	28.12	7.9	11.4	4.9	1.2
14.3	18.1	19.10	17.9	4.4	29.2	—	17.11	24.8	15.2	18.8	28.9
26.10	20.4	7.9	21.3	1.1	31.8	11.3	—	21.9	2.11	22.2	21.12
14.9	19.10	8.2	20.12	25.4	4.4	11.1	18.4	—	17.8	7.3	18.9
28.9	28.12	26.12	7.12	28.1	14.9	23.11	14.3	18.1	—	8.2	18.4
15.2	11.4	2.5	31.8	1.2	21.3	21.12	30.11	14.12	26.10	—	11.1
3.9	5.10	11.4	7.3	7.12	19.10	2.5	18.8	20.4	21.9	24.8	—

DIVISION TWO

	Barnsley	Blackburn R	Brighton & HA	Bristol C	Bristol R	Cambridge	Charlton Ath	Derby Co	Grimsby T	Ipswich T	Leicester C
Barnsley	—	28.3	24.8	19.10	9.11	8.2	29.2	4.4	14.12	14.9	17.9
Blackburn R	16.11	—	2.11	11.1	14.12	1.1	21.3	21.12	26.10	31.8	18.4
Brighton & HA	11.1	14.3	—	1.1	28.9	28.3	1.2	15.4	6.11	12.10	30.10
Bristol C	1.2	24.8	20.8	—	3.9	14.3	30.11	25.4	29.2	18.4	4.4
Bristol R	21.3	7.3	20.4	21.12	—	7.12	2.5	23.11	7.9	17.8	1.1
Cambridge	26.10	22.10	16.11	2.11	28.2	—	15.2	13.9	18.1	21.3	29.9
Charlton Ath	7.12	9.11	19.10	22.2	12.10	23.11	—	31.8	14.3	29.10	25.4
Derby Co	7.9	4.9	21.9	5.10	15.2	1.4	28.12	—	26.12	16.11	30.11
Grimsby T	7.3	8.2	10.3	7.12	4.4	17.8	2.11	29.10	—	28.9	21.12
Ipswich T	31.3	28.12	2.5	21.9	18.1	9.11	26.12	28.3	21.4	—	14.3
Leicester C	11.4	21.9	26.12	7.9	23.10	21.4	5.10	22.2	4.9	2.11	—
Middlesbrough	10.3	22.2	21.3	23.11	25.4	7.3	16.11	1.1	1.2	11.1	14.9
Millwall	22.4	5.10	4.9	11.4	30.11	7.9	14.12	26.10	15.2	1.2	29.2
Newcastle U	22.2	23.11	7.3	8.2	28.12	6.11	18.1	28.9	9.11	18.9	12.10
Oxford U	2.11	7.12	23.11	16.11	18.4	22.2	23.10	18.9	24.8	25.4	26.10
Plymouth Arg	17.8	2.5	22.2	10.3	1.2	29.10	7.9	7.3	31.3	7.12	11.1
Portsmouth	2.5	18.1	7.9	20.4	26.12	21.9	31.3	1.2	11.4	26.10	5.11
Port Vale	27.8	31.3	11.4	31.8	14.3	5.10	20.4	5.11	2.5	1.1	15.2
Southend U	23.11	5.11	7.12	17.8	14.9	21.12	26.10	11.1	28.3	4.4	31.8
Sunderland	1.1	7.9	5.10	21.3	26.10	2.5	11.4	17.8	21.9	10.3	14.12
Swindon T	31.8	19.10	8.2	29.10	17.9	11.1	10.3	12.10	30.11	20.12	17.8
Tranmere R	21.9	20.4	17.1	31.3	23.8	18.10	3.9	14.3	28.12	21.2	27.3
Watford	22.12	11.4	31.3	2.5	28.3	31.8	21.9	7.12	5.10	7.3	9.11
Wolverhampton W	5.10	26.12	28.12	7.3	5.11	11.4	24.8	9.11	22.10	23.11	1.2

Middlesbrough	Millwall	Newcastle U	Oxford U	Plymouth Arg	Portsmouth	Port Vale	Southend U	Sunderland	Swindon T	Tranmere R	Watford	Wolverhampton W
5.11	28.9	30.11	14.3	18.1	12.10	26.12	15.2	20.8	28.12	18.4	3.9	25.4
30.11	25.4	15.2	29.2	12.10	17.8	14.9	10.3	4.4	1.2	28.9	17.9	29.10
9.11	21.12	14.12	15.2	30.11	4.4	18 .9	29.2	25.4	26.10	17.8	14.9	31.8
13.2	17.9	26.10	20.3	6.11	28.9	28.12	18.1	9.11	26.12	14.9	12.10	14.12
5.10	22.2	31.8	21.9	19.10	30.10	2.11	1.4	8.2	11.4	11.1	16.11	11.3
14.12	4.4	10.3	30.11	26.12	17.4	25.4	3.9	12.10	24.8	31.1	29.12	17.9
28.3	7.3	17.8	1.1	4.4	14.9	28.9	8.2	17.9	5.11	21.12	18.4	11.1
21.8	8.2	20.4	11.4	14.12	19.10	11.3	24.8	18.1	2.5	2.11	29.2	21.3
19.10	23.11	21.3	11.1	14.9	17.9	12.10	28.1	18.4	22.2	31.8	25.4	1.1
24.8	19.10	11.4	5.10	29.2	8.2	20.8	7.9	5.11	3.9	30.11	14.12	15.2
1.4	7.12	2.5	8.2	24.8	11.3	23.11	28.12	7.3	18.1	29.1	21.3	19.10
—	17.8	27.8	21.12	18.4	31.8	26.10	2.11	28.9	7.12	17.9	4.4	12.0
18.1	—	21.9	1.4	28.12	2.11	21.3	2.5	24.8	23.10	11.3	26.12	16.11
26.12	18.4	—	19.10	4.9	25.4	7.12	23.10	29.3	14.3	4.4	24.8	14.9
4.9	14.9	1.2	—	28.9	21.3	18.1	26.12	28.12	7.3	12.10	11.3	4.4
21.9	31.8	21.12	20.4	—	1.1	16.11	11.4	23.11	5.10	21.3	26.10	2.11
28.12	14.3	5.10	9.11	22.10	—	24.8	14.12	3.9	28.3	29.2	15.2	30.11
8.2	9.11	29.2	17.8	28.3	11.1	—	21.9	19.10	7.9	13.12	30.11	20.12
14.3	12.10	1.1	29.10	17.9	7.3	14.4	—	22.2	9.11	25.4	1.2	28.9
20.4	11.1	17.11	31.8	15.2	21.12	1.2	30.11	—	1.4	29.10	2.11	29.2
29.2	1.1	2.11	14.12	25.4	16.11	4.4	21.3	14.9	—	15.2	28.9	18.4
10.4	5.11	7.9	2.5	8.11	6.12	6.3	4.10	26.12	22.11	—	22.10	8.2
7.9	29.10	11.1	6.11	8.2	23.11	22.2	19.10	14.3	20.4	1.1	—	17.8
2.5	28.3	21.3	7.9	14.3	22.2	3.9	20.4	7.12	21.9	26.10	18.1	—

DIVISION THREE

	Birmingham C	Bolton W	Bournemouth	Bradford C	Brentford	Bury	Chester C	Darlington	Exeter C	Fulham	Hartlepool U
Birmingham C	—	25.1	15.2	30.11	10.3	17.8	17.9	31.8	23.11	20.12	18.4
Bolton W	7.3	—	31.3	11.4	20.4	21.3	8.2	1.1	22.2	19.10	18.1
Bournemouth	14.12	14.9	—	26.10	22.11	11.2	3.4	17.8	4.1	27.9	12.10
Bradford C	11.2	17.9	8.2	—	2.11	4.1	14.9	7.3	10.3	12.10	31.8
Brentford	5.11	28.9	29.3	14.3	—	8.2	3.3	17.4	22.12	26.4	1.1
Bury	28.12	9.11	30.11	29.2	26.10	—	25.1	25.4	1.2	17.9	28.9
Chester C	11.4	26.10	7.9	31.3	18.1	7.3	—	4.1	11.2	17.8	22.2
Darlington	26.12	3.9	28.12	25.1	21.9	5.10	29.2	—	2.5	30.11	2.11
Exeter C	28.3	11.1	29.2	6.11	24.8	19.10	30.11	12.10	—	25.1	14.9
Fulham	24.8	1.2	20.4	2.5	5.10	11.4	28.12	11.2	7.3	—	20.3
Hartlepool U	21.9	3.3	2.5	26.12	3.9	20.4	11.1	14.3	31.3	9.11	—
Huddersfield T	9.11	28.12	21.9	25.8	26.12	31.3	4.9	14.12	7.9	6.11	11.2
Hull C	3.9	15.2	26.12	3.3	11.4	7.9	9.11	26.10	5.10	14.3	1.2
Leyton O	22.2	26.12	19.10	3.9	28.12	14.12	12.10	14.9	2.11	18.4	4.4
Peterborough U	31.3	29.2	25.1	9.11	2.5	1.1	5.11	28.32	21.9	11.1	26.10
Preston NE	20.4	28.3	3.9	7.9	7.3	2.5	14.3	9.1	18.1	8.2	14.12
Reading	7.9	14.3	5.10	21.9	1.4	31.8	28.3	6.11	20.4	15.2	20.12
Shrewsbury T	5.10	30.11	11.4	20.4	7.9	21.12	15.2	1.2	31.8	3.3	22.11
Stockport Co	2.5	5.11	13.3	5.10	4.1	21.9	18.10	18.1	11.4	27.3	6.3
Stoke C	4.1	12.10	24.8	28.12	22.2	11.3	25.4	4.4	21.3	14.9	18.9
Swansea C	18.1	24.8	8.11	28.3	11.2	22.2	26.12	28.1	14.12	4.4	4.1
Torquay U	14.3	25.4	6.11	1.2	14.12	18.1	28.9	22.2	1.1	31.8	17.8
WBA	26.10	4.4	11.1	15.2	1.2	2.11	18.4	22.12	17.8	1.1	11.3
Wigan Ath	31.1	18.4	3.3	11.1	20.3	22.11	23.8	28.9	26.10	28.2	24.4

Huddersfield T	Hull C	Leyton O	Peterborough U	Preston NE	Reading	Shrewsbury T	Stockport Co.	Stoke C	Swansea C	Torquay U	WBA	Wigan Ath
21.3	1.1	11.1	14.9	28.9	4.4	25.4	12.10	29.2	3.3	2.11	8.2	19.10
17.8	14.12	31.8	4.1	23.11	2.11	11.2	10.3	2.5	21.12	5.10	7.9	21.9
14.4	31.8	1.2	7.3	1.1	25.4	17.9	1.11	21.12	20.3	10.3	22.2	18.1
22.12	18.1	1.1	21.3	4.4	18.4	28.9	25.4	17.8	22.11	19.10	14.12	22.2
31.8	17.9	17.8	12.10	25.1	14.9	4.4	29.2	11.1	30.11	15.2	19.10	9.11
14.9	4.4	15.2	3.9	12.10	26.12	24.8	18.4	5.11	11.1	3.3	14.3	28.3
1.1	21.3	2.5	10.3	2.11	22.11	14.12	1.2	5.10	31.8	20.4	21.9	21.12
15.3	8.2	31.3	22.11	21.3	10.3	19.10	3.3	7.9	11.4	11.1	24.8	20.4
4.4	25.4	14.3	18.4	4.3	28.9	26.12	18.9	9.11	15.2	4.9	28.12	8.2
10.3	2.11	21.9	22.2	26.10	13.12	18.1	22.11	31.3	7.9	26.12	3.9	4.1
30.11	19.10	7.9	8.2	15.2	24.8	28.3	25.1	11.4	29.2	28.12	5.11	5.10
—	4.1	20.4	18.1	1.2	22.2	7.3	25.10	14.3	5.10	2.5	28.3	11.4
29.2	—	28.3	24.8	30.11	28.12	5.11	11.1	25.1	2.5	21.9	20.4	31.3
28.9	23.11	—	25.4	17.9	7.3	4.1	24.8	8.2	10.3	21.3	18.1	11.2
3.3	20.12	5.10	—	17.8	1.2	14.3	15.2	31.8	21.4	30.11	11.4	7.9
19.10	11.2	11.4	28.12	—	4.1	22.2	26.12	21.9	31.3	24.8	5.10	5.11
11.1	17.8	25.1	19.10	29.2	—	8.2	30.11	4.3	1.1	11.4	9.11	2.5
25.1	10.3	29.2	2.11	11.1	26.10	—	20.3	1.1	21.9	31.3	2.5	18.8
7.2	22.2	21.12	13.12	30.8	11.2	8.11	—	20.4	17.8	6.9	31.3	1.1
2.11	7.3	26.10	26.12	18.4	18.1	4.9	28.9	—	1.2	22.11	12.2	14.12
25.4	12.10	3.11	28.9	14.9	3.9	17.4	28.12	19.10	—	8.2	7.3	14.3
12.10	14.4	9.11	11.2	20.12	17.9	14.9	4.4	28.3	26.10	—	4.1	7.3
22.11	28.9	4.3	18.9	25.4	21.3	12.10	14.9	30.11	25.1	29.2	—	31.8
17.9	14.9	30.11	3.4	10.3	11.10	28.12	3.9	15.2	1.11	24.1	26.12	—

DIVISION FOUR

	Aldershot	Barnet	Blackpool	Burnley	Cardiff C	Carlisle U	Chesterfield	Crewe Alex	Doncaster R	Gillingham
Aldershot	—	17.1	5.11	21.12	8.11	6.9	20.4	1.1	14.12	11.2
Barnet	3.3	—	19.10	25.1	28.9	5.11	30.11	17.8	14.9	18.4
Blackpool	10.3	1.2	—	11.1	14.9	21.12	21.3	23.11	14.4	17.9
Burnley	24.8	7.3	22.2	—	4.1	5.10	3.9	7.9	28.12	18.1
Cardiff C	20.3	20.4	31.3	29.2	—	31.8	25.1	21.12	26.10	10.3
Carlisle U	4.4	10.3	24.8	25.4	28.12	—	29.2	26.10	26.12	2.11
Chesterfield	28.9	11.2	9.11	1.1	7.3	4.1	—	14.12	18.1	25.4
Crewe Alex	3.9	26.12	28.3	4.4	24.8	7.2	15.2	—	24.4	28.9
Doncaster R	15.2	31.3	20.9	31.8	8.2	17.8	3.3	5.10	—	19.10
Gillingham	30.11	21.9	11.4	3.3	5.11	14.3	5.10	20.4	1.2	—
Halifax T	17.4	21.3	12.2	2.11	17.9	6.3	19.10	4.1	22.2	12.10
Hereford U	12.10	28.12	18.1	14.9	22.2	28.3	8.2	12.2	7.3	4.9
Lincoln C	2.11	4.9	2.5	26.10	26.12	1.4	21.9	22.2	12.2	4.1
Maidstone	28.12	14.12	4.1	23.11	4.9	12.2	26.12	11.3	12.10	21.3
Mansfield T	11.1	24.8	7.9	21.3	19.10	11.4	28.12	31.3	2.11	23.11
Northampton T	25.1	7.9	5.10	30.11	28.3	21.9	15.10	11.4	3.9	8.2
Rochdale	25.4	23.11	14.12	18.4	4.4	22.2	2.11	18.1	28.9	7.3
Rotherham U	1.2	22.2	20.4	17.8	11.2	1.1	2.5	31.8	10.3	14.12
Scarborough	14.9	26.10	14.3	28.9	14.4	9.11	11.1	1.2	18.9	4.4
Scunthorpe U	29.2	11.4	28.12	15.2	14.3	2.5	31.3	21.9	24.8	26.12
Walsall	26.10	5.10	26.12	1.2	18.1	21.4	11.4	2.5	4.1	22.2
Wrexham	17.9	2.11	8.2	12.10	25.4	19.10	23.11	21.3	3.4	14.9
York C	23.11	2.5	3.9	10.3	14.12	18.1	7.9	7.3	21.3	24.8

Halifax T	Hereford U	Lincoln C	Maidstone	Mansfield T	Northampton T	Rochdale	Rotherham U	Scarborough	Scunthorpe U	Walsall	Wrexham	York C
20.9	2.5	14.3	31.8	21.2	7.3	4.10	18.10	31.3	3.1	8.2	10.4	27.3
9.11	31.8	1.1	15.2	21.12	4.4	28.3	11.1	8.2	17.9	25.4	14.3	12.10
30.11	3.3	13.10	29.2	4.4	25.4	15.2	28.9	2.11	31.8	17.8	26.10	1.1
14.3	31.3	8.2	28.3	9.11	11.2	21.9	26.12	20.4	14.12	19.10	2.5	5.11
11.4	11.1	17.8	1.1	31.1	23.11	7.9	30.11	21.9	2.11	3.3	5.10	15.2
25.1	23.11	14.9	30.11	17.9	18.4	11.1	3.9	21.3	12.10	28.9	1.2	3.3
1.2	26.10	18.4	17.8	31.8	21.12	14.3	12.10	22.2	14.9	17.9	28.3	4.4
28.2	30.11	11.1	5.11	13.9	17.9	3.3	28.12	19.10	18.4	11.10	9.11	25.1
11.1	24.1	30.11	2.5	14.3	1.1	20.4	5.11	11.4	20.12	29.2	7.9	8.11
2.5	1.1	29.2	9.11	28.3	26.10	25.1	15.2	7.9	17.8	11.1	31.3	21.12
—	11.3	25.4	21.12	27.9	17.8	8.2	13.9	22.11	18.1	3.4	13.12	30.8
6.11	—	28.9	14.3	14.12	4.1	9.11	4.4	24.8	25.4	18.4	26.12	18.9
5.10	20.4	—	11.4	7.3	21.3	28.12	24.8	14.12	23.11	11.3	18.1	1.2
21.4	2.11	18.9	—	25.4	18.1	19.10	18.4	7.3	4.4	14.9	22.2	28.9
24.8	15.2	25.1	5.10	—	10.3	2.5	3.3	26.12	8.2	30.11	3.9	29.2
26.12	29.2	9.11	3.3	5.11	—	31.3	14.3	2.5	19.10	15.2	28.12	11.1
26.10	21.3	31.8	1.2	12.10	14.9	—	17.9	11.2	10.3	1.1	4.1	17.8
31.3	7.9	21.12	21.9	18.1	2.11	11.4	—	4.1	21.3	22.11	7.3	25.10
28.3	21.12	15.2	25.1	17.8	12.10	30.11	29.2	—	1.1	31.8	5.11	25.4
3.3	5.10	28.3	7.9	26.10	1.2	5.11	9.11	3.9	—	25.1	20.4	30.11
7.9	21.9	5.11	31.3	11.2	14.12	3.9	28.3	28.12	7.3	—	24.8	14.3
15.2	17.8	3.3	11.1	1.1	30.8	29.2	25.1	10.3	28.9	20.12	—	18.4
28.12	11.4	19.10	20.4	4.1	22.2	26.12	8.2	5.10	11.2	2.11	21.9	—

THE FOOTBALL ASSOCIATION FIXTURE PROGRAMME—SEASON 1991–92

August

3 Sat	Official Opening Season
10 Sat	FA Charity Shield
17 Sat	Football League Season Commences
26 Mon	Bank Holiday
31 Sat	FA Challenge Cup Preliminary Round

September

7 Sat	FA Challenge Vase Extra Preliminary Round FA Youth Challenge Cup Preliminary Round*
10 Tue	England v Germany (U21)
11 Wed	England v Germany (F)
14 Sat	FA Challenge Cup 1st Round Qualifying
18 Wed	EC/ECWC/UEFA 1st Round (1st Leg)
21 Sat	FA Challenge Trophy 1st Round Qualifying
28 Sat	FA Challenge Cup 2nd Round Qualifying FA Youth Challenge Cup 1st Round Qualifying*

October

2 Wed	EC/ECWC/UEFA 1st Round (2nd Leg)
5 Sat	FA Challenge Vase Preliminary Round
12 Sat	FA Challenge Cup 3rd Round Qualifying FA Youth Challenge Cup 2nd Round Qualifying*
13 Sun	FA Sunday Cup 1st Round
15 Tue	England v Turkey (U21)
16 Wed	England v Turkey (EC)
19 Sat	FA Challenge Trophy 2nd Round Qualifying FA County Youth Challenge Cup 1st Round*
23 Wed	EC/ECWC/UEFA 2nd Round (1st Leg)
26 Sat	FA Challenge Cup 4th Round Qualifying

November

2 Sat	FA Challenge Vase 1st Round
6 Wed	EC/ECWC/UEFA 2nd Round (2nd Leg)
9 Sat	FA Youth Challenge Cup 1st Round Proper*
10 Sun	FA Sunday Cup 2nd Round
12 Tue	Poland v England (U21)
13 Wed	Poland v England (EC)
16 Sat	FA Challenge Cup 1st Round Proper
23 Sat	FA Challenge Vase 2nd Round
27 Wed	EC Quarter-Final Round In Groups UEFA 3rd Round (1st Leg)
30 Sat	FA Challenge Trophy 3rd Round Qualifying FA County Youth Challenge Cup 2nd Round*

December

7 Sat	FA Challenge Cup 2nd Round Proper FA Youth Challenge Cup 2nd Round Proper*
8 Sun	FA Sunday Cup 3rd Round

11 Wed EC Quarter-Final Round in Groups
UEFA 3rd Round (2nd Leg)
14 Sat FA Challenge Vase 3rd Round
26 Thu Boxing Day

January

1 Wed New Years Day
4 Sat FA Challenge Cup 3rd Round Proper
11 Sat FA Challenge Trophy 1st Round Proper
FA Youth Challenge Cup 3rd Round Proper*
18 Sat FA Challenge Vase 4th Round
FA County Youth Challenge Cup 3rd Round*
19 Sun FA Sunday Cup 4th Round
25 Sat FA Challenge Cup 4th Round Proper

February

1 Sat FA Challenge Trophy 2nd Round Proper
8 Sat FA Challenge Vase 5th Round
FA Youth Challenge Cup 4th Round Proper*
15 Sat FA Challenge Cup 5th Round Proper
16 Sun FA Sunday Cup 5th Round
19 Wed England v France (F)
22 Sat FA Challenge Trophy 3rd Round Proper
FA County Youth Challenge Cup 4th Round*
29 Sat FA Challenge Vase 6th Round

March

4 Wed EC Quarter-Final Round in Groups ECWC/
UEFA Quarter-Final (1st Leg)
7 Sat FA Challenge Cup 6th Round Proper
FA Youth Challenge Cup 5th Round Proper*
14 Sat FA Challenge Trophy 4th Round Proper
18 Wed EC Quarter-Final Round in Groups
ECWC/UEFA Quarter-Final (2nd Leg)
21 Sat FA Challenge Vase Semi-Final (1st Leg)
FA County Youth Challenge Cup Semi-Final*
22 Sun FA Sunday Cup Semi-Final
25 Wed Czechoslovakia v England (F)
28 Sat FA Challenge Vase Semi-Final (2nd Leg)

April

1 Wed EC Quarter-Final Round in Groups ECWC/
UEFA Semi-Final (1st Leg)
4 Sat FA Challenge Trophy Semi-Final (1st Leg)
FA Youth Challenge Cup Semi-Final*
5 Sun FA Challenge Cup Semi-Final
11 Sat FA Challenge Trophy Semi-Final (2nd Leg)
15 Wed EC Quarter-Final Round in Groups ECWC/
UEFA Semi-Final (2nd Leg)
20 Mon Bank Holiday
25 Sat FA Challenge Vase Final (Wembley Stadium)
29 Wed USSR v England (F)
UEFA Final (1st Leg)

USEFUL ADDRESSES

Football Association: R.H.G. Kelly, FCIS, 16 Lancaster Gate, London W2 3LW.
Scottish FA: J. Farry, 6 Park Gardens, Glasgow G3 7YF.
Irish FA: D. Bowen, 20 Windsor Avenue, Belfast BT9 6EG.
Welsh FA: A.E. Evans, B.Sc., 3 Westgate Street, Cardiff CF1 1JF.
FA of Ireland (Eire): 80 Merrion Square South, Dublin 2.
League of Ireland: E. Morris, 80 Merrion Square, Dublin 2.
Fedération Internationale de Football Association (FIFA): J. Blatter, FIFA House, 11 Hitzigweg, CH-8032 Zurich, Switzerland.
Union des Associations Européenes de Football (UEFA): G. Aigner, Jupiterstrasse 33 PO Box 16, CH-3000 Berne 15, Switzerland.
Football League: J.D. Dent, Lytham St Annes, Lancashire FY8 1JG.
Scottish League: 188 West Regent Street, Glasgow G2 4RY.
Irish League: M. Brown, 87 University Street, Belfast BT7 1HP.
Welsh League: K.J. Tucker, 16 The Parade, Merthyr Tydfil, Mid-Glamorgan CF47 0ET.
GM Vauxhall Conference: P.D. Hunter, 24 Barnehurst Road, Bexley Heath, Kent DA7 6EZ.
Beazer Homes League: D.J. Strudwick, 11 Welland Close, Durrington, Worthing, W. Sussex BN13 3NR.
Northern Premier League: R.D. Bayley, 22 Woburn Drive, Hale, Altrincham, Cheshire WA15 8LZ.
Vauxhall League: N. Robinson, 226 Rye Lane, London SE15 4NL.
The Association of Football League Referees and Linesmen: J.B. Goggins, 1 Tewkesbury Drive, Lytham St Annes, Lancs FY8 4LN.
The Football League Executive Staffs Association: P.O. Box 52, Leamington Spa, Warwickshire.
Women's Football Association: Miss L. Whitehead, 448/450, Hanging Ditch, The Corn Exchange, Manchester M4 3ES.
English Schools FA: C.S. Allat, 4a Eastgate Street, Stafford ST16 2NN.
Professional Footballers' Association: G. Taylor, 2 Oxford Court, Bishopsgate, off Lower Mosley Street, Manchester, M2 3W2.
The Association of Football Statisticians: R.J. Spiller, 22 Bretons, Basildon, Essex.
England Supporters' Association: David Stacey, 66 Southend Road, Wickford, Essex SS11 8EN.
The Football Programme Directory: Editor, David Stacey, 66 Southend Road, Wickford, Essex SS11 8EN.
National Federation of Football Supporters' Clubs General Secretary: 69 Fourth Avenue, Chelmsford, Essex.
Football Trust: Second Floor, Walkden House, 10 Melton Street, London NW1 2EJ.